Applied Mergers and Acquisitions Workbook

Founded in 1807, John Wiley & Sons is the oldest independent publishing company in the United States. With offices in North America, Europe, Australia and Asia, Wiley is globally committed to developing and marketing print and electronic products and services for our customers' professional and personal knowledge and understanding.

The Wiley Finance series contains books written specifically for finance and investment professionals as well as sophisticated individual investors and their financial advisors. Book topics range from portfolio management to e-commerce, risk management, financial engineering, valuation and financial instrument analysis, as well as much more.

For a list of available titles, please visit our Web site at www.WileyFinance.com.

Applied Mergers and Acquisitions Workbook

ROBERT F. BRUNER

WILEY

John Wiley & Sons, Inc.

Published by John Wiley & Sons, Inc., Hoboken, New Jersey.
Published simultaneously in Canada.

For general information on our other products and services, or technical support, please contact our Customer Care Department within the United States at 800-762-2974, outside the United States at 317-572-3993 or fax 317-572-4002.

Wiley also publishes its books in a variety of electronic formats. Some content that appears in print may not be available in electronic books.

For more information about Wiley products, visit our web site at www.wiley.com.

ISBN: 978-0-471-39585-0

10 9 8 7 6 5 4

With gratitude, I dedicate this workbook to my students.

With gratitude, I dedicate this workbook to my students.

Acknowledgments

I am greatly thankful for the contributions of my able research assistants, who prepared questions for this workbook under my direction. The principal assistant for this project was Jessica Chan. Bright, patient, and a tenacious researcher, her work showed great care and dedication. Jessica led a team consisting of herself, Christine Shim, and Baocheng Yang. Christine was especially creative in framing financial problems in realistic terms; she is a champion wordsmith. Baocheng was the champion quant, contributing analytic care, modeling, and real option valuation. The complementary efforts of the three assistants lent flair and precision to the book. I must also recognize Frank Wilmot, Research Librarian at Darden, who gave excellent support in obtaining sometimes obscure data and references. I am truly grateful to them for the creativity and exceptionally hard work they brought to the project. Many of the illustrations in this book draw on the efforts of my earlier research assistants

I am very grateful to the staff of the Darden School for its support in this project. Excellent editorial assistance at Darden was provided by Stephen Smith (Darden's unflappable editor) and Sherry Alston. Betty Sprouse gave stalwart secretarial support. Outstanding library research support was given by Karen Marsh and Frank Wilmot. The patience, care, and dedication of these people are richly appreciated.

I must also acknowledge the great support and encouragement given by my editors (and now friends) at John Wiley & Sons: Bill Falloon, Senior Editor, Finance and Investments; Melissa Scuereb, Editorial Assistant; Robin Factor, Managing Production Editor; and Todd Tedesco, Senior Production Editor. I thank the staff at Cape Cod Compositors as well for their fine attention to detail. Also at Wiley, Pamela Van Giessen, Executive Editor; Joan O'Neil, Publisher, Finance and Investment; and Will Pesce, President, were decisive in my commitment to embark on this project. For the vision and enthusiasm of the Wiley organization, I am very thankful.

Lewis O'Brien of HPS Permissions read everything and gave very helpful advice regarding editorial presentation and support in obtaining permissions.

Of all the contributors, my wife, Barbara McTigue Bruner, and two sons, Jonathan and Alexander, have endured some of the greatest sacrifices to see this book appear. I owe this to them.

All these acknowledgments notwithstanding, responsibility for the final product is mine. I welcome suggestions for its enhancement. Please let me know of your experience with this book either through Wiley or contact me directly.

—Robert F. Bruner
Distinguished Professor of Business Administration
and Executive Director of the Batten Institute
Darden Graduate Business School
University of Virginia
E-mail: brunerr@virginia.edu.

About the Author

Robert F. Bruner is Distinguished Professor of Business Administration and Executive Director of the Batten Institute at the Darden Graduate School of Business Administration, University of Virginia. He teaches the course, "Mergers and Acquisitions" in Darden's MBA program, and is the faculty director of Darden's executive education program, "Mergers and Acquisitions." He has received numerous awards for teaching and casewriting in the United States and Europe. *BusinessWeek* magazine cited him as one of the "masters of the MBA classroom." He is the author or co-author of over 400 case studies and notes, and of *Case Studies in Finance: Managing for Corporate Value Creation*, now in its fourth edition. His research has been published in journals such as *Financial Management*, *Journal of Accounting and Economics*, *Journal of Applied Corporate Finance*, *Journal of Financial Economics*, *Journal of Financial and Quantitative Analysis*, and *Journal of Money, Credit, and Banking*. Industrial corporations, financial institutions, and government agencies have retained him for counsel and training. He has served the Darden School, professional groups, and community organizations in various positions of leadership. Copies of his papers and essays may be obtained from his website, http://faculty.darden.edu/brunerb/. He may be reached via e-mail at brunerr@virginia.edu.

Contents

Introduction to the Workbook

This *Workbook* aims to help you learn faster and more deeply from *Applied Mergers and Acquisitions* by Robert F. Bruner. Its mission is to promote self-instruction about M&A. Its chapters track exactly the content of the chapters in the main book. The problems and answers in this book carry the reader beyond the end-of-chapter questions on the CD-ROM, offering more exercise, stimulating further reflection, and exploring the topics in more depth. Specifically, each chapter in this book can help you:

- **Review** the main ideas in each chapter and a few focused problems and questions.
- **Survey** the ideas in a forthcoming class and chapter reading assignment.
- **Track** the quantitative analysis of M&A issues in a step-by-step fashion.
- **Exercise** spreadsheet models in hands-on fashion.
- **Test** your own grasp of tools and concepts.

Activities such as these are valuable in the effort to gain a solid mastery of M&A.

The *Workbook* has four key features supporting the study of each chapter:

1. *Introduction to the chapter.* Stated in a few sentences, the introduction conveys the main focus of the chapter.
2. *Key ideas.* These are listed at the start of each review chapter in bullet-point fashion to summarize and express key learning points.
3. *Worked-through problems and questions.* These are useful to illustrate key concepts and to test your grasp of lessons.
4. *References to Excel spreadsheet files.* Found on the CD-ROM, these contain the actual models underlying the worked-through problems. You can study these files for the structure of the models and the logic of the analysis.

Chapter 38 of the main book emphasizes the importance of active learning to support one's study. It is not enough simply to *read*: one must *do*. The spirit of this *Workbook* is to help you convert ideas into *best practice* in your daily work.

PART One

Questions

1

Introduction and Executive Summary

M&A (mergers and acquisitions) is one of the most important means by which companies respond to changing conditions. Many firms have no alternative but to merge, acquire, or be acquired.

Although M&A is often portrayed as a gamble that one cannot win, it is possible to succeed in M&A. However, competitive forces may limit the chances of success.

- M&A is a world of contingencies. There are few universal absolute truths about M&A success. For the M&A professional, therefore, there will always be a market for diligent research, sound judgment, and artful execution.
- Success in M&A is driven by both the *structure* of the M&A opportunity one faces and the *conduct* by which one pursues it.
- Elements of *structure* of the M&A environment include:
  - *Economics.* This refers to quantitative drivers of the attractiveness of the opportunity: revenues, costs (both fixed and variable), risk, and required rates of return—these determine cash flow and the net present value of an M&A transaction. They also drive the financial stability and future growth of Newco. Best practitioners in M&A are rigorous analysts of the economics of an opportunity.
  - *Strategy.* Strategic strengths, weaknesses, opportunities, and threats are part of the structure of the M&A environment. Many M&A transactions are motivated by a need to respond to the strategic environment. Careful strategic planning is crucial to success in M&A.
  - *Organization.* Culture, leadership, talent, and organizational architecture of the merging firms have a major influence on the ability of Newco to achieve benefits of the deal. M&A practitioners must therefore lend careful thought to postmerger organizational structure.
  - *Brand.* Large intangible influences in the setting of the M&A opportunity are the reputations of buyer and target. As a brand name affects the thinking of consumers, reputations can shape the expectations and behavior of participants in a merger. Best practitioners seek to create and preserve brand value, and to understand the sources of the counterparty's brand.

  - *Law.* Laws and regulations limit the actions of buyer and target firms. M&A practitioners must manage legal risk exposure and to consider opportunities to shape legislation.
  - *Ethics.* Ethical norms surround everything one does in M&A and are often discovered only after they are broken. Best practitioners in M&A consciously address the ethical dimension in deal development.

- *Conduct* is the behavior of managers in the pursuit of good M&A outcomes and appears in M&A in the form of creativity, interpersonal skills, and elements of personality. Behavior is important because it filters and interacts with the structural elements of a deal. Behavior affects M&A outcomes in areas such as the following:

  - *Search for partners.* Discovery of partners may rely on "networking," which relies on social skills.
  - *Due diligence.* Success in due diligence is tied to the investigator's attitude and personal attributes such as stamina, care, and capacity for critical thinking.
  - *Negotiation and bidding.* Psychology and self-discipline affect the outcomes of negotiation and bidding. Attitudes, appetites, and negotiation tactics have a large influence on deal prices and terms.
  - *Dealing with laws, regulations, and the justice system.* Although laws and regulations may seem like constraints on actions, the M&A practitioner can strive to actually *shape* the structure of the M&A situation.
  - *Deal design.* Deal design entails searching for trade-offs that will result in a win-win deal for both buyer and seller. Often, such a search requires flexibility and creativity from the deal negotiators.
  - *Postmerger integration.* It takes managerial skill to successfully implement postmerger integration.
  - *Deal development process.* Good *process* is one of the key drivers of good outcomes. Conscientiousness in developing a process mind-set lends discipline to thinking and increases the likelihood of a successful M&A outcome.

- The framework reminds us that successful *outcomes* have many dimensions. Best practitioners think in terms of the entire range of outcomes rather than narrowly in just one or two dimensions. One can benchmark the success of a deal against at least seven measures:

  1. *Creation of market value.* This is necessarily the first measure of success because of the obligation of managers and directors to serve the welfare of shareholders. But it is rarely sufficient by itself—to take an extreme example, value created unethically or illegally would be unacceptable.
  2. *Financial stability.* Another measure of success is whether a deal strengthens the financial structure of the firm. Some deals have been so aggressively financed that they led to bankruptcy shortly after closing.
  3. *Improved strategic position.* The deal should serve the mission and strategic objectives of the firm. Best practitioners look for a solid strategic rationale.

4. ***Organizational strength.*** The acquisition of talent, rejuvenation of a worn-out or defeatist culture, improvement of learning or technology transfer, and transformation of the organizational architecture of a firm are examples of ways in which a deal can strengthen the organization.
5. ***Enhanced brand.*** A successful deal may strengthen the esteem for the firm in the eyes of competitors, suppliers, customers, and employees.
6. ***Observance of the letter and spirit of ethical norms and laws.*** Success means more than avoiding criminal indictment: Best practitioners understand that it is important not only to do deals well, but also to do them *right*.
7. ***Improved process.*** Every transaction should sharpen a firm's leadership and business processes. This happens when one conducts a deal with a learning mind-set.

- The *practice* of M&A is continually changing. The chapter outlines several disruptive ideas that will affect the ongoing development of practice:
  - ***A deal is a system.*** Internal consistency is important; one must negotiate the pieces of the deal with a view toward the whole. There may be unanticipated side effects; practitioners must look out for these. There may be many attractive structures, rather than a single best structure, that satisfy the objectives of all parties.
  - ***Find and use optionality.*** Options are pervasive in M&A.
  - ***Study market inefficiency.*** Where markets are integrated and efficient, decision makers can and should refer to market prices for signals about behavior. However, some markets may be inefficient—where this is true, the best practitioner modifies the tools and concepts to adapt to the market circumstances.
  - ***Good governance pays.*** Good governance increases the chances of successful M&A outcomes, though the practices of good governance are still evolving.
  - ***A deal is more than price.*** The practitioner faces a host of choices in designing a transaction, most of which have consequences for the buyer and target company shareholders. Deal design choices can create or destroy value.
  - ***Behaviorism.*** M&A bidding processes, negotiations, and deal design can influence *and* be influenced by behavior.
  - ***No silos.*** The M&A effort will be more successful the more integrated it is across deal design, strategy, and implementation.

CHAPTER 1—WORKBOOK QUESTIONS

Explain why each of the following statements is false:

1. *Success in M&A is determined solely by structural factors.*

2. *In the behavioral realm, success in postmerger integration is influenced more by the conduct and interpersonal skills of managers than by organizational structure.*

3. *Best practice in the legal area of M&A emphasizes only the avoidance of violating laws or regulations so that the pre- and postmerger firms involved in the M&A transaction are not exposed to any legal jeopardy.*

4. *Actions in M&A that are not clearly ethical or that even are unethical will not lead to outright failure as long as they do not violate the law.*

5. *Being able to negotiate and consummate a deal is the hallmark of success in M&A.*

6. *Planning everything with painstaking care ensures a successful outcome.*

7. *The best due diligence processes are those that simply verify facts.*

8. *In M&A, outcomes are more important than processes.*

9. *For every M&A deal, there is one "best" deal design.*

10. *Decision makers should always refer to market prices for signals about behavior.*

CHAPTER 2

Ethics in M&A

Ethical dilemmas are pervasive in M&A.

Unethical business practices are unsustainable; they do not provide a strong foundation for long-term corporate or professional success.

- Companies that are committed to ethical behavior build trust and add meaningful value to their brand. A strong corporate reputation attracts active buyers, intermediaries, advisers, repeat business, and price premiums that ultimately yield attractive profits and higher returns.
- Ethical business practices promote strong leadership and teamwork in organizations. Ethical behavior aligns a company's human capital around a set of shared values, which in turn enhance business processes and capabilities.
- A company committed to ethics will look above and beyond the law to set its standards for good business practices. The law is the lowest common denominator of social norms; it enforces punishment only for illegal behavior.
- Professionals who are guided by their consciences and commitment to ethical standards understand that personal pride and self-respect are invaluable, intangible assets.
- In most, if not all, cases, M&A professionals act as agents on behalf of a company's stockholders and/or stakeholders.
  - The *stockholder theory*, advanced by Milton Friedman (1962), holds that a company must act in the best interests of its owners and strive to maximize shareholders' returns.
  - Alternatively, Edward Freeman's *stakeholder theory* (1984) prescribes a broader view: management should act in the interests of all of its stakeholders, which include constituent groups such as customers, buyers, and employees.
- Moral philosophy offers at least three bases for assessing what is right versus wrong.

1. ***Consequences.*** The first perspective asks who will be affected, and how. This branch of philosophy argues that the "right actions" are those that produce the greatest good for the greatest number. Its best-known proponents include philosophers Jeremy Bentham (1748–1832) and John Stuart Mill (1806–1873).

2. ***Duties or intentions.*** The second perspective focuses on the matrix of duties surrounding the manager and the consistency of one's intentions to fulfill them. An action is deemed as moral if it is intended to benefit and respect others and it is done out of a sense of duty, not self-gain. Perhaps the best-known deontologist is Immanuel Kant (1724–1804).
3. ***Virtues.*** The third perspective asks how an action will affect one's virtue, either in one's own or in others' eyes. A simple test is to imagine how you would feel if the contemplated action were published on the front page of tomorrow's newspaper. Rather than following rules, people are best guided by considering what a paragon of virtue would do. The Greek philosopher Aristotle (384–322 B.C.) prescribed this view.

- Business leadership involves more than an understanding of ethics; it also entails the promotion and practice of ethical behavior, active discussion, and reflection.
- Developing a high-performing culture that is also ethical can be achieved by adopting and enacting personal, corporate, and professional codes of ethics.

CHAPTER 2—WORKBOOK QUESTIONS

Analysis of the 1984 Disney Case

Imagine a conversation among three student philosophers: David, who is focused on duties; Ulyssa, focused on consequences; and Vera, a virtue-ethicist. They are debating the Disney Company's decision to pay greenmail. (For more information about this, see Chapter 2 of the main text.)

1a. *What do you think the three philosophers would say about Ron Miller and the 1984 greenmail situation?*

1b. *In your opinion, which philosopher could most successfully convince you as to whether paying greenmail was ethical and why? How might one philosopher's line of reasoning supersede the others?*

Applying Ethics to Real Business Situations

Case #1

Former majority owners of a manufacturing company, Power Electronics, have filed a lawsuit in federal district court against Systems Integration Corporation (SIC), to whom they recently sold Power Electronics. The plaintiffs claim that the buyer, SIC, ended up paying them about $20 million less than the agreed-upon $220 million for the company after accountants supposedly manipulated the post-closing account. That account included $17 million held in escrow and $4 million in receivables.

The two companies entered into a purchase agreement a year ago. As is standard practice, the seller filed a financial statement at the time of the contract. At the closing, the usual practice is for the buyer to hold back a portion of the agreed-upon price and put it in escrow while it checks the acquired company's books. The acquirer takes possession of the business and produces a final accounting of inventory, receivables, and other assets and liabilities, then often makes a final adjustment to the purchase price from the escrow money.

In the agreement, both companies agreed to use the same rules that conformed to generally accepted accounting principles (GAAP) to avoid any discrepancies regarding inventory and other issues. The two sides hired separate well-known accounting firms. In the event of a dispute, they agreed to use one of the internationally recognized accounting firms as an arbiter.

According to the claimants, the buyer's accountants were intent on finding ways to reduce the purchase price. They claim that the accountants found ways to show that the inventory was lower and that the tax credits would not be fully used because the company's future earnings would be lower than expected.

They are now suing SIC for $25 million, plus legal fees. The plaintiffs have declined to use an arbiter, arguing that they believe that it would be difficult to find one that was objective since many have had dealings with SIC.

On the side of the defense, Systems Integration Corporation's accountants say the company doesn't owe anything to the sellers. According to their audit, the company should not only keep the $17 million in escrow, but should also inform the sellers that they owe another $6 million to SIC.

2. *What ethical issues does this dispute raise? Set aside the legal question of the lawsuit and focus on the frameworks outlined in the chapter.*

Case #2

> *Hershey was a sweet target stuck in a bitter controversy. Dealmakers and M&A lawyers say that there probably never was a controversy of this type plaguing an acquisition, and there may never be again.*
>
> —*Mergers & Acquisitions*, October 2002

On July 25, 2002, the Hershey Trust Company—the primary owner of Hershey Foods and holder of 77 percent of Hershey Foods' voting stock—publicly announced that it wanted Hershey Foods to explore a sale of the entire company. The trust's primary financial and social responsibility is to operate the Milton Hershey School. It had decided that exploring a possible sale of the company "was the most prudent course of action" consistent with its diversification objectives, claiming it needed to diversify its portfolio in order to protect the assets of its beneficiary. When rival food firms like Wrigley and Nestlé inquired about buying the entire stake, the trustees also liked the prospect of receiving a large premium for their control of the company. Wrigley and Nestlé bid $12.5 billion and $11.2 billion, respectively, for Hershey Foods.

Richard Lenny, CEO of Hershey Foods, proposed to buy back the trust's shares over time at a small premium, but Robert Vowler, CEO and president of the Hershey Trust Company, rejected the offer. Robert Vowler released a statement in mid-August 2002 saying, "The board continues to believe this course [of selling its shares in Hershey Foods] is in keeping with its fiduciary responsibility to protect and preserve the Trust, which through the Milton Hershey School serves children in need. We're not talking about making more money. That's not what this is all about. This is about protecting the trust fund in perpetuity, protecting it from risk." But members of the school's alumni association criticized the trust for careless spending, exorbitant salaries, and inadequate oversight of the student facility. Alumni of the Milton Hershey School contended that "modern business temptations, mismanagement, and conflicts of interest have diverted Hershey trustees from the philanthropic and educational mission set down a century ago."

3. *What ethical issues emerge in the controversy over the Hershey Trust's decision to put Hershey Foods up for sale?*

CHAPTER 3

Does M&A Pay?

The degree of success or failure of M&A transactions is of the utmost importance to CEOs, business planners, investors, and government regulators. "Success" can be defined in many ways, but *profitability* from an economic standpoint is the most rigorous and measurable definition. The scientific evidence suggests that M&A *does* pay.

- The best measurable benchmark for evaluating any investment is the investors' required return, also known as the return that investors could have earned on other investment opportunities of similar risk.
  - Value is created when the returns on the investment exceed the required rate of return.
  - Value is destroyed when the investment returns fall short of the return rate required by investors.
  - Value is conserved when investors earn the "required rate of return": that which they expect to receive.
- The primary parties to an M&A transaction are the buying and selling companies. To evaluate value creation, one must consider the economic consequences of M&A transactions on the shareholders of both of the primary parties. These consequences are measured by researchers in four main ways from the standpoint of buyers and sellers.
  1. Event studies
  2. Accounting studies
  3. Surveys of executives
  4. Clinical studies
- Each research method has strengths and weaknesses, and some arguably offer more robust findings than others. The M&A scholar would be well served to look at various studies, using different methods and approaches, in order to glean some patterns of confirmation.
- Event studies, which examine the abnormal returns to shareholders in the period surrounding the announcement of an M&A transaction, yield insights about market-based returns to shareholders of target, buyer, and combined companies. The results of these studies provide the following key findings:
  - Shareholders of target firms receive "average abnormal" positive returns in the 20 to 30 percent range.

  - In the aggregate, market-adjusted returns to buyer shareholders essentially break even and value is conserved. In more than two-thirds of the studies, the buyer shareholders receive zero or positive event returns at the announcements of mergers. This suggests that most of the time the market thinks the investment will at least pay its way.
  - Shareholders who invest in the *combined* entity formed by an M&A transaction receive positive returns. This suggests that the transaction does create new value.
- Accounting studies, which analyze reported financial results of acquiring companies before and after acquisitions against comparable companies that did not make acquisitions, have brought to bear some enlightening points. These include:
  - Buyers outperform their benchmark leading up to an acquisition, which seems to occur near or at the peak of their financial performance.
  - After making an acquisition, buyers tend to perform worse than their peer benchmark on measures such as profit margins, growth rates, and returns on assets.
  - Targets tend to be profitable firms.
  - Anticipated gains of postmerger operating performance drive share prices at the time of a deal's announcement.
- The determinants of M&A profitability can be gleaned from cross-sectional research studies. Some key insights are:
  - Expected synergies are important drivers of wealth creation through merger.
  - When analysts and investors expect synergies, they price the benefits in their valuation.
  - Increased market share achieved through M&A does not create value.
  - Paying with stock is costly; paying with cash is neutral.
  - Hostile deals create more value for buyers than do friendly deals.
  - When managers have a greater economic interest, more value is created.
- The research findings of clinical studies underscore the importance of context and company-specific circumstances that can affect buyers and/or sellers. The role of strategic and organizational issues as well as financial implications should be considered in the evaluation of M&A deals.
- On balance, M&A is economically profitable for buyers, targets, and merging companies combined. M&A does pay. But buyers should be cautious. Though the averages suggest that most deals cover their cost of capital, there is a wide variation in results. Buyers should avoid overpaying and work very hard to achieve projected synergies.

CHAPTER 3—WORKBOOK QUESTIONS

Part I: Short Answer

1. *There are several different research methods of M&A profitability. Please briefly describe four examples, and the advantages and limitations of each method.*

2. *Will accounting-based studies and market return analyses reveal the same information regarding the value created by a merger? Why or why not?*

Part II: Questions on Real Business Situations

Case #1[1]

In October 2001, the J. M. Smucker Co.[2] agreed to purchase Jif peanut butter and Crisco cooking oil and shortening brands from Procter & Gamble[3] for $810 million in stock. P&G shareholders would receive one share of new Smucker stock for every 50 shares they held in P&G. This would shift 53 percent of Smucker stock into the hands of P&G shareholders, and would roughly double its total shares outstanding. However, the new arrangement called for existing Smucker shareholders to retain control over major decisions despite holding a minority share in the company.

Adding Jif and Crisco was expected to double Smucker's projected revenues to an estimated $1.3 billion in fiscal 2003. Due to the acquisition, Smucker's market share would rise to 41 percent in jam, 38 percent in peanut butter, and 24 percent in cooking oils.

At the time of the acquisition, Smucker did not have its own sales force. Because of its small size, it sold its products through brokers. Smucker had recently finished a three-year $35 million overhaul in its inventory and customer-service systems.

Analysts suspected that this would not be Smucker's last acquisition. The company held a cash balance of $67 million and was believed to have borrowing capacity for a further $500 million to $1 billion in debt.

Many expected P&G shareholders to sell their new Smucker shares. Because P&G was heavily owned by many index funds, this large constituent of P&G shareholders would have to unload Smucker stock because unlike P&G, Smucker was not in the Standard & Poor's 500-stock index. Other institutional investors, too, might sell if they believed Smucker would not be actively traded or enjoy good growth prospects.

The deal closed in June 2002. The chart shows the historical price of Smucker between September 2001 and June 2002.

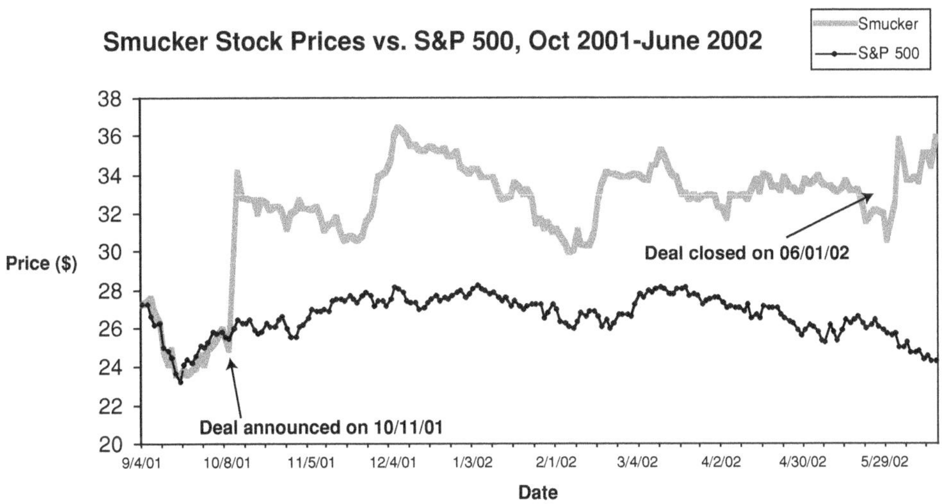

1. *Based solely on the information provided here and the general findings about acquisition returns in Chapter 3 of the main text, do you think this was a good acquisition for Smucker? Why or why not?*

Case #2

In 1997, Quaker Oats Co. agreed to sell Snapple Beverage Corp. to Triarc Cos. for \$300 million—a little over two years after it had spent \$1.7 billion to acquire the specialty drink maker. Three years later, in October 2000, Triarc sold the Snapple brand to Cadbury Schweppes for approximately \$1 billion.

When Quaker made this purchase in 1994, the company believed it would be able to increase the value of the independent beverage producer and to enhance its revenue streams. At the time, however, the growth of the specialty beverage market was slowing, and huge rivals, such as Coca-Cola Co. and PepsiCo, were unleashing new products to compete against Snapple.

After Quaker completed the acquisition, Snapple had more than half of its sales at convenience stores, gas stations, and similar outlets, primarily on the East and West Coasts. Quaker decided to move beyond working with Snapple's small independent distributors in order to leverage its prowess in large-scale market distribution (i.e., supermarkets, mass merchants). Since Quaker's Gatorade drink had been selling well through mass distribution, the company expected that Snapple would meet similar success through those channels.

2. *How did the acquisition of Snapple turn out for Quaker and Triarc, respectively? What might explain Quaker's experience with Snapple? Is past success a good indicator of future experience?*

NOTES

1. *Source: Wall Street Journal*, October 11, 2001.
2. Smucker is the number one U.S. producer of jams, jellies, and preserves, and also makes dessert toppings, peanut butter, juices, and specialty fruit spreads under brand names.
3. Procter & Gamble is a large consumer-goods manufacturer that markets over 250 brands to nearly five billion consumers in over 140 countries. These brands include Tide, Crest, Pantene, Always, Pringles, Pampers, Olay, Folgers, Cover Girl, Downy, Dawn, Bounty, and Charmin.

4
M&A Activity

This chapter explores the drivers of M&A activity in the economy. Of the many possible explanations, the role of "shocks" or economic turbulence offers the greatest traction for the practitioner seeking to understand why M&A appears in waves. The chapter surveys approaches for listening for the forces that drive M&A activity.

- Reflecting on M&A deals of the past helps us to learn and understand the drivers of M&A activity. While past M&A activity does not necessarily reflect the present or predict the future, it does provide key lessons that should be learned and analyzed for future application.
- M&A activity appears in waves, which follow a random walk and show no regularity in terms of period length or amplitude.
- Key points of each M&A wave in the preceding century include:

  Wave 1: 1895–1904
  - Characterized by horizontal mergers.
  - Coincided with a period of economic and capital market growth.
  - Firms sought to build market power in response to overcapacity.
  - Touched a wide variety of manufacturing industries.

  Wave 2: 1925–1929
  - Characterized by vertical integration mergers.
  - Coincided with a booming stock market, ended with the crash of 1929.
  - When large public utility holding companies emerged.
  - U.S. government increased its antitrust enforcement following passage of the Clayton Act of 1914.

  Wave 3: 1965–1970
  - Characterized by conglomerate or diversifying combinations.
  - Concentrated activity among a group of conglomerates and oil companies.
  - Coincided with a strong economy and the 1960s bull market.

  Wave 4a: 1981–1987
  - More hostile takeovers, leveraged deals, and going-private transactions than in prior waves.
  - Broad-based activity: touched virtually all sectors of the U.S. economy.
  - Financial and international buyers became more prominent players.

- Complexity of deals mirrored growing capital market innovation and sophistication.

Wave 4b: 1992–2000

- High M&A activity in banking, health care, defense, and high technology.
- Signaled a paradigm shift with new rules regarding M&A deal design and size.
- Significance of strategic buyers looking for synergies with target companies.

- Explanations for M&A activity are various; any explanation will entail a complicated, multifaceted story. Basically, these stories cluster into four categories:

  1. ***Markets are rational but managers are irrational.*** An example of this view would be the "hubris hypothesis," which holds that managers know that great success in M&A is elusive, but do deals anyway out of sheer arrogance or in the belief that *they* have special capabilities. Markets know better, and punish the share prices of acquirers.
  2. ***Markets and managers are irrational.*** By this view, M&A activity is simply herdlike behavior, much like the swarming of bees or flights of geese.
  3. ***Markets are irrational but managers are rational.*** Share prices occasionally get overvalued. When managers, who have better inside information, see this, they use stock to make acquisitions. At other times they use cash. By this view, the stock market cycle drives M&A activity, an association confirmed by research.
  4. ***Markets and managers are rational.*** M&A activity is driven by profit-seeing behavior on the part of managers and investors. For instance, periodically stimuli like new products, processes, or technologies "shock" the balance of competition in the industry. These shocks stimulate M&A activity. By this view, one should pay attention to forces of turbulence (shocks), such as deregulation, technological innovation, demographic change, trade liberalization, and so on.

- Of the four approaches, only the fourth lends much traction to the practitioner seeking to understand developments and do business. The other three may have some explanatory power at certain times and under certain conditions. But the fourth view, *turbulence*, stimulates an ongoing critical evaluation that can yield useful insights.

- Chapter 4 of the main text describes the turbulence perspective through the writings of four observers of M&A.

  Entrepreneurs: Joseph Schumpeter and "Creative Destruction"

  - Focuses on the role of the entrepreneur, who seeks to profit from new opportunities. This generates "creative destruction" in markets and ensures that market economies are self-renewing.
  - Waves of creative destruction create business cycles.
  - Similarly, creative destruction, in the form of industry "stocks" creates waves of M&A activity. This implies that to understand M&A activity, we should listen for shocks and turbulence at the level of firms and markets, not at the level of the economy.

Naomi Lamoreaux's History of the First Great Merger Wave

- M&A activity was triggered by the entry of new and more powerful technology. This technology hit capital intensive and mass-production firms the hardest.
- Large trusts emerged in response to industry shocks.
- Antitrust policy should have been aimed at minimizing the erection of entry barriers.

Reduction of Agency Costs: Michael Jensen's Explanation

- The wave of M&A activity in the 1980s and 1990s had its roots in problems that built up in the 1960s and 1970s, especially the accumulated effects of inflation, regulation, and the conglomerate merger wave.
- Cited the importance of deregulation, globalization of trade, and organizational innovation as triggers of recent M&A waves.

Practitioners' View: Bruce Wasserstein

- Five pistons drive the merger process: regulatory and political reform, technological change, fluctuations in financial markets, role of leadership, and tension between scale and focus.
- Booms in M&A can be traced to turbulence caused by one or more of the five pistons.

- In order to identify the role of turbulence in stimulating M&A activity, one should look for forms of economic shocks (deregulation, technology change, etc.) in specific industries.
- Capital markets (equity, debt, and derivative markets) are reliable messengers of economic turbulence.

CHAPTER 4—WORKBOOK QUESTIONS

1. *What might explain the association between the cycle of M&A activity and the cycle of the stock market?*

2. *Consider the following quotation from Schumpeter:*

   The fundamental impulse that sets and keeps the capitalist engine in motion comes from the new consumers, goods, the new methods of production or transportation, the new markets, the new forms of industrial organization that capitalist enterprise creates."

   —Joseph Schumpeter, *Capitalism, Socialism and Democracy*, 1942, pp. 82–83

What role does the entrepreneur play in keeping the capitalist engine in motion?

3. *According to Schumpeter:*

   Railroads did not emerge because any consumers took the initiative in displaying an effective demand for their service in preference to the services of the mail

> *coaches. Railroads were forced by producers on consumers who, most often than not, have resisted the change and have had to be educated.*
>
> —Joseph Schumpeter, *Business*, p. 73

Do innovations arise because of consumers' needs or wants, or because the producers force the innovations on the consumer? What are the implications for the entrepreneur?

4. *Read the following fictional case and answer the questions that follow.*

Case

Mara Davis, a broadcast journalist, is interviewing Matthew Adams, the CEO of High Tech Telecom, Inc., an acquisitive telecom company that has been engaged in a few mergers in the past few years.

Background

In 1999, Adams, the CEO of Long Lines Telephone, spent $80 billion to acquire two giant cable companies, Wire Squires and Best Brand Broadband, in order to put Long Lines in the broadband business. Since Long Lines was facing declining margins in its core long-distance business, its stated goal was to achieve operational synergies which could bundle cable, Internet, wireless, and telephone services.

A year later, Long Lines' stock price plummeted with the Internet collapse. Adams decided to restructure the company and break up the consolidated businesses back into separate units, which were sold.

Now, CEO Adams is proposing another mega-merger with another cable giant, Power-line, Inc., which would give Long Lines access to a significant share of the U.S. cable customer base. However, the deal is uniquely designed: The merger would be structured so that the combined cable unit would be spun off as a separate venture. The CEO of Power-line, David Rollins, would be the CEO of this spun-off entity, with Adams at his side as the chairman. Rollins would get 33 percent of the new voting shares.

Shortly after Adams' announcement of this deal, journalist Davis conducted the following interview of Adams:

Interview

JOURNALIST: *A common view that people hold is that M&A activity is dictated by forces of change in the economy that enable companies to take advantage of particularly favorable circumstances and opportunities. However, some people claim that mergers happen because CEOs and senior management really push to complete deals for more personal reasons. What is your take on this?*

CEO: I can say with certainty that my company's acquisitions are motivated by economic and strategic reasons. In fact, I believe that most company mergers are driven for the purpose of creating value, regardless of the hearsay that circulates the market. In particular, acquisitive companies like my own will not put in the time, energy, and resources to complete a deal that does not enhance their business operations and financial results. All it takes is one bad merger to set a company back, and then make it more difficult in the future to transact successful subsequent acquisitions.

JOURNALIST: *Three years ago, you made two significant acquisitions of two cable companies. A year after the acquisitions, you reversed your decision by break-*

ing up the assets of your company. Why did you do this, if you claim your acquisitions are based on sound economic and strategic reasons?

CEO: The two acquisitions we made three years back were made in favorable economic conditions: the stock market was at a peak, interest rates were low, and GDP [gross domestic product] was strong. I expected that the mergers would help us realize significant synergies, better margins, and ultimately, better profits.

However, the economy took an unexpected turn for the worse when the technology bubble burst. Our industry was certainly one that experienced particularly great pains and repercussions of the technology market tumbling. Even though the two acquisitions were made on sound economic and strategic reasoning, conditions changed dramatically. Sometimes drastic changes will dictate that other actions be taken to preserve value. That is what I did when I broke up the assets of the company.

JOURNALIST: *But isn't it possible that managers of acquisitive companies make merger decisions based on their own personal agendas, and just stand behind other outward claims for why a merger is taking place?*

CEO: Good M&A initiatives are based on strategic business goals, not the personal agendas of managers. At Long Lines, we employ strategies for long-term success and value creation. We also realize that our shareholders and the public eye scrutinize all of our M&A transactions and for that reason alone we would not make false outward claims to justify merger decisions.

JOURNALIST: *So explain the reasons for this new proposed merger. Why are you proposing an acquisition of another cable company when you already tried buying two cable companies and ended up selling them shortly after?*

CEO: Well, the circumstances in our industry and the overall economy have changed, and we believe that Long Lines is now in a position to make a successful cable acquisition that will create meaningful value for our company. We do not expect to see another market disruption like the 2001 technology bubble burst. Since 2001, investors have taken on a much more conservative and skeptical view about technology stocks. Even though we would like to restore investor confidence, we believe that the events of the past few years have taken the extreme volatility out of the capital markets. While we may never again see valuations of technology stocks rise at the speed and magnitude of the late 1990s, we also doubt we will see them fall in the same manner.

The proposed merger with Power-line is based on value creation, plain and simple. Cable continues to be a high-margin business, whereas the more mature long-distance telephone and wireless services have been experiencing lower growth and profitability.

4a. *Analyze the interview between the journalist and the CEO. What views or sentiments do the journalist's questions convey? What is the CEO's stance on M&A activity, as revealed in his answers?*

4b. *Which view of M&A activity do you think holds more credence? If you were to enter the conversation, what position would you take? How would you explain what drives M&A activity?*

5. *Read the following case and answer the question that follows. This is drawn from an actual situation.*

Case

In November 2002, Level 3 Communications announced that it would acquire nearly all of Genuity Inc.'s assets. To facilitate the transaction, Genuity filed voluntary petitions for reorganization under Chapter 11 of the Bankruptcy Code.

In December, Level 3 Communications received approval from the U.S. Department of Justice and the Federal Trade Commission to acquire Genuity Inc. Under the Telecommunications Act of 1996, any entity may enter a telecommunications market.

As a result of the transaction, which was completed in February 2003, Level 3 now operates one of the largest Internet backbones in the world and is the primary provider of Internet connectivity for millions of dial-up and broadband subscribers. As of March 2003, the company had a total of 73 markets in service: 57 in the United States and 16 in Europe. This was up sharply from December 2002, when the company had operational facilities in 27 U.S. markets and 9 European markets.

Level 3's CEO attested, "There is a unique and compelling fit between Genuity and Level 3. The transaction combines the assets and operations of Genuity, the company that helped invent the Internet, with Level 3, the company that built the first network fully optimized for Internet Protocol–based communications. . . . Genuity operates an international IP network. Its largest customers are Verizon Communications and America Online. . . . The transaction adds substantial new revenue from high-quality customers and creates value by generating significant network and operating cost synergies for the combined business, as well as reductions in capital expenditures."

The CEO also noted that the agreement with Genuity was consistent with Level 3's overall acquisition strategy, "As we have said in the past, we evaluate every potential acquisition according to its ability to generate positive cash flow from high-quality customers. We look for opportunities to acquire recurring revenues that come predominantly from services we already provide in geographic areas that we already serve, with customers consistent with our existing customer base. Above all we are committed to remaining fully funded to free cash flow breakeven and improving our financial position."

The acquisition was believed to accelerate Level 3's projected time to positive free cash flow to early 2004.

Company Information

Level 3 is an international communications and information services company. It operates the world's first international network optimized end-to-end for IP packet switching technology. Genuity is a leading provider of managed IP networking services for businesses. The company offers a full portfolio of services, including Internet access, Internet security, and Virtual Private Networks (VPNs).

As of July 2002, Genuity Inc. had doubted its ability to stay in business: The company had recently defaulted on a $2 billion line of credit and a $1.15 billion loan from Verizon Communications Corp. The default came after Verizon decided not to exercise its option to take a controlling stake in Genuity.

5. *Identify one or more potential sources of turbulence for Level 3's acquisition of Genuity, Inc., and briefly explain how the turbulence may have created a merger opportunity.*

5

Cross-Border M&A

Countries differ in important ways that will affect the values of firms. Beneath every cross-border valuation analysis is some hidden assumption or "bet" about the future of a country market. Given the ubiquity of cross-border deals, a good M&A practitioner should seek to master cross-border analysis.

- Research has found that cross-border transactions have a different profile compared to domestic deals: Cross-border transactions tend to:
  - Be more related to the buyer's core industry.
  - Be paid for mainly in cash. Many cross-border buyers do not have shares listed for trading in the foreign market. Thus, buyers tend to pay with cash rather than stock.
  - Involve targets that are mainly manufacturing firms with low intangible assets.
- Following are some of the forces that drive cross-border M&A activity:
  - Exploiting market imperfections. Buyers may recognize profitable opportunities to take advantage of cheap labor and raw materials, unmet consumer demand, deregulation, trade liberalization, and country integration of capital and product markets into global markets.
  - Extending the reach of intangible assets. Firms with significant intangible assets such as brand name and patents may want to broaden the scale of their use and preempt others who might be tempted to imitate or appropriate those intangible assets.
  - Reducing tax expense through arbitrage across different tax jurisdictions.
  - Reducing risk through diversification. If economic activity across countries is less than perfectly correlated, geographic diversification can reduce risk.
  - Exploiting differences in capital market and currency conditions.
  - Improving governance. M&A is a means by which companies can exit from a poor governance environment.
- The M&A practitioner must have a "view" about a country in which an acquisition is contemplated. Such a view will be informed by insights about:
  - Expected economic growth in the country and region.
  - Foundations of the country's competitive advantage.
  - Outlook for inflation, interest rates, and exchange rates.

  - Relative valuation of assets.
  - Risks.

- Macroeconomic analysis of a country should cover the following aspects:
  - Fiscal policy.
  - Monetary policy.
  - Exchange rate policy.
  - Intervention policy.
  - Trade policy.
  - Employment and welfare policy.

- Microeconomic analysis of a country considers activity at the level of industries and firms. Michael Porter argues that country performance is essentially a matter of microeconomic performance. His "diamond model" of competitive advantage asserts that the ability to innovate and to improve productivity resides in the following:
  - ***Factor conditions.*** These regard the inputs of production, such as labor, land, natural resources, physical facilities, infrastructure, human resources, and intellectual capital. The analyst should assess how specialized a nation's factors are, and how tailored they are to the needs of the acquisition target.
  - ***Demand conditions.*** The home-market demand for the goods or services of an industry will heavily influence the international success of that industry. The best home demand arises from discerning and sophisticated customers.
  - ***Related or supporting industries.*** Porter maintains that the presence of strong upstream and downstream industries can create industry clusters that in turn enhance a nation's competitive advantage.
  - ***Domestic rivalry.*** Competition tends to strengthen the international competitiveness of local industries. The level of competition can be assessed by measuring concentration ratios, evaluating entry barriers, and analyzing the patterns of competition within an industry/country.

- Institutional economics emphasizes the important role played in national economic growth by a range of institutions that are not direct producers of growth. These institutions include:
  - Banking.
  - Stock markets and investment regulations.
  - Watchdogs: auditors, free press, opposition political parties.
  - Independent judiciary, rule of law, respect for contracts and property rights.
  - Educational system.

- Economic growth may also be influenced by cultural factors such as willingness to pay and receive interest, respect for entrepreneurs, consumerism, emphasis on education, and saving.

CHAPTER 5—WORKBOOK QUESTIONS

1. You are the head of strategic planning for a large U.S. telecommunications firm. In early 2003, you held a planning session with your firm's executive committee in order to flesh out a 10-year vision for your company. The conclusion from that session was that your firm needs to expand overseas if it wants to grow. After analyzing the demographics in several regions, you decide that Southeast Asia offers the greatest growth prospects: It is young, has underserved telecommunications needs, and presents less competition as opposed to the U.S. market.

   You are contemplating either a 100 percent acquisition or a joint venture agreement with a local firm. From having been in the business many years, you have established good relationships with a couple of telecommunications firms in the Philippines and in Thailand. These two countries would therefore be a logical start to your Southeast Asian strategy.

   To begin, you gather some social and economic data as of 2001 and recent economic reports, on the two countries. Now you are ready to perform a preliminary analysis. Here are summary tables of comparative information between the Philippines and Thailand, followed by individual reports and statistics on each country.

1a. *Based on the information here, provide a comparative analysis of both countries.*

1b. *Which country would you invest in? Why? Would you do a 100 percent acquisition or a joint venture? Why?*

1c. *What other information would you like to have, to complete the framework shown in Exhibit 5.12 of the main text?*

	Philippines	Thailand	East Asia & Pacific (Where Available)
Poverty and social			
Population (millions)	85.0	62.0	1,826.0
Surface area (thousand sq. km.)	300.0	513.1	
Population per sq. km.	283.3	119.0	
Population growth	1.90%	0.80%	1.10%
Life expectancy	69	69	69
Population below national poverty line	26%	16.10%	
Urban population as % of total	59	20	37
Infant mortality (per 1,000 live births)	31	28	36
Child malnutrition	32	18	12
Illiteracy (% of population age 15+)	5%	4%	14%
Economics			
GDP (US$ billions)	71	115	
GNI per capita (US$)	1,050	1,970	

(Continued)

	Philippines	Thailand	East Asia & Pacific (Where Available)
Gross domestic investment/GDP	18.0	24.0	
Exports of goods and services/GDP	49.3	66.3	
Gross domestic savings/GDP	19.4	30.1	
Gross national savings/GDP	26.0	28.7	
Current account balance/GDP	6.3	5.4	
Interest payments/GDP	3.5	3.0	
Total debt/GDP	73.3	58.5	
Total debt service/exports	18.7	20.5	
Other			
Form of government	Republic	Constitutional monarchy	
Corruption perceptions index, 2002 (rank out of 102 countries, 1 being the highest)	77.0	64.0	

Sources of data: World Bank web site, "Countries and Regions" section; Transparency International.

Infrastructure	Thailand	Philippines
Telecommunications:		
General assessment	Service to general public adequate but investment in technological upgrades reduced by recession	Good international radiotelephone and submarine cable services; domestic service adequate
Telephone—main lines in use	5.6 million (2000)	3.1 million (2000)
Telephone—mobile cellular	3.1 million (2002)	6.5 million (2000)
Number of Internet users	1.2 million (2001)	4.5 million (2002)
Transportation:		
Railways (km)	4,071	897
Highways (km)		
Total	64,000	199,950
Paved	62,985	39,590
Unpaved	1,615	160,360
Airports (number)	110	275
Number of towns/cities with ports and harbors	7	15

Source of data: CIA web site.

[These spreadsheets can be found in the folder "Key Spreadsheets from the Workbook" located on the CD-ROM.]

The Philippines

Development Progress
The Philippines made significant progress in reducing poverty between 1990 and 1997, when the incidence of poverty fell sharply from 34 percent in 1991 to 25 percent in 1997. Much of this improvement occurred in 1994–1997 when economic growth averaged 5 percent per annum. In contrast, from 1998 to 2001 economic growth averaged only 2.5 percent and poverty reduction stagnated; preliminary data suggest that poverty incidence in 2000 is about 26 percent.

. . .

Recent Developments and Current Challenges
The Philippines had gone through a turbulent political period from 1999 to early 2001, with modest economic growth, weak poverty reduction performance, and faltering investor confidence, undermined by governance concerns. Since a new administration assumed power in January 2001, public confidence has increased with the pursuit of sound macroeconomic policies, and governance and structural reforms. The new administration has also emphasized a "peace and development" approach to conflict-affected Mindanao,* since the resurgence of violence there in 2000.

The Philippines' main challenge for the medium term remains poverty reduction. Poverty is still largely a rural phenomenon, attributed to: high dependence on agriculture where productivity has been declining and per capita economic growth is low; lack of adequate social safety nets, especially for poor women and children; and low educational attainment due to relatively high dropout rates and poor educational quality. Population pressures and a declining natural resource base have exacerbated these problems.

Despite lackluster performance in financial markets domestically and abroad, the real economy has enjoyed relatively robust performance during the first half of 2002 with GDP growing at 4.1 percent annually. Agriculture, trade, and telecommunications performed particularly strongly. The first semester of 2002 saw exports grow by 4.3 percent (year-on-year), while imports grew 3.4 percent, reflecting renewed growth in electronic exports and domestic demand for capital replenishment and consumer durables. Meanwhile, buoyed by strong workers remittances, consumption has played a key role in supporting domestic demand.

Aided by a steady decline in the inflation rate (2.6 percent in July 2002, year-on-year), the monetary authorities were able to lower key interest rates by 800 basis points since the end of 2000, and this has allowed banks to lower lending rates. Moreover, portfolio investment for the first four months of 2002 showed a turnaround from a net negative position of $884 million in 2001 to $1.7 billion this year. Net foreign direct investment also increased (by 86 percent) in the first four months of 2002, to $1.5 billion compared to $808 million for the same period in 2001.

Recent data on the financial market, however, is not as upbeat. Nonperforming

---

*Mindanao is the southern region of the Philippines.

Source of the Philippines country description: World Bank web site, "Countries and Regions" section. *Note:* ". . ." indicates portions taken out. World Bank Online by World Bank.

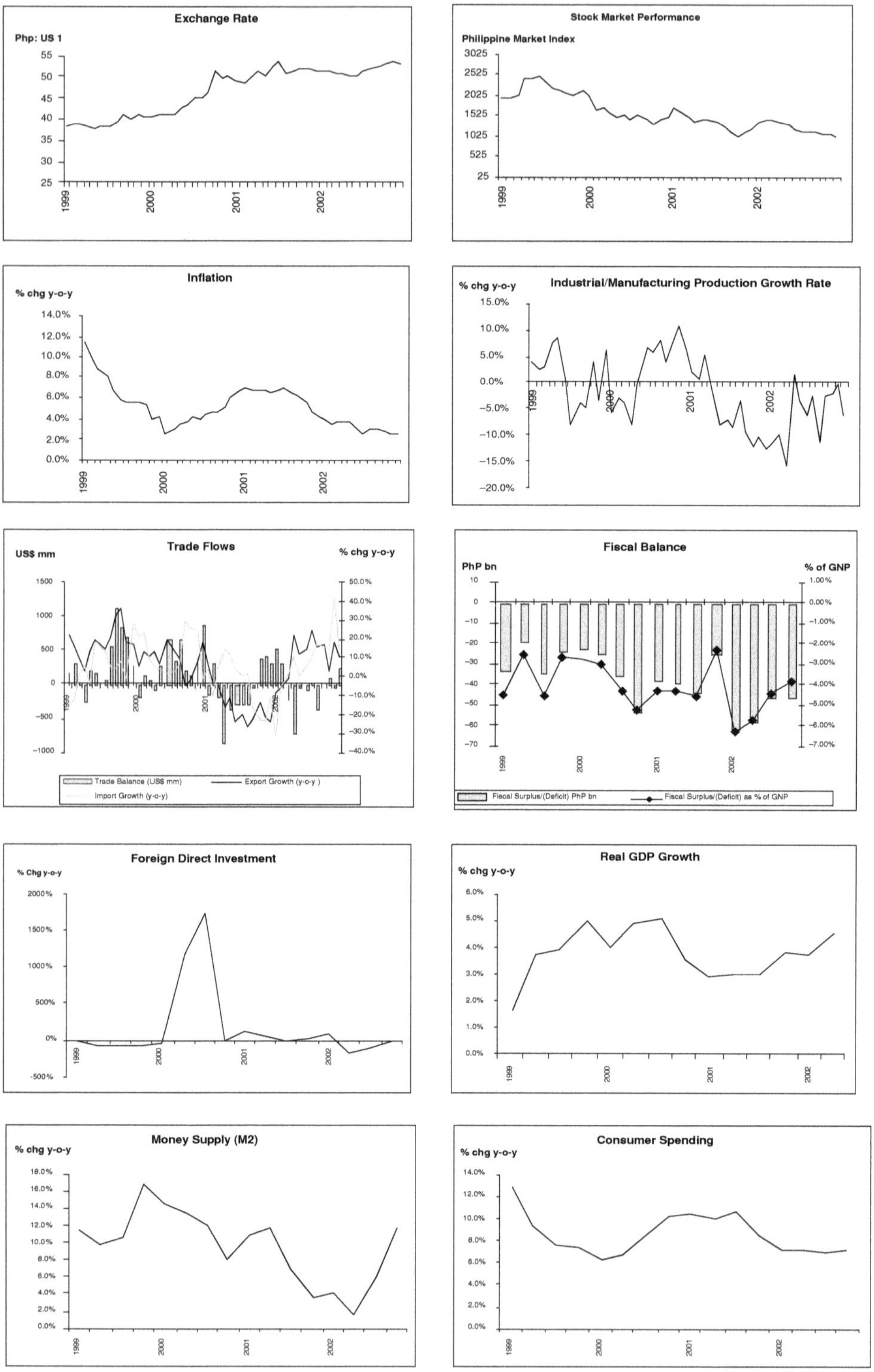

The Philippines Economic Indicators

[This spreadsheet can be found in the folder "Key Spreadsheets from the Workbook" located on the CD-ROM.]

loans (NPLs) of the banking sector have risen to 18 percent in June 2002, from 17 percent a year ago. The Philippine stock market composite index has fallen by 23 percent over the March–August 2002 period, under very thin volumes (average of $5.8 million a day). Spreads on government bonds have also gone up in recent months (e.g., spreads on Eurobonds maturing in 2008 have risen to 460 basis points, after having fallen from 644 in December 2000 to 305 basis points in May 2002). Also, the peso has depreciated slightly since mid-2002.

At the heart of the financial market's concern is fiscal policy discipline. The government budget deficit for the first seven months of 2002 (P133 billion) has already breached its full-year target of P130 billion. Higher spending during the first half of the year to support economic recovery and to maintain the needed basic social expenditures and weak revenue collection have both contributed to the deficit. This revenue shortfall is a key concern of government. Without an improvement in revenue collection, the government will find it hard to sustain the needed expenditures for health, education, and other basic social services, and it will find it hard to absorb increased Official Development Assistance.

In an effort to strengthen fiscal management, the government has continued to work on longer-term structural reforms and efforts to reverse the slide in revenues. In particular, the procurement bill is now at advanced stages of deliberation in the Senate. This will lend strong support to efforts to strengthen expenditure management and to make every peso count. Second, key leaders of Congress recently sponsored a bill to create an Internal Revenue Management Authority (IRMA). The bill proposes to establish an organization that will increase managerial flexibility and strengthen performance review and accountabilities of the primary revenue collection agency of government. These two proposed legislations will help support government's efforts to strengthen fiscal management.

Thailand

Progress in the Last Decade

Following the crisis,* Thailand began to implement deep reform of the financial sector, corporate governance, the secured lending regime, and competition policy to strengthen the incentive for owners of banks and firms to move toward their competitive frontiers. The resilience of the Thai economy facilitated a quick recovery of economic growth and the numbers in poverty began to fall. After contracting by more than 10 percent in 1998, Thailand's economy grew at over 4 percent in 1999 and 2000—and stayed positive at 1.8 percent in 2001, in spite of the global slowdown.

In 1999–2000, aided by the fiscal stimulus and increased external demand, poverty fell by 2 percentage points. Nearly a million people bounced back out of poverty following the recovery of economic growth.

Thailand Government, led by the Prime Minister's Thai Rak Thai party, which has a majority in the Parliament, won the national election on a pro-poor, pro-rural,

---

*The Asian financial crisis that began in 1997.

Source of the Thailand country description: World Bank web site, "Countries and Regions" section. *Note:* ". . ." indicates portions taken out. World Bank Online by World Bank.

and pro-Thailand platform. Notably, this administration is the first to be elected to office under the new Constitution. . . . The Government is in the process of putting forward its medium-term strategies through the Ninth Plan, which focuses on poverty reduction and balanced development.

Thailand's Monarch has set out an agenda for the nation to address the problems of the poor by promoting the idea of a community-driven, self-sufficiency economy. The King has also spoken out against corruption and for the improved management of natural resources. The Senate is playing an increasingly important role as is the new National Social and Economic Council in providing more checks and balances as the country moves forward under the new Constitution.

Current Challenges

Thailand, however, faces a considerably unfinished agenda. With the downturn in the United States and Japan, the country's economic growth has not returned to precrisis levels, although 2002 growth rates are expected to be in the range of 3.5 to 4 percent, assisted by strong domestic consumption. Progress in financial and corporate sector reform has been affected by lagging corporate debt restructuring. . . .

Thailand also faces the challenge of implementing the new Constitution. The Constitution considerably strengthens democratic and accountability institutions such as the National Counter-Corruption Commission, Electoral Commission, and Administrative Courts, but many of those institutions have come under attack. The electoral process has been revamped with a directly elected Senate and a reformed system of parliamentary representation. Civil society has gained greater recognition and voice and is becoming a more powerful participant in the policy debate, and the media is among the freest in the region. However, the public continues to regard weak governance—and in particular corruption—as a major impediment to economic and social development.

The problems of the poor have also been compounded by the crisis. Until the onset of the crisis in 1997, high growth rates in Thailand had pulled poverty rates down from 32.6 percent of the population in 1988 to 11.4 percent in 1996, lifting nearly a million people out of poverty every year. But much of this progress came to a halt in 1997. In a total population of 61 million, the number of poor increased during the crisis from 6.8 million in 1996 to 9.8 million in 1999. The Northeast, the poorest region of the country, experienced a drop in income that was twice the national average.

Substantial environmental damage, a by-product of Thailand's rapid development over the last 30 years and weak environmental institutions, has also hurt the poor disproportionately. One-third of the surface water is unsuitable for human consumption or agricultural use. Half of the forest cover has been lost. Air pollution in Bangkok exceeds standards twofold, and industrial hazardous waste generation has hit 1.6 million tons per year.

The poor in Thailand could also benefit greatly from faster progress in the area of governance, affording them more security, opportunity, and greater voice. Governance is one of the four pillars of the Government's Ninth Plan, which is underpinned by a multifaceted poverty reduction strategy that operates through the four pillars of social protection, competitiveness, governance, and environmental protection in a holistic framework.

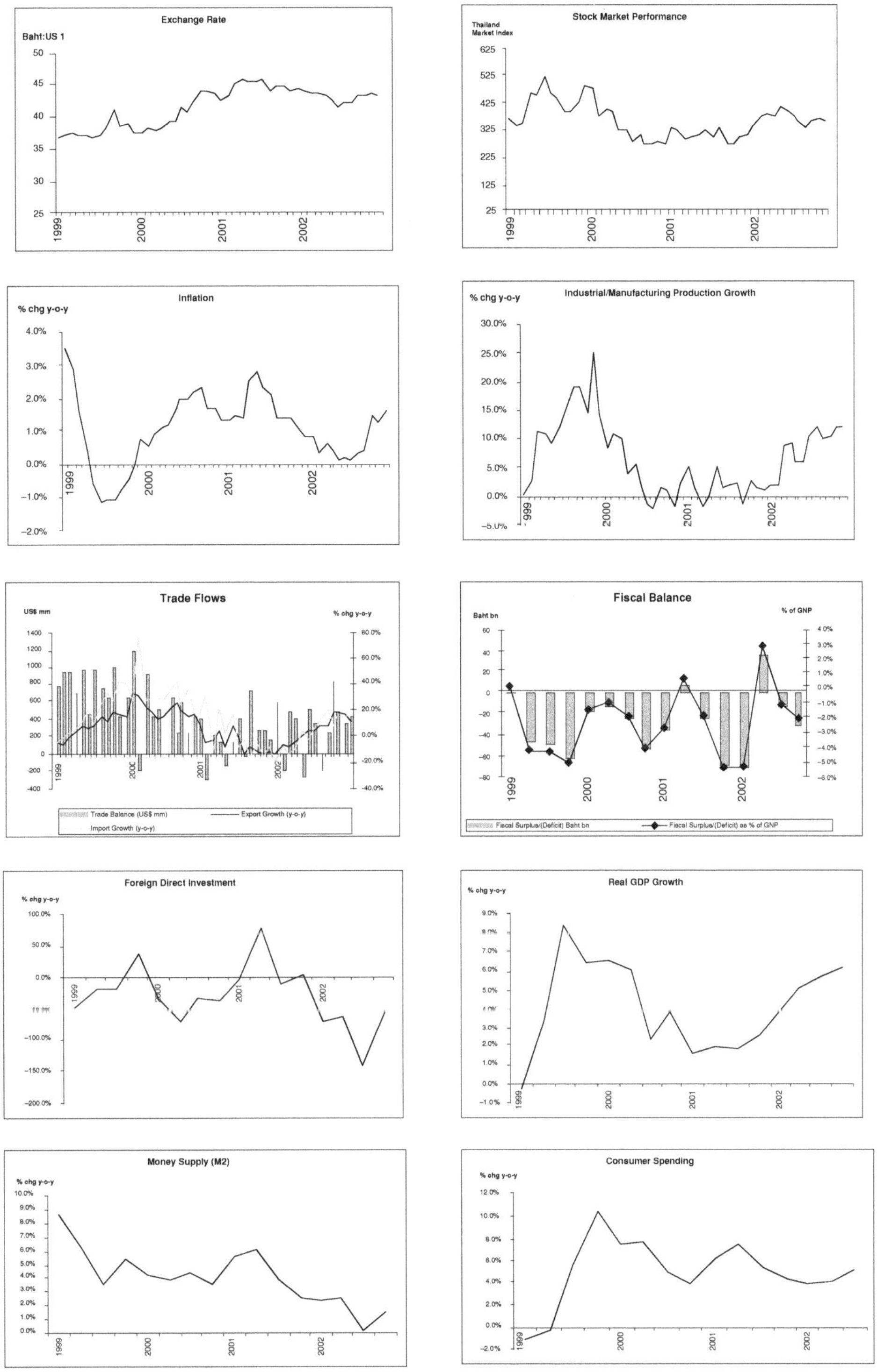

Thailand Economic Indicators

[This spreadsheet can be found in the folder "Key Spreadsheets from the Workbook" located on the CD-ROM.]

CHAPTER 6

Strategy and the Uses of M&A to Grow or Restructure the Firm

M&A is one of the tactical instruments by which a company can pursue an inorganic growth strategy (growth outside of the firm). The various alternatives in addition to M&A include contractual agreements, alliances, joint ventures, and minority investments.

The choice among these alternatives is driven by strategic decisions. Furthermore, the design of good M&A transactions always takes root in good strategy.

- Setting corporate strategy begins with setting the *mission* for the enterprise. A mission defines the business focus of the organization, and implicitly tells what the enterprise does *not* do.
- *Strategic objectives* are overarching goals that flesh out the strategic intent and set the direction of the firm.
- The *corporate strategy* for a firm is its plan for both fulfilling its mission and achieving its strategic objectives.
- The strategic planning process usually begins with an *assessment* of a particular business unit. This focuses both inward on the condition and resources of the unit, and outward on the shape of its environment and the unit's position in the competitive field. The aim of strategic assessment is to draw a profile of the strengths, weaknesses, opportunities, and threats (SWOT) of the business.
- Determining the firm's *position* in its competitive environment and its *internal resources and capabilities* is the foundation for setting strategy. This assessment includes profiling an industry (especially, its competitive structure) and determining a firm's position within it, with particular attention to the intensity of firm rivalry, sources of change and turbulence that may trigger a shift in the industry landscape, and so on.
- A number of analytical tools can be used for strategic planning:
  - The *growth-share matrix* is used to determine and analyze the relative positions of firms in an industry or divisions within a firm along three dimensions: size, growth, and relative share of market. The matrix delineates four broad categories of industry positions: cash cow, star, dog, and problem child (also known as "question mark").

- *Michael Porter's framework* characterizes industry structure and competitive conduct as drivers of competitive success in an industry. Specifically, he highlights the role of *five forces* as driving/influencing economic attractiveness of an industry: (1) barriers to entry, (2) customer power, (3) supplier power, (4) threat of substitutes, and (5) rivalry conduct.
- A *strategic map*, like a growth-share matrix, positions the players in an industry on the basis of size and two other dimensions that are strategically meaningful.
- A *strategic canvas* illustrates in graphic form the similarity or difference among competitors' strategies.
- The *attractiveness-strength matrix* is a tool used to assess both the attractiveness of an industry and the attractiveness of a position in the industry. It addresses the question: "How do returns vary with industry position and industry attractiveness?"
- The *self-sustainable growth rate (SSGR)* is a test of fit between the firm's current capabilities and its aspirations, and the maximum internally sustainable rate of asset growth will be a direct result of the firm's profitability and retention rate.

- All of the strategic analytic tools are *judgment-intensive*. They depend crucially upon proper definition of the "business" and the "peer group" being studied.
- There are *three classic strategies* that seem to yield competitive advantage: low-cost leadership, differentiation, and focus or specialization.
- In considering how to expand a business, executives first must make the classic "make versus buy" decision. They need to decide whether to grow *organically* (i.e., through internal investment) or *inorganically* (i.e., by investing or structuring an affiliation outside the firm).
- Inorganic growth may be employed to:
  - Grow in the context of a maturing product line.
  - Grow by circumventing regulatory or antitrust limits.
  - Create value through horizontal or vertical integration.
  - Acquire unique resources and capabilities.
  - Create value through diversification.
- Diversification might pay if it promotes knowledge transfer across divisions, reduces costs, creates critical mass for facing the competition, and/or exploits better transparency and monitoring through internal capital markets. Diversifying mergers may also have a greater likelihood of success with the following conditions: When there is high relatedness in terms of industry focus between the target and buyer, when managers are properly motivated and rewarded, where the local capital market is less effective, where product markets are experiencing an episode of deregulation or other turbulence, and when one or both firms have significant information-based assets.

- While considering growth by M&A, the executive should also regard the relative costs and benefits of at least four other avenues for inorganic growth: contractual relationships, strategic alliances, joint ventures, and minority stakes.
    1. ***Contractual relationships*** are the simplest of all inorganic expansions. These relationships can take many forms: licensing agreements, co-marketing agreements, co-development agreements, joint purchasing agreements, franchising, and long-term supply or toll agreement.
    2. ***Strategic alliances*** are typically more complicated and express a more serious commitment between the parties. Sometimes alliances entail cross-shareholding agreements between the allies.
    3. ***A joint venture (JV)*** creates a separate entity in which a firm and the counterparty will invest.
    4. A ***minority investment*** is the direct investment into the counterparty firm, rather than into an intermediate firm (like the joint venture).
- Research findings about joint ventures, alliances, and minority equity investments indicate:
    - Alliances are more likely than acquisitions where the risk of the venture is greater than the risk of the partner's core business.
    - Whole ownership is most common when firms coordinate integrated production activities across different locations, transfer technology, and benefit from worldwide tax planning.
    - Like M&A, joint ventures, alliances, and minority equity investments are, on average, profitable for targets, a break-even proposition for purchasers, and, for both target and purchaser combined, an economically positive activity.
    - Joint venture partners do better when buyers have good investment opportunities, the JV increases focus for the buyer, and/or the JV reduces agency costs and returns.
- *Restructuring* is a lengthy process that may entail selling assets, closing plants, streamlining operations, or exiting an industry entirely—all with a goal of improving returns and the prospects for the firm's survival. *Industry turbulence* of the kinds outlined in Chapter 4 of the main text typically stimulates restructuring activity. Other motives could be: to sharpen strategic focus, to correct "mistakes" and harvest "learning," to correct the market valuation of assets, to improve the internal capital market, to reduce tax expenses, to strengthen managerial incentives/align them with the interests of shareholders, to respond to capital market discipline, and to gain financing when external funds are limited.
- The possible transactions to restructure, redeploy, or sell also span a wide range of alternatives: sale of minority interest, sale of joint venture interest, divestiture or asset sale, carve-out, spin-off, split-off or exchange, tracking stock, and financial recapitalization.
- Research studies on the profitability of unit divestitures, asset sales, and liquidation indicate:

  - Announcements of divestitures create value for shareholders of sellers, on the order of a 1 to 3 percent significant abnormal return.
  - It is the redeployment of assets that matters, not merely the sale. The market seems to reward divestitures that focus the firm. Firms selling assets tend to suffer from lower profitability or high leverage.

- Research on the profitability of carve-outs, spin-offs, split-offs, and tracking stock indicates:
  - Investment behavior and financial performance of firms improves following the spin-off.
  - Relatedness matters in the choice of transaction. The more unrelated the unit, the greater the likelihood that it will be separated from the parent.
  - The findings are consistent with benefits of increased focus.
  - The types of transactions do differ in their effects.
  - As with divestitures, deployment of funds raised in these transactions makes a difference.
  - The restructuring has an impact on the rivals of the firm.
  - Firms will favor carve-outs over divestitures when the parent's shares are relatively undervalued and the subsidiary's shares are relatively overvalued. Thus, a sale of equity in the subsidiary would become a signal to investors of the parent's undervaluation.

- Some key considerations in choosing a *decision path for inorganic growth*: (1) benefits from a relationship: learning and coordination gains, (2) need for ownership and control, and (3) management of risk exposure. These three criteria convey the complexity of the choice. These considerations illustrate the following common lessons: one kind of transaction does not fit all needs, the choice among the alternatives is a logical result of balancing important considerations, retain a bias for simplicity, consider starting small, and remember value creation.

- The selection among *alternatives for restructuring* should be influenced by the following considerations: relationship to the core business of the parent, need for control, and whether the business or asset can operate as an independent entity. To complete any strategic analysis of alternatives, one must assess the implications of each choice for shareholder value.

- One of the robust debates today deals with whether and how the strategic efforts to diversify or focus the firm pay. Profitability varies by type of diversification strategy: As firms have moved from great focus (a "single business" strategy) to great diversity (an "unrelated business" strategy), the accounting returns of firms have varied materially by type of strategy. Early studies showed that a strategy of relatedness in diversification yielded higher accounting returns. Recent studies offer a more complicated judgment still somewhat in favor of the benefits of focus and relatedness.

- The practical implication of research is that one should diversify only where there is a sound economic rationale: strong relatedness, strong internal capital markets, where local capital markets are less effective, where there is significant turbulence in the industry, and/or where one or both firms have significant information-based assets. Overall, the value creation discipline is vital.

- The design of good M&A transactions takes root in good strategy. Analysis of positions and capabilities should underpin the effort to profile your firm's strengths, weaknesses, opportunities, and threats (SWOT).
- Restructuring activity is a significant source of M&A activity, but divestiture is only one of the tactical instruments of a strategy of restructuring. Other alternatives include liquidations, minority investments, spin-offs, carve-outs, split-offs, and tracking stock.
- The survey of research establishes that restructuring creates value: divestiture, spin-offs, carve-outs, and tracking stock are associated with significant positive returns at the announcement of those transactions.
- The practitioner should think critically about blanket assertions made about whether there is more value in a strategy of diversification or one of focus. Perhaps the most value is created by responding appropriately (with diversification or focusing) as the situation requires.

CHAPTER 6—WORKBOOK QUESTIONS

1. *What is strategy and why is it important in M&A? How does one use strategy in M&A?*

2. *You are the head of strategic planning for your firm. You are currently trying to analyze three different projects. What strategic analysis tools would you use for each?*

    1. *Your firm has decided to enter a new market to expand the business. You need to assess the ability to earn high returns in that market.*
    2. *You are reassessing the market position of your product relative to its competitors as you prepare to launch an advertising campaign.*
    3. *You are trying to decide whether to keep or sell one of your business units. The decision will depend on your view of how well the unit can compete in its industry, and whether it will survive the competition.*

3. *Identify drivers of value that would influence the choice of diversification versus focus. How do these drivers create value for diversified companies?*

4. *Define organic and inorganic growth. What are the circumstances under which each growth method is particularly appropriate?*

5. *Conventional wisdom says that diversification destroys value. Why has this view been challenged? What evidence is there that shows that diversification may actually create value?*

6. You are the CEO of a publicly listed fast-food chain with both domestic and international operations. Protection and growth of the brand are vitally important to your firm. Therefore, quality control of food and service is paramount. Strength of relationship with the operating units is important as a basis for transferring technology and best practices that build the brand. Domestically, your chain has a presence in every state, and in virtually all profitable locations. You therefore believe that it will be difficult to grow the chain organically, at least in the domestic scene.

   Internationally, there is plenty of growth potential in developing countries. However, high risks of political and economic instability may make greenfield expansion (that is, the construction of brand-new facilities) unfeasible. The need for total control is lower where a local partner can help to manage risks and adapt your firm's best practices.

   In both cases (domestic and international) please recommend alternatives for the company to grow inorganically, and evaluate each. (See Exhibit 6.20 in the main text for a framework for considering the alternatives.)

7. *You are the CEO of a diversified holding company. For a long time you have believed that your stock is undervalued primarily because of a diversification discount. How might you restructure the company to address your perception of the problem? (See Exhibit 6.21 in the main text for a framework that might be of use.)*

8. *What is the framework to be used for choosing a strategy of inorganic growth? Once you arrive at possible inorganic growth alternatives, what guidelines can you use to help make your decision?*

9. *Suppose you are the head of business strategy at Olivia Inc., a consumer foods company. You feel that the company should adopt a focused strategy and shed some of its businesses—right now it has six divisions. A tool that you can use to evaluate strategic issues is the growth-share matrix. Suppose the divisions have the following characteristics; evaluate each using the matrix. Which divisions would you keep, and which ones would you shed? Why? (See the spreadsheet template "Growth Share.xls" found on the CD-ROM.)*

	Growth Rate	Relative Share of Market	Revenues ($ MM)
Division 1	32%	1.50	50
Division 2	15%	0.70	70
Division 3	20%	0.50	150
Division 4	4%	2.00	200
Division 5	24%	0.30	120
Division 6	6%	0.80	100

10. You are the head of a biotech company and have just received the license to manufacture a vaccine to protect from a contagious disease. You estimate that market demand for this product will be explosive. In order to evaluate the financial viability of this product, you need to know accurate information about the cost of manufacturing the vaccine. Because of the difficulty of the process, you plan to start with a low production level, gradually increasing to a higher level. Your intended schedule of production is as follows, where each time period is one month:

Time Period	Cumulative Production (000)
0	0
1	5
2	10
3	20
4	40
5	80
6	160

The base cost for 1,000 doses of vaccine is estimated at $120. Assuming you can reduce the cost by 5 percent, 10 percent, or 15 percent, if your cumulative production doubles, calculate the cost for each period under each scenario and graph the results. What kind of impact will "learning" have on your cost of production?

11. Suppose the CEO of Joy Company, a private company, is determined to achieve 16 percent growth annually in order to compete effectively and to survive in its industry. The following table summarizes the modeling assumptions and results:

Joy Company Self-Sustainable Growth Rate Analysis	Assumptions and Result
Dividend payout ratio	40%
Target debt/equity ratio	30%
Expected return on equity	15.00%
Expected return on total capital	12.46%
Expected after-tax cost of debt	4%
New issues of common equity	Nil
Self-sustainable growth rate	9.00%

But Joy Company can self-sustain a growth rate of only 9 percent. How can the CEO increase the firm's self-sustainable growth rate? Assume you are hired by the CEO as a consultant, list several possible alternatives. Which would you recommend to the CEO?

12. You are the CEO of a diversified company that has three divisions in different industries. The following table shows each division's annual sales, and the industry average ratio of total capital to sales:

	($ MM)	Total Capital/Sales (Industry Average)
Division 1 sales	12	2.00
Division 2 sales	44	1.28
Division 3 sales	30	1.76
Total capital	120	

Based on market capitalization, the total value of your company's capital is $120 million. Is there a diversification discount? If so, how much is it?

CHAPTER 7

Acquisition Search and Deal Origination: Some Guiding Principles

M&A transactions may spring from a *search* process by a buyer or from an *origination* process by an intermediary, such as a banker. The acquisition search process is essentially an intelligence-gathering operation. As such, the search process needs to be structured so as to enhance the quality of information acquired.

- It is helpful to keep the following ideas in mind with respect to the acquisition search process:
  - The most valuable information is private.
  - Networks are valuable. Networking can be profitable.
  - Investing in building a search network is like investing in options.
  - Information about deal opportunities is often dispersed through the market. As such, studies of the speed and impact of dispersion may yield insights about the pathway of information that can help buyers in the search process.
- In performing an acquisition search, focus on *information*, rather than on transactions. This is another variation on a theme that is repeatedly offered in this book—focus on *process*, rather than outcomes.
- Markets discount ambiguous information. In contrast, what the market knows clearly is fully priced. Public information gets impounded into security prices rapidly and without bias—this is the cornerstone of the efficient markets hypothesis. Therefore, private knowledge of high return opportunities is a crucial ingredient for creating value through M&A. Deal searches should be structured to generate private information before it becomes widely known.
- In a world of adverse selection (where the seller has an incentive to misrepresent the item to be sold), costly attributes (such as a promise to pay dividends) will tell buyers things that mere words will not.
- Usual acquisition screening criteria include:
  - Industry and buyer's and target's position in it.
  - Strategic capabilities.

- Size of the business (usually in terms of sales or assets).
- Profitability.
- Risk exposure.
- Asset type.
- Management quality.
- Prospective control.
- Organizational fit.
- Prospective control.

- Acquisition search involves dynamic learning by doing. The searcher *learns* through experience, revising targets and expectations over time. One must allow for a certain degree of opportunism, since opportunities help clarify strategy.
- Invest in social networks: They make search more efficient and effective. What you seek may be closer than you think. Through social connections, the research on the "small world" phenomenon suggests that we are separated from distant strangers by a relatively small number of connections. Paradoxically, there is strength in weak ties: The connections most likely to help you are those people who are least like you.
- Information first disseminates slowly, then spreads explosively. For this reason, the searcher should seek to position him/herself early or "upstream" in the flow of news about investment opportunities. *Primary* research is the best and safest way of positioning oneself upstream.
- Cultivating strong relationships with "navigators" helps position a searcher upstream. Navigators are intermediaries in the flow of information. They include:
  - *Gatekeepers*—those who provide access to information and deals. Investment bankers who have an exclusive engagement to sell a firm are among the most important gatekeepers.
  - *River guides*—industry or regional specialists who highlight emerging trends that might affect the availability of investment opportunities.
- Attributes of the best navigators include:
  - Control over an existing base of customers or suppliers.
  - Intellectual property rights.
  - Ability to innovate better than other navigators.
  - First-mover advantages.
  - Low-cost provider of search services.
  - Reputation and brand name image.
- A search or origination team that is flexible and consistent with the complex external environment has the highest probability of succeeding in a rapidly changing world.

- Persistence and repeated effort in acquisition search pays. The probability of a positive payoff from an acquisition search can be increased by:
  - Choosing promising arenas—those where there is uncertainty about who knows what information.
  - Increasing the total number of deal opportunities reviewed.
  - Increasing the frequency of reviews.
  - Optimizing the network infrastructure to yield valuable information.
- The acquisition search process requires proactivity.

CHAPTER 7—WORKBOOK QUESTIONS

Part I: True or False

1. *Asymmetry and ambiguity of information about an asset can affect the price of that asset.*

2. *In performing an acquisition search, one should focus on information rather than on transactions.*

3. *What the market knows clearly is fully priced.*

4. *High-quality information is costly.*

5. *If information about an acquisition opportunity is fully public, there is a high likelihood that the opportunity is fully priced.*

6. *If information about an acquisition opportunity is fully public, there is a high likelihood that the buyer can tailor the pricing and terms to greater advantage.*

7. *It is all right for some acquisition searchers to look for unusual capabilities rather than market positions.*

8. *Focusing on distressed targets can be a search strategy.*

9. *There is no place for opportunism in acquisitions. Every acquisition must be a result of careful reflection on strategy, rather than the availability of a target.*

10. *Deal-rich information is public.*

Part II: Short Answer

1. *Go to www.cs.virginia.edu/oracle. Play the "Oracle of Bacon" game. Type in names of actors or actresses to see how close their connection is to Kevin Bacon; include international actors and actresses in your experiment, too! Were you surprised by the results? What does this game tell you about connectivity? How can you tie this idea in to the M&A search process?*

2. *What implications does the Granovetter study on how people find jobs have for the M&A search process?*

3. *Navigators are intermediaries of information—people like investment bankers, consultants, lawyers, and accountants. What are some attributes of the best navigators in the realm of M&A?*

Part III: Target Assessment Cases

In May 2003, a large food and beverage manufacturer is searching for an acquisition target. This buyer is a manufacturer of a variety of carbonated and noncarbonated drinks, and of snack foods. In general, its products are in the convenience and impulse foods category. Annual revenues are over $20 billion. The buyer, which has operations all over the world, believes that the U.S. market is mature and that foreign markets offer greater growth potential.

The buyer's ideal target would have the following characteristics:

- At least $50 million in sales.
- At least 12 percent in operating margins.
- Accretive to EPS in the first year.
- Products that fit the buyer's ambient and/or chilled distribution system.
- Products that are in the "good for you" food category.

1. *Suppose you are a business developer just hired by the buyer for this assignment. Draw up a short list of potential targets, and assess each according to the criteria provided by the buyer. Also consider other issues such as industry position, shareholder structure, and so on—you may want to use the discussion in Chapter 7 of the main text as reference. Do not focus on pricing, valuation, or accounting issues for now. Concentrate on the rationale.*

CHAPTER 8

Due Diligence

"Know what you are buying." The lack of knowledge of potential problems in an acquisition is one of the more common causes of failure in M&A.

- "Due diligence" is research. Traditionally, it has been aimed at revealing risks in the target company that a diligent buyer should understand. This chapter defines due diligence to include a search for *both* risks and opportunities.
- Excellence in due diligence begins with the *right mind-set.* The essence of the mind-set can be summarized in the following elements:
  - ***Avoid a compliance mentality and adopt an investor mentality.*** One of the recurrent themes in the book is *think like an investor.*
  - ***Generally, one should conduct due diligence broadly.*** Broad due diligence will reveal more about risk and opportunity than will narrow due diligence. Ultimately, the trade-offs between broad and narrow due diligence boil down to "surprises now" versus "surprises later."
  - ***Be fact-based but knowledge-oriented.*** Due diligence builds from the bottom up—from data to information, to knowledge.
  - ***Communication should be clear and documented.*** Communicate the output in plain-language briefings for managers, but leave a detailed paper trail.
  - ***Leadership matters.*** The due diligence process requires strong skills of leadership and process management. Link the process and conclusions to the valuation, negotiation, and postmerger integration processes.
- Broad due diligence encompasses knowledge of:
  - Risks *and* opportunities.
  - The past, present, *and* future.
  - The firm *and* its partners such as key customers and suppliers.
  - The financial condition *and* the business that generated it.
  - Internal conditions of the firm *and* external conditions of the firm's environment.
  - The basic data of the target *and* the refined opinions of the experts.
- Within the buyer's due diligence team there must be formalized understanding of deadlines, assignments of responsibility, and objectives of specific tasks, through memos or other written messages. Progress must be monitored, and quality checked.

- From the target's side, management of the due diligence process entails organizing, planning, and controlling the process to satisfy the buyer's due diligence needs with least disruption to the target's operations. An important means for this is the "data room," a location where the requested documents are placed for inspection by the buyer's diligence team.
- Some important issues to explore as part of the due diligence process are:

Legal issues	Proper incorporation, legal standing, compliance with laws, shareholding/voting structure, procedures for electing directors, involvement in legal proceedings, and potential litigation issues.
Accounting issues	Compliance with GAAP, any unusual accounting practices, any unusual trends in the target's financial results, and comparison of target's accounting processes and results with peers.
Tax issues	Compliance with tax laws, accrued unpaid taxes, and opportunities for tax reduction.
Information technology	Adequacy of target's management information systems and compatibility with buyer's, and investments necessary to achieve compatibility.
Risk and insurance issues	Adequacy of target's insurance policies and liability coverage, possible exposures to natural hazards, business interruption, technological change, and change in government policy.
Environmental issues	Compliance with environmental laws, and possible exposures to environmental liabilities.
Market presence and sales issues	General image of the firm, strength of its brand franchise, compatibility of market segment with buyer's, competitors, strength of target's sales and marketing organizations, and outlook for revenues and future trends.
Operations	Strength of target's operational processes in terms of cost, quality, efficiency, and flexibility; compatibility of target's operational processes with buyer's; streamlining for cost synergies; exposure to technological change; and labor issues.
Intellectual and intangible assets	Value of intangible assets, how well they are protected, and potential exposures to infringement claims.
Finance	Soundness of financial policies, creditworthiness and solvency, and likelihood of cash flow problems.
Cross-border issues	Exposure to foreign currency fluctuations and to foreign laws and regulations, and cultural differences.
Human resources	Depth of talent and leadership pool, compensation policies, levels of turnover and employee satisfaction, union issues, and pension liabilities.
Cultural issues	The target's beliefs, mission, values, norms, and traditions; leadership and communication styles; and cultural compatibility with buyer.
Ethics	Compatibility of ethical norms and practices between target and buyer.

- Cultural due diligence should assess congruence on three dimensions:
  1. Between actions and aspirations (i.e., as expressed in statements about mission and values). Is the culture of the target company consistent with the aims of the firm?
  2. Between the cultures of buyer and target.
  3. Between the target's culture and its strategic threats and opportunities. Acquisitions fail when the buyer makes demands on the target inconsistent with the target's culture. The main text summarizes the research of Christopher Luis, who finds that strategic cultures tend to cluster around:
     - Customer service cultures
     - Product uniqueness cultures
     - Cost orientation cultures
     - Preeminence cultures
- Public sources can be used to help:
  - Obtain basic financial information about a target and assess the target's industry and peer firms.
  - Identify economic forces affecting the target, such as deregulation, technological change, demographic change, and trade liberalization.
  - Gauge the view of peers and investors about the target.
  - Develop a basic factual foundation about the target.
- In summary, excellent due diligence is:
  - *Fact-based.* Avoids guesses or opinions.
  - *Inquisitive.* Avoids a compliance or checklist mentality.
  - *Knowledge-focused.* Goes beyond mere data.
  - *Systems-focused.* Seeks the links to valuation, negotiation, and closing.
  - *Undertaken with initiative.* Begins as soon as the possibility of a transaction arises.
  - *Managed to take enough time.* Plans ahead and avoids errors from too little time.
  - *Multidisciplinary.* Seeks to understand the target firm in all its aspects.
  - *Drawn from both formal and informal resources.*
  - *Careful to avoid surprises.* Due diligence is, in part, risk management. If you must have surprises, you should want them early rather than later.
  - *Written.* Good due diligence creates a careful written record of findings that can be retrieved if disputes arise later.

CHAPTER 8—WORKBOOK QUESTIONS

Part I: Concept Questions

1. *Why is it important to think like an investor when conducting due diligence?*
2. *Discuss the tension between broad and narrow due diligence.*

3. *Why is it important to focus on knowledge when conducting due diligence? How are data, information, and knowledge different from each other?*

Part II: Mini-Cases

CUC-HFS[1]

In December 1997, Cendant Corporation was created by a $14 billion merger between HFS Inc. and CUC International Inc. HFS was run by a well-known deal maker, Henry Silverman, and owned hotel brands Ramada, Days Inn, and Howard Johnson, car-rental company Avis, and real estate brokers Coldwell Banker and Century 21. CUC was in the business of selling memberships in clubs that offered travel, shopping, and dining discounts. The merger was predicated on cross-selling products and services to the combined (massive) customer database of the two companies. However, just four months later, it was discovered that CUC had been engaging in accounting fraud since 1995: About $500 million of revenues reported from 1995 to 1997 was made up, and 61 percent of CUC's 1997 net income was fictitious.

> *In sworn affidavits taken by Cendant investigators . . . [two former CUC managers] said they had been told to record millions of dollars of phony orders. Mr. Sabatino said he had been told to arbitrarily adjust revenue up or expenses down. He had raided reserves set up for merger costs to cover revenue shortfalls. In short, the men alleged that they had cooked the books to order for CUC executives, and specifically named . . . CUC's former senior vice president of finance and controller . . . [and] CUC's chief financial officer.*[2]

CUC had had accounting problems before. In 1989, it changed its accounting methods after being criticized by investors for "spreading out the cost of recruiting new members over three years instead of reflecting those costs right away. In 1991, the SEC questioned the completeness of CUC's financial documents and required numerous amendments to them."[3]

After the merger was announced, Henry Silverman began requiring daily cash reports and detailed monthly financial statements about operations, which had not been required at CUC. These were slow in coming. Frustrated, Silverman finally assigned two HFS finance officials to CUC's case. It was at this point that anomalies began to be discovered, prompting further investigations that ultimately revealed evidence of fraud since 1995. Tactics employed by CUC had included making up or reclassifying revenues, overstating membership renewal rates, claiming bogus merger reserves, falsifying expenses, and delaying recognition of insurance claims. One investigation uncovered "several million dollars in questionable expenses over three years, including about $550,000 in undocumented cash advances between . . . 1995 and 1997."[4] In addition, CUC, despite being a large company, appeared not to have highly automated accounting systems. For instance, most revenues and expenses had to be entered manually.[5]

Silverman's due diligence on CUC had been based almost purely on public information. Although the merger deal was friendly, CUC had refused to share some nonpublic data. Silverman has insisted many times that there was no way he could have known about the fraud at the time of merger negotiations.

1. *In light of the facts given, do you think the problems associated with this deal could have been uncovered with due diligence? If so, how? Or do you agree with Mr. Silverman's position?*

Quaker Oats–Snapple

On November 2, 1994, Quaker Oats announced it had agreed to acquire Snapple Beverage Corp. for $1.7 billion. Quaker believed it could build Snapple into a vibrant, growing brand, just as it had done with Gatorade. It believed that synergies could be exploited by integrating the Snapple operation into its Gatorade organization. Just two years and five months later, Quaker agreed to sell Snapple for $300 million, taking a $1.4 billion charge on the loss.

Quaker had planned to streamline distribution in order to exploit cross-selling opportunities between Snapple and Gatorade—in fact, reconfiguring distribution had been a basic tenet of the postmerger plan. Snapple had employed a distribution scheme that relied on more than 300 independent distributors to service supermarkets, restaurants, gas stations, and other "convenience chains and mom-and-pop markets" within their respective territories (to which they had exclusive rights). Gatorade, in contrast, distributed its product directly from its bottling plants to the warehouses of supermarket chains. The postmerger plan aimed to swap distribution rights: Quaker would grant Snapple's independent distributors rights to deliver Gatorade to the convenience chains and mom-and-pop stores. In exchange, Quaker wanted the distributors to hand over their supermarket accounts and let Quaker sell Snapple directly to the supermarkets.

A journalist wrote, "The uproar was immediate. The plan gave Quaker the benefit of an already established Snapple supermarket business in exchange for a small-store Gatorade trade that had yet to be built."[6] Further, the independent distributors were making $4-per-case margins on Snapple—double what they would have been able to make on Gatorade. Quaker was forced to shelve its plans to streamline distribution, a linchpin of its merger program. *Forbes* magazine wrote, "Only after it bought Snapple did it [Quaker] fully realize that Snapple's distribution system is completely different from Gatorade's."[7]

Other problems appeared after the merger. For one, it was discovered that much of Snapple's growth before the acquisition had come from cramming its distribution pipeline full of inventory. In addition, Quaker ran into problems with Snapple's manufacturing systems. Snapple had employed a production scheme whereby it outsourced bottling operations to independent contractors. This procedure not only slowed production, but also locked Snapple into contracts that required minimum bottling quotas even when sales slowed. Quaker had to take a $30 million charge to buy out these bottling contracts. In addition, Quaker encountered stock-out problems at Snapple, where it took weeks rather than days to fill orders.

Finally, there was the problem of slowing sales, signs of which emerged *before* the definitive agreement had been signed. Late in the merger discussions, Snapple revealed to Quaker that sales and profits for the year had plummeted, and that weakness was expected to continue throughout the year. In addition, Snapple's owners insisted on an all-cash deal despite the stock-and-cash plan originally put forward.[8] Despite this, Quaker agreed to buy Snapple for $1.7 billion in cash.

2. *Do you think faulty due diligence was a cause of merger failure in this case? Explain.*

Medical Care–Critical Care

On September 9, 1992, Medical Care America was formed by a merger between two of the largest and fastest-growing providers of outpatient health care services in the United States: Medical Care International, Inc. (MCI), an operator of outpatient surgery centers, and Critical Care America, Inc. (CCA), a provider of "home-infusion therapies" (i.e., programs in which outpatients are supplied with equipment and training to administer their own drugs, therapies, and recovery programs at home). Examples of infusion therapies include chemotherapy, nutrition support, IV antibiotics, and so forth.

The merger received overwhelming shareholder approval, with at least 80 percent of each company's shareholders voting in favor. Analysts lauded the deal as well. But merely 16 days after the merger announcement, the new company declared that its third-quarter earnings would be flat, as opposed to market expectations of 30 percent profit growth. On that day, Medical Care stock dropped 57 percent. Two months later, the chairman of Medical Care resigned.

More bad news was to come: In the fourth quarter of 1992, Medical Care's earnings fell 25 percent below the previous year. In the first quarter of 1993, net income dropped 32 percent from the previous year's comparable period. The surgery centers—that portion of the business contributed by the former Medical Care International—were doing well; revenues were growing briskly. It was the infusion business (formerly of Critical Care) that was faltering.

Only after the merger was it learned just how badly competitive pressures were pushing prices down in the infusion industry, and how badly Critical Care had been falling behind in the changing health-care environment. Its prices were as much as 26 percent higher than those of its rivals, due to its propensity to "provide high-level service regardless of the cost. . . . Founder Patrick S. Smith . . . had been so eager to prove that his company could provide many of the same services available in hospitals that he spared no expense in assembling the staff and equipment needed to treat medical problems such as cancer, cardiac disease and bone-marrow transplants."[9] In addition, Critical Care's sales force had focused almost solely on marketing to physicians (who would then send their patients to Critical Care's centers) rather than to managed-care networks and insurance companies, which increasingly dominated the health market, and whose profit margins depended on low costs. Because of Critical Care's uncompetitive prices and its refusal even to negotiate them, it often was bypassed by HMOs and insurers.

After the earnings disappointments were revealed, 15 shareholders filed a lawsuit against Medical Care, charging that "Critical Care's problems were so severe that managers had to have known about them."[10] But a senior vice president of Medical Care asserted, "We were very surprised by the problem and had no idea of the problem on September 9."

3. *Do you think the problems would have been uncovered with better due diligence?*

NOTES

1. This account draws from Emily Nelson and Joann Lublin, "Buy the Numbers? How Whistle-Blowers Set off a Fraud Probe That Crushed Cendant," *Wall Street Journal*, August 13, 1998, p. A1. *Wall Street Journal.* Eastern Edition [staff produced copy only] by Emily Nelson and Joann Lublin. Copyright © 1998 by Dow Jones & Co. Inc. Reproduced with permission of Dow Jones & Co. Inc. in the format textbook via Copyright Clearance Center.
2. Ibid.
3. Ibid.
4. Ibid.
5. Amy Barrett, "Cendant: Who's to Blame? A Loose Accounting Culture May Lie at the Core of the Debacle," *BusinessWeek*, August 17, 1998, p. 70.
6. Nancy Millman, "Quaker Stumbles over Snapple," *Raleigh News and Observer*, September 12, 1996, p. C7.
7. Zina Moukheiber, "He Who Laughs Last: Was Quaker Oats Taken When It Paid $1.7 Billion for Snapple?" *Forbes*, January 1, 1996, p. 42.
8. Millman, "Quaker Stumbles over Snapple," p. C7.
9. Robert Tomsho, "Medical Care America Tries to Regain Investor Faith," *Wall Street Journal*, November 2, 1992, p. B6.
10. Stephanie Anderson Forest, "Operating Room Mishap—A "Brilliant Idea" Led to Medical Care America. So What Happened?" *BusinessWeek*, September 20, 1993, p. 77.

CHAPTER 9

Valuing Firms

Mastery of valuation is important, not only because it is a primary concern in M&A, but also because an understanding of valuation can guide managerial action. This chapter introduces techniques for valuing firms on a stand-alone basis, and outlines the mind-set necessary for creating value.

- In valuation, remember:
  - Think like an investor; that is, focus on economic reality, focus on future expectations, focus on cash flow, get paid for risks, account for the time value of money and for opportunity cost, consider any information advantages, and diversify efficiently.
  - Intrinsic value is unobservable; it can only be estimated. One should therefore triangulate from many estimates. One should also work with ranges of value, rather than with point estimates.
  - An opportunity to create value exists where price and intrinsic value differ—in other words, when the concept of value additivity is violated. Value additivity means that the value of the whole should equal the sum of the values of the parts.
  - Have a view about the various estimators of value. Understand the strengths and weaknesses of each and how relevant each is to your situation.
  - Find key value drivers and the inherent bets in the acquisition. Some tools for helping to find the key value drivers are sensitivity analysis, scenario analysis, break-even analysis, and Monte Carlo simulation.
  - Think critically; triangulate carefully. To "triangulate" is to converge on a range of value within which intrinsic value probably resides.
  - Focus on process, not on product. Thoughtfully attend to the steps of valuation analysis rather than trying to push the analysis to justify an outcome.
- Some of the methods ("estimators") used to estimate value are:
  - *Accounting book value.* Value is based on amounts recorded in the financial statements.
  - *Liquidation value.* Sums the values that might be realized in a liquidation of the firm today.
  - *Replacement cost valuation.* Value is estimated by determining the cost to replace the assets of the firm piecemeal today.
  - *Current trading or market value.* Sum of the market values of debt and equity.

- *Trading multiples.* Applies the valuation multiples of peer firms to the target.
- *Transaction multiples.* Multiples based on actual prices paid for firms in comparable transactions are applied to the target firm.
- *Discounted cash flow approaches.* Value is based on the present value of cash flows discounted at an appropriate cost of capital.
- *Venture capital/private equity approach.* Value of the business is equal to the present value of the target's exit value.
- *Option valuation.* Value of business is based on the value of equity as a call option on the value of the business.

- *Enterprise value* is the value of the whole firm, while *equity value* is the value of the residual claim on the firm's assets.
- There are three types of discounted cash flow approaches. Theoretically, each approach should yield the same firm value, but in practice it is rare to obtain the same answer under all three approaches due to imperfections in data, models, or procedures.

	Discounted Cash Flow (DCF) Method	Residual Cash Flow (RCF) Method	Adjusted Present Value (APV) Method
Cash flows discounted	Cash flows before financing effects (i.e., flows available to both debt and equity holders)	Cash flows to equity	Free cash flows assuming 100% equity financing, adjusted for the value of debt tax shields
Discount rate used	Weighted average cost of capital (WACC)	Cost of equity	Unlevered cost of equity for free cash flows; cost of debt for debt tax shields

- Two general approaches for estimating the cost of equity are the *dividend growth model* and the *capital asset pricing model*:
  - Dividend growth model: $K_e = \frac{DIV_1}{P_0} + g\infty$
  - CAPM: $K_e = R_f + \beta\,(R_m - R_f)$
- If an acquirer intends to lever up or lever down the target significantly, beta should be unlevered and then relevered.

$$\beta_{\text{Unlevered}} = \frac{\beta_{\text{Levered}}}{\left[1 + (1-t)\frac{D}{E}\right]}$$

$$\beta_{\text{Levered}} = \beta_{\text{Unlevered}}\left[1 + (1-t)\frac{D}{E}\right]$$

- When bidding, the opening bid is typically bounded on the low side by the recent market price range of the target. The walk-away bid should be bounded on the high side by the intrinsic value of the target. The intrinsic value of the target to the buyer should include synergies.

CHAPTER 9—WORKBOOK QUESTIONS

1. Sober Brews Corporation is a holding company composed of the following subsidiaries:

   - *Sober Brews Beer Corporation* produces, markets, and sells various beer products. Beers produced appeal to a wide range of consumer taste and price preferences.
   - *Sober Brews Foods Corporation* produces, markets, and sells meat products for household consumption.
   - *SBC Brews Packaging Corporation* produces, markets, and sells packaging products, including bottles, aluminum cans, and cardboard boxes.
   - *SBC Properties, Inc.* develops and sells commercial and residential properties.
   - *SBC International, Inc.* acts as the holding company for all of Sober Brews' international operations, which are concentrated in Eastern Europe and China.

   You have performed a DCF analysis on each of the subsidiaries, with the following results:

	Equity Value ($ MM)
Sober Brews Beer Corporation	713.70
Sober Brews Foods Corporation	396.50
Sober Brews Packaging Corporation	237.90
SBC Properties, Inc.	95.16
SBC International, Inc.	142.74
Total	1,586.00

   Sober Brews currently trades on the New York Stock Exchange at $32.8 a share, and has 36.2 million shares outstanding. Debt on Sober Brews' balance sheet totals $396 million.

   Would you recommend taking any action with regard to Sober Brews? If so, what course of action would you take?

2. *What is wrong with each of these statements?*

   a. *Value can be created when price and intrinsic value are the same.*
   b. *All estimators must be used when determining a company's value.*
   c. *To arrive at a company's value, one must pick a point estimate arrived at after using the various estimators.*

d. Intrinsic value can be observed by looking at a company's stock market price.

3. Red Hill Vinegar Company is going out of business due to fierce competition in the condiments industry. Jack Mueller, an independent appraiser, has been hired to estimate the liquidation value of Red Hill's assets.
   How much will be left to the owner of Red Hill after liquidation?

	Book Value ($000)	Percent Recoverable
Cash	$ 123.8	100
Receivables	619.0	75
Inventory	309.5	55
PPE	879.0	60
Other assets	92.9	90
	$2,024.1	
Debt	$1,763.3	
Equity	$4,114.7	

[This spreadsheet can be found in the folder "Key Spreadsheets from the Workbook" located on the CD-ROM.]

4. Pellagia Inc. is a nationwide retail chain specializing in women's apparel. The company's most popular lines are Aura and Home. Aura offers executive wear for women in the middle to high-end markets, and Home features casual but stylish clothes, also targeted at women in the middle to high-end markets. The company has 135 million shares outstanding, 30 percent of which are publicly traded with a current market price of $5.63 per share. The company is expected to net $38 million in the next 12 months. Forecast sales and EBITDA are $633 million and $57 million, respectively. Debt outstanding is $120 million.

   a. What is the current enterprise market value of Pellagia?

   b. Suppose you are asked to value Pellagia Inc. given the following information. What is your estimate of equity value? Of enterprise value?

	Price to Earnings	Price to Sales
Abercrombie & Fitch	13.04	1.58
Ann Taylor Stores Corp.	26.10	0.78
Bebe Stores Inc.	15.36	1.41
Gap Inc.	N/A	0.76
Limited Brands Inc.	18.59	0.96
Talbots Inc.	14.11	1.06

[This spreadsheet can be found in the folder "Key Spreadsheets from the Workbook" located on the CD-ROM.]

5. *What is wrong with the following equations?*

a.
$$V_{\text{Enterprise}} = \frac{\text{FCF}}{K_e}$$

b.
$$V_{\text{Equity}} = \frac{\text{Dividends}}{\text{WACC}}$$

6. Tel-Talk Inc. is a company that provides domestic and international long distance, regional and local communications services, cable (broadband) television, and Internet communications services. For the past two years, it has paid an annual dividend of $2.31 per share; however, the compound rate of growth in dividends per share over the past 10 years has been 6.2 percent. The beta of Tel-Talk stock measured over the past three years is 1.10. Its debt, which makes up 32 percent of total capital, currently yields 7.28 percent, while long-term Treasury bonds are yielding 5.63 percent. The market risk premium (geometric) is at 5.9 percent. Tel-Talk shares are currently trading at $46.25 per share.

Calculate Tel-Talk's cost of equity using both the CAPM and the dividend growth model.

7. Trigeorgis Partners, a leveraged buyout firm, is considering an investment in a national retail bookseller. The target is attractive to Trigeorgis because of its low level of debt, which at present makes up just 9.5 percent of the company's total capital. The partners at Trigeorgis believe that the debt level can be raised to as much as 30 percent of capital. Although this might mean a lowering of the credit rating from AAA to AA, or even to A, the Trigeorgis partners believe that the interest tax shields would more than offset higher costs of borrowing. The bookseller's average beta for the past year has been 0.98, and its marginal tax rate is 35 percent.

How would beta change if Trigeorgis completed the acquisition and raised the bookseller's debt to 30 percent?

8. The following is a five-year discounted cash flow (DCF) forecast for Middlestates Electric, Inc., an electric utility company:

($ MM)	Year 1	Year 2	Year 3	Year 4	Year 5
Operating income	2,039	2,325	2,169	2,430	2,615
Taxes	712	813	777	870	937
Depreciation and amortization	1,299	1,413	1,470	1,527	1,584
Change in working capital	(169)	294	(223)	163	(205)
Capital expenditures/asset sales	(1,754)	(3,432)	1,180	(2,720)	(2,133)
Free cash flow	703	(213)	3,819	530	924

[This spreadsheet can be found in the folder "Key Spreadsheets from the Workbook" located on the CD-ROM.]

Cash flows over the next five years are expected to fluctuate significantly due to key acquisitions and restructuring measures planned by Middlestates. After the fifth year, however, cash flow is expected to stabilize. Economists expect the long-term inflation rate to stabilize at 1.5 percent, and Middlestates expects real growth in sales to be 1.5 percent or less. Management has determined that the cost of capital is 9.28 percent.

Estimate Middlestates' enterprise value.

9. Vanguard Office Supplies is a nationwide retail chain that offers office supplies and office furniture. Company management has decided that, from both a competitive and a cost-cutting standpoint, Vanguard should offer its own private-label brands for products like student notebooks, fillers, ledgers and journals, bond and linen paper, and other products. To accomplish this objective, Vanguard is considering the purchase of Omega Paper, a manufacturer of paper products and notebooks. A five-year income forecast for Omega is given, along with other pertinent information. Vanguard plans to keep Omega's debt-equity ratio at its current level.

   Calculate the equity value per share of Omega using the discounted cash flow method.

Five-Year Forecast ($ MM)	**Year 1**	**Year 2**	**Year 3**	**Year 4**	**Year 5**
Revenue	957.9	972.2	986.8	1,001.6	1,016.6
Cost of goods sold	862.1	875.0	888.1	901.4	915.0
SG&A	67.0	68.1	69.1	70.1	71.2
EBIT	28.7	29.2	29.6	30.0	30.5
Interest expense	12.5	13.4	13.8	14.1	14.4
EBT	16.2	15.7	15.8	16.0	16.1
Taxes	5.5	5.3	5.4	5.4	5.5
Net Income	10.7	10.4	10.5	10.5	10.6
Other projections:					
Change in net working capital	(5.7)	(5.8)	(5.9)	(6.0)	(6.1)
Capital expenditures	28.7	29.2	80.3	62.2	30.5
Depreciation	52.7	53.5	54.3	55.1	55.9
Tax rate	34.0%				
Book value of debt ($MM)	192.3				
Book value of equity ($MM)	364.9				
Share price ($)	10.5				
Beta	0.76				
Shares outstanding (MM)	51.5				
Interest rate on company debt	6.5%				
Current bond yields on similarly rated companies	6.1%				
10-year T-bond rate	5.0%				
Inflation	2.5%				
Market risk premium	6.0%				

[This spreadsheet can be found in the folder "Key Spreadsheets from the Workbook" located on the CD-ROM.]

10. Refer to problem 7. See the forecasts for the next five years given here. Assume that the new debt level will total $400 million at an interest rate of 6 percent and that this debt will be the perpetual amount of debt of the firm.

    Calculate the equity value of the bookseller to Trigeorgis using the adjusted present value approach.

($ MM)	Year 1	Year 2	Year 3	Year 4	Year 5
Sales	3,271.2	3,387.9	3,537.4	3,777.5	3,966.4
EBIT	171.4	191.9	210.3	235.9	238.0
Depreciation and amortization	83.5	95.3	96.2	103.0	112.0
Changes in working capital	(32.7)	(37.3)	(17.7)	(41.6)	(39.7)
Capital expenditures	(159.2)	(141.2)	(90.7)	(100.0)	(120.0)
Risk-free rate	5%				
Risk premium	6%				
Terminal value growth rate	3%				
Shares outstanding	75 million				

[This spreadsheet can be found in the folder "Key Spreadsheets from the Workbook" located on the CD-ROM.]

CHAPTER 10

Valuing Options

The world of M&A has been influenced greatly by options concepts; these concepts help explain behavior and deal features that were previously difficult to understand. There are six important determinants of an option's value: asset price, exercise price, volatility, time to expiration, interest rate, and dividends. The value of options can be calculated by analytical and numerical methods. Option-pricing theory can be used to value securities as different as loan guarantees, bonds, common stock, and real assets.

- Some terminology:
  - An *option* is the right, not the obligation, to do something.
  - A *call* option is the right to buy and a *put* option is the right to sell an asset at certain price within a certain time period.
  - An *American option* can be exercised at any moment before expiration; a *European option* can be exercised only at expiration.
  - A *long position* gives the investor the *right* to exercise an option; a *short position commits* the investor to perform if the option is exercised.
  - A call option is *in the money* if the current stock price is higher than the exercise price; it is *out of the money* if the stock price is lower than the exercise price. A put option is *in the money* if the stock price is lower than the exercise price; it is *out of the money* if the stock price is higher than the exercise price.
- The value of a firm consists of its stand-alone value plus the value of options. Long options are assets; short options are liabilities.

$$V_{\text{Enterprise, option-adjusted}} = V_{\text{DCF of enterprise}} + V_{\text{Long options}} - V_{\text{Short options}}$$

- A *payoff* is the flow of cash to the parties to an option contract at the time of exercise of the option. Profit differs from payoff by recognizing the outlay necessary to establish the option position. Payoffs are not to be confused with profits—profits reflect the cost of buying (or the revenue from selling) the option while payoffs do not. Payoffs for different option positions are:

	Call	Put
Long	Payoff = Max(S – Ex, 0)	Payoff = Max(Ex – S, 0)
Short	Payoff = – Max(S – Ex, 0)	Payoff = – Max(Ex – S, 0)

S = Underlying asset price; Ex = Exercise price.

By using various combinations of these four simple positions, one can achieve more complex payoff structures.

- *Put-call parity* refers to the relationship between the price of a put option and the price of a call option on the same underlying asset with the same expiration date. The equality of the two sides hypothesizes that at equilibrium there will be no arbitrage opportunities.

$$P_t - C_t = E/(1 + R_f)^{T-t} - S_t$$

- Option value consists of two parts: *intrinsic value* and *time value*. Intrinsic value refers to the payoffs that can be obtained by exercising an option. Time value derives from the chance that the option will be in the money at some point in the future. As long as the option holder does not have to exercise the option immediately, the option will have some time value.
- The *Black-Scholes option pricing model* estimates the value of an option. The basis of the model is that a risk-free hedge is created, and once the risk-free hedge is created we can then set the cost of the hedge equal to the present value of the hedge payoff discounted at the risk-free rate, in order to arrive at an option value. The Black-Scholes model is popular because of its simplicity.
- The table describes the drivers of option values:

Increase In	Call Option Value	Put Option Value
Underlying asset price	Increase	Decrease
Exercise price	Decrease	Increase
Time to expiration	Increase	Increase
Risk (volatility)	Increase	Increase
Dividend yield	Decrease	Increase
Risk-free rate	Increase	Decrease

- Some applications of option-pricing theory include:
  - Value the residual claim on a firm's assets. Equity can be treated as an option on the assets of the firm, with the exercise price equal to the par value of the debt, and expiration equal to the maturity of the debt.
  - Value a firm's debt, which should be equal to the present value of a risk-free zero coupon bond less the value of a put option written on the firm's assets:

$$V_{\text{Bond}} = Ee^{-rt} - V_{\text{Put}}$$

  - Value loan guarantees, subordinated debt, and equity-linked debt, to design securities and to assess capital investments, too.
- Options permeate M&A transactions and affect the attractiveness of a deal. Good analysis based on an appropriate consideration of options drives good deal design and helps both parties converge to a better deal.

CHAPTER 10—WORKBOOK QUESTIONS

1. Mr. Jones holds a biotech stock in his portfolio. The stock has been a highflier for several years, and Mr. Jones thinks it will continue to go up in value because it has a couple of drugs in the pipeline. But he also worries about the uncertainty of future Food and Drug Administration (FDA) approvals. Therefore, he is thinking about using options to hedge his position. He wants a minimum return of 30 percent and is willing to give up any returns above 50 percent in two years. The stock trades at $80 today.

   a. Draw the payoff diagram illustrating Jones' objectives.

   b. Decompose this into discrete option positions (long/short; put/call) and cite the exercise prices that will allow Jones to meet his goals.

2. *Mrs. Chelsea is a business manager at Company ABC, and is considering purchasing the right to drill an oil well. The right will allow ABC to drill the well anytime in the next five years and then extract any oil in perpetuity. The initial cost for drilling will be around $8 million. The expected value for the total sales from the well is estimated at $10 million with a standard deviation of 40 percent. Given a 7 percent risk-free rate for five-year government bonds, what is the value of this right?*

3. Suppose a stock has an equal chance of moving up by 20 percent or down by 15 percent over the next year—the probability of either outcome is 50 percent. The current stock price is $100.

   a. Calculate the one-year at-the-money call and put option payoff at the expiration, assuming exercise prices for both at $100.

   b. Estimate the appropriate risk-free rate that makes put-call parity hold.

4. Suppose a stock is trading at $50 today. A one-month call option on this stock with an exercise price of $55 is quoted at $.50, and a one-month put option at the same exercise price is quoted at $6.00. The annualized one-month Treasury-bill rate is 8 percent.

   Is there an arbitrage opportunity? If so, what position should you take to exploit it?

5. *In words, explain:*

   a. Why an investor would exercise an American call option before expiration if the stock pays a dividend.

   b. Why put-call parity does not hold for American options.

6. *List the six drivers of option value and illustrate the corresponding price movements for call and put options with the decrease of each driver.*

7. *You can use beta to characterize the risk of stocks; can you calculate the beta of an option? If so, how would it compare to the beta of the underlying stock?*

8. *Consider stock ABC, trading at $80 with an historical volatility of 25 percent annually. The one-year risk-free rate is 9 percent. Calculate the value of the following investment alternatives:*

   a. *Call option with an exercise price of $90, expiring in one year.*

   b. *Put option with an exercise price of $75, expiring in one year.*

   c. *The combination of a call and a put option with an exercise price of $80, expiring in one year. What is the purpose of combining the two options this way?*

   d. *Assuming stock ABC pays a $3 dividend next year, recalculate the prices for a, b, and c.*

9. *Mr. Brian, a loan officer at a midsize local bank, is reviewing the file for Acme Programs, a computer software company. Acme is applying for a $5 million subordinated long-term loan from Mr. Brian's bank. The company has a market capitalization of $30 million and already has $10 million of senior debt on its balance sheet. The book value of assets is only $10 million. What is your recommendation to Mr. Brian about this loan? Please state your reasons and concerns qualitatively and illustrate your recommendation using a graph.*

CHAPTER 11

Valuing Synergies

The word "synergy" refers to an increased result from the combination of efforts compared to what could be obtained from the two efforts alone. In M&A, the defining feature of a synergistic transaction is that it creates value for shareholders that they would be unable to create on their own through combination of shares in a portfolio.

- *Synergies* can be of two kinds: synergies "in place" and synergies that are contingent (i.e., that have optionlike characteristics).
- Payoffs on *in-place synergies* are reasonably predictable. Discounted cash flow valuation is well suited for valuing synergies of this kind. In-place synergies include:
  - Revenue enhancement synergies.
  - Cost reduction synergies.
  - Asset reduction synergies such as through the disposal of idle or redundant assets.
  - Tax reduction synergies such as through an increase in depreciation tax shields or through a transfer of net operating losses.
  - Weighted average cost of capital (WACC) reduction synergies.
- WACC reduction synergies may occur in two ways, neither of which is necessarily a straightforward path to value creation.
  - Optimization of debt tax shields (i.e., increasing the use of interest-bearing debt). But unless there are imperfections in capital markets, tax shield optimization may not be doing something for shareholders that they cannot already do on their own through "homemade leverage."
  - Coinsurance effects (i.e., combining two cash flow streams that are less than perfectly correlated to produce a joint stream that is less risky and that will therefore reduce capital costs). Shareholders can duplicate the effect of coinsurance on WACC through their own portfolio changes; therefore, it likely does not do something for shareholders they cannot already do on their own. However, coinsurance may expand the debt capacity of the firm, permitting greater exploitation of debt tax shields, and therefore the creation of value.
- *Contingent synergies* are those that depend on a triggering event—a right that is exercised—to produce payoffs. Examples of contingent synergies include growth option synergies, exit option synergies, and options to switch.

- When valuing synergies, one must:
  - Choose a discount rate consistent with the risk of the synergy. One size does not fit all: Riskless synergies should be discounted at the risk-free rate; highly speculative synergies should be discounted at a high rate, such as the return required by venture capitalists. Synergy cash flows as risky as earnings before interest and taxes (EBIT) could be discounted at the cost of debt; synergies as risky as dividends could be discounted at the cost of equity.
  - Reflect inflation, real growth, taxes, and a reasonable life span.
  - Use a terminal value to reflect life of the synergies beyond the forecast horizon.
- Back-solving for required synergies is useful for decision makers. In back-solving, one asks what synergies are necessary in order for a deal to be economically attractive, given a certain price.
- Synergies are:
  - Highest in horizontal deals; middling in vertical combinations; lowest in conglomerate deals.
  - Highest in "in-market" deals; lower in market extension deals.

CHAPTER 11—WORKBOOK QUESTIONS

1. *What discount rates would you choose to value the following synergy cash flows? Please explain for each whether you would use WACC, K_e, K_d, or R_f as the discount rate, and why.*

   a. *The merger between Pfizer and Pharmacia in July 2002 created a pharmaceutical giant with combined annual revenue of $48 billion. Potential cost savings were the biggest impetus for the merger: The combined company was expected to realize $2.5 billion in annual savings by 2005.*[1]

   b. *In June 2000, the French water supplier Vivendi S.A. announced its plans to acquire Seagram. Vivendi was also in the television and telecommunications businesses, and intended to bolster its presence in these areas by combining them with Seagram's Universal Studios. Vivendi intended to deliver Universal's entertainment through its (Vivendi's) digital delivery systems (i.e., wireless telephones and Internet). What discount rate would you use to value possible revenue synergies from this business combination?*

   c. *In June 1998, the Canadian Imperial Bank of Commerce (CIBC) and Toronto Dominion Bank announced a $14 billion merger. Executives of both companies said that the banks' complementary strengths made for a good fit: CIBC was strong in retail and investment banking, while Toronto Dominion had strong discount-broker and mutual-fund operations. The ability to cross-sell products of the two banks would result in revenue synergies. The executives also said that they anticipated eventual cost savings of about 10 percent a year.*[2]

2. UniMart and Harry's were two big supermarket chains operating in the southeastern United States. The two chains recently agreed to merge in response to increased competition within the industry. The feasibility of the merger hinged very much on the potential cost savings that could be achieved through greater purchasing power. The CFOs of both chains agreed that cost savings of 2 percent of annual revenue could be achieved. Around $50 million would have to be spent on redecorating the stores and putting up new signs. Revenues were expected to grow at an annual nominal rate of 4 percent. Both chains' cost of debt currently stood at 6.5 percent. Profits were taxed at a rate of 35 percent.

   What is the value of the synergies?

3. April 6, 1998, saw the announcement of the then biggest merger in history: the $83 billion deal between Travelers Group Inc. and Citicorp. The deal "brought forth a colossus—Citigroup—with a commercial bank (Citibank), an insurance company (Travelers), an investment bank (Salomon Brothers) and a retail brokerage firm (Smith Barney) all under one roof."[3] Executives at both companies bet that the one-stop-shop format would lure customers in. Cost savings were also an important part of the deal: An estimated 8,000 employees were to be laid off by the completion date. Given are stand-alone earnings forecasts for Travelers and Citicorp. Suppose that revenue synergies were forecast at 5 percent of projected revenue, that annual cost savings of $400 million were expected, and that operating margins were forecast at 12.2 percent of revenue.

Stand-Alone Summary Earnings Models

	1998F	1999F	2000F	2001F	2002F	2003F
Revenues						
Travelers	41,829	43,653	46,804	49,847	52,837	56,008
Citicorp	23,525	26,139	28,194	30,449	32,733	35,188
	65,354	69,792	74,998	80,296	85,570	91,196
Operating earnings						
Travelers	4,035	4,420	5,035	5,234	5,548	5,881
Citicorp	4,273	4,806	4,973	5,329	5,728	6,158
	8,308	9,226	10,008	10,563	11,276	12,039

Note: 1998–2000 figures taken from report by Judah Kraushaar and Amy Butte, "Citigroup: A New Model for the Millennium," Merrill Lynch, July 10, 1998. F = Forecast.

   Calculate the present value of the expected synergies. (Assume a tax rate of 35 percent, a discount rate of 10 percent suitable for the cost and revenue synergies combined, and inflation of 3 percent. Assume also that the transaction is completed at the end of 1998.)

4. On behalf of Bridgewater Corporation you are negotiating to acquire Coastal Inc., a large competitor. The two sides cannot agree on price. However, the negotiator for the other side argues that the combination of the two firms will produce financial synergies that will make Newco worth $2.5 billion more than your analysis suggests. The negotiator hands you the following table in support of her analysis.

	Buyer (Before)	Target (Before)	Sum of Buyer and Target (Before)	Newco	Value Impact
Weighted average cost of capital, before the acquisition	9.1%	11.1%	9.1%		
Newco's weighted average cost of capital, after the acquisition				8.3%	
Total capital of buyer and target, before the acquisition	$26,723	$581		$27,304	
Dollar cost of capital	$ 2,424	$ 64	$2,488	$ 2,278	$ 210
Implied Present Value of Financial Synergies from Acquistion					**$2,521**
Calculation of Newco's Cost of Capital after Acquistion					
Cost of equity estimate =	**10.6%**	**14.2%**		**9.8%**	
Beta of buyer, before the acquisition	1.02				
Beta of target, before the acquisition		1.62			
Unleverered beta	0.84	1.13		0.84	
Adjustment in Newco asset beta because of covariance unanticipated by market				−0.15	
Market value weight of buyer in Newco (%)	98%				
Market value weight of target in Newco (%)		2%			
Beta of Newco				0.89	
Risk-free rate of return	4.5%	4.5%		4.5%	
Equity market risk premium	6.0%	6.0%		6.0%	
Cost of equity from CAPM	10.6%	14.2%		9.8%	
Cost of debt estimate =	**4.4%**	**6.3%**		**4.9%**	
Current *pre-tax* yields on debt, at rating and tenor of Newco	6.8%	9.8%		7.5%	
Marginal tax rate for Newco	35.0%	35.0%		35.0%	
After-tax cost of debt for Newco	4.4%	6.3%		4.9%	
Weights in target capital structure for Newco					
Targeted weight of debt (%)	25%	40%		30%	
Targeted weight of equity (%)	75%	60%		70%	

What questions or observations might you raise?

5. Phantom Computing and Ghostly Notebooks, formerly competitors in the computing industry, have agreed to merge. Phantom's management is fairly certain that the projected cost synergies—mostly to come from layoffs and restructuring—are achievable. It is less certain about the achievability of the revenue enhancements, which are expected to come from greater market power and from cross-selling the products and services of both firms. Management estimates that the net present value (NPV) of revenue synergies, discounted at a WACC of 10 percent, should be worth at least $1.2 billion in order to ensure that the deal is value enhancing.

   Based on the following information, how much should the annual revenue enhancements (in constant dollars) be in order to achieve the desired NPV?

Expected inflation rate	2%
Growth rate of FCF (nominal), in perpetuity	3%
Discount rate	10%
Ongoing investment revenue (year 1+)	2%
Operating cost revenues	90%
Tax rate	38%

6. Two auto parts manufacturers have agreed to merge. By streamlining operations, the merger is projected to generate pretax cost savings of $63 million in the first year, $118 million in the second year, $183 million in the third year, and thereafter growing at the rate of inflation. To achieve these cost savings an investment of $480 million must be made at the outset. Sales of redundant equipment and property are expected to bring in pretax gains of $63 million in the first year and $48 million in the second year. There is a high probability that these projections will materialize. The merged company's cost of capital is forecast at 9.6 percent; borrowing cost is expected to be 7.8 percent. Inflation is 2.5 percent.

   What is the present value of savings? (Assume a marginal tax rate of 35 percent.)

7. Sirius Technologies, a manufacturer of personal digital assistants (PDAs), is looking to acquire Leonid Corporation, a weaker competitor. Sirius believes Leonid's PDAs are of inferior quality, but is optimistic about a technology being developed by Leonid that would allow PDAs to measure human body temperatures and pulse rates. Sirius estimates the present value of cash flows from this new technology to be $388 million. Leonid is roughly eight months away from bringing this new technology to market. To launch the product, Sirius would need to spend approximately $272 million. The CFO of Sirius has qualms about the Leonid acquisition. He believes that while the new technology could give Sirius a first-mover advantage, it is not sophisticated enough and will be easily replicated/improved upon by competitors. Accordingly, he thinks the projected $871 million in cash flows may have a standard deviation of as much as 90 percent.

   If the current risk-free rate is 4.5 percent, what would be the value of this new technology to Sirius?

8. Refer to problem 7. Leonid wants Sirius to pay $270 million for the company. The CFO of Sirius believes that revenue synergies will be insignificant, while cost synergies will be merely $8 million a year. Here is a forecast of Leonid's financial performance, excluding the new technology:

	Year 1	Year 2	Year 3	Year 4	Year 5
Revenue	$58.00	$75.40	$90.48	$99.53	$104.50
Cost of goods sold and operating expenses	51.62	67.86	82.34	92.56	97.19
Operating income	$ 6.38	$ 7.54	$ 8.14	$ 6.97	$ 7.32
Taxes	2.23	2.64	2.85	2.44	2.56
Net income	$ 4.15	$ 4.90	$ 5.29	$ 4.53	$ 4.75
Other items:					
Capex			(20.00)		
Depreciation	1.74	2.26	2.71	2.99	3.14
Change in net working capital	(2.32)	(3.02)	(3.62)	(3.98)	(4.18)

Assuming a tax rate of 35 percent, discount rate of 12 percent, and inflation of 2.5 percent, is Leonid worth $270 million to Sirius?

NOTES

1. Scott Gotlieb, "Mergers Won't Cure Diseases," *Wall Street Journal*, July 17, 2002, p. A16.
2. Mark Heinzl, "CIBC to Merge with Toronto Dominion," *Wall Street Journal*, April 20, 1998, p. A3.
3. Ron Chernow, "The Birth of a Bureaucratic Mastodon?" *Wall Street Journal*, April 9, 1998, p. A22.

CHAPTER **12**

Valuing the Firm across Borders

Going across borders affects many of the valuation assumptions in M&A. Analysts must think carefully about factors such as inflation, exchange rates, tax rates, the timing of cash remittances, political risk, market segmentation, governance, accounting principles, and social/cultural issues. Analysts must have a view, not merely about the forecast assumptions for the target firm, but also about the country and local market in which the target firm competes.

- The Fisher Equation decomposes nominal rates into inflation and a real growth rate:

$$(1+R_{\text{Nom}})^n = (1+R_{\text{Real}})^n (1+Inf)^n$$

where R_{Nom} = Nominal interest rate.
R_{Real} = Real interest rate.
Inf = Inflation rate.

- The spot rate is the exchange rate today between two currencies. The forward rate is the expected exchange rate at some future point in time. Forward exchange rates can be projected using the idea of interest rate parity, using these formulas. The relation between them supposes a constant real rate of return as suggested in the Fisher Equation.

$$\frac{SPOT_{\frac{\text{Foreign currency}}{\text{Dollar}}}}{FWD_{\frac{\text{Foreign currency}}{\text{Dollar}}}} = \frac{(1+R_{\text{Dollar}})}{(1+R_{\text{Foreign currency}})}$$

$$FWD_{\frac{\text{Foreign currency}}{\text{Dollar}}} = SPOT_{\frac{\text{Foreign currency}}{\text{Dollar}}} \left[\frac{\left(1+Inf_{\text{Foreign currency}}\right)^n}{\left(1+Inf_{\text{Dollar}}\right)^n} \right]$$

- Different countries have different tax and accounting systems. With respect to tax systems, some countries may use the territorial tax system; others may use the worldwide tax credit system. Accounting treatments may be very different from U.S. GAAP.

- There are two ways to adjust DCF calculations for higher political risk in a foreign market than your home market: (1) by "haircutting" the cash flow estimates, or (2) by raising the discount rate.
- Segmented markets are those that have a low degree of integration with the global markets. Segmentation may be created by a variety of factors such as foreign exchange controls, controls on investment by foreigners, high and variable inflation, lack of a high-quality regulatory and accounting framework, lack of country funds or cross-listed securities that provide benchmarks for arbitrage, small size of market, poor credit ratings, or absence of credit ratings. In segmented markets, a beta versus the global equity market index will poorly explain returns.
- Research suggests that equity markets of emerging markets exhibit (1) higher average returns and higher volatility than developed markets, (2) lower correlations with developed market returns, and (3) variable volatility and correlation across time.
- Cross-border DCF valuations may be approached in two ways:
  1. Convert local currency flows into dollars using forward exchange rates, and discount such flows at a dollar rate.
  2. Forecast in local currency and discount at a local WACC.

  Note: The two approaches will produce identical estimates only if assumptions are consistent.
- Nominal cash flows must be discounted at nominal rates; real cash flows must be discounted at real rates. Note that under the nominal cash flow/nominal discount rate approach, the distortion of historical cost assets causes cash flows to be less than they would be with current cost assets. The real/real approach ignores this distortion.
- Aside from the simple CAPM, other methods can be used to estimate the cost of equity:
  - ***Multifactor model*** considers the exposure of a stock to various factors, both macroeconomic and firm-specific, such as world stock market price risk, country stock market risk, industry risk, foreign exchange rate risk, political risk, and liquidity risk.

$$(R_i - R_f) = \alpha_i + \beta_{i/W}(R_W - R_f) + \beta_{i/C}(R_C - R_f) + \beta_{i/I}(R_I - R_f) + \beta_{Ex}(R_{Ex} - R_f) + \beta_D(R_C^D - R_{AAA}) + \beta_L(R_L^{Lo} - R_L^{Hi}) + \varepsilon$$

where:
R = Return.
β = Regression coefficient.
i = Specific company.
f = Risk-free.
W = Global equity market portfolio.
C = Country equity market portfolio.
I = Industry equity market portfolio.
Ex = Portfolio of foreign currency deposits.
D = Sovereign debt instrument of home country, C.
AAA = Highest-rated sovereign debt instrument.
L = Portfolio of low or high liquidity bonds.
ε = Regression residual indicating company-specific variability of returns (unsystematic risk).

- *CAPM*, the capital asset pricing model, suggests that the relevant measure of a stock's risk is how it covaries with the equity market portfolio. This can be expressed in its domestic or global versions (the ICAPM). The domestic version is based on the home equity market portfolio; the global version is based on the global equity market portfolio.

  CAPM: $k_e = R_f + \beta_i \cdot (R_{\text{Market}} - R_f)$

  ICAPM: $k_e = R_f + \beta_i^W \cdot (R_m^W - R_f)$

- *Credit model* relies on non–equity market measures.

  $$K_{i,t+1} = \gamma_0 + \gamma_1 \times \ln(\text{Country credit risk rating}_{it}) + \varepsilon_{it+1}$$

- *Adjusted CAPM* adjusts cost of equity for segmentation and political risks.

  $$k_e = R_f^{US} + \pi + (\beta_i^{Foreign} \cdot \beta_{Foreign}^{US}) \cdot (R_m^{US} - R_f^{US})$$

CHAPTER 12—WORKBOOK QUESTIONS

1. Following is an income statement projection for an acquisition target in a developing nation. The forecasts are in the local currency, and have been projected using an expected real rate of growth of 5 percent, which is also the expected perpetual growth rate. The local sovereign debt yields are currently at 8 percent, which factors in expected inflation of 3 percent.

   What is the NPV of these cash flows?

   Assume that the cost of capital for this company is a nominal 13 percent, and that net working capital requirements will increase by 0.5 percent of sales each year, and that depreciation and capital expenditures offset each other. Depreciation is based on historical book values.

($ MM)	Year 1	Year 2	Year 3	Year 4	Year 5
Sales	68,776	72,215	75,826	79,617	83,598
Cost of goods sold (65.5% of sales)	45,048	47,301	49,666	52,149	54,756
Gross profit	23,728	24,914	26,160	27,468	28,841
Operating expenses (24.5% of sales)	16,850	17,693	18,577	19,506	20,481
Operating income	6,878	7,221	7,583	7,962	8,360
Interest expense	741	631	712	753	771
Income before taxes	6,137	6,590	6,871	7,209	7,589
Taxes (@34%)	1,964	2,109	2,199	2,307	2,428
Net income	4,173	4,482	4,672	4,902	5,160

[This spreadsheet can be found in the folder "Key Spreadsheets from the Workbook" located on the CD-ROM.]

2. On September 1, 1997, the exchange rate between the U.S. dollar and the Philippine peso was US$1:PhP30.4. The one-year Philippine Treasury bill rate at this time was 15 percent, while the yield on the one-year U.S. Treasury was 5.52 percent. The expected inflation rate for the Philippines was 8 percent, and for the United States it was 2.5 percent.

   a. *Using interest rate parity, what is your estimate of the peso-dollar exchange rate one year hence as implied by the Treasury bill yields in the two countries?*
   b. *Use equation (5) in Chapter 12 of main text to estimate the forward rate one year hence as implied by the expected exchange rates in the two countries.*

$$FWD_{\frac{\text{Peso}}{\text{Dollar}}} = SPOT_{\frac{\text{Peso}}{\text{Dollar}}}\left[\frac{(1+Inf_{\text{Peso}})^n}{(1+Inf_{\text{Dollar}})^n}\right]$$

   c. *Did you get the same answers to a and b? Why or why not?*

3. Assume you have acquired manufacturing equipment for $500 million, and that it has a useful life of 10 years. Depreciation, calculated on a straight-line basis, will be $50 million per year. Inflation is 3 percent, the real discount rate is 4.85 percent, and the tax rate is 40 percent.

   a. *What would be the present value of the depreciation tax shields from year 1 to year 5? Use the nominal discount rate to calculate present value.*
   b. *Now assume that you can inflate depreciation expense at a rate of 3 percent annually. Using the same discount rate, what is the present value of depreciation tax shields from year 1 to year 5?*
   c. *Go back to (a). This time, use the real discount rate to calculate the present value of the tax shields. What do you observe? How would you interpret the results?*

4. Following is a free cash flow estimate and valuation for a Brazilian company. Values are given in Brazilian reals (R$), and the NPV is translated into U.S. dollars at the current exchange rate of US$1:R$3.54.

(R$, in millions)		2003	2004	2005	2006	2007	2008
Free cash flows		R$1,505	1,990	2,674	3,153	3,780	8,219
Terminal value						103,247	
Cash flows including terminal value		R$1,505	1,990	2,674	3,153	107,028	
Present value in reals	**R$62,578**		32.21%	34.37%	17.95%	19.88%	
Present value in U.S. Dollars	**$17,677**						

[This spreadsheet can be found in the folder "Key Spreadsheets from the Workbook" located on the CD-ROM.]

Translate the cash flows into U.S. dollars and find their present value. Assume the following:

Inflation rate, United States	2.4%
Inflation rate, Brazil	8.4%
Exchange rate at time 0 (reals per dollar)	R$3.54
Real discount rate	5.0%

Did you come up with the same present value? What rate did you use to discount the U.S. dollar flows? What assumptions are necessary to obtain equivalency between the approach of converting local flows into dollars and discounting at a dollar rate and the approach of forecasting in local currency and discounting at a local rate?

5. You are trying to determine the cost of equity for a target located in a developing country whose cash flows you have projected in dollars. You have the following data:

10-year rate, U.S. dollar denominated sovereign bonds	7.25%
Beta of target versus foreign country stock index	0.97
Beta of foreign country stock index versus U.S. index	1.28
Market risk premium, United States	6.00%
Market risk premium, foreign country	8.00%

[The spreadsheet can be found in the folder "Key Spreadsheets from the Workbook" located on the CD-ROM.]

What would be your estimate of this firm's cost of equity?

6. In late April 2003, you are attempting to determine Singapore Airlines' cost of equity for valuing cash flows in Singapore dollars. Its beta versus the global equity portfolio was 1.02 over the past 12 months. You estimate, based on the past 17 years of data, that the equity market premium on the global portfolio is 5.8 percent. Currently, the Singaporean Treasury bond yield is at 4.5 percent.

   a. *What is your estimate of Singapore Airlines' cost of equity based on the preceding data?*
   b. *Estimate the cost of equity for Southwest Airlines and American Airlines using a risk premium of 5.6 percent for the United States. Based on stock price performance over the past 12 months, the betas for the two companies versus the S&P 500 index are 1.10 and 2.16 respectively. The yield on the 10-year U.S. Treasury bond in April 2003 is 3.8 percent.*
   c. *Are the costs of equity among the three airlines comparable? What are the drivers of the differences among their costs of equity?*

7. *For each of the following situations, what method(s) might you use for calculating the cost of equity? Write out the equation for each method you choose, and explain why you think it is appropriate.*

a. You work for a large conglomerate that has holdings in companies in more than 50 different countries; most of the investments are in consumer goods manufacturers. Currently your firm is evaluating a potential Malaysian target. What method would you use to calculate the cost of equity for the Malaysian company?

b. You have just set up your own private equity firm in Canada and are evaluating your first investment—in the United States. The target is small and privately held. What method would you use to calculate the cost of equity for this company?

8. Telekom Malaysia BHD is a provider of telecommunication and related services in Malaysia.

Calculate the U.S. dollar cost of equity for the company under the different approaches. You are given the data you will need for each approach.

a. ICAPM:

U.S. risk-free rate	5.43%
World risk premium	5.70%
Telekom Malaysia beta vs. world portfolio	0.31

b. CAPM adjusted for segmentation and political risk:

Return on U.S. 10-year T-bond	5.43%
U.S. equity market premium	5.70%
Beta, Malaysia vs. S&P	0.39
Beta, Telekom Malaysia vs. Malaysia market	1.34
Country credit spread	1.47%

c. Compare your results from the two methods. How do you interpret the differences?

CHAPTER 13

Valuing the Highly Levered Firm, Assessing the Highly Levered Transaction

High leverage presents special challenges for M&A practitioners and analysts. Because of the relatively low volume of highly leveraged transactions (HLTs), this is an area of M&A in which sound judgment comes at a super-premium. Having a rigorous view of the way to analyze these deals and their wealth-transfer possibilities is vital.

- Highly levered transactions appear in corporate finance in three classic forms:
  1. *Leveraged buyout (LBO).* In this transaction a private group of investors acquire a company (or division) financed with a mixture of high-ratio debt and equity. In the LBO, the management of the target is usually retained, and often takes an equity interest in Newco—hence the alternative name for this transaction, management buyout. In addition, it is also called a going-private transaction. A typical LBO candidate would have most of the following features: (1) strong cash flow, (2) low level of capital expenditures, (3) strong market position, (4) stable industry, (5) low rate of technological change (and low R&D expense), (6) proven management with no anticipated changes, (7) relatively low (or under-) valuation in the stock market, and (8) no major change in strategy.
  2. *Leveraged recapitalization.* In a "recap" the company dramatically levers itself and uses the proceeds of the financing to pay an extraordinary dividend or to repurchase shares. The leveraged recapitalization is similar to the LBO except that the company continues to be publicly owned.
  3. *Reorganization in distress or bankruptcy.* In bankruptcy the value of the firm's assets is less than the value of its debt. Under protection of a court, the firm reorganizes its debt and equity claims.
- The buyout boom gained momentum in the early 1980s, peaked in 1988 with the massive buyout of RJR Nabisco, and receded somewhat in the 1990s.
- Typically the LBO offers a sizable abnormal return to shareholders of target companies. Also, shareholders of the buyer group typically earn large absolute returns. The large returns to target and buyer shareholders stem from significant improvements in operating efficiency.

- Leverage has two offsetting effects on firm value. The first is the benefit of *debt tax shields*—literally, the savings in free cash flow owing to a lower tax bill. The second effect is the *default risk*, which will offset the value created by borrowing as the borrowing of the firm increases.

- It is difficult to value highly levered firms because costs of bankruptcy and distress are unobservable. There is no fluid market in which these costs are isolated, priced, and may be observed from one day to the next. The analyst can look for some guidance from two sources: debt market yields and put option valuation. The difficulty of estimating the value of the highly levered firm poses two chief implications for the M&A practitioner. First, analytic rigor is even more important in the instance of highly levered transactions (HLTs), not less. Second, the ambiguities about valuing the highly levered firm mean that there will be many opportunities to transfer value from some players (e.g., creditors) to others (e.g., equity holders) in the design of the transaction.

- To use the adjusted present value approach to valuation, follow these steps:
  1. Project the book value balance sheets before and after the transaction.
  2. Estimate the market value of the enterprise before the transaction by adding together the book value of liabilities and the market value of equity of the firm.
  3. Estimate the present value of the firm's debt tax shields before the HLT.
  4. Solve for the implied market value of the firm's long-term business assets before the HLT.
  5. Solve for the market value of equity of the firm after the HLT including new debt tax shields.
  6. Estimate the new price per share as equal to the new market value of equity, plus any extraordinary dividend to be received, divided by the number of shares.

- The key lesson of the highly levered transaction is the need for a "*whole deal*" perspective, which looks at the risks and returns to all the players in the transaction. The whole deal perspective includes asking four kinds of questions:
  1. Is the purchase price for the target appropriate? Begin by valuing the target of the HLT. If the price is greater than intrinsic value, one should go no further with the HLT.
  2. What are the sources of positive NPV? If the first step suggests that the intrinsic value of the target is greater than purchase price, one should scrutinize the assumptions to identify *key value drivers*.
  3. Can the firm sustain the debt it will assume? This third question focuses on *financial feasibility*, as measured by analyses of asset coverage, interest coverage, and covenant coverage.
  4. What are the prospective returns to various providers of funds in the deal? Too often analysts focus only on the NPVs or internal rates of return (IRRs) of their own firm's investment in the target, rather than on the allocation of

profits among all the players. This final analysis focuses on possible *wealth transfers* among participants.

- The methodology and results of the risk analysis offer some important lessons about debt capacity and capital adequacy. Capital adequacy should be measured by the ability of expected cash flows to cover debt service requirements. In setting capitalization targets, point estimates of coverage are of limited value. What matters is the *probability of default.*
- Highly levered transactions are a prominent fixture on the M&A landscape. The analysis of HLTs uses discounted cash flow based on rates reflecting the classic risk-and-return relationship of modern financial theory. Yet these transactions require careful scrutiny for nonlinearities in the estimation of beta, for circularities in respect to capital structure assumptions, and for changing capital structures.

CHAPTER 13—WORKBOOK QUESTIONS

Case: Deep-Sea Tuna[1]

In 1984, Laurel Everett, the managing lending officer of Drake and Hollinger Bank (D&H Bank) was approached by Crawford & Co. to help finance $59 million for a management-led leveraged buyout of Deep-Sea Tuna Inc. from its parent company, Felicity Foods, Inc.

Crawford was looking to find an institutional investor to purchase $7 million in senior subordinated debt, which included the right to buy a 20 percent equity stake in the new company for an additional $1 million. The remaining $2.3 million in equity would be divided between the Felicity management team and Crawford. D&H Bank would be the sole creditor; thus, Felicity agreed to take back $15 million in junior subordinated notes.

Proposed Financing Structure

Senior Secured Bank Notes

Amount:	$37 million
Rate:	16%
Maturity:	7 years
Amortization:	Debt to be paid down as quickly as profits allow

Senior Subordinated Notes (Institutional Investor)

Amount:	$7 million
Rate:	16%
Maturity:	15 years
Amortization:	20% of face amount in years 11 through 15
Security:	Inventory and receivables, no trademarks

Junior Subordinated Notes

Amount:	$15 million
Rate:	12%
Maturity:	5 years
Amortization:	End of: 6 months, $1.5mm; 12 months, $1.5mm; 18 months, $2.0mm; 3 years, $2.5mm; 4 years, $2.5mm; 5 years, $5.0mm
Security:	Trademarks, Puerto Rican cannery leasehold, inventory, and receivables
Subordination:	Subordinated to principal and interest payments of senior bank debt and interest payments of senior subordinated notes

Common Equity

Amount:	$3.3 million
Investors:	Institutional investor of senior subordinated notes ($1.0mm buys 20%) Crawford & Co. ($2.0mm buys 40%) Management ($0.3mm buys 40%)

In early 1984, the managers of Felicity Foods decided to divest Deep-Sea Tuna because the tuna operation did not fit well with the company's overall business strategy. Felicity managers approached Deep-Sea Tuna to propose a possible management buyout. In addition, Felicity Foods hired/retained an investment bank to solicit bids from other interested buyers. None of their bids, however, exceeded Deep-Sea's net book value and therefore Felicity Foods decided to focus its efforts on the Deep-Sea management group. To facilitate the deal, the parent company even agreed to charge only the risk-free interest rate of 12 percent on the $15 million junior subordinated debt. To reduce the risk, the junior notes were scheduled to retire in five years, significantly sooner than the retirement of the senior subordinated notes.

Two years earlier, Deep-Sea had begun to experience difficulties after Felicity management had decided to expand capacity by entering into long-term contracts and by purchasing the largest tuna fleet in the industry. Felicity's strategic intent was to gain market share nationally. However, Felicity's decision unfortunately coincided with a period of overcapacity and stable demand in the tuna industry. Deep-Sea managers had to take cost-cutting measures soon thereafter, thus relinquishing the goal of capturing national market share in order to maintain their foothold in traditional markets. They also contracted their business by discontinuing certain operations and closing down plants. After the company incurred some initial losses due to discontinued operations, the overall cost cuts began to improve its bottom line.

Management believed that they could help continue this positive trend and that further improvement would follow. In particular, the proposed new managers estimated that $9.6 million in annual savings would be realized.

Refer to the following exhibits before answering the questions.

DEEP-SEA TUNA, INC.
Pro Forma Balance Sheets
(in millions $)

	1985	1986	1987	1988	1989	1990	1991	1992
Cash	0.0	0.0	0.0	0.0	0.0	0.0	0.0	0.0
Other receivables	1.1	1.1	1.1	1.1	1.1	1.1	1.1	1.1
Accounts receivable	0.0	10.9	11.0	10.9	10.9	11.7	11.7	11.7
Inventory	54.7	56.6	57.4	56.6	56.8	61.2	61.2	61.2
Other current assets	4.0	4.0	4.0	4.0	4.0	4.0	4.0	4.0
Total current assets	$59.8	$72.6	$73.5	$72.5	$72.8	$78.0	$78.0	$78.0
Plant, prop., and equip.	0.5	0.8	1.1	1.6	2.1	2.6	2.9	3.2
Other assets	2.0	2.0	2.0	2.0	2.0	2.0	2.0	2.0
Total assets	$62.3	$75.4	$76.6	$76.1	$76.9	$82.6	$82.9	$83.2
Accruals and payables	0.0	10.5	10.6	10.5	10.5	11.3	11.3	11.3
Current portion LTD	3.0	2.0	2.5	2.5	5.0	0.0	0.0	0.0
Total current liab.	$ 3.0	$12.5	$13.1	$13.0	$15.5	$11.3	$11.3	$11.3
Debt: Sr. bank	37.0	36.4	32.8	27.7	22.7	22.4	11.9	0.0
Sr. sub. notes	7.0	7.0	7.0	7.0	7.0	7.0	7.0	7.0
Jr. sub. notes	12.0	10.0	7.5	5.0	0.0	0.0	0.0	0.0
Total liabilities	$59.0	$65.9	$60.4	$52.7	$45.2	$40.7	$30.3	$18.4
Equity	3.3	3.3	3.3	3.3	3.3	3.3	3.3	3.3
Retained earnings	0.0	6.2	12.9	20.1	28.4	38.6	49.3	61.5
Total liabilities and owners' equity	$62.3	$75.4	$76.6	$76.1	$76.9	$82.6	$82.9	$83.2
Capital expenditures		$0.6	$0.8	$1.1	$1.1	$1.1	$1.1	$1.1
Depreciation		$0.3	$0.5	$0.6	$0.6	$0.6	$0.8	$0.8

DEEP-SEA TUNA, INC.
Pro Forma Income Statement
(in millions $)

	1986	1987	1988	1989	1990	1991	1992
Sales	$208.9	$211.9	$208.7	$209.5	$225.7	$225.7	$225.7
Cost of goods sold	169.2	171.6	169.0	169.7	182.8	182.8	182.8
Gross profit	$ 39.7	$ 40.3	$ 39.7	$ 39.8	$ 42.9	$ 42.9	$ 42.9
Distribution	5.0	5.1	5.0	5.0	5.4	5.4	5.4
Selling	10.2	10.4	10.2	10.3	11.1	11.1	11.1
General and admin.	8.4	8.5	8.3	8.4	9.0	9.0	9.0
Operating income	$ 16.1	$ 16.3	$ 16.1	$ 16.1	$ 17.4	$ 17.4	$ 17.4
Interest expense	8.8	8.4	7.6	6.5	5.4	4.7	3.0
Profit before taxes	7.2	7.9	8.5	9.7	12.0	12.7	14.4
Income taxes	1.1	1.2	1.3	1.5	1.8	1.9	2.2
Net income	$ 6.2	$ 6.7	$ 7.2	$ 8.2	$ 10.2	$ 10.8	$ 12.2
Assumed interest rates:							
U.S. bank debt	16.0%	Tax rate			15%		
Junior debt	12.0%						

Calculation of Cash Flows to Equity

	1986	1987	1988	1989	1990	1991	1992
Net income	$ 6.2	$ 6.7	$ 7.2	$ 8.2	$ 10.2	$ 10.8	$ 12.2
Plus depreciation	0.3	0.5	0.6	0.6	0.6	0.8	0.8
Less capital expenditures	(0.6)	(0.8)	(1.1)	(1.1)	(1.1)	(1.1)	(1.1)
Less additions to working capital	(2.3)	(0.8)	0.9	(0.2)	(4.4)	0.0	0.0
Less debt amortization	(3.6)	(5.6)	(7.6)	(7.5)	(5.3)	(10.5)	(11.9)
Cash flow to equity[1]	$ 0.0	$ 0.0	$ 0.0	$ 0.0	$ 0.0	$ 0.0	$ 0.0

1. Leveraged buyouts are usually designed so that debt service absorbs virtually all of the cash flow of the firm.

[These spreadsheets can be found in the folder "Key Spreadsheets from the Workbook" located on the CD-ROM.]

1. *Estimate the equity value of Deep-Sea Tuna Company. Refer to Exhibit 13.4 in the main text and to the Chapter 13 Questions and Answers located on the CD-ROM as guides for your calculations. Use a terminal (perpetual) growth rate of 2.5 percent.*

2. *Is the deal attractive from the perspective of a senior mezzanine investor?*

3. *Is the deal attractive from the perspective of a senior-secured debt investor?*

4. *What is your overall analysis of this deal? With all relevant parties in mind, is it a well-structured management buyout?*

NOTE

1. This problem is a disguised synopsis of an actual leveraged buyout case study prepared by Robert Bruner and Peter Hennessy.

CHAPTER 14

Real Options and Their Impact on M&A

Real options are usually unique, derived from nonfinancial assets such as land, plant and machinery, patents, and artistic property. These are usually challenging to value. Nonetheless, having a real options mind-set (i.e., looking for real optionality in any business situation) can lend important insights into the structure and valuation of deals.

- Analysts and executives should strive to master real options thinking for at least four reasons:
  1. Real options are pervasive in the business environment.
  2. Real options can have a material influence on firm value.
  3. One can easily create and destroy real option value.
  4. Discounted cash flow and other cash flow methods alone fail to capture qualities about an asset that are not reflected in the projected cash flows.
- Real options can be difficult to value because the parameters are not always clear. For instance, the exercise price, expiration date, and underlying value of the asset may be contingent. Or the option may actually consist of a cluster of options.
- Best practice in M&A draws on real option theory to:
  - Refine estimates of value.
  - Structure thinking about M&A opportunities, particularly for setting strategy and planning integration.
  - Guide deal design and negotiation problem solving.
- Some generic types of real options include:
  - Entry or growth options.
  - Exit or abandonment options.
  - Timing options: rights to delay or accelerate.
  - Switching options.
- Real options may appear in the field of M&A in strategic planning, deal design, and postmerger integration:
  - In strategy, real options appear in decisions about flexibility versus irreversibility of actions; insurance; learning and competencies (e.g., the acquisition of

strategic capabilities); and planning. Possible applications of real options in strategy might focus on:

- Buying a minority interest versus total control.
- Buying a built-up company versus building up the same assets yourself.
- Moving first, as opposed to following.
- Rights to exploit an uncertain resource.
- Acquisition search.

- Real options often appear in deal design through the exchange offer, breakup terms, liquidity and control features, contingent payment schemes, transaction risk management, and the adoption of takeover tactics.
- In postmerger integration, real options may appear in the organizational design and operational architecture of the firm, the structuring of contracts for human resources, and the selection among competing capabilities.

- Despite the pervasiveness of "rights," not all of them are options—some rights are better classified as "opportunities" rather than options. You may have the right to sell lemonade at the curbside in front of your house, but it's an opportunity rather than an option. Options exist where asset values are uncertain, the rights are exclusive, the decision can be freely and rationally made, and the rights are costly to acquire.
- Chapter 14 of the main text outlined steps to assess the impact of real options:

1. Find and specify the option. Anything that creates the right to "get" is a *call* option. The right to give away in return for payment is a *put* option. Anything that provides flexibility is a *long* position. Any commitment is a *short* position.
2. Options and their values can be assessed for three considerations:
   - ***Direction.*** Who holds the option? Who is the counterparty? Does the option create or destroy value for your position?
   - ***Materiality.*** Will the option make a material difference? Where the decision is important, the valuation analysis based on discounted cash flow seems close, and/or the assets under option are sizable, the option values will make a difference.
   - ***Key value drivers.*** What attributes of the asset are its main value drivers?
3. Model and value the option. There are four possible approaches for valuing options:
   - Value the real option in the framework of an existing equation (e.g., the *Black-Scholes option pricing model*).
   - Fit the option in the framework of a *binomial* lattice.
   - Fit the option in a *decision tree* framework.
   - Value the option using *simulation analysis*.
4. Interpret the results and develop implications.
   - Examine real option estimates against some test of reasonableness.
   - Examine one's confidence level in the estimated values.
   - Ask "so what?"

CHAPTER 14—WORKBOOK QUESTIONS

1. *Where can you find real options in the field of M&A?*

2. *List four methods of estimating real option value, and consider where each method could be used.*

3. *Assume you are a general manager of a professional sports club. You have just built a new stadium for the club, with $5 million remaining in your budget. Your architect proposes four ways to use the $5 million: upgrading a section of seats to private luxury rooms; building a multimedia center that will hold more than 50 journalists; upgrading the court to a multifunction one so that it can be used for basketball, ice hockey, and even arena football matches; and installing a flexible lighting and sound system that allows the stadium to be used for concerts or other events. Among these, which one seems like an option to you? Please explain why.*

4. Mr. Jones is a top professional basketball player. His agent just signed a deal with the New York Knicks. He will be given $25 million for the next three years, with an option to extend his contract for one more year at a salary of $8 million. Normally, after two years, if he plays well, he will get a contract extension for several years and forfeit the one-year extension. Based on current market demand and on his health, he estimates that the possibility of getting a contract extension is about 60 percent. If he does not get the contract extension, he thinks there is a 50 percent chance that he will be able to sign a contract with another team for a yearly salary of $10 million, and a 50 percent chance of getting a contract for $5 million a year. In the first instance, he will definitely forfeit his extension option and go for the $10 million. And in the latter instance, he may exercise his extension option in order to get the $8 million salary.

   From this information, draw a decision tree and value the extension option for Mr. Jones. (Do not consider the time value of the money.)

5. Referring to problem 4, assume that there is another clause in the agreement that allows the club to buy out the last two years of Mr. Jones' contract for $10 million after the first year or buy out the last year of his contract for $6 million if he does not perform well. The total value of the contract was $25 million—the payout schedule being $7.5 million, $8.5 million, and $9 million respectively for years 1, 2, and 3. Given his track record and the current team structure, there is a 75 percent chance that Mr. Jones will play well in the first year. If that happens, the probability of playing well in the second year will be 80 percent.

   Assuming there is no monetary benefit to the team keeping him if he does not perform well, what is the value of the club's option to buy out Mr. Jones' contract? Use a discount rate of 10 percent and assume that the payment is made in the beginning of each year. (Consider the time value of money.)

6. Your company is considering acquiring a patent for an innovative hard drive from a computer hardware company. The seller agrees to give you the right to purchase the patent after three years for $10 million. Based on market research data, the estimated value of the patent today is $8 million. But uncertainty about

this patent's success leads you to conclude that its value has a future volatility of 25 percent.

Given a three-year risk-free rate of 7.5 percent, please value this right. (Use the file "Option Valuation.xls," found on the CD-ROM, for your calculations.)

7. Bockhaus Industries is developing a joint venture deal with a local company in an emerging market. Due to industry regulations, Bockhaus Industries can own only 50 percent of this joint venture at the moment. The gradual deregulation of the domestic industry will allow Bockhaus Industries to have a maximum 75 percent share after three years and 100 percent ownership in five years. Therefore, Bockhaus Industries is planning to sign an agreement with its partner to give it the right to buy the rest of the company at its current market price of \$20 million. The annual volatility of the venture is 20 percent, and the risk-free rate is 5 percent (assume this is constant).

   What is the maximum value that Bockhaus Industries should be willing to pay? (Using the binomial method, draw the tree and fold it back to calculate the present value of this portfolio of European options.)

8. Company ABC, a leading chip maker, is considering engaging in a joint venture deal with a semiconductor company XYZ, which just developed an innovative photolithography technology. Due to the complexity and uncertainty of this new technology, the deal is structured in the following way:

   Stage one: ABC will pay \$10 million up front to fund R&D for one year.

   Stage two: After XYZ develops the first prototype of chips using this technology, ABC agrees to pay another \$10 million as milestone payment. Developing the first prototype will take one year.

   Stage three: If the beta test of this technology is successful, ABC will pay another \$10 million. Beta testing will take one year.

   Stage four: Finally, if test marketing is successful ABC will pay \$25 million. It will take half a year to finish test marketing.

   Based on market research data and responses to this technology, the management team made four estimates about the probabilities of success and size of profits:

   1. XYZ has an 80 percent chance of successfully developing the prototype.
   2. XYZ has a 75 percent chance of passing the beta test if stage one is completed.
   3. There is a 90 percent chance that test marketing will be successful if stage two is completed.
   4. Based on forecasts of the market, there is a 70 percent chance of earning a profit of \$200 million and a 30 percent chance of earning \$100 million if stage three is completed.

   If ABC is seeking 60 percent of the joint venture, how much, in terms of NPV, will it earn from this investment? Draw the decision tree and calculate the NPV of the project assuming a 10 percent discount rate.

9. Consider the following expansion project. Utility company ABC can sign a deal with the Chinese government to build an oil-based power plant. An investment of \$10 million will be required today. During the first three years, company ABC is entitled to 100 percent of the profits from the power plant. After three years, it will hand the plant back to the Chinese government. Forecasted revenue for the first year follows a normal distribution with a mean of \$50 million and a standard deviation of \$25 million. Revenues are projected to increase by 5 percent annually for years 2 and 3. The expected profit margin is 20 percent. A discount rate of 25 percent has been assigned to this project.

    a. *Should the company invest in this project? Explain using both quantitative and qualitative reasons.*

    b. *Suppose the Chinese government allows company ABC to increase its capacity after the first year if revenues reach \$50 million. An investment of \$1.5 million will be needed to increase capacity. If this additional investment is made, any revenues in excess of \$50 million will grow by 20 percent, on top of the 5 percent natural growth of the industry. (The original \$50 million will still grow by 5 percent annually.) In addition, the profit margin for the entire operation will increase to 21 percent. Under these conditions, how much is this project worth to company ABC?*

CHAPTER 15

Valuing Liquidity and Control

Liquidity and control can have sizable effects on shareholder value. They are rights that may be assessed for their option value. Illiquidity requires a discount from liquid values, and minority status requires a discount from value with control. Volatility and time produce material variations in estimates of the premiums and discounts.

- The value of a target firm consists of its stand-alone value plus synergy value plus a premium or discount for liquidity and control:

$$\text{Maximum payment for target} = V_{\text{Stand-alone}} + V_{\text{Synergies}} + \pi_{\text{Liquidity and control}}$$

- "Liquidity" implies the ability to find a ready price and counterparty for a transaction to purchase or sell an asset. Illiquidity commands a discount sufficient to induce investors to buy the nonmarketable asset rather than an identical marketable asset.
- Liquidity is valuable. This is found in many studies of illiquid securities such as letter stock, entrepreneurs' restricted shares, private placements before public transactions, initial public offerings, and so on. Its value varies with volatility, time to maturity, and other factors.
- The value of liquidity can be modeled as the value of a European put option with a strike price equal to the share price at date of issue. Volatility, the length of the restriction period, the risk-free rate, and the stock's dividend yield significantly determine the discount.
- "Control" is the right to direct the strategy and activities of the firm, to allocate resources, and to distribute the economic wealth of the firm.
- When shares are widely dispersed among shareholders, effective control may be achieved with a relatively small block of shares. Voting power (that determines control) is determined by the likelihood that a stockholder or group of stockholders might become the decisive factor in the outcome of a vote. Voting power can be estimated using the Shapley Value, which measures the number of times each player in a contest would be pivotal to the voting outcome.
- Research tells us that owning a controlling interest commands a premium; owning a minority interest commands a discount relative to the controller. Some research findings provide evidence of the value of controlling power:

- ***Dual-class shares.*** Research finds that the class with superior voting rights trades at a material premium relative to the junior class for firms that have two classes of common stock outstanding.
- ***Block trades.*** Studies show that trades of large blocks of stock can alter the ownership structure of a firm. Blocks have been found to trade at a 20 percent premium, reflecting the voting power of the block.
- ***The private benefits of control, pyramids, and cross-shareholdings.*** One reason that control might be valuable is that it presents the opportunity for the majority to expropriate wealth of the minority. Benefits not shared by all shareholders are private benefits. Private benefits can be achieved through control, pyramids, and cross-shareholdings.
- ***M&A transactions.*** Research suggests that acquiring a majority position commands a premium 20 to 30 percent higher than the price paid for a minority position.

- The conventional multiplicative approach for estimating the joint impact of illiquidity and lack of control is:

$$V_{\text{With discount}} = V_{\text{Base}}\,[(1 - d_L) \times (1 - d_C) - 1]$$

where V_{Base} = Value of the firm without accounting for illiquidity or lack of control.
d_L = Percentage discount for illiquidity.
d_C = Percentage discount (premium) for lack of control (control).

- The discounts or premiums are typically determined by studying a sample of comparable transactions. Given the dissimilarity among transactions, considerable judgment is involved in developing a suggested discount or premium. Chapter 15 of the main text emphasizes that since control and liquidity are options, their effects may well interact. The conventional adjustment outlined earlier assumes no such interaction.

- Discounts or premiums have meaning only relative to some base case. It is vital to clearly describe the base case when discussing any discount or premium. Chapter 15 assumes as a convention that the base case would be a firm whose shares are actively traded on a public stock exchange (and therefore "liquid"), and among whose shareholders there was no *control asymmetry*, meaning that no shareholder or group of shareholders had controlling power over the firm and that therefore no control premium or discount could be applied to the value of the shares.

- Four reasons why liquidity and control may interact are:

  1. Liquidity may bring with it transparency, which may reduce the value of control.
  2. Liquidity may be associated with more dispersed shareholdings.
  3. Control positions tend to be sticky. Controlling shareholders tend not to trade shares actively, and if they decide to sell control intact, may experience delays in selling. Thus, liquidation of a control position occurs only after

you have tried to create value through strategic choice. This time sequencing of control and liquidation choices suggests that the decision to liquidate depends on the prior choice of strategy.

4. With control, any decision to liquidate is complicated by the right to choose the most attractive strategy.

- If, as Chapter 15 argues, control and liquidity are options, then using a standard discount or premium for all transactions is inappropriate. Such adjustments should be tailored carefully to the situation of the specific target company. One size does not fit all.

CHAPTER 15—WORKBOOK QUESTIONS

1. Not only do liquidity discounts and control premiums permeate the M&A world, they are everywhere in our daily lives, from baseball card trading to your election bid for the student body president position and so on. Think about examples in your personal life when you have had to pay a premium or discount for something.

   Why did you have to pay the premium/discount?

2. Suppose you are purchasing a private company that has a value of $50 million today. The acquisition agreement does not allow you to sell the equity until the end of the third year. Your estimated volatility of the firm's value for the next three years is 22 percent, and the risk-free rate is 3 percent.

   Should you ask for a liquidity discount from the owner? If so, by how much? Assuming risk neutrality, use the binomial pricing model to value the discount. Assume that the length of each period in the binomial model is one year.

3. Refer to problem 2. Assume that you can sell your equity stake only after five years. Assume the same volatility and risk-free rate for the next five years.

   How much of a discount should you deduct from the base value? Compare your result to that in problem 2 and explain the difference.

4. You are the CEO of a private company and are negotiating a deal with a potential buyer. The base value of your firm using the DCF method assuming full liquidity is around $10 million. Based on current market conditions, you and the buyer agree that it would be very difficult for the buyer to resell your firm to another party or to launch a public offering in two years. You are asking for $9 million for your firm and the buyer wants to pay only $8.5 million. Given a two-year Treasury bond yield of 5 percent, explain the difference in asking prices between buyer and seller. Assume that both estimate the same base values for your firm, and that no synergies are considered.

   Use the Black-Scholes model to find the implicit volatility in your asking price and the bidder's offering price.

5. Assume you have just been hired as the CEO of a public company. The board of directors offers you a compensation package that includes call options on

100,000 shares of the company's stock at an exercise price equivalent to today's trading price of $40. The options expire in five years and cannot be exercised in the first two years, which is a "lockup" period for you. You find some data from several sources: The two-year Treasury rate is at 6 percent, the six-year T-note yields 7.5 percent, the historical volatility for the stock is 20 percent, and the company does not plan to pay any dividends in the near future.

How much are the options worth? Use the Black-Scholes model to find an approximate value.

6. In Chapter 15 of the main text, the Shapley Value is introduced to assess the voting power of any given type of shareholder. The file "Power.xls," found on the CD-ROM, can be used to calculate the power index and power ratio for scenarios where there are two major shareholders and the rest are oceanic shareholders.

   a. Assume the oceanic shareholders have 50 percent control of the company; by varying the ratio between the two major shareholders, calculate the corresponding power index.

      What conclusion can be drawn from the results?

   b. Assume the oceanic shareholders have 10 percent control of the company; by varying the ratio between the two major shareholders, calculate the corresponding power index.

      What conclusion can be drawn from the results?

7. You are the CEO of a trading firm considering a merger with another trading firm. After the merger you will have full control of the company, so you start thinking about how to implement your aggressive strategy in the target company. The target has $100 million in capital. By acquiring control of the target, you gain the right to impose a new strategy on the firm. At present, the new strategy is economically unattractive. But if conditions improve sufficiently, the new strategy would be very attractive. Specifically, if the S&P 500 index's annual return is 15 percent or lower, the target's $100 million in capital will increase by whatever the return on the index is. However, if the S&P 500 return exceeds 15 percent, the $100 million capital will increase by 15 percent plus twice the excess returns beyond 15 percent.

   Assuming 20 percent historical volatility for the return of S&P 500, a 13.5 percent historical return for the past 10 years, a three-year time horizon, and a risk-free rate of 7 percent, use the binomial pricing method to value the control right over the strategy of this firm.

8. *Refer to problem 7. Use the Monte Carlo simulation method to value control. Compare the results from problems 7 and 8 and explain the difference.*

9. As the CEO of a leading children's toy company, you are considering a 100 percent acquisition of a midsize children's clothing company. You believe that by co-branding the toys and clothes, it might be possible to create synergy value with a mean present value of $20 million and a volatility of 25 percent. Your CFO indicates that the investment necessary to co-brand is $25 million, pro-

ducing a negative NPV ($20 – $25 million) for the co-branding project. Nevertheless, you believe the control right for co-branding is valuable. You have a two-year window in which to launch this product.

Assuming a risk-free rate of 8 percent, use the Black-Scholes model to estimate the value of control in this case. (Also assume there is no difference between the value of a European call option and an American call option.)

10. You are the CEO of a private company and want to buy it. There is one major shareholder who owns 51 percent of the firm. The remaining 49 percent is held by oceanic shareholders. Based on a DCF model, you estimate the base value of the firm to be $100 million. This excludes any liquidity discount and/or control premium. Based on your observations of the market, liquidity discounts are about 25 percent and control premiums are about 20 percent for similar deals. Your firm has 50 million shares outstanding.

    What would you offer to pay per share to the controlling shareholder? To the oceanic shareholders?

CHAPTER 16

Financial Accounting for Mergers and Acquisitions

Accounting rules can shape the conduct of firms in M&A. Because there is some latitude in the interpretation and implementation of accounting rules, firms may engage in earnings management that can be either conservative (to produce the appearance of smooth and stable performance) or aggressive (to produce the appearance of supernormal financial results). In either case, earnings management is wrong. Best practitioners seek to tell the truth. Investors should exercise caution in interpreting financial results surrounding an acquisition.

- The Financial Accounting Standards Board (FASB) issued Financial Accounting Statements 141 and 142, which became effective after June 30, 2001. These landmark rules changed the method of accounting in the United States for mergers and acquisitions, most significantly by:
  - *Eliminating the pooling-of-interests method of accounting.* Today, all business combinations must be accounted for by the purchase method, whereby the target firm is recorded on the buyer's books at the purchase price. No retroactive restatement of the buyer's past financial results is permitted.
  - *Eliminating amortization of goodwill.* Instead, the FASB now requires that goodwill be tested at least annually for impairment. In addition, goodwill must first be allocated to a reporting unit.
  - *Tightening the recognition of intangible assets.* The new accounting standards require intangible assets to be recognized apart from goodwill if they meet the contractual-legal criterion and/or the separability criterion.
  - *Revising rules on amortization of intangible assets.* Intangible assets may have indefinite useful lives and need not be amortized under the new rules. However, intangible assets whose lives are finite must be amortized over their useful lives.
- Depending on the percentage of shares acquired, there are three methods of accounting for acquisitions under purchase accounting:

Method of Accounting	Ownership Percentage of Shares	Particulars
Consolidation method	>50%	• The buyer records 100% of the target company's assets at fair market value. A "Minority Interest" account is created on the liabilities side representing the portion of the firm not owned by the buyer. • Any portion of the difference between purchase price and book value that is not allocable to any other asset is recorded as goodwill. • 100% of the target's income statement flows would be reflected on the buyer's income statement, with a deduction for the minority investors' interest in the profits or losses of the target.
Equity method	20 to 50%	• The buyer records its acquisition of the target in an account called "Investment in Target Company," which shows up as an asset on the balance sheet. The amount recorded reflects the cost of purchasing the shares. • The buyer's share in the target's earnings/losses is reflected on its income statement in an account called "Income from Minority Interest," as well as on its balance sheet as an addition/deduction from the "Investment in Target Company" account.
Cost method	Less than 20%	• The buyer records the investment on the balance sheet sheet, typically in an account called "Investment in Affiliate," as the cost of acquisition. The investment is revalued regularly, and any unrealized gains or losses are reflected not in the income statement, but rather in the buyer's owner's equity account. Dividends, however, are recorded in the buyer's income statement.

- Accounting choices may affect the long-term value of the firm. For instance, asset allocation choices will affect the future depreciation/amortization tax shields, which in turn will affect the value of the firm.
- Managers of a buyer firm will often evaluate an acquisition by comparing the buyer's expected earnings per share (EPS) for the current year to the pro forma EPS for the same year, assuming consummation of an acquisition. A reduction in EPS is *dilution*, and an increase is *accretion*. The extent of dilution or accretion can be influenced by accounting choices. Sometimes, excessive focus on EPS dilution/accretion may distract managers from focusing on value creation and the real economic effects of a deal instead.
- M&A accounting choices can also affect and likewise be influenced by:
  - *Measures of financial leverage*. Measures such as debt/equity ratios, interest coverage, and so on can in turn affect the ability of the firm to borrow funds in the future.

  - *Profit margins.* The allocation of the purchase price to different asset categories can affect margins.
  - *Measures of asset efficiency.* Recording the acquisition of a target using the consolidation method versus the equity method will have different results in terms of returns on assets and equity.
  - *Liquidity.* Larger allocations of the target purchase price to current assets will enhance the appearance of liquidity of Newco.
- Managers may employ accounting tactics to engage in earnings and EPS enhancement games, credit enhancement games, price maximization games, and tax management games. Such games can raise serious ethical questions.
- Successive discoveries of accounting fraud at large corporations led to the drafting of the Sarbanes-Oxley Act in 2002. The Act seeks to discourage fraud by:
  - Requiring the CEO and CFO to certify financial reports.
  - Requiring public companies to appoint independent directors to audit committees within their boards of directors.
  - Requiring enhanced financial disclosures by corporations.
  - Prohibiting auditors from providing ancillary services such as consulting, legal, and corporate financial advisory services.

CHAPTER 16—WORKBOOK QUESTIONS

Exercises in Accounting for Acquisitions

Suppose Bed Bath & Beyond, a chain of stores selling bed linens, bath items, and home and kitchen furnishings, decides to acquire Pier 1 Imports, Inc., a retail chain that sells furniture and home furnishings, dining and kitchen goods, and bath and bedding accessories. At the end of fiscal year 2001, Pier 1 has 96.3 million shares outstanding, currently trading at $17.05 apiece. Suppose Bed, Bath & Beyond pays $21.31 per Pier 1 share. At its current share price of $33.90, Bed Bath & Beyond will have to issue 60.5 million shares to pay for the acquisition. Here are income statements and balance sheets for both companies.

Bed Bath & Beyond

Income Statement ($ Millions)	**2002**	**2001**
Net Sales	2,928.0	2,396.7
Cost of sales	1,720.4	1,410.2
Gross profit	1,207.6	986.5
SG&A	861.5	713.6
Operating profit	346.1	272.8
Interest income (expense)	11.0	9.0
Earnings before taxes	357.1	281.8
Provision for taxes	137.5	109.9
Net earnings	219.6	171.9
Earnings per share	0.76	0.61
Weighted average shares outstanding	289.7	283.9

Balance Sheet ($ Millions)	**2002**	**2001**
Assets		
Current assets:		
Cash and equivalents	429.5	239.3
Merchandise inventories	754.0	606.7
Other current assets	43.2	39.7
Total current assets	1,226.7	885.7
Investment securities	51.9	—
Property and equipment, net	361.7	302.7
Other assets	7.2	7.4
Total assets	1,647.5	1,195.7
Liabilities and Shareholders' Equity		
Current liabilities:		
Accounts payable	270.9	192.4
Accrued expenses and other current liabilities	190.9	128.8
Income taxes payable	49.4	32.0
Total current liabilities	511.3	353.2
Deferred rent and other liabilities	41.9	25.5
Total liabilities	553.2	378.7
Shareholders' equity:		
Common stock	241.6	183.9
Retained earnings	852.8	633.2
Total shareholders' equity	1,094.4	817.0
Total liabilities and shareholders' equity	1,647.5	1,195.7

Pier 1 Imports, Inc.

Income Statement ($ Millions)	**2002**	**2001**
Net sales	1,548.6	1,411.5
Operating costs and expenses:		
Cost of sales	898.8	817.0
SG&A	448.1	399.8
Depreciation and amortization	42.8	43.2
	1,389.7	1,260.0
Operating income	158.8	151.5
Nonoperating income and expenses:		
Interest and investment income	2.5	1.9
Interest expense	(2.3)	(3.1)
	0.2	(1.3)
Income before taxes	159.0	150.2
Provision for taxes	58.8	55.6
Net income	100.2	94.7
Earnings per share	1.06	0.98
Average shares outstanding	94.4	96.3

Balance Sheet ($ Millions)	**2002**	**2001**
Assets		
Current assets:		
Cash and equivalents	235.6	46.8
Other accounts receivable, net	6.2	8.4
Inventories	275.4	310.7
Prepaid expenses and other current assets	87.9	111.2
Total current assets	605.2	477.1
Properties, net	210.0	212.1
Other noncurrent assets	47.6	46.6
	862.7	735.7
Liabilities and Shareholders' Equity		
Current liabilities:		
Current portion of long-term debt	0.4	—
Accounts payable and accrued liabilities	208.0	144.1
Total current liabilities	208.4	144.1
Long-term debt	25.4	25.0
Other noncurrent liabilities	43.3	34.7
Total liabilities	277.0	203.8
Shareholders' equity:		
Common stock	100.8	100.8
Additional paid-in capital	140.2	139.4
Retained earnings	429.9	344.8
Cumulative other comprehensive income	(4.7)	(3.2)
Treasury stock	(80.5)	(49.9)
Total shareholders' equity	585.7	531.9
Total liabilities and shareholders' equity	862.7	735.7

[These spreadsheets can be found in the folder "Key Spreadsheets from the Workbook" located on the CD-ROM.]

1. Assume Bed Bath & Beyond acquires 100 percent of Pier 1, and that the transaction takes place at fiscal year end 2001.

   Prepare a consolidated balance sheet to reflect the acquisition. Then, prepare an income statement for fiscal year 2002, the year following the acquisition.

   Assume that:

   - The book values of Pier 1's assets and liabilities are equal to their fair market values.
   - There is a total of $500 million in identifiable intangible assets, which will be amortized for 20 years using the straight-line method.
   - The tax rate is 38 percent.

2. *Compute the following for Bed Bath & Beyond, pre- and postmerger, and fill in the appropriate parts of the table that follows:*

   - *Gross margin*
   - *Operating margin*
   - *Net margin*
   - *EPS*

		With Merger	
Ratios for Bed Bath & Beyond	Without Merger	100% Stock	60% Stock, 40% Cash
Gross margin			
Operating margin			
Net margin			
EPS			
% Dilution (accretion)			

3. Now assume that the terms of the deal have changed—that Bed Bath & Beyond will pay 60 percent of the consideration price in stock and the rest in cash, to be funded with a 10-year debt obligation at a fixed annual rate of 7 percent. It will also assume Pier 1's existing liabilities.

   Redo the consolidated balance sheet and income statement to reflect this new structure.

4. *Compute the following for Bed Bath & Beyond, postmerger, and fill in the rest of the table in problem 2:*

   - *Gross margin*
   - *Operating margin*
   - *Net margin*
   - *EPS*

Think about the following:

- *Do the ratios improve following the deal?*
- *Is the deal accretive or dilutive to Bed Bath & Beyond's EPS?*
- *How do the ratios differ between the all-stock deal versus the part-stock, part-cash deal? Can you explain the differences?*

5. Now assume that Bed Bath & Beyond acquires a 40 percent stake in Pier 1 at the same price ($21.31 per share), and pays for its investment by issuing shares. Assume that the transaction takes place at fiscal year end 2001.

    Use the equity method of accounting to prepare a balance sheet reflecting the acquisition. Then, prepare an income statement for fiscal year 2002, the year following the acquisition. Use the same assumptions given in problem 1.

CHAPTER 17

Momentum Acquisition Strategies: An Illustration of Why Value Creation Is the Best Financial Criterion

The strategy of momentum acquisition has appeared episodically over the years, most recently in the late 1990s. Some of the telltales of this strategy are a focus on EPS (or revenues), a relatively large number of acquisitions increasing in size over time, an aggressive growth trajectory, and a high price/earnings multiple reflecting investor expectations of continued growth. Regardless of the temporary attractiveness of momentum acquisition approaches, growth strategies based on momentum end in disappointment. Focusing on value creation rather than earnings momentum better promotes the survival and prosperity of the firm.

- Momentum acquisition strategies commonly focus on EPS and revenue momentum.
  - EPS has been the traditional focus of momentum acquirers, based on the belief that stock prices are driven by changes in EPS and that therefore steady and aggressive growth in EPS will result in high stock prices (and high P/E multiples).
  - In some industries, the momentum focus is on revenues instead of earnings per share due to the fact that a significant portion of the market value of firms in these industries derives from their growth options; some analysts therefore advocate using revenue multiples as a basis for valuing these firms.
- The common argument for momentum acquiring is that stock market investors appear to reward momentum. It appears that firms with momentum enjoy higher valuation multiples than other firms. And "momentum investing" attracted specialist investment managers in the 1990s. But the existence of such specialists was no proof of the superiority of momentum investing. And, in fact, the research evidence tends to reject the ability of momentum investors to earn supernormal returns. Arguments *against* momentum acquiring include the following:
  - Momentum is unsustainable indefinitely because the annual acquisition volume cannot get bigger forever; the world is finite, and unexpected events can happen at any time in the future to halt growth.

- Momentum invites a focus on accounting cosmetics rather than on economic reality. Central to the momentum acquisition approach is the maintenance of a steady path of growth in EPS, revenues, or assets. Because of the difficulties of maintaining the growth trajectory, the incentives to use accounting cosmetics increase. Purchase accounting for M&A transactions entails various judgments about the fair market value of assets, the allocation of purchase price, the creation of reporting units, and the impairment of assets. Finally, momentum acquirers will be highly sensitive to the factors that drive EPS dilution: the growth rate of the buyer's shares relative to the target's percentage addition to the buyer's earnings, the P/E ratio embedded in the bid relative to the P/E ratio of the buyer, and the size of the target relative to the size of the bidder.
- Momentum strategies can promote uneconomic deals and reject good ones.
- Value creation is the best criterion for acquisition strategies because it focuses on the longer-term future, accounts for the time value of money, focuses on economic reality, focuses on risk and return, and accounts for opportunity costs. Further, the use of NPV directly measures changes in investors' welfare. Although difficult to apply, value-based acquisition strategies have the ultimate virtue of weeding out bad deals more effectively than other approaches.
- Momentum acquiring is a dangerous path for both corporate managers and their investors. On the contrary, value maximization is a superior foundation for acquisition planning.

CHAPTER 17—WORKBOOK QUESTIONS

1. In Chapter 17 of the main text, Tyco International, Ltd., is introduced to illustrate the application of a momentum acquisition strategy. After the restructuring announcement on January 22, 2002, by CEO Dennis Kozlowski, various market participants had different responses.

   Using the critique of momentum acquiring in the chapter, what prompted Tyco to stop acquiring more companies and restructure? How did the market respond?

2. The strategy of momentum acquisition has swung in and out of favor over the years.

   What are the arguments for and against momentum acquiring? What should be the criteria used to evaluate the success of an acquisition strategy?

3. The momentum acquisition approach focuses on the maintenance of a steady path of growth in EPS, revenue, or assets. Therefore, how to manage the earnings dilution or accretion is essential to the success of this strategy.

   Please briefly explain how dilution (or accretion) occurs and identify the factors that drive EPS dilution.

4. Assume that a buyer and target agree to a stock-for-stock acquisition. The buyer has 1.5 million shares outstanding and $3 million in earnings. Its current

P/E ratio is 25. The target has one million shares outstanding and $1 million in earnings. The target's current P/E ratio is 20. Suppose the buyer is willing to offer a 20 percent premium for the target, and a purchase-related transaction charge of 0.5 percent of total purchase price is expected. (You will find the Excel file, "Momentum.xls," on the CD-ROM to automate your calculations on this problem.)

a. *Calculate the earnings per share for Newco after the merger and the percentage change in the buyer's EPS.*
b. *Assuming the deal is paid by cash, which is funded by an issue of new debt by the buyer at an annual interest rate of 5 percent, calculate the EPS for Newco after the merger and percentage change in the buyer's EPS assuming a tax rate of 35 percent.*
c. *Refer to problem 4a. By changing the bid price for the target, the buyer can avoid dilution. Please calculate the percentage dilution or accretion for purchase premiums of 0 percent, 5 percent, 15 percent, 25 percent, 35 percent, and 45 percent. Now recalculate the percentage dilution or accretion, varying the target's earnings according to the following schedule: $500,000, $1,000,000, $1,500,000, $2,000,000, $2,500,000, $3,000,000, and $3,500,000. Explain the results.*

5. Assume you as the CEO of a publicly listed company are considering an acquisition. There are two opportunities available. Company A is a high-growth firm that invests heavily in R&D. But it also demands a higher premium than Company B, which has lower growth potential. Both companies have 2 million shares outstanding, and projected earnings for this year for both companies are the same at $3 million. Company A's stock trades at $40, and Company B's stock trades at $18. After due diligence research, you estimate that earnings of Company A will grow at a rate of 25 percent and those of Company B will grow at only 5 percent. You estimate your own firm's earnings will grow at 10 percent. Assume that the earnings of Newco after the merger will be just the simple arithmetic addition of the forecasted earnings of your firm and the target. There are 5 million shares outstanding for your firm; projected earnings for this year are $6.5 million. Your firm's stock trades at $28.

   If Company A asks for a 60 percent premium over its market price and Company B asks for only a 20 percent premium, which company would you acquire? Use quantitative evidence to back up your decision. (Refer to "Momentum.xls" on the CD-ROM for calculating your answers.)

CHAPTER 18

An Introduction to Deal Design in M&A

Designing a deal is more than setting a price. As Bruce Wasserstein says, "Implementing a deal is a blend of psychology, business judgment, and technical dexterity. While taxes, accounting, and corporate law provide the skeletal frame of a transaction, *optimizing position* is the purpose of direct negotiation."[1] One must optimize across a range of goals, and within a series of constraints.

- Deals are solutions to economic problems. To design deal terms, begin with an understanding of the economic problems: the constraints and competing objectives under which the deal designer must try to "optimize position."
- Classic objectives of M&A deal design include:
  - Creating value.
  - Improving reported financial results; avoiding EPS dilution.
  - Improving control; avoiding voting dilution.
  - Building financial flexibility.
  - Hedging security price risk.
  - Improving competitive standing.
  - Managing signals to the capital markets.
  - Managing incentives.
  - Shaping impact on employees and communities.
- Some deal terms and how they can be used to achieve objectives:
  - *Price* is a key instrument for claiming value. Be careful, however, not to focus exclusively on price—multi-issue bargaining generally leads to more successful outcomes than does single-issue bargaining.
  - *Form of payment* considers whether the payment should be "fixed" or "contingent." There may also be "side" payments.
  - *Fixed payments* use cash or senior debt securities. They can resolve uncertainty for the target shareholders about the value they will receive; however, they could also have an adverse signaling effect—their use could be interpreted as a lack of confidence by target shareholders in the buyer's future management of the enterprise (i.e., thus prompting them to demand fixed payments).

- *Contingent payments* use mezzanine or "junk" debt securities, preferred stock, and common stock. These permit target investors to participate in the combined entity's upside potential, and may also be used when the buyer does not have the cash or senior debt capacity to finance the acquisition. Earnouts, warrants, convertible bonds, contingent value rights, puts, guarantees, caps, collars, and floors are usually used to resolve strong disagreements about the value of the target firm, and to limit the adverse effects of stock price changes between announcement and consummation of a deal.
- *Side payments* are payments to parties other than the owners of the target firm, parties that may have some influence on the success of the firm post-merger. Examples of side payments are golden parachutes, warrants, bonuses, buyouts of employment contracts, and consulting commitments to managers of the target firm. Sometimes, side payments might also be made to municipal, state, and national governments.
- *Timing and deadlines* are important, as the speed of closing will affect the present value of cash flows to investors. Acquisitions might be full and immediate, or partial and staged over time.
- *Commitments* are promises by the target and/or buyer to make good on previous agreements; for instance, the buyer commits to assuming the target's liabilities, the target commits to handing over all tangible and intangible assets to the buyer, and so on. Commitments may also include warranties from either side to the other that certain conditions exist, and that if not, reparations will be made.
- *Control and governance* affect the balance of power among the shareholders of the firm, as well as the degree of managerial discretion. Important deal terms with respect to control and governance include the relative proportions of share ownership and voting rights, and the makeup of the new board and executive management.
- *Transaction hedges* are special terms that mitigate risks that the transaction may not be consummated. For instance, walk-away fees when either party reneges are usually part of the deal terms.
- The *form of transaction* (e.g., merger of equals, "type A" reorganization, etc.) has implications for tax exposure, exposure to liabilities, control, and value creation.
- The *form of financing* has implications for tax shields, default risk, and the financial flexibility of the firm.
- *Social issues* include agreements about the composition of the board, executive management, headquarters, corporate name, and so on.

- Each deal is a system—deal terms are linked to one another. The terms of an M&A transaction cannot be set independently of each other.

- Some important concepts for the deal designer to remember:
  - *There is no single best feasible deal.* Rather, there is an *area* within which feasible deals exist for both buyer and seller. This area is called the zone of potential agreement (ZOPA).

- *Deal design involves trade-offs.* The process of optimization is simply a matter of comparing the desirability of one set of terms against another. Desirability is measured in terms of the value attached to each attribute.
- *Deal design is a learning process.* Trial and error and feedback are intrinsic to the learning process.

CHAPTER 18—WORKBOOK QUESTIONS

Part I: Mini-Problems

1. Genesis Corp., a biotech company, has approached R_x Pharmaceuticals, a large drug manufacturer, to acquire a minority equity interest in Genesis for funding drug development. In return for the equity investment, Genesis will commit to a co-marketing agreement with R_x for those drugs. R_x thinks Genesis has a promising lineup of drugs, but all are still in Phase II clinical trials, meaning that there remains a substantial risk that the drugs might not receive approval for release to the public. Also, R_x has a strategic interest in the drugs that Genesis is proposing to bring to market, and would be disadvantaged if a competitor bought a stake in Genesis. The CEO of Genesis is optimistic about the prospects for regulatory approval and for sales revenue of the new drugs.

   a. *What are the deal design problems here? Where might R_x and Genesis find helpful trade-offs that produce a win-win deal to both?*

   b. *Suppose R_x decides to make an equity investment in Genesis, but buyer and target differ widely in their valuation of the target. How might the parties bridge the gap?*

2. Company B has agreed to be acquired by Company A. However, Company B shareholders are only willing to accept cash payment. However, paying in cash would affect Company A's credit ratings.

   a. *Can a deal be designed such as to satisfy both parties' requirements?*

   b. *Suppose Company B agrees to a stock acquisition, but wants to protect the value of stock against fluctuations in Company A's stock price. How might Company B protect itself? On the other hand, Company A wants to ensure it does not give away too much value. How can Company A do this? What is the resulting structure called?*

   c. *Although Company B has agreed to be acquired by Company A, the latter knows that the former continues to be pursued by several other interested parties. What can Company A do to prevent Company B from reneging on its agreement?*

   d. *Company A needs to retain the top managers at Company B because their knowledge of the business is key to postmerger success. What provisions might Company A include in the deal terms to increase the chances that the target's managers will stay?*

Part II: Mini-Case

During the 1980s, the economy of Texas nearly collapsed due to a prolonged downward spiral in oil prices. This downturn severely affected Texas' banking industry, causing many local banks to fail. One of the most serious cases involved the $41 billion First Republic Bank, the largest bank in Texas. The Federal Deposit Insurance Corporation (FDIC) chose not to bail out First Republic Bank, and invited large financial institutions to take over the bank. North Carolina National Bank (NCNB) won the takeover contest over rivals such as Citicorp and Chase Manhattan by coming up with a creative structure for the deal. As a result, in August 1988, NCNB acquired 20 percent of First Republic, with the FDIC acquiring the remaining 80 percent. Some of the key deal terms were:[2]

Control	• NCNB's 20 percent equity interest is composed of 100 percent of the voting stock. • The FDIC's 80 percent equity interest is in the form of nonvoting common stock.
Option to purchase	• NCNB has an exclusive option to purchase stock owned by the FDIC immediately or at any time within the next five years.
Option purchase prices:	
First year	The pro rata amount of the FDIC's original investment plus 115 percent of the net increase in book value of the acquired entity.
Second year	The pro rata amount of the FDIC's original investment plus 120 percent of the net increase in book value of the acquired entity.
Third to fifth year	The pro rata amount of the FDIC's original investment plus 125 percent of the net increase in book value of the acquired entity.
Sale by FDIC	• The FDIC is not permitted to sell its shares other than to NCNB until after November 22, 1993. • In the event that NCNB has not raised its ownership percentage to 51 percent or more by the end of the fifth year, the FDIC may sell its shares to whomever it chooses.
Special Asset Division	A Special Asset Division was created within Newco to absorb substandard loans acquired or originated prior to August 29, 1988, or loans that had been charged off prior to November 22, 1988. • Through December 31, 1989, NCNB could transfer to the division, *in unlimited amounts*, loans acquired prior to August 29, 1988. • During 1990, NCNB could designate additional loans as division assets subject to a $750 million limitation. • The FDIC would provide as assistance the estimated loss amount. The FDIC would also reimburse NCNB for the costs of funding and administering division assets. • Neither NCNB or any of its subsidiaries would share losses that might be suffered by the Special Asset Division, but NCNB would be entitled, in the event of gains by the division, to receive incentive payments that could range from 3 percent to 20 percent of such gains.

1. *Was the control structure advantageous for NCNB? What were the reasons for why the control structure was designed the way it was? Why would the FDIC agree to this structure?*

2. *Describe NCNB's purchase option. What advantages did NCNB gain from this structure? What risks did this structure protect NCNB against? Why did the purchase option price ratchet up over time?*

3. *What was the purpose of the Special Asset Division? What did it effectively do for NCNB? What kind of economic rewards did NCNB get from administering the Special Asset Division?*

4. *Putting aside price considerations, was this an attractive deal for NCNB? Why or why not?*

NOTES

1. Quoted from Bruce Wasserstein, *Big Deal* (New York: Free Press, 1998). (Emphasis added.)
2. *Source:* NCNB Form 10-K as filed with the Securities and Exchange Commission (SEC) on March 31, 1989, modified for instructional purposes. (Emphasis added.)

CHAPTER 19

Choosing the Form of Acquisitive Reorganization

Mergers and acquisitions often result in a *legal reorganization* of one or both of the partners to the deal. There are several forms of reorganization, each with peculiar advantages and qualifying conditions. Transactions are designed in ways to meet those qualifying conditions and to achieve desired outcomes. Through an understanding of the forms of organization, one can see that transaction design has big implications for issues that concern deal designers and senior executives, such as taxes, control, transfer of liability, risk exposure, form of payment, legal standing, and other issues. A careful understanding of the buyer's and seller's goals should drive the choice of the reorganization structure.

- The choice of reorganization structure will affect and be affected by at least five considerations:

  1. *Taxation.* Is this proposed deal taxable or tax deferred? To whom is it taxable? What are the tax consequences for the buyer and seller? How large is the tax exposure? Will the seller be subject to double taxation?
  2. *Risk exposure.* Will this structure isolate the hidden liabilities of the target from the buyer?
  3. *Control.* Will this require a vote of shareholders of the target and/or the buyer? How will the voting control of Newco be affected by this structure?
  4. *Continuity.* Which, if any, firm survives as an ongoing entity? What implications does this have for the ability to assign leases and licenses, for corporate identity, and for social issues such as headquarters location?
  5. *Form of payment.* What form of payment is required to achieve objectives for taxation, risk exposure, control, and continuity?

- The possible types of acquisitive reorganization and their definitions follow along with a summary providing more detailed information pertaining to each structure.

Type of Reorganization	Description
Cash purchase of assets	The buyer exchanges its cash for the assets of the target. The target's liabilities are not transferred to the buyer without explicit agreement. After the transaction, the target may or may not liquidate.
Cash purchase of stock	The buyer exchanges its cash for shares of the target's voting common stock. The target company remains in existence. The buyer will be shielded from the target's known and unknown liabilities.
Reverse triangular cash merger	The buyer forms a subsidiary (Newco) and capitalizes it with cash sufficient to acquire the target's stock. Newco merges into the target. The target company survives, as do its tax attributes and liabilities.
Forward triangular cash merger	The buyer forms a subsidiary (Newco) and capitalizes it with cash sufficient to acquire the target's stock. The target merges into Newco and ceases to exist, although its liabilities have been transferred to Newco.
Statutory merger ("A" reorganization)	In a statutory merger one company absorbs the other. Target shareholders exchange their shares for the buyer's stock and other consideration. The target company ceases to exist. The buyer assumes the liabilities of the target.
Statutory consolidation ("A" reorganization)	In a statutory consolidation, two or more corporations combine into one new corporation. The preexisting corporations cease to exist as legal entities.
Forward triangular merger ("A" reorganization)	The target company merges into a subsidiary of the buyer (Newco). Payment must consist of at least 50 percent of the parent corporation stock to qualify as "tax-free."
Reverse triangular merger ("A" reorganization)	The buyer's subsidiary (Newco) merges into the target, leaving the target company in existence as a subsidiary of the buyer. At least 80 percent of the consideration must be paid in the buyer's parent corporation voting stock to qualify as "tax-free."
Voting stock-for-stock ("B" reorganization)	To qualify as "tax-free" the buyer must exchange only voting stock and afterward control at least 80 percent of the votes. No merger occurs, as the target is retained as a wholly (or partially) owned subsidiary.
Voting stock-for-assets ("C" reorganization)	The buyer offers shares of its voting stock in return for substantially all of the assets of the target company. The target company must liquidate after the transaction.

Note: "Tax-free" is common usage for "tax deferred until disposition or sale of the stock."

Summary of Features of Various Transaction Types

	Tax Implication for Seller	Buyer's Exposure to Target's Liabilities	Need for Target Shareholder Vote	Need for Buyer Shareholder Vote	Minority Freeze-Out?[1]	Does the Target Company Survive?	Form of Payment
Cash purchase of assets	Immediately taxable	Low	Maybe	No	No minority	Uncertain	No restriction; usually cash
Cash purchase of stock	Immediately taxable	High	No	No	No	Yes	No restriction; usually cash
Cash merger	Immediately taxable	Low if target merged into a subsidiary	Yes	Maybe	Yes	No if forward triangular merger Yes if reverse triangular merger	No restriction; usually cash
Statutory merger or consolidation ("A" reorganization)	Tax-free[2]	High	Yes	Yes	Yes	No	Buyer's stock and typically no more than 50% "boot"
Forward triangular merger ("A" reorganization)	Tax-free[2]	Low—limited by sub	Yes	No[3]—unless need to authorize more shares	Yes	No	Buyer's stock and typically no more than 50% "boot"
Reverse triangular merger ("A" reorganization)	Tax-free[2]	Low—limited by sub	Yes	No[3]—unless need to authorize more shares	Yes	Yes	Buyer's voting stock of at least 80% and the rest in "boot"
Voting stock-for-stock ("B" reorganization)	Tax-free[2]	Low	Maybe	No[3]—unless need to authorize more shares	No	Yes	100% in buyer's voting stock
Voting stock-for-assets ("C" reorganization)	Tax-free[2]	Low	Maybe	No[3]—unless need to authorize more shares	No minority	No	At least 80% buyer's voting stock in value and the rest in "boot"

1. A "minority freeze-out" seeks to eliminate *direct* interests in the target firm held by a minority of shareholders (who are possibly dissidents) following the completion of the deal. This is ordinarily accomplished by merging the target into the buyer.
2. "Tax-free" is common usage for "tax deferred until disposition or sale of the stock." Also, any "boot" in the tax-free transactions may create an immediate tax liability to the extent of any gain implicit in the boot.
3. Stock exchanges and legal counsel may require a vote of the buyer's shareholders on material transactions. Asset sales and spin-offs could create adverse tax consequences.

CHAPTER 19—WORKBOOK QUESTIONS

1. Sam Goodman, founder and CEO of fast-food chain Uncle Sam's Fried Chicken, is set to retire in a few months. Two parties have approached him offering to buy the chain. Party A has offered an all-cash deal, while party B has offered an all-stock deal. Sam reckons that the nominal value of the two offers is about the same, so he wants to base his decision on which of the deals would be more tax-efficient.

   Which deal would you advise Sam to take? Why?

2. Phil Welch, owner of a midsize trucking service, recently purchased some secondhand trucks and containers for cash. His discount rate for these assets was 10 percent. The assets, which were on the seller's books for $483,000, were sold to him for $511,000. Phil estimated that the new equipment had a useful life of eight years, and expected annual tax savings of $20,528 on a marginal tax rate of 34 percent.

   Is Phil correct that the expected annual tax savings is $20,528? What is the present value of the tax shields?

3. Escape Cruise Lines is seeking to expand its operations in the Caribbean by acquiring Grupo Viva Cruise Lines in either a stock-and-cash deal, or an all-stock deal. Escape's risk-averse CEO is concerned above all about keeping Escape insulated from Grupo Viva's liabilities.

   Knowing this, what forms of reorganization might you recommend to Escape's CEO? Please explain.

4. Refer to problem 3. Escape's CEO wants to make sure that the deal qualifies as tax-free, and wants to "freeze out" a troublesome shareholder of Grupo Viva.

   For each type of reorganization that you suggested in problem 3, what requirements must be met for the deal to qualify as tax-free? Knowing these requirements, does any form of reorganization from among those you suggested stand out as being most favorable?

5. Refer to problems 3 and 4.

   If Grupo Viva's shareholders want some cash, can the transaction be structured to meet their requirements and still be tax-free? If so, what types of reorganization are possible?

6. Consumer products manufacturer Holden & Caulfield wants to acquire Sally's Delectable Dinners, a manufacturer of frozen microwave dinners. Holden & Caulfield plans to integrate Sally's into its own microwave dinner operating division, and then spin the division off within two years. The shareholders of Sally's want a tax-free deal.

   What forms of acquisitive reorganizations are possible in light of these conditions?

7. Refer to problem 6. It turns out that Holden & Caulfield had earlier purchased a toehold position in Sally's Delectable Dinners.

Does this narrow down the possible forms of reorganization you suggested in problem 6?

8. Decadence, a manufacturer of premium ice cream, wants to acquire Bright Ice, a specialty maker of sherbets. Bright Ice is 82 percent owned by the O'Shaughnessy family, who are willing to sell only their shares of stock, not the assets of the company. Eight years ago, the company underwent financial difficulties, prompting founder Maurice O'Shaughnessy to sell 15 percent of the company to a multimillionaire, Leonardo Fox. (Other shareholders own the remaining 3 percent.) Over the years, Fox has repeatedly badgered the O'Shaughnessy family, asking for increasing dividend payments or constantly criticizing Maurice O'Shaughnessy's decisions. Therefore, Decadence wants to make sure it gets rid of Fox when it purchases Bright Ice. Also, Decadence wants to isolate the liabilities of Bright Ice in a subsidiary.

   What acquisition structures would you recommend to Decadence?

9. *What is a "minority freeze-out"?*

CHAPTER 20

Choosing the Form of Payment and Financing

Form of payment and financing are major deal design dimensions that have implications for each other, and for returns to shareholders. Choices along these dimensions merit careful analysis.

- The form of payment chosen in an M&A transaction can lead to large differences in shareholder returns. Studies find that:
  - Payment in cash is associated with lower (but still large and positive) returns to targets, and close to zero returns to buyers.
  - Payment in stock is associated with higher returns to targets and significantly negative returns to buyers.
- Over the years following a deal, share-for-share transactions yield lower returns to investors than do cash deals.
- Stock payments tend to be used when:
  - A deal is friendly.
  - The buyer's stock price is buoyant.
  - Ownership is not concentrated.
  - Deals are larger in size.
  - The buyer has less cash.
- Stock payments are used with greater frequency when the stock market is buoyant. This contributes to the appearance of merger waves during economic booms. This phenomenon supports the notion that overvaluation is an important motive for using stock as a medium of payment.
- Choice of form of payment is driven by a range of considerations:
  - *Perspectives of buyer and seller.* To the selling shareholder, form of payment is an *investment* issue; to the buyer, form of payment is a *financing* issue. The form of payment must result in a good investment decision from the seller's standpoint and a good financing decision from the buyer's standpoint.
  - *Possibility of competing bidders.* The form of payment can strongly influence the target and thus preempt competing bidders. The form of payment chosen must be consistent with the probability of entry by competitors.

- *Taxes.* Cash and stock deals differ in their tax exposures for the target shareholders and buyer firm. The decision maker must consider the interests of the selling shareholders, as well as opportunities for value creation arising from tax shields or deferred taxes.
- *Control.* Cash and stock differ in their impact on the voting control of Newco.
- *Financing.* The choice of form of payment must consider the impact on present and future funding capacities of both buyer and target. The type of financing employed will also have future implications for taxes and control.
- *Transaction costs.* Different forms of payment may entail a wide variety of transaction costs. Generally, a cash payment made directly from the buyer's cash accounts entails the least costs, while a stock payment made by issuance of new equity will be the most costly.
- *Size.* The absolute and relative sizes of target and buyer can have implications for the form of payment, transaction costs, financing, control, and expected synergy value.
- *Asymmetric information.* The managers of the buyer and target may each have differing views on the values of their own firms and of any expected synergies. Such views will have an impact on the form of payment chosen.

- Seven dimensions describe transaction financing:

1. *Classes of capital.* The mix of classes of capital to be used for acquisition financing may be influenced by several factors, such as the firm's current debt-equity mix; the CFO's preference for different kinds of financing (pecking order); opportunistic responses to hot, cold, or segmented markets; and the asset base of the firm.
2. *Maturity.* A risk-neutral maturity structure would equate the life of the firm's assets with the life of the firm's liabilities to reduce exposure to reinvestment risk and refinancing risk.
3. *Basis for the yields.* Management's outlook for interest rates will determine whether rates of payment on debt will be fixed or floating. Whether the issuer's returns vary with fluctuations in interest rates will also affect this choice.
4. *Currency.* A firm's exposure to foreign exchange rate fluctuations, unusual financing possibilities in global capital markets, and management's views about the future movement of exchange rates will affect the choice of currency used to finance a deal.
5. *Exotic terms.* Securities can be highly tailored in cases where there is some disagreement between issuers and investors about a firm's prospects.
6. *Control features.* Financing choices will affect issues surrounding control, such as *who* might exercise control (e.g., creditors or shareholders); the *degree* of control exercised by various players; and the *control trigger* (e.g., tightness of loan covenants, default on a loan covenant, etc.).
7. *Distribution.* Choices about distribution of securities include retail versus institutional, domestic versus international, and full commitment versus best efforts. The decision is influenced by (1) how the firm wants to mar-

ket itself through its securities (e.g., where the shares are sold, how liquid the shares are) and (2) how the firm delivers value (i.e., returns capital) to its investors.

- A framework that is helpful for evaluating financing alternatives is the *FRICTO* framework:
  - F lexibility—the ability to meet unforeseen financing requirements as they arise.
  - Risk—the predictable variability in the firm's operating cash flow.
  - Income—the effect of financing choice on value creation.
  - Control—the effect on financing choices on ownership.
  - Timing—the suitability of the financing choice given current capital market conditions.
  - Other—examples include issues like signaling effects, investment liquidity of the owners, estate-planning considerations, and so on.

CHAPTER 20—WORKBOOK QUESTIONS

Part I: True or False

1. *Form of payment is often related to the size of a deal.*

2. *Payment in cash is associated with higher returns to targets than payment in stock.*

3. *Choices in form of payment and financing vary with the economic cycle.*

4. *Taxable deals are for stock, and "tax-deferred" deals are for cash.*

5. *From the seller's standpoint, cash deals are more likely to be more tax efficient.*

6. *Issuing new debt of higher seniority can allow buyers to bid more than their assessment of the intrinsic value of the target.*

7. *The more highly levered the target, the lower will be the total payment required to acquire the target's equity.*

8. *Financing choices can have effects on taxes and control.*

9. *When a target firm knows its value better than does the acquirer, the acquirer will prefer to offer cash.*

10. *Bidders that are optimistic about the value of merger synergies will tend to offer cash.*

11. *The fraction of the acquisition value funded by bank debt has no effect on announcement returns.*

Part II: Questions

1. Company A is thinking of acquiring Company B. The CEO of Company A is optimistic about the value of merger synergies, but less confident about the stand-alone value of Company B. With respect to Company A's own shares, the CEO thinks they are currently fairly valued. The ratio of Company A's debt to total capital is currently 20 percent. At present, interest rates are attractive.

   What are the advantages of using cash or stock as the form of payment for the acquisition?

2. Company A has been eyeing Company B for some time, and believes now is the time to complete an acquisition. Company A's stock is at an all-time high. At the same time, it has a large cash reserve and substantial debt capacity.

   Given his outlook on the economic cycle, the CEO of Company A believes that the valuation of Company A's stock may soon recede. Would you recommend a cash or stock payment? If the latter, how do you think the market might react, assuming the purchase price is reasonable? Why?

3. Company A wants to acquire Company B. Fifty percent of Company A is owned by its founder, Jeff Smith. Twenty percent is owned by another major stockholder, and the remaining portion is held in small amounts by individual shareholders (also called "oceanic shareholders"). Company B is 80 percent owned by its founder, Angus Pierce, who is known to be brilliant, but hotheaded. The remaining 20 percent is owned by oceanic shareholders. Jeff Smith values Pierce's talent, but is wary of Pierce owning a large enough block of shares that might upset the balance of power. Smith insists on controlling a stake in Newco that is at least twice as large (in percentage terms) as Pierce's.

   Assuming 0.5 shares of Company A are exchanged for each share of Company B, and that A and B have 100 million shares and 60 million shares outstanding, respectively, would a share-for-share deal be acceptable to Smith?

4. Company A wants to launch a hostile bid for Company B. A competitor analysis leads the CEO of Company A to conclude that two other bidders may jump into the fray after Company A announces its bid.

   What strategy would you advise for the CEO of Company A in terms of price, form of payment, and financing so that the likelihood of a successful bid increases?

5. *Explain how the cost of overpaying for a target might be borne by creditors.*

6. The table at the top of the opposite page lists the number of cash and stock transactions in the United States for deals above $100 million for two different time periods: 1990–1992, and 1998–2000.

   What do you think might explain the change in proportion between cash and stock deals from the earlier period to the latter?

	1990–1992	1998–2000
Completed deals > $100 million:		
Cash	691	2,558
Stock	196	1,343
	887	3,901
% of cash deals	78%	66%
% of stock deals	22%	34%

Source of data: Thomson Financial Securities Data Corporation.

7. Going back to our example in Chapter 16 of this workbook ("Financial Accounting for Mergers and Acquisitions"), suppose Bed Bath & Beyond wants to acquire Pier 1 Imports. Let's examine the impact of choosing a 100 percent stock payment versus a 100 percent cash payment that is funded entirely with debt.

   Note: A spreadsheet has already been built for you, showing primary data for Bed Bath & Beyond (BB&B), Pier 1, results for a 100 percent stock deal, and results for a 100 percent cash deal. Please see it in "Chapter 20 Workbook.xls" on the CD-ROM, and answer the following questions.

   a. *Assuming a 25 percent purchase premium, fill in the following table. What observations can you make about the impact of form of payment on the ratios?*

		With Merger	
Ratios for BB&B	**Without Merger**	**100% Stock**	**100% Cash**
Gross margin			
Operating margin			
Net margin			
EPS			
% Accretion/(dilution)			
Debt-equity ratio			
Interest cover (EBIT/Interest expense)			

   b. *Build data tables that show the EPS impact of purchase premiums of 20 percent, 25 percent, 30 percent, 35 percent, and 40 percent under both the all-stock and all-cash transactions. Calculate the percentage accretion/dilution for all cases. What do you observe?*

   c. *Under the 100 percent stock transaction, build a data table showing how the exchange ratio, number of new shares issued, and control change under purchase premiums of 20 percent, 25 percent, 30 percent, 35 percent, and 40 percent.*

CHAPTER 21

Framework for Structuring the Terms of Exchange: Finding the "Win-Win" Deal

In an M&A transaction, neither the buyer nor the seller wants to be worse off financially after the deal. A range of exchange ratios can be derived such that both buyer and seller will be better off after the deal, though this may not always be possible.

- The exchange ratio is the number of shares of the buyer's stock to be received for each share of the target firm's stock:
  - The buyer will set a *maximum* exchange ratio, below which the buyer will be willing to acquire the target.
  - The seller will have a *minimum* exchange ratio, above which it will be willing to be acquired.

  It is possible that in a deal negotiation there will be a range of exchange ratios between the buyer's maximum and the seller's minimum that will allow both parties to emerge better off after the deal. This is the win-win zone of outcomes.
- The maximum and minimum exchange ratios of buyer and seller, respectively, depend on the estimated value of Newco. But because the value of Newco is uncertain, the analyst needs to assess the minimum and maximum exchange ratios across a range of possible values for Newco. Two ways to do this are by: (1) focusing on the likely price/earnings ratio of Newco and (2) estimating the likely discounted cash flow (DCF) value of the equity of Newco. Refer to Chapter 21 of the main text for the formulas for calculating minimum and maximum exchange ratios under different parameters.
- Deal boundaries have three important applications:
  1. Given a view about the DCF value or P/E of Newco, one can identify a negotiation range and some likelihood of agreement.
  2. Given a proposed exchange ratio, one can identify P/E or DCF break-even assumptions necessary to permit a mutually beneficial deal.
  3. Given both a proposed exchange ratio and view of DCF value or P/E of Newco, one can evaluate the adequacy of a proposal.
- There are four possible outcomes based on the deal boundaries:
  1. Both win; the exchange ratio is below the buyer's maximum and above the seller's minimum. Here, the deal creates value for the buyer and seller.

2. Target wins, buyer loses.
3. Both lose. Here, the deal destroys value for the buyer and seller.
4. Buyer wins, target loses.

- In situations where the zone of potential agreement (the win-win region) is large, the following are the factors that tend to determine the outcomes:
  - Bargaining power.
  - Control premium in comparable transactions.
  - Focal points based on relative contribution of the two firms.
  - Social issues.
- Synergies create flexibility for the deal designer. Value creation through synergies can raise the buyer's maximum exchange ratio boundary and lower the target's minimum.

CHAPTER 21—WORKBOOK QUESTIONS

1. Suppose Microsoft Corporation (MSFT), the largest software company in the world, wants to acquire ExxonMobil (XOM), the largest oil and gas company in the world. Microsoft is currently trading at $25.96, and ExxonMobil, at $38.31 per share. Microsoft's earnings are at $9.6 billion, and Exxon's, at $15.4 billion. Synergies of $1.25 billion are expected. Shares outstanding are 10.7 billion and 6.68 billion for Microsoft and Exxon, respectively.

   What minimum price/earnings ratio for Newco will make a deal just feasible for both parties?

2. Suppose ExxonMobil thinks Newco will trade at a P/E ratio of 22 times and that Bill Gates says, "How can Exxon think that by merging with us it can raise its P/E to 22 times? Microsoft thinks Newco will trade only at 18 times. If ExxonMobil wants to make the deal work, it needs to convince Microsoft to increase its P/E estimate for Newco." This is a test of negotiating skills!

   Without changing its own view that the postmerger P/E will be 22 times, what P/E level must ExxonMobil convince Microsoft that Newco will trade at in order for Microsoft to agree to a deal?

3. Suppose Microsoft wants to acquire ExxonMobil and thinks that Newco's DCF value will be $550 billion. (Currently, Microsoft and ExxonMobil's market capitalizations are at $278 billion and $256 billion, respectively.) Suppose ExxonMobil thinks, however, that because the two companies' businesses are so unrelated, Newco will suffer a diversification discount, and will have a DCF value of only $500 billion—even *less* than the sum of the two companies' current market capitalizations.

   What is the minimum DCF value for Newco that Microsoft must convince Exxon is possible in order for there to be a possibility for a win-win deal?

4. Assume that the hypothetical Microsoft-ExxonMobil deal is going to be a cash-for-stock deal.

   Calculate the minimum and maximum exchange ratios for P/E ratios ranging from 19 to 25 times. Graph the results. What P/E ratio must Newco trade at in order for the deal to be economically attractive to both firms?

5. *Still assuming a cash-for-stock deal, calculate the exchange ratios for the hypothetical Microsoft-Exxon deal using the DCF method, and graph the results. (Assume DCF values ranging from $400 billion to $800 billion.) What DCF value will make a deal between Microsoft and Exxon feasible?*

6. *Why is it that the minimum acceptable payment in a cash-for-stock transaction is constant regardless of the expected P/E or DCF value of Newco?*

7. Two companies are in merger negotiations. The buyer's and target's share prices are currently trading at $35 and $20, respectively. The buyer is projected to earn $200 million, and the target, $150 million. Synergies of $10 million are expected from the deal. Each party has 80 million shares outstanding. Both buyer and target expect Newco to trade at a price/earnings ratio of 11 times.

   Is a deal attractive to both parties feasible at this P/E ratio? Calculate the maximum and minimum exchange ratios for P/E ratios from 11 to 17 times and graph your results.

8. *Refer to problem 7. Still assuming that Newco will trade at a P/E ratio of 11 times, what amount of synergies would make a deal feasible? Using this new amount of synergies, calculate the maximum and minimum exchange ratios for P/E ratios ranging from 9 to 15 times. Graph your results, superimposed on the graph you drew in problem 7. Interpret the results.*

9. Two companies are in merger negotiations. The buyer's and target's shares are currently trading at $35 and $20, respectively. The buyer is projected to earn $200 million, and the target, $150 million. No synergies are expected from the deal. Each party has 80 million shares outstanding.

   Calculate the maximum and minimum exchange ratios for DCF values ranging from $3 billion to $7 billion and graph your results. If the projected stand-alone DCF value is $5 billion, can a deal be feasible?

10. Refer to problem 9. Assume that the DCF value of synergies of $1 billion is expected from the deal.

    Will the graph that you drew in problem 9 change? Explain. What does change?

11. On June 6, 2003, Oracle Corporation, a provider of software solutions, announced a hostile tender offer for PeopleSoft, a company specializing in software solutions for business. PeopleSoft's stock was trading at $15.11; Oracle offered to pay $16.00 per share. Oracle's own stock was trading at $13.36 a share. Some data about the two companies follows:

Data for Fiscal Year 2002 (in Millions)	Oracle	PeopleSoft	% Contribution Oracle	% Contribution PeopleSoft
Revenues	$ 9,673	$1,949	83.2%	16.8%
Operating expense	$ 6,102	$1,696	78.2%	21.8%
Operating income	$ 3,571	$ 253	93.4%	6.6%
Net income	$ 2,224	$ 183	92.4%	7.6%
Operating margin	36.9%	13.0%		
Net margin	23.0%	9.4%		
Total assets	$10,800	$2,849	79.1%	20.9%
Total shareholders' equity	$ 6,117	$1,956	75.8%	24.2%
Outstanding shares	5,518	311		
Market capitalization on May 15, 2003	$71,237	$5,038	93.4%	6.6%

[This spreadsheet can be found in the folder "Key Spreadsheets from the Workbook" located on the CD-ROM.]

Use contribution analysis to calculate the exchange ratios, assuming the contributions are based on each company's net income. Is a deal feasible?

12. On June 16, 2003, Oracle raised its bid for PeopleSoft to $19.50 a share.

Would a deal be feasible now?

CHAPTER 22

Structuring and Valuing Contingent Payments in M&A

Earnouts are options. The option analogy highlights two important design aspects that are worth careful attention by the negotiators: the time period and triggers (exercise prices) for the earnout. Ultimately the design and evaluation of earnouts depend on the assessment of uncertainty. Incentive payment plans can be extremely useful devices for breaking deadlocks by bridging the perspectives for both buyer and seller.

- Incentive payments are pervasive in M&A activities. They can take many forms: bonus payments to sellers, escrowed funds, holdback allowances, stock options, targeted stock, and earnout plans. In this chapter, "earnout" refers generically to all forms of incentive payments.
- Earnouts are used mostly in the acquisitions of privately held targets, of service businesses, and of high-tech companies. Smaller acquirers are more likely to use earnouts than larger acquirers.
- Although earnouts are quite useful in bridging the valuation gap and retaining and motivating shareholders or managers, they also pose challenges in postacquisition integration and in defining the earnout formulas and performance goals.
- Earnout provisions are call options on the benefits of future performance by the target firm. Like the more standardized option, the earnout can be described in terms of some of its key value drivers: exercise price, price of the underlying asset, interim payout, term, and uncertainty. It must be tailored to the specific deal and therefore can help in bridging the differences in perspectives between an optimistic seller and a pessimistic buyer.
- To structure an effective earnout, the following key elements must be tailored to the expectations of the two sides:
  - *Earnout amount.* Most earnout values range from 20 percent to 70 percent of the total purchase price.
  - *Earnout period.* Earnouts typically run for a period of between one and five years.
  - *Performance goals.* Common performance milestones are cast in terms of revenues, gross margin, pretax profit, cash flow, or earnings before interest, taxes, depreciation, and amortization (EBITDA). Often the goals are tailored to rise over time.

- *Payment schedule.* This can be structured as periodic payments or a lump-sum payment at the end of the earnout period. Different schedules have different motivational effects on the sellers.
- *Operational integration.* The earnout contract must clearly define the business criteria being measured, and the responsibilities of decision makers.
- *Accounting rules and performance measurement.* The earnout agreement should specify the accounting policies that will be followed when measuring the target's performance.
- *Additional issues.* Availability of financing, management process, change in control, liquidity, and impact on the buyer's financial structure should be considered.

- Under purchase accounting for M&A, the earnout must be included as part of the total consideration paid to acquire the target. It brings up a series of legal and accounting implications. Careful consideration of the tax implication of earnout structure is important to reduce friction between the parties.

- The right approach to valuing earnouts is to value them as derivative instruments rather than as predictable streams of cash. The Monte Carlo simulation method is a simple and effective numerical valuation approach. Under this method, the buyer and seller are allowed to input their own assessments of key value drivers, leading to different valuations of the same earnout structure for the two parties and therefore giving both parties a negotiating window.

- An acceptable earnout will satisfy both sides. To the buyer, the earnout and fixed payment will be *equal to or less than* the value of the target to the buyer. To the seller, the earnout and fixed payment will be *equal to or greater than* the target's value. Stated mathematically, a satisfactory deal should meet both equations simultaneously:

$$\text{Enterprise value according to buyer} \geq \text{Dollars at closing} + \text{Buyer valuation of earnout}$$

$$\text{Enterprise value according to seller} \leq \text{Dollars at closing} + \text{Seller valuation of earnout}$$

CHAPTER 22—WORKBOOK QUESTIONS

1. Earnouts are very useful in bridging differences between buyers and sellers. However, they are also difficult to implement.

   Please briefly explain the advantages and disadvantages of using earnouts in M&A.

2. Suppose you as CEO of your firm are negotiating an acquisition deal with Company ABC. The deal structure is proposed as follows: You will pay \$5 million in cash to ABC's shareholders now; if ABC's profit reaches \$1.5 million after five years, ABC's shareholders will be awarded any amount that exceeds \$1.5 million. By checking ABC's financial statements over the past several years, you estimate that the revenues of the firm have a volatility of 35 percent.

ABC has $10 million in revenue this year, and its profit margin is estimated at 10 percent for the next five years.

Given a 6 percent risk-free rate, how much is the value of the earnout plan? Use a binomial tree to value the earnout.

3. Refer to problem 2. Different assessments of volatilities and future profit margins will create huge discrepancies in the valuation of the firm.

   What is the value of the earnout plan assuming sales volatilities of 25 percent, 30 percent, 35 percent, 40 percent, and 45 percent?

   What is the value of the earnout plan assuming profit margins of 8 percent, 9 percent, 10 percent, 11 percent, and 12 percent?

   Build a matrix with the different profit margins and sales volatilities and calculate the corresponding earnout values. What do you observe?

4. *Refer to problem 2. If the earnout begins after three years rather than five years, how does the value of the deal change assuming all other parameters are the same?*

5. *Refer to problem 3. Changing the start of the earnout from five years to three years, build the matrix with the different profit margins and sales volatilities, and calculate the different values of the earnout. Give your observations.*

6. Assume a buyer plans to acquire a target company that has $12 million in sales. The buyer's estimation of the enterprise value of the target firm is $5 million, while the target values itself at $7 million. To bridge the gap between the target and buyer, an earnout plan is proposed: The buyer will pay $2 million at closing; the earnout, which is based on the target's profit, will be good for five years. In the first year, the earnout will be triggered when the firm reaches a profit of $500,000—any profit in excess will be paid to the target shareholders. The same procedure will be followed every year for five years, except that the earnout trigger will increase by $500,000 every year; therefore, for year 2, for instance, target shareholders will be paid any profit in excess of $1 million, for year 3, $1.5 million, and so forth. Sales growth follows a normal distribution with a mean of 12 percent and a standard deviation of 3 percent. The profit margin also follows a normal distribution with a mean of 12 percent and a standard deviation of 2 percent. The five-year risk-free rate is 7 percent.

   What is the economic cost of the earnout to the buyer?

7. *Refer to problem 6. The target estimates that sales growth will follow a normal distribution with a mean of 20 percent and a standard deviation of 5 percent, and profit margins will follow a normal distribution with a mean of 14 percent and a standard deviation of 3 percent. What is the economic value of the earnout to the seller?*

8. Refer to problems 6 and 7. Different assessments of revenue growth rates and profit margins will lead to completely different valuations.

Do a sensitivity analysis using means of 10 percent, 11 percent, 12 percent, 13 percent, and 14 percent for revenue growth, and means of 10 percent, 11 percent, 12 percent, 13 percent, and 14 percent for profit margins. In what combinations will the buyer not take this deal?

9. *Now from the seller's perspective, do a sensitivity analysis using means of 16 percent, 18 percent, 20 percent, 22 percent, and 24 percent for revenue growth, and means of 12 percent, 13 percent, 14 percent, 15 percent, and 16 percent for profit margins. In what combinations will the seller not take this deal?*

CHAPTER 23

Risk Management in M&A

M&A is risky activity. The appropriate goal for investors should be to at least get paid for the risk one does take. The advice to novices and seasoned practitioners is to pay attention to the uncertainties embedded in a transaction, and use risk management devices where warranted.

- The value at risk in the failure of a deal is not trivial and probably grows over time, reaching its maximum at the closing. Strategic options, synergies, and other opportunity costs amplify the value at risk. For the frequent buyer or participant in M&A activity, reputation considerations will amplify the value at risk.
- Some sources of risk to the transaction:
  - Decline in the buyer's share price or financial performance.
  - Preemption by a competing bidder.
  - Disappointed sellers.
  - Appearance of formerly hidden product liabilities.
  - Loss of key customers by the target.
  - Problems in the target's accounting statements.
  - Regulatory intervention.
  - Litigation by competitors.
  - Disagreements over social issues.
  - Failure to get shareholder approvals.
  - Controversy or lack of credibility.
- Risk management devices that are available to the deal designer appear in three time periods around an M&A transaction:
  1. Before the public announcement of the deal: The investment in cash and attention by each side is relatively small.
     - Toehold stake.
     - Antitakeover defenses.
  2. Between announcement and consummation: The investment of the two sides grows dramatically during this period.
     - Breakup and "topping" fees.
     - Lockup options.
     - Exit clauses.

- Representations and warranties.
- Due diligence research.
- Caps, floors, and collars.

3. After consummation:
   - Escrow accounts and post-transaction price adjustments.
   - Contingent value rights.
   - Earnouts and other contingent payments.
   - Staged investing.
   - Cash payment.

- A collar is simply a way to hedge uncertainty about the value of the buyer. Deals that incorporate collars are significantly more likely to succeed (i.e., to close) than are straight stock or cash offers. In addition, the announcement returns to the buyer's shareholders are not materially affected by the use of collars.
- Stock-for-stock deals may be grouped into four classic profiles:
  1. *Fixed exchange ratio deal.* No matter what happens, the target shareholder receives X *shares* of the buyer per target share.
  2. *Fixed value deal.* No matter what happens, the target shareholder receives X *dollars* of value in buyer stock per target share.
  3. *Floating collar.* Within limits, the value the target shareholder receives varies with changes in the buyer's stock price.
  4. *Fixed collar.* Within limits, the value the target shareholder receives is fixed and does not vary with changes in the buyer's stock price.
- A collar mitigates the impact of uncertainty about the buyer's share price through either a transfer of cash or an adjustment in the exchange ratio. To value a collar, as in the AT&T/MediaOne case given in Chapter 23 of the main text, simulate the expected value based on the three factors:
  1. *The life of the collar.* This depends on the closing date for the transaction. Uncertainty about regulatory approvals, shareholder votes, and the absence of potential competitors make the closing date and the life of the collar uncertain.
  2. *The expected future share price at the date of the consummation of the deal.* The buyer's shares are the assets underlying the collar. The price of the buyer's shares is uncertain and can be modeled using the estimated volatility of the buyer's shares.
  3. *The risk-free rate of return.*
- Contingent value rights (CVRs) (see the case of Rhône-Poulenc's acquisition of Rorer given in Chapter 23 of the main text) may be regarded as *fixed collars* that live well beyond the closing date of the transaction. Contingent payments tended to appear in acquisitions involving a large potential difference between the target transaction prices of buyers and sellers or when the sellers were seeking some protection for the remaining minority shareholders against unfair treatment by the acquirer.

- Staged investing structures a series of options over time. The Genzyme/GelTex deal described in Chapter 23 of the main text illustrates the use of *staged investing* (as opposed to lump-sum investing) as a means of hedging the risk associated with FDA approval.
- Risk management in M&A will be more valuable while the value at risk is greater; the ability of buyer or seller to bear those risks is lower; the uncertainty is greater; they create the right incentives for behavior; and they create reasonable signals of expectations to employees and the capital markets.

CHAPTER 23—WORKBOOK QUESTIONS

1. *What are some possible sources of risk to the M&A transaction?*

2. Assume you are the CEO of a publicly listed company who is considering a purchase of a manufacturing company, Fine-Machinery. The most attractive asset in Fine-Machinery is its newly updated Baltimore factory, which has a book value of $15 million and a market value of $20 million. You estimate that extensive due diligence research on Fine-Machinery and other deal development expenses have amounted to almost $3 million. To mitigate your risk, you propose a lockup option to be incorporated into the purchase agreement. This lockup option allows you purchase the Baltimore factory at $15 million if another bidder comes in and acquires the target. You estimate the probability of a competing bid to be 25 percent.

   Please identify the type of this option and calculate its value.

3. As the CEO of a big information technology (IT) consulting firm, you are considering acquiring several small financial consulting firms to enter the financial services market. You reached a tentative agreement with one of the potential targets. You will pay a 25 percent premium over its market value of $24 million for the target's equity. After extensive due diligence, you conclude that the acquisition will generate $10 million present value of synergies. Because the major asset of the financial consulting firm is human capital, you and the target also agree on an exit clause, which allows you to cancel the deal if more than 30 percent of the target's key employees decide to leave the firm before the closing of the deal—loss of these employees would make the target worth $5 million less. The probability of its happening is estimated at 20 percent.

   Please identify the optionality of this exit clause and calculate its value.

4. As the CEO of a hotel chain management firm, you are considering a potential purchase. After preliminary study, you identified one target that suits your overall market positioning and strategy very well. The rough estimate of the value of the target is $50 million. But there are some uncertainties around its accounting methodologies employed for the past several years' financial statements that are used to determine the value of the target. You are considering hiring an independent auditing firm to conduct a thorough audit of its financial reports. The estimated cost of an audit is $500,000. Assuming the accounting

is okay, you believe the deal will generate an NPV of \$20 million. You believe that there is an 85 percent chance that the accounting is okay. But if the accounting is as bad as rumored, it would not only wipe out the synergies, but create an NPV (negative) of –\$10 million. The agreement allows you to exit from the deal if an audit uncovers accounting irregularities.

If you invest in an audit of the target, what kind of option are you acquiring? What is the option worth?

5. Assume the fixed exchange ratio in a deal is 1.4:1. The buyer and seller agree to a floating collar, which has a low trigger of \$20 and a high trigger of \$40. Thus, the exchange ratio is 1.4 to 1, unless the buyer's stock price falls below \$20, in which case the exchange ratio will be equal to \$28 divided by the buyer's share price; if the buyer's share price is greater than \$40, the exchange ratio will equal \$56 divided by the buyer's share price.

   Calculate and graph the number of shares issued for one share of the seller's stock, assuming the following share prices for the buyer: \$0.01, \$10.00, \$15.00, \$20.00, \$30.00, \$40.00, and \$50.00. Also calculate and graph the value of the bid with the collar at these prices. (Use the spreadsheet "Collars Analysis.xls" found on the CD-ROM.)

6. Assume a seller and buyer have agreed on an acquisition, in which the seller will receive a payment in buyer's stock worth \$40 per seller share. In addition, buyer and seller agree to a collar, which has a low trigger of \$20 and a high trigger of \$60. Thus, the cash payment will be \$40 for each share of the seller's stock, unless the buyer's stock price falls below \$20, in which case the exchange ratio would be equal to two shares of buyer stock; or unless the buyer's share price is greater than \$60, in which case the exchange ratio will equal 0.67 shares of stock.

   Please calculate and graph the number of shares issued for each share of the seller's stock, assuming the following share prices for the buyer: \$0.01, \$10.00, \$20.00, \$30.00, \$40.00, \$50.00, \$60.00, and \$70.00. Also calculate and graph the value of the bid with the collar at these prices. (Use the Excel spreadsheet "Collars Analysis.xls" found on the CD-ROM.)

7. Assume that you—the CEO of a big pharmaceutical company—have been approached by a small biotech company to discuss an acquisition. After preliminary research, you and the target reach a tentative agreement on a \$20 million purchase price for the target's equity although there is some disagreement on the value of the promising product of the target, a potential cancer treatment drug. Because the drug is still in the early development stage and the target cannot provide detailed information to you, it is very hard to estimate the drug's true value. Therefore, you propose a staged investment: You will pay \$15 million in cash now; later, if the value of the drug is proved, you will pay another \$5 million if its value is above \$50 million in present value terms (you will pay no more if its value is below \$50 million).

   Assume that the probability distribution for the value of the drug is a normal distribution with a mean of \$60 million and a standard deviation of \$15 million. What is the total cost of the deal to you, and what is the probability of paying the added \$5 million?

8. Assume you are negotiating a deal with Company ABC. The tentative agreement proposed is:

   - You will pay ABC shareholders $45 cash for each ABC share right now, which equals 1.5 shares of your stock.
   - Besides the cash payment, each share of ABC stock will also get 1.5 share contingent value rights, which will give ABC's shareholders the right to some cash payment at the end of one year if Newco's stock does not perform well during this period. Assume one share of Newco is worth $30 today. The contingent value right will permit a holder of Newco to receive a cash payment equal to the difference between $42 and the stock price of Newco after two years, *if* Newco's stock trades below $42. The cash payment will be capped at $10 for each share of Newco's stock.

   Use the Excel spreadsheet "Collars Analysis.xls," found on the CD-ROM, to estimate values using Monte Carlo simulation for the questions.

   a. *Given a risk-free rate of 4.8 percent with a 16 percent volatility and estimated volatility of 15 percent for Newco's stock, what does the deal cost the buyer in terms of each share of ABC's stock?*
   b. *Assuming the time period for this contingent value right is not certain and has a triangular distribution, the best guess is two years with a minimum of one year and maximum of three years. The volatility of interest rates is 16 percent. What is the expected value of this right?*

9. Company Macrosofft, a leading computer software developing company, is considering engaging in a joint venture deal with a small software firm Red Dragon, which just developed an innovative voice recognition software package. Macrosofft believes this technology, using the digitalization of voice patterns, may have application to ultra-secure computing environments. For instance, voice recognition might be a substitute for complex passwords or scans of retinas or thumbprints. Due to the complexity and uncertainty of this new technology, the deal is structured in the following way:

   Stage one: Macrosofft will pay $20 million up front to fund continuous R&D to expand its application to security market. Upon Red Dragon's completion of the first prototype of its security system using this technology, Macrosofft will invest another $10 million as a milestone payment. Developing the first prototype will take a half year.

   Stage two: If the beta test of this technology is successful, Macrosofft will pay another $10 million. Beta testing will take another half year.

   Stage three: Finally, if test marketing is successful, Macrosofft will pay another $5 million, which is the final payment. It will take three months to finish test marketing.

   Based on market research data and responses to this technology, the management team made four estimates about the probabilities of success and size of profits:

   1. Red Dragon has a 75 percent chance of successfully developing the prototype.

2. Red Dragon has an 85 percent chance of passing the beta test if stage one is completed.
3. There is a 90 percent chance that test marketing will be successful if stage two is completed.
4. Based on forecasts of the market, the projected profit follows a normal distribution with a mean of \$250 million and a standard deviation of \$50 million if stage three is completed.

If Macrosofft is seeking 75 percent of the joint venture, how much, in terms of NPV, will it earn from this investment? Please draw the decision tree and calculate the NPV of the project assuming a 15 percent discount rate.

CHAPTER 24

Social Issues

The term *social* is meant to distinguish a set of issues and deal terms from economic issues such as price, form of payment, and generally the returns to shareholders. These issues define the management and governance of Newco, including designation of the CEO and senior management team, makeup of the board of directors, and location of the headquarters. In many cases, social issues have a complicated impact on the buyer, target, and newly combined company.

- Deal-related social issues are often the first terms to be negotiated in a friendly acquisition. The likelihood of consummating a deal is typically contingent on the settlement of social issues.
- While they are sometimes difficult to quantify, social issues can have an economic impact. They can impose a direct cost on the buyer and/or target firm's shareholders. And they may stimulate side payments and complex trade-offs with other terms of the acquisition.
- Social issues cluster into at least nine categories:
  1. Designation of the management team of Newco.
  2. Payments to retain key employees.
  3. Severance payments.
  4. Leadership succession.
  5. Organization design of Newco.
  6. Control options and the composition of the new board of directors.
  7. Structure of transactions: merger of equals (MOE) or other.
  8. Corporate name for the new company.
  9. Geographic location of headquarters.
- Research shows that top management turnover increases significantly following an M&A transaction. In particular, studies have revealed a correlation between the degree of firm underperformance and management changes following merger transactions. Problems arising from corporate culture differences between buyer and target firms explain a significant variation of the top management turnover rate in the first year after the transactions.
- *Retention payments* are the terms of compensation for managers continuing with the new company.

  - They come in varying forms: increased salaries, extraordinary retention bonuses, and so on.
  - They are intended to keep key executives and employees from leaving the firm prior to the completion of the deal. To that end, they usually include contingencies regarding continued employment for a set period of time after the merger closes.
- *Severance payments* are given to departing managers in lump sum, usually according to some predetermined formula set by the firm. Sometimes severance payments are accompanied by *perquisites*: nonmonetary benefits like the use of a company office, car and/or airplane; administrative assistance; country club membership; and so on.
- Regarding the organization design of the new company, the lines of reporting and accountability will convey the degree of the target's independence.
- The determination of the new board of directors will be of particular interest for the directors of the buyer and target firms. The composition of the new board will convey the relative influence of the buyer and target firm's shareholders.
- Structuring a transaction as a merger of equals seeks to give the buyer and target firms equal influence in Newco. MOEs usually involve an exchange of shares with low or zero implied acquisition premiums.
- Naming the new company is no small task; it may signal the relative power and continuity of the buyer and target firms.
- The new headquarters location is often dictated by the firm with more dominance or greater size. Because a buyer is usually much larger than the target, it most likely will endeavor to retain its existing headquarters while closing that of the target firm. Sometimes the two firms will maintain different regional headquarters, in which they share the various headquarters functions.
- In order to understand the transfer of value in a deal, it is important to determine all the relevant parties who will benefit from the resources spent on social terms. These include shareholders, managers, and employees of the buyer and target firms.
- Incentives provided by social terms can influence the present value of expected cash flows, attributable to better operating performance. The business practitioner should not double-count the incentive effect if it is already priced in with estimates of synergy cash flows.
- Adding social terms to the deal may affect the price, reflecting the trade-off between economic and social issues.

CHAPTER 24—WORKBOOK QUESTIONS

1. In early 1998, the CEOs for Daimler-Benz and Chrysler met to discuss a potential merger between the two companies. Study the case ("Daimler and Chrysler: Cross-Border Merger of Equals") outlined in Chapter 24 of the main text and respond to the following questions:

a. In addition to structuring the transaction as a merger of equals, what were the key social issues included in the DaimlerChrysler merger agreement?

b. Did these issues reflect a merger of equals? Why or why not?

c. What were issues that were controversial in negotiations?

d. Do you think that there were any particular issues that could become problematic after the merger closed? If so, which one(s) and why?

2. *How can social issues create value? How can social issues destroy value?*

3. Roberta has been working for nine years as a managing architect in the landscaping division of Best Homes, Inc., which has recently become a target for acquisition by Urban Living, Inc. Both companies are home design and decorating firms; Best Homes mainly serves a rural and suburban clientele, while Urban Living caters to city dwellers. If Best Homes is acquired by Urban Living, there is a high probability that Roberta's job will be eliminated. However, there is also a chance that Roberta will continue with the new company in a different job role. Roberta has been one of the best-performing managing executives at her firm.

   How might a golden parachute and severance package induce Roberta to stay with the target firm, even if her future at the firm is threatened by a merger?

4. In February 1997, investment bank Morgan Stanley and brokerage firm Dean Witter announced their plans to merge; their combination would represent the biggest ever in the securities business. Each firm was to have equal representation on the board of the new company. Dean Witter chief executive Philip Purcell would become chairman and chief executive of the new firm, to be called Morgan Stanley Dean Witter Discover (MSDWD). John Mack, current president of Morgan Stanley, would be the new company's president.

   The cultural integration was expected to be critical to the success of the merger. Some say the deal would not have been consummated had Mack not agreed to let Purcell be CEO. One thing Mack would have going for him was that most of the firm's business would report to him. In the new MSDWD, Purcell would directly control Dean Witter's mutual funds and its credit card operations. Mack would oversee all of Morgan Stanley's former businesses as well as Dean Witter's retail sales force of 9,000 brokers.

   Reconciling the two firms' cultural differences would involve sorting out compensation issues, because Morgan Stanley executives tended to make much more than their Dean Witter counterparts. The employees of the investment bank wanted to make sure it would get to pick the chair of the new company's compensation committee.

   The proposed transaction received large majority approval from the two company's shareholders. At Morgan Stanley, shareholders representing about 83 percent of the common shares outstanding approved the merger; at Dean Witter, the merger was approved by stockholders representing about 87 percent of the shares outstanding. Both stocks rose on the merger announcement.

The deal carried a $250 million termination fee, according to an SEC filing. If either Dean Witter or Morgan Stanley should strike a better deal with another partner, that firm must immediately pay the other $250 million.

In addition to the breakup fee, each firm would give the other an option to acquire a substantial amount of its own stock—equal to 19.9 percent of its currently outstanding shares—if a higher bidder came along. Dean Witter gave Morgan Stanley an option to buy 63.9 million shares of Dean Witter's stock at $38.13 a share. Morgan Stanley gave Dean Witter an option to buy 31.5 million shares of Morgan Stanley's stock at $62.92 a share.

The two companies said that they were not going to integrate everything. For example, Dean Witter would keep its headquarters in the World Trade Center, while Morgan Stanley would remain in its offices in Times Square.

Based on the information given, do you think the proposed merger was a merger of equals? Why or why not?

CHAPTER 25

How a Negotiated Deal Takes Shape

The key to understanding best practice in shaping a deal is the concept of *risk management*. The shaping process is riddled with uncertainties. Anecdotal evidence from seasoned M&A professionals suggests that only small percentages of M&A proposals result in a consummated deal. The process of striking a deal is more like a game of poker than an engineering problem. Law structures the game. Economics adds powerful incentives and motivates strategic behavior. Psychology influences how the game is played.

Good deal process management involves using the legal framework to hedge risk exposure and stimulate good behavior. In general, a deal takes shape through the following process:

1. *Strategic planning, search, and target identification.* Months, or maybe years, of purposeful search culminates in an internal decision by the buyer's managers to approach the target firm. Often this decision entails a formal presentation and discussion supported by strategic and financial analysis.
2. *The initial contact.* The CEO or other senior representative of the buyer approaches the target firm's CEO with a proposal to talk. This brief discussion must give a compelling reason for the combination of two firms that speaks to the needs of target shareholders and management. If the target responds positively to the initial contact, further talks will be scheduled. At the top of the agenda will be social issues.
3. *Confidentiality agreement and related documents.* Very early in the discussions, the two sides will negotiate agreements that outline the behavior of the two sides in the deal shaping process. These agreements address respect for the confidentiality of information, exclusivity of discussions, standstill in the purchase of target shares, and the conditions for terminating discussions.
4. *Term sheet and letter of intent.* When the two sides reach a sufficient degree of alignment on the general terms of a deal, they may memorialize their understanding in a term sheet and/or a letter of intent. These serve to confirm a growing level of commitment and guide the lawyers in drafting a definitive agreement.
5. *Due diligence and negotiation of a definitive agreement.* The next phase entails drafting a definitive agreement that will depend on detailed assertions about the condition of the target, and perhaps the buyer. The defini-

tive agreement binds the two sides to consummate a transaction. Due diligence research becomes a vital step underlying both the definitive agreement and the closing.

6. ***Affirmative vote by the board of directors.*** The definitive agreement likely requires approval of the target's board of directors, and may require approval by the buyer's board as well. If a vote of the shareholders is required, the board can only recommend that they approve the deal. Usually around this stage, the merger negotiations are disclosed to the public and to regulators.
7. ***Disclosure to the public and to regulators.*** Securities regulations and court decisions require firms to disclose to shareholders news about events that is material and probable. When to make the announcement and what to say are matters of judgment, and therefore two of the most delicate issues faced in managing the deal shaping process.
8. ***Antitrust filings and permission.*** Part of the process of releasing information about the deal entails required disclosure to antitrust authorities as part of gaining their permission to consummate the transaction. Filings under the Hart-Scott-Rodino Act (HSR) must reveal the likely degree of Newco's industry concentration following the deal.
9. ***Informing the shareholders and gaining an affirmative vote.*** Merger proposals require the approval of shareholders. Thus, the target and sometimes the buyer will issue a merger prospectus that informs shareholders about the deal, and a proxy statement that requests their votes in support of the deal. The document preparation and voting process take three to six months.
10. ***Closing.*** The M&A agreement commits the two firms to conclude a transaction under various terms and conditions, such as gaining shareholder votes and regulatory approvals. At the closing the two sides document that they have met the representations, warranties, and covenants outlined in the agreement. Payment is made and ownership is assumed by the buyer.
11. ***Postmerger integration.*** Except for terms of the definitive agreement that specifically extend beyond closing, the focus thereafter is on combining the two companies to realize the economic benefits hypothesized at the outset. Indifference to integration is a leading cause of M&A failure. Planning for integration ideally commences early in the process such as at the signing of the letter of intent.

- Factors that may derail the deal process are:
  - *Bad chemistry.* CEOs/management teams do not get along.
  - *Social issues, control.* Disagreements arise about who becomes CEO or chairman of the board; there are culture clashes.
  - *Pricing.* Target and buyer do not agree on the purchase price/valuation.
  - *Market trends.* Adverse moves in the stock market or interest rates may affect the value of the buyer's offer or ability to finance the transaction.
  - *Skeletons in the closet.* Previously unknown or undisclosed facts or events relating to either party surface during negotiations.

  - *Material adverse change.* There are sudden changes in the businesses of the buyer or target.
  - *Regulatory or antitrust constraints.* Regulatory bodies may not approve merger for antitrust reasons.
  - *Competing bidder.*
  - *Shareholders vote "no."*

- First-round documents help deal designers manage risks such as leakage of information, double-dealing, buyer backing out, and so on. Examples of first-round documents include the term sheet, exclusivity agreement, engagement letter, confidentiality agreement, standstill agreement, and letter of intent.
- Generally, executives and boards are obligated to disclose material news to investors. "Materiality" will depend on:
  - Significance of the transaction to the company.
  - Probability of the transaction occurring.
- An attitude of risk management should guide the deal shaping process. One must focus on good process and trust that in doing so a good outcome will emerge.

CHAPTER 25—WORKBOOK QUESTIONS

1. Family Mart, a medium-sized supermarket chain in the Carolinas, has been approached by Mighty Mart, the largest supermarket chain in the Southeast, for a possible merger. In his excitement, the CEO of Family Mart says during the initial meeting, "This sounds like a winner! I will instruct my CFO and chief auditor to provide all the information you need. You can start immediately!"

   Comment on the action of the CEO of Family Mart.

2. Refer to problem 1. At the conclusion of the initial meeting, the CEO of Family Mart tells the CEO of Mighty Mart, "Our bylaws require board approval for these kinds of transactions. But don't worry—I give you my word that the directors will vote in favor of our merger."

   Comment on the action of the CEO of Family Mart.

3. Camelot, Inc., a large publisher, is planning to acquire Little Pete's House, a specialty publisher of children's books. Based on his business development team's analysis, the CEO of Camelot, Hans Olsen, believes that the acquisition will be a big win for his company. Confident that Camelot's directors will agree with him, he proceeds to make a presentation to Little Pete's management without first informing his own board. The two CEOs agree to a merger, and go through the necessary procedures (e.g., signing of confidentiality agreements, due diligence, discussion of tax and accounting treatment, etc.).

   If you were in Olsen's shoes and likewise believed that the acquisition would be a big win, would you go about the deal process in the same fashion as Olsen?

4. Refer to problem 3. Suppose that Little Pete's CEO vehemently opposes Olsen's proposal to merge. Olsen, however, continues to believe that a merger would be favorable to both companies, and refuses to give up.

   What alternatives does Olsen have? Explain.

5. Refer to problem 4. Suppose word gets out that Little Pete's has been approached by Camelot, and that this results in unusual trading activity in Little Pete's.

   Does Little Pete's have an obligation to disclose that it has received an unwanted offer?

6. *What risk does a standstill agreement manage?*

7. Two large telecommunications companies have agreed in principle to a merger of equals. Both companies think that the merger may be challenged by outside parties (competitors and activist shareholders), and therefore want to keep discussions private for as long as they can. Many of the main merger terms (i.e., price, form of payment, structure, social issues) have already been worked out.

   Should the companies formalize their understanding with a letter of intent?

CHAPTER 26

Governance in M&A: The Board of Directors and Shareholder Voting

"Governance" is the action of controlling or directing. In a corporate setting, governance entails a system of oversight and delegation of decisions that reaches from the owners of the firm (the shareholders) to the board of directors, and from there to senior, middle, and front-line managers. While good governance may be challenging to achieve because of complexity, size, diffuse ownership, conflicting interests of owners and agents, and moral hazard, the evidence suggests that good governance pays.

- The board of directors plays a key role in promoting shareholder interests in the management of the firm. A company's board of directors exercises governance through the processes of executive hiring and firing, compensation, auditing, review of financial performance, and approval of major decisions.
- Agency costs arise when managements promote their own interests at the expense of shareholders. Good governance is necessary for the minimization of agency costs.
- Governance reduces agency costs by:
  - *Designing compensation structures* that align the interests of managers and shareholders.
  - *Monitoring financial performance* and taking actions necessary to improve shareholder wealth.
  - Binding managers through contracts aimed at achieving goals. This is known as *financial contracting.*
  - Building a coalition among directors and shareholders to influence managers. This is known as *jawboning.*
- Shareholders exercise their influence through votes, lawsuits, and jawboning. Foundational documents (e.g., articles of incorporation and bylaws) lay out guidelines such as procedures for voting, creation of new shares of stock, how resolutions may be presented to shareholders, and so on, and are therefore also a means by which shareholders can exercise their influence. Bylaws, in particular, can be changed only by a vote of the shareholders. Provisions such as supermajority voting requirements, and straight or cumulative voting for directors all influence the potency of shareholder votes.

- Good governance pays in the sense of being associated with higher returns to shareholders, higher corporate valuation, and higher financial performance. Alignment of the interests of managers and shareholders is associated with shareholder value creation.
- The corporate charter and bylaws specify how shareholders can vote. The two classic approaches are *straight voting*, in which shareholders wield votes equal to the number of shares on each candidate independently, and *cumulative voting*, in which a shareholder is granted votes equal to the number of shares held times the number of directors to be elected, and can allocate votes at will (in the extreme giving all his or her *cumulative* votes to just one director). The cumulative voting system makes it easier for cohesive, but minority, groups of shareholders to gain representation on the board.
- The actions of directors are measured against three doctrines of rising degrees of intervention by courts: the business judgment rule, enhanced scrutiny, and entire fairness.

  1. ***Business judgment rule.*** This rule holds that courts are unlikely to intervene if directors and officers fulfill their duties in good faith—that is, if they are not conflicted, are informed, and act in rational belief. Directors must adhere to the duties of loyalty and care.
  2. ***Enhanced scrutiny.*** In certain instances, such as hostile tender offers and auctions, the courts have acknowledged that some business problems may warrant a higher level of judicial scrutiny. Before applying the business judgment rule, the court will first examine the directors' decision-making process and the reasonableness of the action. The *Revlon duties* fall under enhanced scrutiny, and require the directors to auction the firm when the firm is for sale and more than one bidder is competing to acquire it.
  3. ***Entire fairness.*** The highest level of court intervention occurs when an actual conflict of interest affects a majority of directors approving a transaction. In these cases, the defendants (directors) must show that the challenged action was entirely fair to the corporation and its shareholders: fair in terms of "fair dealing" and fair price.

CHAPTER 26—WORKBOOK QUESTIONS

1. *For challenging the decision of directors to sell a firm, which laws govern?*
   - *Laws of the state in which the company is headquartered.*
   - *Laws of the state in which the company is incorporated.*
   - *Delaware state laws.*
2. *What is the difference between straight voting and cumulative voting?*
3. The Addams family owns 70 percent of Addams' Apple, a manufacturer of apple juice, apple cider, apple chips, and other apple-related products. The remaining 30 percent is publicly traded, with Gordon Echo, a raider, owning 100,000 of the publicly traded shares. The company has 1 million shares out-

standing and eight directors on its board. A shareholders' meeting is coming up, and Gordon wants to get at least one of his nominees on the board.

a. Under straight voting, does Echo have a chance?

b. What about under cumulative voting?

4. The directors of XYZ Corporation met for 20 minutes to discuss the sale of the company, and then voted.

   Assuming they held no other meetings or viewed no other reports, which duty would this violate?

5. The CEO of Starstruck Corporation submitted a management buyout proposal to his board of directors, offering to buy the company at a small premium to current market value. Privately, the CEO promised each board member they would remain on the board of the company, and that directors' salaries would be raised.

   Does voting to approve this transaction violate any of the rules that govern directors' conduct?

6. Tom Kane sits on the board of Walking Shoes, Inc. He has headed the board's audit committee for seven years, and has been instrumental in designing Walking Shoes' financial reporting and monitoring systems. He has great confidence in the system of checks and balances he has built, and has therefore become more relaxed in his review of financial results. Lately he has limited his involvement to reading the firm's quarterly financial statements.

   Under which duty might Tom have an obligation to do more?

7. Special Delivery, Inc., offers domestic courier services via ground transportation across the United States. Its board of directors has just voted to approve the sale of the company to Fly-by-Night, Inc., a provider of overnight courier service throughout the country. There are compelling synergies in support of the merger. The financial advisers believe that Special Delivery is receiving a fair price at $55 per share. The price represents nearly a 30 percent premium to the current market price of $43.50.

   Upon learning of the deal, Jet Courier, a competitor, quickly assembles an offer to buy Special Delivery at $60 per share. Jet Courier expects to realize even greater synergies.

   Is it possible that Special Delivery, Inc. is in "Revlon mode" at this point in time?

8. The directors of Pizza Joe's, a nationwide fast-food chain, have agreed to a merger of equals with Mexican Delight, another nationwide fast-food chain. The directors of both boards believe that significant cost synergies can be achieved through economies of scale in purchasing ingredients and equipment, and through savings in rent and leases by having both franchises in each location. Both boards have reviewed internal studies exhaustively and have consulted independent financial and legal advisers. Fairness opinions have been obtained, and the directors believe that the terms of agreement are fair to both parties.

   Are courts likely to intervene in this case? Why or why not?

CHAPTER 27

Rules of the Road: Securities Law, Issuance Process, Disclosure, and Insider Trading

The practice of M&A is vastly influenced by securities laws and regulations. The aim of these laws is to inform investors, prevent manipulation, produce more efficient markets, and achieve a level playing field. M&A practitioners should be knowledgeable about these laws. Ignorance of the laws is no defense for failing to observe them.

- Key rules of disclosure include these:
  - If a deal is material and probable to investors in public firms, one must disclose the proposed transaction to the public.
  - One must control information about a deal and avoid insider trading.
  - One must observe correct procedures regarding deadlines and filings.
- The *Securities Act of 1933* requires that new securities be registered with the Securities and Exchange Commission (SEC), grants the SEC rule-making authority, and sharply limits the trading of unregistered securities. The significance of this act lies in the concept of *registration*, through which the SEC can impose standards of disclosure of information by means of a prospectus.
- The *Securities Exchange Act of 1934* lays out rules regulating securities exchanges and the securities traded in the public markets. It also requires corporations with assets greater than $10 million and more than 500 shareholders to register with the SEC. These companies are called reporting companies.
- The *Williams Amendment* requires hostile bidders to disclose information to the public and target shareholders in connection with a bid. The Williams Amendment imposes four important rules of the road:

1. *Early warning.* A buyer must notify the SEC within 10 days upon the accumulation of 5 percent or more of a target's shares.
2. *Open for 20 days.* The buyer's tender offer must be open for 20 business days before shares may be purchased.
3. *Equal treatment.* All target shareholders must be treated equally by the buyer.
4. *Cash offers, too.* Cash tender offers are also subject to the antifraud and registration requirements that govern share-for-share exchanges.

- Private placements are exempt from registration under certain rules.
- States are permitted to have jurisdiction over securities registration as long as they don't conflict directly with the provisions of the 1934 Act.
- Court law directs the decision maker to consider the following disclosure guidelines:
  - ***Materiality.*** Do not omit material facts. The Supreme Court states, "An omitted fact is material if there is a substantial likelihood that a reasonable shareholder would consider it important in deciding how to vote."
  - ***Probability.*** Disclosure of merger negotiations is not required if the merger is unlikely to go through.
  - ***Commit and disclose.*** When an agreement has been reached, release a definitive agreement or a letter of intent to the public.
  - ***Expectations in the market.*** A firm has a "duty to update" where recent actions depart from past pronouncements.
  - ***"No comment."*** Do not deny rumors if negotiations are serious.
  - ***Abstain from trading or disclose.*** Abstain from trading during merger negotiations. If abstention is not possible, disclose merger negotiations.

CHAPTER 27—WORKBOOK QUESTIONS

1. *Joe says to John, "The aim of securities law is to build security for companies and individuals." Is Joe right?*

2. *You are adviser to Pearl Ronaldman, a raider. She wants to commence a hostile tender offer for Mary Stuart Living, Inc., a producer and marketer of products for homemakers and other consumers. Pearl already purchased 4.99 percent of Mary Stuart in the open market 15 days ago. She has four friends, consciously acting together, who have each purchased another 4.99 percent of the company. Pearl is planning to offer higher prices to shareholders who tender more than 100,000 shares apiece and lower prices to those who tender less. Her offer will be open for 10 days because she wants to try to stampede investors into tendering. Will her strategy create any legal exposure?*

3. *In another situation, Pearl makes a hostile two-tier offer for a furniture company. The offer is as follows: $50 in cash to investors who tender the first 50 percent, and in the second stage, five shares of Ronaldman Corp. stock, which is currently trading at $10 per share. Does this violate the Williams Amendment?*

4. *Fitness Buff, Inc., a maker of fitness equipment, is in serious talks to be acquired by Olympic Life, a company that operates fitness centers across the United States. The two parties are very close to signing a merger agreement. Rumors that Fitness Buff is for sale begin to spread. In response to journalists' questions, the company issues a press release denying it is for sale. By means of its public denial, has Fitness Buff created any legal exposure for itself? Explain.*

5. *Jack Siegel tells his long-time friend Sam Denver in confidence that his (Siegel's) company has been approached by a competitor wishing to initiate friendly merger discussions. Siegel also tells Denver that he believes a well-known raider is accumulating a significant percentage of shares in his company, and that a bidding war might ensue between the raider and the "friendly" competitor. The next day Denver asks his broker to buy 20,000 shares in Siegel's company. Do Denver and Siegel have any legal exposure? Explain.*

6. *Myer-Goodwill-Milo wants to acquire independent filmmaker La Primavera Pictures, and approaches the latter's 22,000 shareholders with an offer for a share-for-share exchange. Myer-Goodwill-Milo's shares are privately held and unregistered, but the firm will file a registration with the SEC in two months. Is Myer-Goodwill-Milo in any legal trouble?*

7. *Myer-Goodwill-Milo wants to acquire 18th Century Fox. Myer-Goodwill-Milo offers the five wealthy people who own 18th Century a share-for-share exchange. Myer-Goodwill-Milo does not intend to register its shares issued in this exchange. Is it in any legal trouble?*

CHAPTER 28

Rules of the Road: Antitrust Law

The goal of antitrust law in the United States is to preserve and promote competition within industries, reflecting the public policy view that active competition produces efficiency, innovation, and prices that are fair to consumers. It is important for M&A practitioners to gain familiarity with current antitrust attitudes, to anticipate possible objections, and to creatively work to revise a deal to satisfy regulators.

- According to the Federal Trade Commission (FTC), for a merger to be ruled *anticompetitive* it must substantially concentrate the market for a product and make it difficult for new firms to enter.
- The *Sherman Act* outlaws anticompetitive behavior. It considers illegal (1) contracts that attempt to restrain trade or commerce among the different states and foreign countries, and (2) attempts to monopolize trade among the states or with foreign nations. Violations of the Sherman Act are punished by fines and/or imprisonment. The Antitrust Division of the Department of Justice (DOJ) handles violations of the Sherman Act.
- The *Clayton Act* specifically addresses mergers and acquisitions, preventing combinations that would restrain trade. The Clayton Act forbids acquisitions whose effect may be "substantially to lessen competition or tend to create a monopoly."
- The *Hart-Scott-Rodino Act* requires combinations above a certain size threshold to submit information to the DOJ and FTC in advance of consummating the deal. This law grants the federal government a right of advance regulatory refusal on M&A deals.
- *Horizontal mergers* occur among peer competitors in an industry, and are motivated by the potential for greater market power and increased economies of scale. *Vertical mergers* occur among firms within the value chain. Vertical mergers may help firms increase revenue through greater product offerings and reduce costs through greater control of the supply chain. *Conglomerate mergers* occur among firms unrelated by value chain or peer competition. They help buyer firms grow in size. They may also be motivated by the belief that the central office has key know-how in allocating capital and running the disparate businesses better than they can be run independently.
- Regulatory agencies use two quantitative measures when assessing the impact of horizontal mergers. These are the *cross elasticity of demand* and the

Herfindahl-Hirschman Index (HHI). The cross elasticity of demand measures how closely related demand is for two different goods. The relationship is measured as the change in demand for one good in response to a change in the price of another good. The Herfindahl-Hirschman Index measures market concentration based on market shares of players in the relevant market.

$$\text{Elasticity} = \frac{\%\ \text{Change in quantity demanded of good B}}{\%\ \text{Change in price of good A}}$$

$$HHI = \sum_{i}^{n}\left(\frac{\text{Sales or output of Firm } i}{\text{Total sales or output of market}} \times 100\right)^2$$

- Regulatory agencies also use other guidelines to decide whether to approve or disapprove horizontal mergers:
  - Whether the merger will forestall entry by other firms.
  - Whether the merger efficiency gains are credible.
  - Whether either of the merger partners is a failing firm.
- Antitrust agencies challenge nonhorizontal mergers under two theories:
  1. ***Theory of potential competition.*** Nonhorizontal mergers may have adverse effects on competition in indirect ways by eliminating potential entrants into a market.
  2. ***Barriers to entry from vertical mergers.*** Some vertical mergers could reduce competition in a market through the erection of significant barriers to entry.

CHAPTER 28—WORKBOOK QUESTIONS

1. *Goods X and Y have a cross elasticity of –1.2. If the price of X increases, what do you think will happen to the demand for Y? Provide examples of goods with negative cross elasticities. How would you characterize the relationship between such goods?*

2. Firm A, a large processor of beefsteaks, wants to acquire Firm B, a processor of lamb chops. The Federal Trade Commission wants to determine the economic relationship between beef and lamb. A review of prices over the past 10 years reveals that demand for lamb chops rises 0.25 percent for every 1 percent increase in the price of beefsteaks.

   Calculate the cross elasticity of demand and interpret the results

3. Listed are the 10 largest U.S. electronics, audio, and appliance stores, ranked according to fiscal year 2000 revenue:[1]

	FY 2000 Revenues ($ MM)
Best Buy Co. Inc.	12,494.0
Circuit City Stores Inc.	10,599.4
RadioShack Corporation	4,794.7
The Good Guys Inc.	860.5
Intertan Inc.	484.2
Rex Stores Corp.	464.3
Tweeter Home Entertainment	404.7
Ultimate Electronics Inc.	385.0
Sound Advice Inc.	177.3
Harvey Electronics Inc.	34.4

Suppose RadioShack Corporation wanted to acquire The Good Guys, Inc. Here are descriptions of both companies:

> *RadioShack Corporation*
>
> *RadioShack operates 5,109 company-owned stores located throughout the United States. These stores . . . are located in major malls and strip centers, as well as individual storefronts. Product lines include electronic parts and accessories, cellular and conventional telephones, audio and video equipment, direct-to-home satellite systems, and personal computers. . . . In addition, the company has a network of 2,090 dealer/franchise outlets, including 54 located outside of the U.S.*[2]
>
> *The Good Guys, Inc.*
>
> *The Good Guys, Inc. is a leading specialty retailer of consumer electronics products. The company currently operates 72 stores in California, Nevada, Oregon, and Washington. These stores offer some 4,600 products from 240 vendors. The company's merchandising strategy is to provide shoppers with a broad selection of brand name consumer electronics products, with an emphasis on more fully featured merchandise.*[3]

Calculate the Herfindahl-Hirschman Indexes premerger and postmerger. Do you think the FTC would approve this acquisition?

4. In December of 2000, PepsiCo agreed to acquire Quaker Oats. By doing so, PepsiCo gained access to Gatorade, which controlled 84.1 percent of the sports-drink market. Coca-Cola's Powerade was second, with a share of 10.9 percent, while PepsiCo's All Sport was third at 2.8 percent. Other brands accounted for the remaining 2.2 percent.[4] Total market revenues were $2.658 billion.

   Compute the HHI in terms of revenue before and after the deal, determine the change in the index, and interpret the results.

5. *Firm A wants to acquire Firm B. Firm A has assets of $398 million; Firm B has assets of $82 million. Is Firm A required to file a report with the DOJ and FTC in advance of the acquisition? Why?*

6. Blue Skies Airways wants to acquire Eagle Airlines. This combination would make the airline industry even more highly concentrated than it already is: Together the two airlines would control 38 percent of the air travel market. The post-transaction HHI would be 2,738 and the change in HHI would be 137 points. Eagle, which has a workforce of approximately 18,000, is teetering on the edge of bankruptcy.

   Is there a chance that the FTC might approve this deal?

7. Satellite Communications Inc. and The Alpha Digital Group have agreed to a merger of equals. The companies submitted filings to the FTC and the DOJ on July 5, 2002. A month later they had not received a response from either of the agencies.

   Can Satellite and Alpha proceed to consummate their merger?

NOTES

1. Jack W. Plunkett, *Plunkett's Entertainment & Media Industry Almanac 2002–2003*, Houston, TX: Plunkett Research Ltd. p. 89.
2. Ibid., p. 391.
3. Ibid., p. 250.
4. Skip Wollenberg, "Gatorade-plus: PepsiCo Snack Foods, Juice Sales to Be Sweeter after Quaker Deal," *Houston Chronicle*, December 5, 2000.

CHAPTER 29

Documenting the M&A Deal

First-round documents lay out terms of engagement among parties privy to a deal. The purpose of first-round documents is to address risks that may arise before a definitive agreement can be reached. First-round documents include confidentiality agreements, engagement letters, exclusivity/termination agreements, standstill agreements, a term sheet, and a letter of intent. In contrast to first-round documents, the definitive agreement contractually binds the buyer and target to consummate the deal. This agreement is a device for managing risks that may arise between signing the contract and actually consummating the deal.

- *Engagement letters* for advisory work must deal with the following considerations:
  - Scope of the engagement.
  - Compensation.
  - Tail provision (whether the obligation to compensate extends to events after possible cessation of talks).
  - Indemnification of adviser against liabilities.
  - Length of engagement.
  - Method of terminating the engagement.
- A *confidentiality agreement* commits the buyer to hold in confidence all nonpublic information received from the target and to use it for no other purpose than consummating the transaction. The agreement also lays out the information to be provided and the channels through which it is to be accessed. The target may seek relief in the event that the agreement is violated.
- An *exclusivity agreement* binds a target to not share information or seek discussions with other potential buyers over a specified period of time during which the merger agreement is being negotiated and the buyer is performing due diligence.
- A *standstill agreement* prevents a buyer from purchasing more target shares without approval from the target's board of directors. Its objective is to prevent the buyer from pressuring the target by short-circuiting merger negotiations through open market purchases or a direct tender offer to shareholders.
- A *term sheet* contains a brief summary of terms of the deal such as price, form of payment, structure, and social issues. Although not a binding agreement, the

term sheet establishes a sense of alignment between the two parties, and provides a framework on which to draft the definitive agreement.

- A *letter of intent* is an agreement on the intent of the deal negotiations up to that point. Some M&A advisers advise against signing an LOI because it is not contractually binding, and because it may trigger some disclosure obligations. On the other hand, it can serve the following useful purposes:
  - Confirm understanding between the two parties.
  - Express commitment.
  - Preempt market rumors.
  - Test investor sentiment.
  - Help get financing for a deal.
  - Start to shape integration efforts.
  - Deter competitors.
- Most *definitive agreements* contain the following sections/information:
  - ***Parties to the deal.*** This section defines who the parties to the transaction are, thereby ensuring clarity about who has commitments to perform under the agreement. Defining the parties to the deal also establishes exclusivity.
  - ***Recitals.*** These tell the reader what the parties want to accomplish, and are easily identified by clauses that begin with "Whereas." The risk management aspect of the "Recitals" section is to frame the transaction as being in the best interests of shareholders.
  - ***Definition of terms.*** The risk management content of the "Definitions" section is to prevent or reduce misunderstanding. Formal definitions also help reduce the length and complexity of the document.
  - ***Description of the basic transaction: purchase or sale of assets or equity, or merger.*** The "Transactions" section lays out the terms of the merger and contains information about how the deal will be consummated. Details provided in this section will usually include the form of exchange, the price or the exchange ratio, information about the treatment of options and warrants, the merger structure, the targeted closing date, and social issues.
  - ***Representations and warranties.*** This section contains disclosures about the condition of the buyer and seller at the time of the transaction. In effect, this section provides a snapshot of the buyer and seller as of a certain date. A representation is a statement of fact, while a warranty is a commitment that a fact is or will be true. The reps and warranties can trigger an exit with no liability if the other party's representations and warranties are shown to be false. By the same token, this section gives a foundation for indemnities after the closing of the deal.
  - ***Covenants.*** Covenants are promises, forward-looking commitments. In the covenants section, the buyer and seller promise to do or not do certain things between the signing of the agreement and the closing date. Covenants prevent opportunistic behavior by either party.
  - ***Conditions to closing.*** This section lists the conditions that each side must observe in order to consummate the transaction. Standard closing conditions

include shareholder approvals, regulatory approvals, absence of material litigation, and consents from third parties (such as landlords and creditors where necessary).
- *Termination.* This gives the circumstances under which the parties can unilaterally or mutually terminate the transaction. These may include mutual consent to terminate, the failure to receive regulatory or shareholder approvals, the expiration of a completion date, material adverse change in the business, or breach of reps, warranties, or covenants.
- *Indemnifications.* The "Indemnifications" section specifies damage payments in the event of losses discovered after closing, or even breach of provisions in the agreement. Typical structures of indemnification are "basket," threshold, ceiling, clawback, and escrow or deferred payment.
- *Miscellaneous items.*

- Corporations and shareholder groups send out solicit proxies from shareholders to gain authority to vote on behalf of shareholders.
- In the context of a vote to approve a merger, the proxy statement chiefly aims to disclose the terms, history, and effects of the merger. At their most basic level, merger proxy statements contain information about terms of the proposed deal (e.g., price, form of exchange, organizational structure), rationale and background of the deal, financial and tax impact of the deal, requirements for consummation, proof of financing for buyer, fairness opinions, regulatory matters, and conditions of termination.
- Merger proxy statements do not tell investors everything they want to know. The proxy statement is drafted in a way to help stockholders vote wisely, yet not divulge valuable information to competitors. Merger proxy statements contain very few forward-looking statements. Careful scrutiny of the merger proxy statement and independent analysis are needed to make wise decisions about deals.

CHAPTER 29—WORKBOOK QUESTIONS

1. Harry, the president of a stock brokerage and research firm called Motley Players, has initiated merger talks with Close Call, another stock brokerage firm. Sally, the president of Close Call, is interested in continuing discussions, but is worried that Motley Players, which already has an 11 percent stake in Close Call, will preempt negotiations and launch a tender offer.

   What can Sally do to address this? Explain.

2. In view of problem 1, Sally insists early in the negotiations that Harry sign a standstill agreement, as well as a confidentiality agreement. Harry tells his financial adviser, "That's outrageous!" to which the financial adviser replies, "Not if we can get something in return."

   What might the financial adviser be thinking of?

3. Predator Bank has been hired to act as financial adviser for Close Call. In the engagement letter proposed by Predator, the latter asks for the right to be com-

pensated even if the deal is not consummated. The clause states that Predator has the right to receive the agreed-upon fees as long as Close Call consummates a merger (with any party) within four years of termination of its engagement with Predator. Sally blows up when she reads this clause.

Is Sally's reaction reasonable? Explain.

4. The engagement letter between Predator Bank and Close Call includes the following terms:

   - Compensation: 5 percent of the first $1 million (or part thereof) of the total purchase price, 4 percent of the second $1 million (or part thereof) of the total purchase price, 3 percent of the third $1 million (or part thereof) of the total purchase price, 2 percent of the fourth $1 million (or part thereof) of the total purchase price, and 1 percent of the remainder of the total purchase price.
   - Length of engagement: 120 days.
   - Tail provision: Close Call agrees to remunerate Predator for the fees cited above if Close Call consummates a merger with any other party within four years of termination of its engagement with Predator.
   - Indemnification: Predator shall be indemnified against possible liabilities arising from the engagement.

   Is the engagement letter missing any important features?

5. Harry has requested a period of 60 days to conduct due diligence research. Sally is in a hurry to consummate the transaction and insists on completing due diligence within two weeks. Sally's company conducts business in 15 countries, sometimes through wholly owned subsidiaries and other times through joint ventures with local partners.

   Comment on this situation.

6. After conducting due diligence, Harry presents Sally with a first draft of the definitive agreement. The portion on "Merger Consideration" reads:

   > *Each share of the Common Stock, par value $0.001 per share of Close Call . . . shall be converted into, and become exchangeable for 0.42 shares of Motley Players, subject to the following adjustment: If the average of the Motley Players market price 20 days before the closing date is greater than $38.6522, the exchange ratio shall be adjusted to 0.41 shares, and shall decrease by 0.01 for each subsequent 5 percent upward movement.*

   Sally is outraged upon reading this. She tells Harry, "We never said anything in our preliminary term sheet and letter of intent about adjusting the exchange ratio!"

   Is Harry under any obligation to adhere to the terms set out in the earlier documents?

Answer the following questions based on the eBay/PayPal merger agreement found at this web address: www.sec.gov/Archives/edgar/data/1065088

/000089161802003151/0000891618-02-003151.txt (You'll have to scroll down a little to get to the merger agreement.)

7. *Who are the parties to the deal?*

8. *Fill in the following term sheet:*

Purchase Price
Implied price per share
Resulting PayPal ownership of eBay
Transaction fees
Exchange ratio
Cap

Format of Payment
Consideration
Number of shares to be issued

Form of Transaction and Tax Considerations

Transaction Process Requirements
Termination penalties
Shareholder vote
Closing date

Social Issues
Organization structure
Executives
Board seats
Headquarters
Name
Workforce

---

9. *When was the merger agreement dated? What defines the closing date? What defines the effective date?*
Explain the organizational structure of the merger. Please also diagram the transaction.

10. *What information can you glean from the Recitals section?*

11. *Whose bylaws will apply to the surviving entity?*

12. *Who will serve as the directors of the surviving entity? Who will serve as the company officers? What is the impact of this structure?*

13. *In what form will the target receive payment? What are the terms of exchange?*

14. Go over the "Representations and Warranties" section briefly.
What do you observe as the most common or most important issues addressed? Why are these issues included?

15. *Describe some of the covenants in the merger agreement and how they serve as risk-management tools.*

16. *What are some of the conditions deemed by eBay and PayPal to be necessary for the consummation of the merger? How do these conditions manage risk?*

17. *When is termination of the agreement possible?*

The following material contains excerpts from a merger proxy statement. Read this material and then address questions 18 to 31 that follow. [Note that ". . ." indicates the intentional omission of material not deemed relevant to this chapter.]

SCHEDULE 14A

(Rule 14a-101)
INFORMATION REQUIRED IN PROXY STATEMENT

SCHEDULE 14A INFORMATION

Proxy Statement Pursuant to Section 14(a) of the Securities Exchange Act of 1934

Filed by the Registrant [ ]

Filed by a Party other than the Registrant [X]

Check the appropriate box:

[ ] Preliminary Proxy Statement

[X] Definitive Proxy Statement

[ ] Definitive Additional Materials

[ ] Soliciting Material Pursuant to

240.14a-11(c) or 240.14a-12

[ ] Confidential, for Use of the Commission Only (as Permitted by Rule 14a-6(e)(2))

Echlin Inc. (Name of Registrant as Specified In Its Charter)

SPX Corporation (Name of Person(s) Filing Proxy Statement, if other than Registrant)

SPX CORPORATION

Solicitation Statement

to Call a Special Meeting of Shareholders

of

ECHLIN INC.

SPX Corporation, a Delaware corporation ("SPX"), is asking you to help it call a special meeting of shareholders (a "Special Meeting") of Echlin Inc., a Connecticut corporation (the "Company"), for the purpose of voting to remove the current members of the Board of Directors of the Company and replace them with SPX's nominees.

On February 17, 1998, SPX delivered a letter to the Company containing a proposal for a strategic business combination of the Company with SPX (the "Proposed Business Combination"), in which shareholders of the Company would receive for each of their shares of common stock, par value $1.00, of the Company ("Shares") (together with the associated preferred stock purchase right (the "Rights")), the amount of $12.00 net in cash and 0.4796 share of SPX's common stock, par value $10.00 ("SPX Common Stock") (the "Consideration"). The SPX Common Stock component had a value of $36.00, and the total Consideration had a value of $48.00, based on the $75-1/16 closing price on the New York Stock Exchange of a share of SPX Common Stock on February 13, 1998, the last trading date preceding the date of the public announcement of the Proposed Business Combination, and the SPX Common Stock component had a value of $36.12, and the total Consideration had a value of $48.12, based on the $75-5/16 closing price on the New York Stock Exchange of a share of SPX Common Stock on March 5, 1998, the last trading date preceding the date of this Solicitation Statement. At the time the Proposed Business Combination is consummated, the transaction may have a market value that is greater or less than either of those two amounts depending upon the market price of a share of SPX Common Stock at such time. At a total value of $48.12, the Consideration represents a 24% premium over the $38-7/8 price at which a Share closed on the New York Stock Exchange on February 13, 1998, and a 32% premium over the average trading price at which a Share closed on the New York Stock Exchange during the 30 trading days preceding February 17, 1998, the date of the public announcement of the Proposed Business Combination. Immediately following the consummation of the Proposed Business Combination and after giving effect to the issuance of the SPX Common Stock in the transaction, shareholders of the Company (other than SPX) would own approximately 70% of the then outstanding shares of SPX Common Stock.

SPX believes that the Proposed Business Combination would be advantageous to the shareholders of both companies. See "The Proposed Business Combination, the Exchange Offer, and the Merger." The Company, however, in past meetings and correspondence with SPX, has consistently advised SPX that the Company and its Board of Directors have no interest in pursuing discussions with SPX.

The Company has Rights outstanding, issued pursuant to a Rights Agreement dated as of June 30, 1989, between the Company and The Connecticut Bank and Trust Company, N.A., as rights agent (the "Rights Agreement"), which purports to prevent SPX from consummating the Proposed Business Combination without the approval of the Company's Board of Directors. Likewise, Sections 840-845 of the Connecticut Business Corporation Act (the "Connecticut Business Act") governing business combinations (the "Business Combination Statutes") present certain obstacles to the consummation of the Proposed Business Combination absent Board approval. See "Reason to Call a Special Meeting" below.

Consequently, SPX is asking its fellow shareholders to join SPX in executing written demands upon the Company that a special meeting be called and held ("Demands") in order to remove the entire Board of Directors of the Company and elect SPX's nominees to the Board in their place. SPX expects that if SPX's nominees are elected, they will act to facilitate the consummation of the Proposed Business Combination, subject to their fiduciary duties as directors of the Company and the general statutory standards applicable to any person serving as a director of a Connecticut corporation as required by Section 756 of the Connecticut Business Act. In particular, the provisions of Section 756(d) of the Connecticut Business Act require directors of a Connecticut corporation, when considering a business combination such as a plan of merger or share exchange, to consider the interests of constituencies other than shareholders, including creditors, customers, suppliers, employees and the communities in which any office or other facility of the corporation is located. SPX's three nominees who are also executive officers of SPX, if elected to the Company's Board of Directors, may find themselves faced with a potential conflict of interest due to their current positions with SPX. If that occurs, such directors will act in compliance with law, including the aforementioned provisions of the Connecticut Business Act and the provisions of the Connecticut Business Act relating to directors' conflicting interest transactions.

Under applicable law, the Special Meeting must be held if holders of outstanding Shares representing in the aggregate at least 35% of all the votes entitled to be cast on any issue proposed to be considered at the Special Meeting demand in writing that a special meeting of shareholders be held. According to a shareholder list provided to SPX by the Company, as of February 17, 1998, the Company had 63,248,939 Shares outstanding. SPX owns 1,150,150 Shares, or approximately 1.82% of the outstanding Shares.

This Solicitation Statement and the GOLD DEMAND CARD are first being mailed or furnished to the Company's shareholders on or about March 6, 1998.

AT THIS TIME SPX IS SOLICITING YOUR WRITTEN DEMAND THAT A SPECIAL MEETING OF SHAREHOLDERS BE CALLED AND HELD. SPX IS NOT SOLICITING YOUR PROXY TO VOTE ON THE REMOVAL OF THE EXISTING DIRECTORS OR THE ELECTION OF SPX'S NOMINEES IN THEIR PLACE. ONCE THE SPECIAL MEETING HAS BEEN CALLED, YOU WILL BE SENT SEPARATE PROXY MATERIALS URGING YOU TO TAKE SUCH ACTION. THOSE PROXY MATERIALS WILL CONTAIN SIGNIFICANTLY

MORE DETAILED INFORMATION CONCERNING THE PROPOSED BUSINESS COMBINATION, INCLUDING RELEVANT PRO FORMA FINANCIAL INFORMATION.

IMPORTANT NOTE: If you hold your shares in the name of one or more brokerage firms, banks or nominees, only they can exercise the right with respect to your Shares to make a written demand that the Special Meeting be called and held, and only upon receipt of your specific instructions. Accordingly, it is critical that you promptly sign and date the GOLD DEMAND CARD and mail it in the envelope provided by your broker, bank, or nominee so that they can exercise the right to make a Demand on your behalf.

A registration statement relating to the securities of SPX to be issued in connection with the Exchange Offer has been filed with the Securities and Exchange Commission but has not yet become effective. Such securities may not be sold nor may offers to buy be accepted prior to the time the registration statement becomes effective. This Solicitation Statement shall not constitute an offer to sell or the solicitation of an offer to buy nor shall there be any sale of these securities in any state in which such offer, solicitation or sale would be unlawful prior to registration or qualification under the securities laws of any such state.

. . .

SPX Common Stock trades on the New York Stock Exchange and the Pacific Stock Exchange under the symbol "SPW." On March 5, 1998, the last trading day before the date of this Solicitation Statement, the closing price of a share of SPX Common Stock was $75-5/16.

THE PROPOSED BUSINESS COMBINATION

SPX has proposed to enter into the Proposed Business Combination with the Company pursuant to which the shareholders of the Company would receive for each Share (together with the associated Right) the Consideration in the amount of $12.00 net in cash and 0.4796 share of SPX Common Stock. The Consideration had a total value of $48.00, based on the $75-1/16 closing price on the New York Stock Exchange of a share of SPX Common Stock on February 13, 1998, the last trading date preceding the date of the public announcement of the Proposed Business Combination, and a total value of $48.12, based on the $75-5/16 closing price on the New York Stock Exchange of a share of SPX Common Stock on March 5, 1998, the last trading date preceding the date of this Solicitation Statement. At the time the Proposed Business Combination is consummated, the transaction may have a market value that is greater or less than either of those two amounts depending upon the market price of a share of SPX Common Stock at such time. At a total value of $48.12, the Consideration represents a 24% premium over the $38-7/8 price at which a Share closed on the New York Stock Exchange on February 13, 1998, and a 32% premium over the average trading price at which a Share closed on the New York Stock Exchange during the 30 trading days preceding February 17, 1998, the date of the public announcement of the Proposed Business

Combination. Immediately following the consummation of the Proposed Business Combination and after giving effect to the issuance of SPX Common Stock in the transaction, shareholders of the Company (other than SPX) would own approximately 70% of the then outstanding shares of SPX Common Stock.

At present, it is contemplated that the Proposed Business Combination would be effected by means of (i) an exchange offer in which SPX is offering to pay the Consideration in exchange for each Share (together with the associated Right) validly tendered and not properly withdrawn (the "Exchange Offer"), and (ii) a subsequent merger of a subsidiary of SPX into the Company (the "Merger") in which each Share (together with the associated Right) not purchased in the Exchange Offer would be converted into the right to receive the Consideration. The transaction would be taxable to exchanging shareholders. The Exchange Offer is conditioned upon, among other things, the amendment by the Company of the Rights Agreement to render it inapplicable to the Proposed Business Combination, the Exchange Offer and the Merger, and the inapplicability of the restrictions contained in the Business Combination Statutes to the Proposed Business Combination, the Exchange Offer and the Merger. The Merger would be conditioned, among other things, on the consummation of the Exchange Offer. See "The Proposed Business Combination, the Exchange Offer, and the Merger." SPX has filed exchange offer materials with the Securities and Exchange Commission and will commence the Exchange Offer as soon as the registration statement included in those materials has become effective. With its letter to the Board of Directors of the Company setting forth the Proposed Business Combination, SPX delivered a proposed merger agreement to the Company in contemplation of arriving at a negotiated transaction. That agreement provides for a single-step "cash election" merger of the Company into a subsidiary of SPX in which each outstanding Share would be converted into the right to receive the Consideration (with shareholders able, instead, to elect to receive all cash, in the amount of $48.00 per Share, or all stock, in the amount of 0.6395 share of SPX Common Stock per Share, subject to proration) in a partially tax-free reorganization.

The Merits of the Proposed Business Combination

In SPX's letters to the Company, SPX set forth various benefits of the Proposed Business Combination to the shareholders, customers, suppliers, and employees of the Company and to the constituencies of both companies. See "Background."

Demand for a Special Meeting.

SPX is asking the Company's shareholders to demand a Special Meeting for the following purposes: (i) to repeal any provision of the Company's By-Laws or amendment to the Company's By-Laws adopted by the Board of Directors of the Company or any Committee thereof at any time after April 3, 1997 (the date of the last set of By-Laws publicly filed by the Company) and before the effectiveness of the last of the proposals to be voted on at the Special Meeting; (ii) to vote upon a proposal to remove all of the members of the Board of Directors of the Company; (iii) to vote upon a proposal to amend the By-Laws of the Company to fix the number of directors of the Company at five; and (iv) to elect SPX's five nominees to the Board of Directors of the Company.

Reasons for the Demand.

Despite repeated urgings by SPX to the Chief Executive Officer of the Company and then directly to the Board of Directors of the Company, the Company has steadfastly turned down requests by SPX to meet with and make a presentation to the Company's Board of Directors to discuss any and all aspects of a proposed business combination. The Company has informed SPX that it and its Board of Directors have no interest in pursuing a business combination.

In its February 17, 1998 letter to the Company's Board of Directors, SPX reaffirmed its desire to enter into a negotiated transaction with, rather than to effect a unilateral acquisition of, the Company. However, if the Company's Board of Directors remains adamant in its refusal to enter into discussions with SPX, the only way that the Proposed Business Combination can proceed is for the present members of the Board of Directors of the Company to be removed and SPX's nominees to be elected in their place. See "Reason to Call a Special Meeting." SPX expects that SPX's nominees, if elected as the new Board of Directors, will act to facilitate the consummation of the Proposed Business Combination, subject to their fiduciary duties as directors of the Company and the general statutory standards applicable to any person serving as a director of a Connecticut corporation as required by Section 756 of the Connecticut Business Act.

Proposed Shareholder Action

SPX's Exchange Offer to the Company's shareholders and the merger proposal to the Company are conditioned upon, and will not be effected without, certain action being taken by the Company's Board of Directors. If the current Board of Directors persists in its position that it will not enter into a negotiated transaction with SPX, the only way that SPX's Proposed Business Combination can be effected is for the existing Board to be replaced with SPX's nominees.

Under applicable law, holders of outstanding Shares representing in the aggregate at least 35% of all the votes entitled to be cast on any issue proposed to be considered at the Special Meeting have the right to demand that a Special Meeting be held. By signing and sending the GOLD DEMAND CARD, you are merely demanding that a Special Meeting be called and held. Signing and sending the GOLD DEMAND CARD will NOT give SPX the right to vote your Shares at the Special Meeting.

SPX is not asking in this solicitation that the Company's shareholders remove the existing Board and replace it with its nominees. Thus, the current Board members may still reverse their position and determine to enter into discussions with the Company for a negotiated transaction. HOWEVER, THE FAILURE TO SIGN AND RETURN THE GOLD DEMAND CARD WILL HAVE THE SAME EFFECT AS OPPOSING THE CALL OF A SPECIAL MEETING, IN WHICH EVENT THE PROPOSED BUSINESS COMBINATION WILL NOT BE ABLE TO PROCEED.

Timing; Assistance

We ask that you sign and date the GOLD DEMAND CARD and mail it in the enclosed envelope as soon as possible and, preferably, before March 31, 1998. If you have any questions or need assistance, please call D.F. King & Co., Inc. at (212) 269-5550 (collect) or (800) 758-5378 (toll free).

PURPOSE OF THE SOLICITATION

SPX is soliciting Demands for the Company to call and hold a Special Meeting. SPX has made a proposal for a business combination with the Company, which SPX believes would provide exceptional value to the Company's shareholders. See "The Proposed Business Combination, the Exchange Offer, and the Merger." The Proposed Business Combination, the Exchange Offer and the Merger are conditioned upon, among other things, the Board of Directors of the Company amending the Rights Agreement so as to render it inapplicable to the Proposed Business Combination, the Exchange Offer and the Merger, and the Board taking such other action as may be necessary so that the restrictions contained in the Business Combination Statutes are not applicable thereto. See "Reason to Call a Special Meeting" and "The Proposed Business Combination, the Exchange Offer, and the Merger." The Company has advised SPX that the Company and its Board have no interest in pursuing discussions with SPX. Accordingly, if the Proposed Business Combination is to proceed, the present members of the Company's Board of Directors will have to be removed and new directors elected in their place who will take all action necessary to facilitate the consummation of the Proposed Business Combination, the Exchange Offer and the Merger, subject to their fiduciary duties as directors of the Company and the general statutory standards applicable to any person serving as a director of a Connecticut corporation as required in Section 756 of the Connecticut Business Act.

The purpose of this Solicitation Statement is to solicit Demands from the shareholders of the Company holding outstanding Shares representing in the aggregate at least 35% of all the votes entitled to be cast on any issue proposed to be considered at the Special Meeting, demanding that the Company call and hold a Special Meeting. According to a shareholder list provided to SPX by the Company, as of February 17, 1998, there were 63,248,939 Shares outstanding; based on that number, Demands from holders of an aggregate of 22,137,129 Shares would be required. SPX owns 1,150,150 Shares or 1.82% of the outstanding Shares.

If SPX is successful in this solicitation, the Company will be required to call and hold a Special Meeting at which the shareholders will be asked (i) to repeal any provision of the Company's By-Laws or amendment to the Company's By-Laws adopted by the Board of Directors of the Company or any Committee thereof at any time after April 3, 1997 (the date of the last set of By-Laws publicly filed by the Company) and before the effectiveness of the last of the proposals to be voted on at the Special Meeting (the "By-Law Repeal Proposal"); (ii) to vote upon a proposal to remove all of the members of the Board of Directors of the

Company (the "Proposal to Remove the Directors"); (iii) to vote upon a proposal to amend the By-Laws of the Company to fix the number of directors of the Company at five (the "Proposal to Amend the By-Laws of the Company"); and (iv) to elect SPX's five nominees (the "SPX Nominees") to the Board of Directors of the Company.

. . .

REASON TO CALL A SPECIAL MEETING

The reason to demand that a Special Meeting be called and held is simple. Unless the Board of Directors of the Company takes action to remove certain obstacles, described below, to the Proposed Business Combination, the Proposed Business Combination, the Exchange Offer, and the Merger will not proceed. Thus far, the present Board of Directors of the Company has indicated that it has no interest in pursuing discussions with SPX.

Rights Agreement. Under the Rights Agreement, if SPX were to acquire beneficial ownership of 20% or more of the Shares, unless the Rights are redeemed or invalidated or are otherwise inapplicable to the Proposed Business Combination, each holder of record of a Right (other than SPX) would, upon exercise of the Right, have the right to purchase, at the exercise price of the Right, Shares having a value at the time equal to twice the exercise price. As a result, the Rights could make SPX's acquisition of the Company prohibitively expensive by severely diluting SPX's equity interest and voting power.

The Rights Agreement provides that the Board of Directors may redeem the Rights at any time prior to a person becoming an "Acquiring Person." An Acquiring Person generally means a person who, together with his or her Affiliates and Associates (each term as defined in the Rights Agreement), beneficially owns 20% or more of the Shares outstanding, subject to certain exceptions. Once a person has become an Acquiring Person the Board of Directors may only redeem the Rights if there are "Continuing Directors" in office and a majority of such "Continuing Directors" concur in authorizing redemption of the Rights. A "Continuing Director" means a director, while a member of the Board, who either (A) was a member of the Board prior to an Acquiring Person becoming such or (B) subsequently became a member of the Board, is not an Acquiring Person or its Affiliate or Associate, representative or nominee, and whose nomination for election or election to the Board was recommended or approved by a majority of the Continuing Directors. In any event, the Board of Directors may not redeem the Rights after the tenth day following the day on which a person has become an Acquiring Person.

The Board of Directors may amend the Rights Agreement prior to the earlier of (i) the first date a public announcement is made that a person has become an Acquiring Person, or (ii) the close of business on the tenth business day (or such later date as the Board may determine prior to such time as any person becomes an Acquiring Person) following the commencement of a tender offer or exchange offer which would result in a person becoming an Acquiring Person). Neither of those events has yet occurred. The commencement of the Exchange Offer will result in the Board of Directors of the Company no longer being able to amend the Rights Agreement after the end of the ten business day period unless the Board of Directors takes action to extend such period.

If elected to the Board of Directors of the Company, the SPX Nominees intend to amend the Rights Agreement so that the Rights Agreement will not be applicable to the Proposed Business Combination, the Exchange Offer or the Merger, or, if the Rights Agreement can no longer be amended, to cause the redemption of the Rights, in each case subject to their fiduciary duties as directors of the Company and the general statutory standards applicable to any person serving as a director of a Connecticut corporation as required in Section 756 of the Connecticut Business Act.

Business Combination Statutes. Pursuant to Section 844 of the Business Combination Statutes, a corporation may not engage in any business combination with an "Interested Shareholder" (defined as the beneficial owner of 10% or more of the voting power of a company) for five years following the date on which the Interested Shareholder became such (the "Stock Acquisition Date") unless the acquisition which resulted in the Interested Shareholder becoming such (the "10% Acquisition"), or the business combination, is approved by the board of directors and by a majority of the non-employee directors, of which there shall be at least two, before the date of the 10% Acquisition.

Pursuant to Sections 841 and 842 of the Business Combination Statutes, any business combination with an Interested Shareholder that was not approved by the board of directors prior to the 10% Acquisition must be approved by the board of directors, 80% of the voting power and two-thirds of the voting power not controlled by the Interested Shareholder or meet certain conditions regarding minimum price and type of consideration.

On March 4, 1998, Raised Bill No. 5695 was introduced into the Connecticut House of Representatives, which, if enacted, would (i) amend the Connecticut Business Act to restrict the ability of shareholders of a public company to remove directors, (ii) amend Section 844 of the Business Combination Statutes to require the approval of a majority of "continuing directors," rather than the approval of the board of directors, and (iii) amend Section 842 of the Business Combination Statutes to provide that the failure to obtain approval of a majority of "continuing directors", rather than the failure to obtain the approval of the board of directors, would trigger the requirements of Section 842 discussed above.

If elected to the Board of Directors of the Company, the SPX Nominees intend to approve the Proposed Business Combination, the Exchange Offer and the Merger or seek to take such other action so that the restrictions contained in the Business Combination Statutes will not be applicable thereto, subject to their fiduciary duties as directors of the Company and the general statutory standards applicable to any person serving as a director of a Connecticut corporation as required in Section 756 of the Connecticut Business Act.

Shareholders of the Company are urged to execute the GOLD DEMAND CARD to demand that the Special Meeting be called and held. Making a Demand and causing the Special Meeting to be called and held is not a vote at the Special Meeting or a vote in favor of the Proposed Business Combination. Shareholders will have the opportunity to vote on the Proposal to Remove the Directors and the election of the SPX Nominees at the Special Meeting. Moreover, shareholders will be able to elect whether or not to tender their Shares into the Exchange Offer; execution of a Demand does not constitute a tender of the shareholder's Shares or obligate the shareholder to tender his or her Shares in the Exchange Offer. However, the failure to obtain Demands from holders of the requisite 35% of the outstanding Shares to call the Special Meeting is a dispositive vote against the Proposed Business Combination because without the Special Meeting, the shareholders will not be able to override the Board's refusal to negotiate with SPX and enter into the Proposed Business Combination. THE FAILURE TO SIGN, DATE, AND MAIL A GOLD DEMAND CARD HAS THE SAME EFFECT AS OPPOSING THE DEMAND FOR A SPECIAL MEETING TO BE CALLED AND HELD.

THE PROPOSED BUSINESS COMBINATION, THE EXCHANGE OFFER AND THE MERGER

By letter dated February 17, 1997 to the Company's Board of Directors, SPX has proposed a business combination with the Company. In the Proposed Business Combination, shareholders of the Company would receive for each of their Shares (together with the associated Right) Consideration in the amount of $12.00 net in cash and 0.4796 share of SPX Common Stock, for a total value of $48.00 based on the $75-1/16 closing price on the New York Stock Exchange of a share of SPX Common Stock on February 13, 1998, the last trading date preceding the date of the public announcement of the Proposed Business Combination, and a total value of $48.12 based on the $75-5/16 closing price on the New York Stock Exchange of a share of SPX Common Stock on March 5, 1998, the last trading date preceding the date of this Solicitation Statement. At the time the Proposed Business Combination is consummated, the transaction may have a market value that is greater or less than either of those two amounts depending upon the market price of a share of SPX Common Stock at such time. At a total value of $48.12, the Consideration represents a 24% premium over the $38-7/8 price at which a Share closed on the New York Stock Exchange on February 13, 1998, and a 32% premium over the average trading price at which a Share closed on the New York Stock Exchange during the 30 trading days preceding February 17, 1998, the date of the public announcement of the Proposed Business Combination. Immediately following the consummation of the Proposed Business Combination and after giving effect to the issuance of the SPX Common Stock in the transaction, shareholders of the Company (other than SPX) would own approximately 70% of the then outstanding shares of SPX Common Stock.

The Proposed Business Combination would be effected by means of (i) the Exchange Offer, in which SPX is offering to pay the Consideration in exchange for each Share (together with the associated Right) validly tendered and not with-

drawn, and (ii) the Merger, in which each Share (together with the associated Right) not purchased in the Exchange Offer would be converted into the right to receive the Consideration.

SPX has today filed Exchange Offer materials with the Securities and Exchange Commission and intends to make the Exchange Offer as soon as its registration statement has been declared effective by the Securities and Exchange Commission.

The Exchange Offer will be conditioned, among other things, upon the following:

The Minimum Condition. The number of Shares validly tendered and not withdrawn before the expiration date of the Exchange Offer, together with the Shares owned by SPX and its affiliates as of such time, must represent at least 66-2/3% of the Shares outstanding on a fully diluted basis (the "Minimum Condition"). According to a shareholder list provided to SPX by the Company, as of February 17, 1998, there were 63,248,939 Shares outstanding. Based on publicly available information, as of December 31, 1997, options to acquire 2,044,284 Shares were also outstanding. SPX owns 1,150,150 Shares. See Schedule II. For purposes of the Exchange Offer, "fully-diluted basis" assumes that all outstanding stock options are presently exercisable and exercised.

Based on the foregoing and assuming no additional Shares have been or will be issued after February 17, 1998 (other than Shares issued pursuant to the exercise of the stock options referred to above), and no options, warrants or rights exercisable for, or securities convertible into, Shares have been or will be issued after December 31, 1997, the Minimum Condition would be satisfied if at least 42,378,666 Shares were validly tendered into and not withdrawn from the Exchange Offer.

The Rights Condition. SPX must be satisfied, in its sole discretion, that a Distribution Date has not occurred under the Rights Agreement, and that the Rights have been invalidated or are otherwise inapplicable to the Exchange Offer and the Merger (the "Rights Condition"). See "Reason to Call a Special Meeting - Rights Agreement."

The Business Combination Statutes Condition. SPX must be satisfied, in its sole discretion, that the restrictions contained in the Business Combination Statutes will not apply to the Proposed Business Combination, the Exchange Offer, the Merger or any other business combination to which SPX and the Company are directly or indirectly parties (the "Business Combination Condition").

The Business Combination Condition may be satisfied if the Board of Directors of the Company duly approved the Exchange Offer and the Merger prior to consummation of the Exchange Offer, or if SPX, in its sole discretion, were satisfied that the Business Combination Statutes were invalid or their restrictions were otherwise inapplicable to SPX in connection with the Exchange Offer and the Merger for any reason, including, without limitation, those specified in the Business Combination Statutes.

Financing Condition. SPX must have obtained, on terms satisfactory to it in its sole discretion, sufficient financing to enable the Exchange Offer and the Merger to be consummated. SPX estimates that the total amount of financing that will be required to pay the cash component of the Consideration in the Proposed Business Combination, to refinance outstanding debt of SPX and of the Company, to pay fees and expenses related to the Proposed Business Combination and to provide working capital will be approximately $2.4 billion. SPX has received a "highly confident" letter from Canadian Imperial Bank of Commerce and its affiliate CIBC Oppenheimer Corp. ("CIBC Oppenheimer"), dated February 13, 1998, in which the two entities state that they are highly confident of their ability to raise the financing in the credit markets in an amount sufficient to consummate the acquisition of the Company, refinance existing debt of SPX and the Company, pay fees and expenses related to the Proposed Business Combination and provide working capital. SPX has not had access to, and therefore has not been able to review, any of the documents governing any indebtedness of the Company. Some or all of these documents may contain provisions for acceleration of the Company's indebtedness upon a change in control of the Company. In determining the amount of financing necessary to effect the Proposed Business Combination and in arranging for receipt of the "highly confident" letter with respect thereto, SPX has assumed that all of the indebtedness of the Company would need to be refinanced.

SPX Stockholder Approval Condition. Pursuant to the rules promulgated by the New York Stock Exchange, approval by stockholders of SPX is required prior to the issuance of additional shares of SPX Common Stock if the number of shares to be issued is or will be equal to 20% or more of the number of shares of SPX Common Stock outstanding before the issuance of the additional shares. Since the number of shares of SPX Common Stock that would be required to be issued in the Exchange Offer exceeds such 20%, consummation of the Exchange Offer will be conditioned upon receipt of the requisite approval by SPX's stockholders of the issuance of the shares of SPX Common Stock in the Exchange Offer and the Merger (the "SPX Stockholder Approval Condition"). Under the rules of the New York Stock Exchange, assuming there is a quorum present at the stockholders meeting at which the matter is being considered (consisting of over 50% of the stock issued and outstanding and entitled to be voted at the stockholders meeting), the issuance of the additional shares must be approved by a majority of the votes entitled to be cast by the holders of SPX Common Stock that are present or represented by proxy at the stockholders meeting. SPX has not commenced a solicitation of its stockholders to approve the issuance of the shares in the Exchange Offer and the Merger and does not intend to do so at least until the required number of Demands have been received to call the Special Meeting.

The timing of the consummation of the Exchange Offer and the Merger will depend on a variety of factors and legal requirements, the actions of the Board of Directors of the Company, and whether the Minimum Condition, the Rights Condition, the Business Combination Statutes Condition, the Financing Condition and the SPX Stockholder Approval Condition are satisfied or (if permissible) waived. On January 6, 1998, SPX made its HSR Filing under the HSR Act.

The waiting period under the HSR Act expired at 11:59 p.m. on February 5, 1998. Accordingly, satisfaction of the pre-merger notification and waiting period requirements of the HSR Act is not a condition of either the Exchange Offer or the Merger.

SPX reserves the right to amend the terms of the Exchange Offer and/or the Merger (including amending the number of Shares to be purchased in the Exchange Offer, the nature or amount of the Consideration to be paid in the Exchange Offer and/or in the Merger, and the surviving entity in the Merger) at any time, including upon entering into a merger agreement with the Company. SPX further reserves the right to negotiate and enter into a merger agreement with the Company (and has delivered a draft of such a merger agreement with its February 17, 1998 letter to the Board of Directors (See "Background")) pursuant to which there would be no Exchange Offer but rather a "single-step" merger in which the Shares would be converted into the right to receive the Consideration, or all cash, in the amount of $48.00 per Share, or all stock, in the amount of 0.6395 share of SPX Common Stock per Share, subject to proration, or cash and SPX Common Stock in such other amounts as are negotiated between SPX and the Company; provided that SPX does not presently intend to reduce the aggregate amount of the consideration to be paid in respect of the Shares from the amount of the Consideration proposed to be paid in the Exchange Offer and the Merger, although the taking of certain actions by the Company's current Board of Directors, such as an extraordinary dividend, might lead SPX to reduce the amount of consideration to be paid. SPX has repeatedly stated to the Company's Board and management, including in its February 17, 1998 letter to the Board, that if the Company is able to substantiate more value in the Company, SPX is prepared to recognize such additional value in the context of a negotiated transaction.

A registration statement relating to the shares of SPX Common Stock to be issued in connection with the Exchange Offer has been filed with the Securities and Exchange Commission but has not yet become effective. Such securities may not be sold nor may offers to buy be accepted prior to the time the registration statement becomes effective. This Solicitation Statement shall not constitute an offer to sell or the solicitation of an offer to buy nor shall there be any sale of these securities in any state in which such offer, solicitation or sale would be unlawful prior to registration or qualification under the securities laws of any such state.

In the February 17, 1998 press release announcing the Proposed Business Combination and in certain slides utilized by SPX regarding the Proposed Business Combination, copies of which were filed as supplemental materials to the Preliminary Solicitation Materials of SPX, certain cautions were given regarding the forward-looking statements contained therein. To the extent these materials are deemed issued in connection with the proposed Exchange Offer, it should be noted that the safe harbor provisions of the Private Securities Litigation Reform Act of 1995 do not apply to tender or exchange offers.

SPECIAL MEETING PROPOSALS

If SPX is successful in its solicitation of Demands and a Special Meeting is called and held, the following matters will be proposed for action by the shareholders at the Special Meeting:

Repeal of By-Laws Adopted Subsequent to April 3, 1997. The By-Law Repeal Proposal is designed to prevent the Board of Directors of the Company or a Committee thereof from taking actions, by means of amending the Company's By-Laws, to attempt to nullify the actions to be voted on by the shareholders at the Special Meeting or to create obstacles to the consummation of the Proposed Business Combination, the Exchange Offer and the Merger. According to publicly available information, the most recent version of the Company's By-Laws was adopted on April 3, 1997 and no amendments subsequent to that date have been publicly disclosed. If the Board of Directors of the Company or any Committee thereof has adopted since April 3, 1997, or adopts prior to the effectiveness of the proposals that are to be voted on at the Special Meeting, any amendment to the Company's By-Laws, this proposal would repeal such amendment. The purpose of this amendment is to remove any existing undisclosed obstacles, and to prevent the Board or any Committee thereof from creating new obstacles, to the consummation of the Proposed Business Consummation, the Exchange Offer, and the Merger. Assuming there is a quorum (consisting of a majority of the votes entitled to be cast on the matter (a "Quorum")) at the Special Meeting, the By-Law Repeal Proposal will be adopted, and the By-Laws and By-Law amendments covered thereby will be repealed, if the number of votes cast in favor of adopting the proposal exceeds the number of votes cast against such proposal.

Removal of Directors of the Company. Unless the Board of Directors of the Company takes action to remove certain obstacles, the Proposed Business Combination, the Exchange Offer, and the Merger will not proceed. Thus far, the current Board has shown no interest in negotiating with SPX. . . .

Amendment of the By-Laws of the Company. The Company's By-Laws currently provide that the Board shall consist of not less than three members and not more than 12 members, with the exact number of directors to be determined from time to time by a resolution of the Board. According to publicly available information, the Company currently has nine directors. At the Special Meeting, SPX will propose that the By-Laws of the Company be amended to fix the number of directors of the Company at five by replacing the first sentence of Article II, Section 1, which currently provides that

"The Board of Directors shall consist of not less than three nor more than twelve members, the number to be as the directors shall from time to time direct.",

with the following sentence:

"The Board of Directors of the Corporation shall consist of five members."

Assuming there is a Quorum at the Special Meeting, the By-Laws will be amended if the number of votes cast in favor of amending the By-Laws exceeds the number of votes cast against the amendment.

Election of SPX Nominees as Directors. SPX will propose at the Special Meeting that the shareholders of the Company elect the following persons, all of whom are nominees of SPX, to the Board of Directors of the Company: . . . If the SPX Nominees are elected, SPX anticipates that the SPX Nominees will act to facilitate the consummation of the Proposed Business Combination, including the actions with respect to the Rights Agreement and Business Combination Statutes discussed above (see "Reason to Call a Special Meeting"), subject to their fiduciary duties as directors of the Company and the general statutory standards applicable to any person serving as a director of a Connecticut corporation as required by Section 756 of the Connecticut Business Act. Assuming there is a Quorum at the Special Meeting, directors are elected by a plurality of the votes cast by the shareholders entitled to vote at the Special Meeting. Shareholders of the Company do not have cumulative voting rights.

Each SPX Nominee, other than the three executive officers of SPX, will receive $25,000 from SPX for his services as a nominee for election as a director of the Company, and, if elected, as a director of the Company, and each SPX Nominee will be reimbursed his reasonable out-of-pocket expenses incurred in the performance of his service as a nominee and, if elected, as a director of the Company. SPX has agreed to indemnify each SPX Nominee from and against any losses, claims, charges, liabilities, costs or expenses (including reasonable legal fees and expenses) arising out of any claim, action, suit or proceeding to which the SPX Nominee is or is threatened to be made a party (i) by reason of his being a nominee and a "participant in a solicitation" (as defined in the Securities Exchange Act of 1934) or (ii) arising out of or in connection with his service as a Company director. SPX may, but is not obligated to, obtain insurance policies covering any portion of such indemnification.

SPX does not expect that any of the SPX Nominees will be unable to stand for election if the Special Meeting is held, but, in the event that any vacancy in the slate of SPX Nominees should occur, SPX will name a substitute nominee. In addition, SPX reserves the right (i) to nominate additional nominees to fill any director positions created by the Board of Directors of the Company prior to or at the Special Meeting and (ii) to nominate substitute or additional persons if the Company makes or announces any changes to its By-Laws or takes or announces any other action that has, or if consummated would have, the effect of disqualifying any or all of the SPX Nominees.

If the Special Meeting is called, shareholders of the Company will be furnished proxy materials relating to the foregoing proposals. These proxy materials will contain significantly more detailed information concerning the Proposed Business Combination, including relevant pro forma financial information.

DEMAND PROCEDURES

Under the Connecticut Business Act and the Company's By-Laws, a special meeting of the Company's shareholders may be called by one or more holders of Shares representing in the aggregate at least 35% of all the votes entitled to be cast on any issue proposed to be considered at the Special Meeting. According to the Company's By-Laws, each holder of Shares is entitled to one vote per Share held. According to a shareholder list provided to SPX by the Company, as of February 17, 1998, there were 63,248,939 Shares outstanding. Based on such number and the fact that SPX owns 1,150,150 Shares, Demands from holders of an aggregate of at least 20,986,979 Shares in addition to SPX will be required to call the Special Meeting. The By-Laws of the Company provide that, upon written request of the requisite holders, the President of the Company shall call a Special Meeting. Following receipt of the requisite Demands, SPX will deliver the Demands to the Secretary of the Company and request that officer forthwith to cause appropriate notice of the Special Meeting to be given to the Company's shareholders entitled thereto.

Under the Connecticut Business Act, a company's by-laws may fix or provide the manner of fixing the record date for one or more voting groups in order to determine, among other things, the shareholders entitled to demand a special meeting (the "Demand Record Date"). The Connecticut Business Act provides that, if not otherwise fixed by the by-laws or the board of directors, the record date for determining shareholders entitled to demand a special meeting is the date the first shareholder signs the demand. On February 17, 1998, SPX delivered its written Demand to the Secretary of the Company. Accordingly, SPX believes that the Demand Record Date is February 17, 1998.

You may revoke a previously executed Demand at any time before the delivery of Demands from holders of Shares representing in the aggregate the requisite 35% vote to the Secretary of the Company by delivering a written notice of revocation to SPX, care of D.F. King & Co., Inc. ("D.F. King"), 77 Water Street, 20th Floor, New York, New York 10005. Although such a revocation is also effective if delivered to the Secretary of the Company or to such other recipient as the Company may designate as its agent, SPX requests that either the original or photostatic copies of all revocations be mailed or faxed to SPX, care of D.F. King, so that SPX will be aware of all revocations and can more accurately determine if and when enough Demands have been received from requisite holders.

Under the Connecticut Business Act, the Connecticut Superior Court may summarily order a special meeting to be held if notice of the special meeting is not given within 30 days after the date the demand is delivered to the corporation's secretary or if the special meeting is not held in accordance with the notice. Moreover, a corporation must notify shareholders of the date, time, and place of the special meeting no fewer than ten nor more than 60 days before the meeting date. The Demands contain a request that the Special Meeting be scheduled 35 days after delivery of the Demands so as to provide shareholders the opportunity to vote on the Special Meeting proposals in a reasonably prompt timeframe.

BY EXECUTING THE GOLD DEMAND CARD AND RETURNING IT TO SPX, YOU ARE NOT COMMITTING TO CAST ANY VOTE IN FAVOR OF OR AGAINST, NOR ARE YOU GRANTING ANY PROXY TO VOTE ON, ANY OF

THE PROPOSALS TO BE BROUGHT BEFORE THE SPECIAL MEETING. MOREOVER, EXECUTION AND DELIVERY OF THE GOLD DEMAND CARD WILL NOT OBLIGATE YOU IN ANY WAY TO SELL YOUR SHARES PURSUANT TO THE EXCHANGE OFFER OR ANY OTHER OFFER.

SOLICITATION OF DEMANDS

This solicitation of Demands is being made by SPX. Demands may be solicited by mail, facsimile, telephone, telegraph, the internet, in person and by advertisements. Solicitations may be made by certain directors, officers, and employees of SPX, none of whom will receive additional compensation for such solicitation.

SPX has retained D.F. King for solicitation and advisory services in connection with this solicitation, for which D.F. King will receive a fee not to exceed $50,000, together with reimbursement for its reasonable out-of-pocket expenses. SPX has also agreed to indemnify D.F. King against certain liabilities and expenses, including liabilities and expenses under federal securities laws. D.F. King will solicit Demands from individuals, brokers, banks, bank nominees and other institutional holders. SPX is requesting banks, brokerage houses and other custodians, nominees and fiduciaries to forward all solicitation materials to the beneficial owners of the Shares they hold of record. SPX will reimburse these record holders for their reasonable out-of-pocket expenses in so doing.

CIBC Oppenheimer is acting as financial advisor to SPX in connection with the Proposed Business Combination, and will act as Dealer Manager of the Exchange Offer, for which services SPX has paid a fee of $500,000 and has agreed to pay additional fees, up to a maximum of $8,500,000 in the aggregate (in addition to any fees which may be paid to it in connection with arranging or participating in the financing of the transaction), a substantial portion of which is contingent upon the consummation of the Proposed Business Combination. SPX has also agreed to reimburse CIBC Oppenheimer for its reasonable out-of-pocket expenses, including reasonable legal fees up to a specified maximum, and to indemnify CIBC Oppenheimer and certain related persons against certain liabilities and certain expenses in connection with its engagement, including certain liabilities under the federal securities laws. In connection with CIBC Oppenheimer's engagement as financial advisor, officers and employees of CIBC Oppenheimer may communicate in person, by telephone or otherwise with a limited number of institutions, brokers or other persons who are shareholders of the Company for the purpose of assisting in the solicitation of Demands for the Special Meeting. In addition, CIBC Oppenheimer, together with CIBC, has issued a "highly confident" letter regarding the financing of the Proposed Business Combination. See "The Proposed Business Combination, the Exchange Offer, and the Merger - Financing Condition." CIBC Oppenheimer will not receive any fee for or in connection with such solicitation activities or for the issuance of such letter apart from the fees which it is otherwise entitled to receive as described above.

The entire expense of soliciting Demands is being borne by SPX. SPX does not currently intend to seek reimbursement of the costs of this solicitation from the Company. Costs of this solicitation of Demands, including the fees referred to above, are expected to be approximately $2,000,000 (exclusive of costs represented by salaries and wages of regular officers and employees) of which approximately $1,150,000 have been incurred to date.

. . .

IMPORTANT

Your action is important. No matter how many Shares you own, please join SPX in demanding that the Special Meeting be called and held by:

MAILING the enclosed GOLD DEMAND CARD TODAY in the envelope provided (no postage is required if mailed in the United States).

If you hold your Shares in the name of one or more brokerage firms, banks, nominees or other institution, only they can exercise the right with respect to your Shares to make a written demand that the Special Meeting be called and held, and only upon receipt of your specific instructions. Accordingly, it is critical that you promptly sign and date the GOLD DEMAND CARD and mail it in the envelope provided by your broker, bank or other nominee so that they can exercise the right to make a Demand on your behalf.

If you have any questions or require any additional information concerning this Solicitation Statement, please contact D.F. King at the address set forth below.

D.F. King & Co., Inc. 77 Water Street New York, New York 10005 Call Toll Free (800) 758-5378 Banks and Brokers Call (212) 269-5550 (Collect)

DEMAND TO CALL A SPECIAL MEETING OF SHAREHOLDERS OF ECHLIN INC.

THIS REVOCABLE DEMAND AND REQUEST IS SOLICITED BY SPX CORPORATION

To the President and Secretary of Echlin Inc.:

The undersigned is a shareholder of common stock, par value $1.00 per share (the "Shares"), of Echlin Inc., a Connecticut corporation (the "Company"). Pursuant to Article I, Section 3 of the Company's By-Laws and Section 696 of the Connecticut Business Corporation Act, the undersigned hereby requests and demands that the President of the Company call a special meeting of the shareholders of the Company (a "Special Meeting") for the purposes described below, fix the date, time and place of the Special Meeting and give notice of the Special Meeting (together with a description of the purposes for which the Special Meeting is being called) to shareholders of the Company entitled to vote thereat.

A. To repeal any provision of the Company's By-Laws or amendments thereto adopted by the Company's Board of Directors or any Committee thereof subsequent to April 3, 1997 and prior to the effectiveness of the last of the proposals to be voted on at the Special Meeting.

B. To consider and vote upon a proposal to remove all of the directors of the Company.

C. To consider and vote upon a proposal to amend the By-Laws of the Company to fix the number of directors of the Company at five.

D. To consider and vote upon a proposal to elect five persons nominated by SPX Corporation to the Board of Directors of the Company.

The undersigned further requests that the Special Meeting be held 35 days after such date as the Company has received demands to call a Special Meeting for the purposes listed above from shareholders who, in the aggregate, hold at least 35% of the Company's outstanding Shares, unless such 35th day is not a business day in Connecticut, in which case it is requested that the Special Meeting be called for the first such business day after such 35th day.

The undersigned hereby authorizes SPX Corporation or any agent thereof to collect and deliver this demand to the Company.

This demand supersedes, and the undersigned hereby revokes, any earlier dated revocation which the undersigned may have submitted to SPX Corporation, the Company or any designee of either.

Dated:_______________ __, 1998

____

(Signature)

____

(Signature, if held jointly)

Title: ______________________

Please sign exactly as your shares are registered. When Shares are held by joint tenants, both should sign. When signing as an attorney-in-fact, executor, administrator, trustee or guardian, give full title as such. If a corporation, sign in full corporate name by president or other authorized officer. If a partnership, sign in partnership name by authorized person. This demand will represent all Shares held in all capacities.

PLEASE SIGN, DATE, AND MAIL IN THE ENCLOSED ENVELOPE PROMPTLY.

[______________________ **end of proxy statement** ___________________________]

18. *Who is filing the proxy statement, the target or the buyer?*

19. *What specifically is SPX asking Echlin's shareholders to vote for in the proxy statement? What percent of votes does SPX need?*

20. *What class/classes of Echlin securities has/have voting rights?*

21. *What condition(s) of the Business Combination Statutes must be met for SPX to be able to acquire Echlin? How do these impact SPX?*

22. *What defense mechanism does Echlin have against unwanted takeover attempts? How do these hinder SPX's attempt to acquire Echlin?*

23. *Do you think Connecticut is a state friendly to hostile takeovers? Why or why not?*

24. *What organizational form is SPX proposing for its acquisition of Echlin?*

25. *What form of payment is SPX proposing? Is the deal going to be taxable for Echlin's shareholders? At SPX's current share price, how big a premium is it paying to Echlin shareholders? Has SPX filed a registration statement with the SEC? Is its registration effective?*

26. *If the merger is consummated as described, what percent of SPX stock will Echlin shareholders hold?*

27. *The SPX offer is conditioned upon certain things. What are these conditions? For each condition, explain the risk that SPX is trying to mitigate.*

28. *How much financing does SPX estimate it needs to consummate the deal? Has SPX received confirmation that it has access to such funding?*

29. *What is the significance of this clause?*

> *SPX further reserves the right to negotiate and enter into a merger agreement with the Company . . . pursuant to which there would be no Exchange Offer but rather a "single-step" merger in which the Shares would be converted into the right to receive the Consideration, or all cash, in the amount of \$48.00 per Share, or all stock, in the amount of 0.6395 share of SPX Common Stock per Share, subject to proration, or cash and SPX Common Stock in such other amounts as are negotiated between SPX and the Company.*

30. *What matters will SPX propose for action if a special shareholders' meeting is called? Why is SPX proposing each of these actions?*

31. *What will it take to get one of Echlin's current directors removed from the board?*

30

Negotiating the Deal

The bargaining entailed in designing the agreement to merge or acquire can have a material influence on the outcome. Success in M&A is not determined solely by excellent analysis. One must also master the processes of negotiation by which deals are obtained. This chapter outlines some of the considerations in setting a negotiating strategy for the deal.

- To prepare for a merger negotiation:
  - Assess the current strategic position and alternative strategic actions for buyer and target.
  - Value the target using a variety of approaches.
  - Explore your best alternative to a negotiated agreement (BATNA).
  - Decide on an opening and a reservation price—these bound the *range* in which you aim to settle on price.
  - Identify the relevant players and their interests.
  - Anticipate trade-offs.
  - Consider motivations and aspirations.
  - Work through possible negotiation scenarios in advance.
  - Assess the impact of bargaining costs.
  - Check the reputation of your counterparty.
  - Reflect on persuasion, its sources, and its impact.
- The midpoint between the opening and asking prices is often a fair predictor of the settlement price, as long as it falls within the zone of potential agreement (ZOPA). Knowing this effect, a seller might seek to *anchor* the buyer's thinking by quoting a high asking price—this has the effect of elevating the range of prices within which the buyer believes a deal is possible. The use of tactics such as anchoring can influence outcomes.
- How to manage a negotiation:
  - Conduct multi-issue, parallel bargaining, not single-issue, serial bargaining.
  - Distinguish claiming value from creating value.
  - Look for trade-offs.
  - Consider using a strategy of openness.
  - Don't let stalemates simmer.

- Master the tactics (anchoring, making offers, ultimatums, number and rate of change of offers).
- Remember that time matters.
- Turn negotiation into a corporate capability.
- Use contingent payments to bridge a gap between two positions.
- Respect the other party's culture.
- Manage the politics within your own team.

CHAPTER 30—WORKBOOK QUESTIONS

Identify the mistakes in the following situations based on what you have learned about negotiations:

1. *Nova Water is in talks to acquire Seattle Springs, a small water bottler in the Pacific Northwest. Nova and its financial advisers have come to the conclusion that the target is worth between $290 million to $330 million. Seattle Springs and its advisers have settled on a range of $320 million to $350 million. During the negotiations, Nova opens with an offer of $80 million. Seattle Springs' chief gets up without a word and leaves the room. What happened? Why?*

2. *Refer to problem 1. Suppose that instead of opening at $80 million, Nova opens at $330 million. Is this a good strategy?*

3. *Suppose that two other bidders are competing with Nova for Seattle Springs. The sale is to take place through a sealed-bid first-price auction. Nova has hired an investment bank to do a competitor analysis. The bankers are closely acquainted with the bottled water industry and are almost certain that Rings of Saturn, one of the other bidders, will offer a price close to $350 million. The bankers have come to this conclusion based on Rings of Saturn's past bidding patterns and on the value that the bankers think Rings of Saturn can derive from Seattle Springs. Thinking of the amount Nova has already spent putting its bid together, its CEO says, "We've put so much work into this that it would be stupid to abandon the deal now. Go ahead and bid $360 million." As an adviser to the CEO of Nova, what would be your counsel?*

4. *Sea Horse Inc., a large cargo shipping company, is looking to expand its presence in Asia by acquiring a majority position in a Taiwanese shipping concern. Arthur Sprouse, CEO of Sea Horse, flies to Taiwan to meet with CEO Te-Hua Chang. Their meetings go well enough that Sprouse decides to leave the negotiations to his CFO and financial advisers, despite having been advised in advance that Asians place particular importance on rank. Is there any problem with this?*

5. *The CEO and CFO of a large pharmaceutical company are preparing to negotiate with a target. The CFO insists that price, form of payment, and issues regarding the makeup of the board can all be negotiated as a bundle. The CEO*

disagrees, and orders the CFO to negotiate only the price first. Is there any problem with this?

6. *A large soft drink company, fearful of being left behind by the competition, wanted to quickly create a presence in the fast-growing noncarbonated beverages segment. It estimated the cost of building a noncarbonated beverages business was $400 million invested annually over five years. Its cost of capital was 10 percent. However, when word went around that one of the players in the noncarbonated beverages business was looking to sell, the soft drink company initiated discussions. The soft drink company ended up paying $2 billion for the target. Has the soft drink company ignored a basic tenet?*

7. *Dan Settles wanted to acquire a string of distributorships in the Southeastern United States in a "roll-up" strategy. In his first negotiation he behaved in an intimidating, aggressive manner, and was able to acquire the target for a cheap price—the target was a weak player in the market with an owner eager to sell. Settles thought, "The intimidating approach worked pretty well. I am going to adopt that approach in my next negotiations." He boasted to the local newspaper, "I always get the terms I want." The next week, a local trade magazine referred to Settles in an uncomplimentary fashion. What may be the result?*

8. *John Bailey negotiated a definitive agreement that was within the bounds of the range his CEO had instructed him. The seller and Bailey shook hands on the deal. Bailey's CEO had offered no other guidance. When Bailey finished presenting the acquisition terms to the CEO, the latter erupted, "They'll be moving the headquarters to Toledo, Ohio! I can't stand that place! Get that fixed or you're fired."*

CHAPTER 31

Auctions in M&A

An understanding of the basics of corporate auctions is vital to successful bidding in M&A. Different types of auctions will affect the behaviors of buyers and sellers in different ways. M&A practitioners must not only see auctions as rational processes driven by price, but must also be alert to the dynamics of strategy and psychology inherent in auctions.

- An auction is a public event at which an asset is sold through a bidding process to the highest bidder. Auctions in M&A can vary dramatically from this conventional definition of auctions.
- Five methods of sale and their advantages and disadvantages are:

Method	Description	Advantages	Disadvantages
Beauty contest	Interested buyers are invited to present themselves to the target. Choice of buyer is made behind closed doors.	Judges have greater ability to obtain information from buyers.	Slow, opaque, and vulnerable to lobbying.
Lottery	Seller specifies sale price; winner is selected by random drawing.	Speed: quick to set up and conclude.	No price discovery by seller. No chance to evaluate buyer on other criteria such as fit, competence, and so on.
First come, first served	First buyer to show up gets to acquire target.	Straightforward to conclude.	No price discovery or chance to evaluate buyer on other criteria.
Auction	Sale is awarded to highest bidder.	Reveals prices, transparent, fast, draws more potential buyers.	Likely is costly to buyer.
Friendly, noncompetitive negotiation	Buyer persuades target to sell in friendly negotiations.	No hostility or nettlesome events that might hinder integration. Target has greater say in structuring the deal.	No price discovery.

- Auctions may be open versus sealed, single versus double, and common value versus private value. In an open auction bids are made public, while in a sealed-bid auction, only the seller sees the bids. In a single auction, only the buyers bid, while in a double auction, buyers bid and sellers offer prices at which they would be willing to consummate a deal. In a common value auction, the asset being sold has similar use to all buyers. In a private value auction, values differ depending on their uses to the buyer.
- Types of auctions include the English auction, the Dutch auction, the first-price sealed-bid auction, and the second-price sealed-bid auction.

Method	Description	Advantages	Disadvantages
English auction	Open bidding. Asset is sold to highest bidder.	• Price discovery and revenue maximization for seller. • Transparency. • Speed.	• Bidding frenzy may result in overpayment by buyer. • Reduces flexibility for seller. No chance to evaluate buyer on other criteria such as fit, competence, and so on. • Vulnerable to collusion. • "Winner's curse."
Dutch auction	Seller begins with arbitrarily high price and reduces it until a bidder accepts.	• Does not "leave money on the table." • Speed.	• Reduces flexibility for seller. No chance to evaluate buyer on other criteria.
First-price sealed-bid auction	Each bidder has only one chance to offer—and outside the view of other bidders.	• Price discovery. • Speed.	• Bidders have no chance to counteroffer. • Revenues to seller are not maximized.
Second-price sealed-bid auction	Same as first-price sealed-bid auction, but winner pays second-highest price rather than highest price.	• May encourage more bidders and higher prices. • Speed.	• Bidders have no chance to counteroffer. • Revenues to seller are not maximized.

- Auctions can be advantageous because they allow sellers to maximize revenue, motivate buyers to bid with speed and at higher prices, and are relatively fast, fair, and transparent. But the disadvantage of auction is that it reduces the flexibility and discretion of the seller by committing the seller to a specific process. Auctions may also be subject to manipulation by buyers. Finally, auctions may discourage entry by prospective bidders because auctions are so successful in maximizing revenue to the seller.
- In an auction sellers rationally seek to reduce uncertainty about the process and to draw many bidders into the contest. Buyers rationally seek to bend or break the rules to gain some special advantage in the process, using tactics such as pressure, aggressive bids, use of the press, and bluffing and threats.

- An auction is an advisable method of sale if the asset for sale is limited or unique.
- Auctions are not always settled solely by price. Price is just one consideration within the bundle of attributes that constitutes the M&A deal.

CHAPTER 31—WORKBOOK QUESTIONS

1. *If bidders are affiliated with or know each other, what auction method is most advisable to use? Explain.*

2. *Plexus Energy has decided to focus solely on electricity distribution and to wind down its business in power generation. Hence it is selling its generation assets that serve the New York and New Jersey areas. Management believes that given the high concentration of population and businesses in these areas, the assets will be highly coveted by several bidders. What method of sale would you recommend? Explain.*

3. *Selectiv, Inc., seeks to sell a minority equity stake and can identify only two other firms that might be interested in making the investment. Factors other than price are important to the founders: reputation, cultural fit, and past experience. The CEO of Selectiv wonders whether an auction would be the best approach to making the sale. What would you recommend?*

4. *What advantage does a Dutch auction have over an English auction? Explain.*

5. *Why might a second-price sealed-bid auction be more advantageous than a first-price sealed-bid auction?*

6. *An English auction was held recently for the sale of Culpeper, Inc. The winning bidder, Virginia, Inc., wound up paying a very high price—beyond even its reservation price. What is it about auctions that might lead to this outcome?*

7. *Refer to problem 6. After Virginia, Inc. was defined as the winner in the English auction, the two sides entered negotiation of the definitive agreement. What is the power of each side at this round of deal design?*

8. *What would be the strategy of a target that wants to hold an auction? What would be the strategy of a bidder that is faced with the announcement of an auction?*

32

Hostile Takeovers: Preparing a Bid in Light of Competition and Arbitrage

A hostile tender offer ("takeover") begins with an unsolicited offer by a bidder to purchase a majority or all of the target firm's shares. The bidder will set the offer for a particular period of time, price, and form of payment, and may attach conditions to the offer. Economic motives for hostile takeovers may include redirection of underperforming firms and exploitation of synergies.

- An unsolicited offer is one of several tactics aimed at motivating the target's management and board of directors to negotiate with the bidder. Thus, it is part of a buyer's bargaining strategy.
- Takeovers are *games*: This lends the foundation for understanding, analyzing, and designing or repelling hostile tender offers. One can understand these events and the behavior of their participants by studying them as a game. One should try to gain the perspective of the various players in the takeover scenario, their motives and behaviors; master important rules and defenses that constrain the players; and anticipate the paths that outcomes may take.
- The outcome of takeover attempts is highly uncertain. A quarter of takeover attempts succeed; another 45 percent result in the target remaining independent; and the final 30 percent result in the target being acquired by another firm.
- A target may seek to defend itself by searching for a white knight buyer, developing a recapitalization plan, or mounting other defenses.
- A hostile takeover often involves more than just the bidder and the target. Other players include arbitrageurs, free riders, other potential buyers (e.g., white knights and white squires), and factions within the target firm (e.g., managers versus directors, inside versus outside directors, large versus small shareholders).
- The arbitrageur is the consummate economic actor. The arb's outlook is rationalistic, impatient, and always oriented toward value maximization. Once a takeover is announced, arbs become a major influence on the outcome of the contest, typically absorbing available shares in the market and betting that the target's share price will rise.
- Arbs evaluate the likelihood of a deal being consummated and structure an investment position based on that view. The arb will seek to create a hedged position whose risk is determined by the deal rather than by general market

conditions. A typical arbitrage position following a hostile takeover announcement would be to take a "long" position in the shares of the target company and a "short" position in the shares of the bidder—this reflects the typical movement of share prices at the announcement of hostile bids, but the structure also cushions the arb against general movements in the stock market.

- An arb's returns are highly sensitive to the length of the waiting period and the size of the payoff.
- In a takeover attempt with a two-tiered offer, bidders benefit and target shareholders lose by the asymmetric structure of payoffs and the difficulty of taking joint action among target shareholders.
- Target shareholders should be willing to accept a tender offer if the value of tendering is greater than the expected value of not tendering (EVNT).
- EVNT is the expected value of share prices under all possible "not tendering" outcomes, though for illustration we focus on two uncertain outcomes: (1) no shares are tendered to the raider, the takeover fails, and share prices subside to the *ex ante* price; and (2) no shares are tendered to the raider, but they are tendered to a higher competing bidder who buys the firm.
- Hostile bidders should take actions that shorten the time to outcome, that forestall collaboration among target shareholders, that preempt potential competitors, that reduce investor uncertainty about the value of the bid, and that generally pressure the target board to cooperate. The target firm should do the opposite: delay, explore restructuring and white knight bidders, cast uncertainty on the hostile bidder and its bid, and generally pressure the target board not to cooperate.

CHAPTER 32—WORKBOOK QUESTIONS

1. *On October 8, 2002, Arthur Knight announced an unsolicited bid for the Empire State Construction Company. On October 20, a competing bidder entered the contest with a bid that was significantly higher than Knight's. Shareholders who had previously tendered to Knight now wanted to back out. Is this possible? Explain.*
2. *Will an M&A arbitrageur always tender to the bidder with the highest offer?*
3. *What is a two-tiered offer? Why might a bidder resort to a two-tiered offer?*
4. *Explain how a two-tiered offer can be likened to the "prisoner's dilemma."*
5. *As a shareholder, what strategy is best when faced with a two-tiered offer?*
6. In the face of a hostile bid, the restaurant chain Bacon and Eggs announced a recapitalization plan to buy back 30 percent of its shares at $58 per share pro rata among all shares. The stub shares (the shares that remain outstanding after

a share buy-back) are estimated to trade at approximately \$52 per share after the recapitalization is completed. An arb holds 10,000 shares of the company with an average cost of \$51.50.

What is the value of the arb's shares based on the recapitalization plan?

7. *What is a leveraged recapitalization? How does it fend off a hostile bid?*

8. Scott Siegel, manager of an M&A hedge fund, picked up his copy of the *Wall Street Journal* on September 4, 2001, and was greeted by a front-page headline reading "H-P Reaches Accord to Acquire Compaq for \$25 Billion in Stock."[1] The article reported that Hewlett-Packard had agreed to acquire Compaq in a merger-of-equals all-stock deal that valued the latter at around \$25 billion. Each Compaq share would be exchanged for 0.63 share of Hewlett-Packard. The previous trading day, Hewlett-Packard shares had declined 19 cents to \$23.32, while Compaq fell 34 cents to \$12.35.
   a. *Calculate the effective purchase price. What do you think of the acquisition premium?*
   b. *The acquisition involved a fierce proxy fight and was not completed until eight months after the date of announcement. Hewlett-Packard's share price on the closing date was \$18.22. Assume that Siegel had purchased 125,000 shares of Compaq at \$12.35 per share, and shorted 32,000 shares of Hewlett-Packard at \$23.32 each on the day the acquisition was announced. Assuming a borrowing cost of 6 percent, calculate the return on Siegel's investment for the holding period and on an annualized basis.*

9. CleanPack, Inc., a manufacturer of flexible packaging solutions, wants to acquire its fiercest rival, EasyPack. CleanPack has determined that its purchase price should not exceed \$114.40 per EasyPack share. The shares currently trade at \$74.10 apiece. EasyPack's officers occupy all board seats and are determined to keep the company within their control. They have drawn up a restructuring plan that, by their estimates, could raise the value of EasyPack to \$117 a share—over a period of two years. An aggressive raider named Lou Barrymore is reportedly going to join the bidding contest. CleanPack thinks Barrymore will place a bid of \$91. CleanPack estimates a 50 percent chance that EasyPack will win the bid, a 30 percent chance that Barrymore will win, and a 20 percent chance that neither scenario will materialize.

   Should CleanPack put in a bid? If so, for how much? Draw a decision diagram facing the investor.

NOTES

1. Nikhil Deogun, Gary McWilliams, and Molly Williams, "Computer Deal: H-P Reaches Accord to Acquire Compaq for \$25 Billion in Stock—Hit by Global PC Slowdown, Firms Aim for Growth in the Services Business—Carly Fiorina Places Her Bet," *Wall Street Journal*, September 4, 2001, p. A1.

CHAPTER 33

Takeover Attack and Defense

Firms employ certain tactics for both takeover attack and defense. In general, the power of tactics is derived from their ability to: (1) accelerate or delay a takeover deal, (2) increase/decrease the costs to the buyer, and (3) change the perceptions of certainty to the investor.

- Use of defensive tactics is widespread: Over 80 percent of public companies have adopted some kind of defenses to deter potential bidders from making hostile takeover attacks.
- Defense tactics empower a target firm's board of directors and management team with increased control options. These are call options on the strategy of the target firm. Defensive tactics increase in value with longer delay and greater uncertainty.
- Tactics of attack attempt to neutralize or nullify defense control options by accelerating outcomes and removing uncertainties.
- The most persuasive takeover attack is a high offering bid; the best defense against takeovers is a high stock price.
- There are two views about the targets of takeovers. The first is that they are underperforming firms that have attracted capital market discipline—this is the *inefficiency hypothesis*, which holds that takeovers are motivated by a desire to correct and profit from target company inefficiency. Another view, the *investment opportunities hypothesis*, suggests that targets simply offer investment and growth opportunities to prospective buyers.
- Many studies portray a strong relationship between the strength of the target's corporate governance and the market reaction to the announcement of takeover defenses. Where the board of directors is strong, independent, and effective, the reaction is positive. Where corporate governance is weak, the reaction is negative.
- Studies also reveal a positive correlation between the alignment of a CEO's interests and the market reaction to takeover defenses. The market reaction is positive when CEO's interests are strongly aligned with shareholders, and negative when they are not.
- Tactics of takeover attack:
  - Purchase of shares directly in the market.
  - Offer directly to the target board of directors.

  - Tender offer directly to target shareholders.
  - Coercive tender offer structures.
  - Proxy contest and consent solicitation.
  - Challenge the target's defenses through litigation.
- Tactics of takeover defense:

  Proactive Defenses
  - Charter amendments.
  - Golden parachutes.
  - Employee stock ownership plans (ESOP) and labor agreements.
  - Poison pills.

  Deal-Embedded Defenses
  - Breakup and topping fees.
  - Toehold stakes.
  - Asset lockup options: the "crown jewels."
  - Stock lockup options.

  Reactive Defenses
  - Litigation.
  - Counter tender offer: "Pac Man."
  - Share repurchases and leveraged recapitalization.
  - Asset restructuring.
  - White knight or white squire.
  - Going-private transaction/leveraged buyout.
  - Greenmail or targeted share repurchase.
- Having a combination of different defenses leads to better defense success than having just one defense tactic.

CHAPTER 33—WORKBOOK QUESTIONS

1. *Why are takeover defenses likely to help shareholders of well-managed "good" firms, and why might takeover defenses harm shareholders of poorly managed "bad" firms? What is the reason for the discrepancy, and what can you deduce from this difference?*

2. *Describe the various forms of charter amendments. What, if any, findings have there been regarding their effects on shareholder wealth, and on the probability of takeovers?*

3. Company A is considering a hostile takeover of Company B. After some initial due diligence, Company A estimates that the intrinsic value of Company B is \$460 million. Company A's investment bank advisory fee is 2 percent of the total deal, and the legal fees are fixed at \$10 million. Based on Company A's

planned bid price of $450 million, it estimates the probability of a successful takeover to be 60 percent.

Given this information, is it profitable for Company A to make an offer for Company B?

4. K-Wells Industries is a target company with a $30 stock price and 1.5 million shares outstanding. Currently, it has a poison pill in place, which allows investors to buy $200 worth of shares for each share that they own. The shares could be purchased at an 80 percent discount to the prevailing the market price of the stock. The poison pill will be triggered when a shareholder purchases 12 percent or more of K-Wells Industries' stock.

   Please estimate the total economic dilution to the raider from triggering the poison pill. (The Excel spreadsheet "Poison Pill Dilution.xls," found on the CD-ROM, can assist in computing the raider's dilution.)

34

The Leveraged Restructuring as a Takeover Defense: The Case of American Standard

The leveraged restructuring is a classic defensive response to hostile takeover bids. The aggressive use of debt financing can create value through the exploitation of debt tax shields. But it also increases default risk. The net impact of the restructuring on the takeover attempt is to raise the floor for bidding. Used in combination with other defenses, the restructuring can help to form an effective deterrent to takeover.

- Successful defense against hostile takeover attempts does not depend entirely on preestablished defenses. How well a target company employs defensive tactics *in response* to the attack has a large influence on the overall success of the defense. A company can protect itself against a hostile takeover bid with various defense tactics that can be employed simultaneously or in succession.

- As outlined in Chapter 33 of the main text, the panoply of defensive tactics includes defenses that can be established in advance, such as the poison pill and golden parachute. Leveraged restructurings include leveraged recapitalizations and leveraged buyouts—these are typically undertaken in response to an announced attack. As Black & Decker Company's hostile takeover attack of American Standard illustrates, defense strategies such as parachutes, pension lockups, and poison pills are not "bullet-proof" because they are all subject to judicial review. These "shark repellent" defenses do buy time for a target's management to develop other alternatives to the raider's bid.

  - To date, a golden parachute has never defeated a hostile bid. Nevertheless, more than 350 firms of the Fortune 500 have golden parachutes. Having a golden parachute marginally raises the takeover cost, creating an additional hurdle for a buyer. And it keeps management on board during difficult times. A company making a hostile takeover attempt can sue to disarm a golden parachute. Black & Decker made such a suit against American Standard, which resulted in a temporary immobilization of the parachute.

  - There has been no instance thus far in which the target of a hostile raid has swallowed a poison pill. Like the golden parachute, the poison pill can be contested. Black & Decker sued to challenge American Standard's poison pill and successfully disarmed this defense tool in court. Thus, while poison pills are "showstoppers" in the sense that they have never been deliberately triggered, they are not invulnerable.

- A management buyout (MBO) is a going-private transaction whereby a company's management team purchases the company with funds that are mainly borrowed. MBOs allow companies to keep information private and save on public reporting costs. With MBOs, equity shares become illiquid securities. Evidence shows that the announcement of MBOs and leveraged recaps is associated with positive abnormal returns to target shareholders. A few sources of value creation include:
  - Substantial increase in corporate leverage, which affords the company the benefits of increased debt (i.e., tax shield).
  - Reduction in agency costs through the realignment of interests between managers and shareholders.
  - Improvements in operating efficiency and sale of redundant assets.
- Leveraged recapitalizations (discussed in Chapters 13 and 20 of the main text) can be viewed as synthetic MBOs that provide similar benefits to shareholders without taking the company private. The prerequisites for executing a leveraged recapitalization include these:
  - The target company must have substantial unused debt capacity.
  - The proposed restructuring must be able to provide the value that the target might have realized through synergies with takeover bidding companies.
  - The target management team must be highly effective.
- With all forms of leveraged restructuring, the target company must be able to finance a sizable amount of debt. For the recapitalization, the debt finances an extraordinary dividend or share repurchase. In a leveraged buyout, the company must be able to sustain the debt financing, *and* management must be able to finance its equity purchase and assume the related risks.

CHAPTER 34—WORKBOOK QUESTIONS

1. *Why did American Standard decide to restructure?*
2. *Why can one view a leveraged recapitalization as a "synthetic MBO"?*
3. *Why are the wealth effects for shark repellent defenses and leveraged restructurings vastly different?*
4. *Some corporate advisers argue that it is important for companies to erect elaborate defenses as a precaution against unforeseen takeover bids. Is the case of American Standard consistent with this view? Why or why not? What might be a counterargument?*

5. This question is based on the American Standard case, discussed in Chapter 34 of the main text. In order to solve this problem, you will need to make the following assumptions:

   - Suppose that management contemplates a defensive leveraged restructuring under which it issues debt and pays a one-time dividend in cash equal to the amount of the new borrowing.
   - American Standard can borrow $1,486,201,000 in new debt.
   - The maximum amount of debt the firm might be able to borrow is equal to six times its market value of equity outstanding.
   - The firm's marginal tax rate is 37.5 percent.
   - The tax shield equals the tax rate times total debt resulting from the deal.
   - American Standard's shares were trading at $50 before the takeover announcement.

Also suppose the following financial information:

American Standard's Balance Sheet
Prior to Black & Decker's Hostile Bidding
for American Standard (January 1988)

Current assets	$1,347,954
Property, plant, and equipment	$ 912,772
Goodwill	$ 55,700
Other assets	$ 81,812
Total assets	$2,398,238
Current liabilities	$ 897,790
Long term debt	$ 279,506
Deferred taxes	$ 370,316
Total liabilities	$1,547,612
Preferred stock	$ 1,046
Common stock	$ 837,722
Other	$ 11,858
Total shareholder equity	$ 850,626
Total shareholder equity and liabilities	$2,398,238
Number of outstanding shares	30,962,513
Share price	$ 50.00
Tax rate	37.5%

[This spreadsheet can be found in the folder "Key Spreadsheets from the Workbook" located on the CD-ROM.]

With this information, complete the following:

a. *Calculate the value of the restructuring to American Standard's shareholders.*

b. *Next, recalculate the amount of debt that American Standard must borrow in order to fund a recapitalization plan that will defend against Black & Decker's various increasing bids (of $65, $68, $73, $77) after the initial bid of $56.*

c. *In light of your answers to problem 5b, to what extent is it true that a firm's unused debt capacity is an antitakeover defense?*

35

Communicating the Deal: Gaining Mandates, Approval, and Support

Effective deal presentation promotes good corporate governance. Failure to communicate a transaction effectively to investors and decision makers may result in uneconomic deal outcomes. The timing, depth, and focus of deal presentations affect investor perceptions, as well as the ability of senior managers and boards of directors to evaluate the transaction.

- There are four classic kinds of deal presentations: (1) a "concept" presentation to a CEO or senior executive seeking approval to begin negotiations; (2) a formal presentation to a firm's board of directors seeking approval for negotiated terms; (3) an announcement of the deal to the financial markets; and (4) presentation of the deal to employees.
- Usual challenges to effective presentation include:
  - *Conflicting objectives.* Start with a clear sense of what you are trying to accomplish with the deal presentation. Often you will uncover aims that may conflict, such as achieving transparency and preserving flexibility.
  - *Differing perspectives.* You and your audience may bring different points of view to the presentation. It is important to anticipate the impact of these differences.
  - *Balancing secrecy and disclosure.* Secrecy is important in the early stages of transaction development in order to preempt competitors (e.g., rival bidders) and to avoid unnecessary volatility in the capital markets. However, secrecy until consummation of the deal is not advisable. Instead, target and buyer firms ought to disclose the transaction at the point in time that the consummation of the deal looks probable. Deal presenters need to balance between telling too much and too little.
  - *Bandwidth.* Humans are limited in their ability to absorb information. Therefore, a deal presenter should edit information about the deal, and focus on the aspects that matter.
  - *Objectivity versus advocacy.* Sometimes, deal presenters become invested in the goal of gaining acceptance for their particular deal rather than in ensuring that the right decision is made or that the deal is value-enhancing.
  - *Market expectations.* In presenting a deal to shareholders, one has an opportunity to communicate with investors and shape expectations in the public arena.

- All communications should be guided by prudence, ethical norms, and the law.

Summary Comparison of Types of Deal Communications

	Concept Proposal	Board Presentation	Public Announcement	Employee Communication
Key audience	CEO	Independent directors	"Lead steer" investors	Managers, supervisors, rank-and-file employees
Predominant interest of the audience	Fit with his/her vision; resource allocation.	Execute well duties of loyalty and care.	Economic insight on which to base trading intentions.	"Me issues"; rationale for the deal: Why us? Why now?
Focus of communication	An opportunity; themes; the payoff. Key issues are strategy, valuation, and setting negotiation goals.	A definitive agreement. Key issues are valuation, implications for stakeholders, and strategy.	Either letter of intent or definitive agreement. Key issues are deal terms, motives, and probabilities.	Letter of intent or definitive agreement, eventually followed by integration plan for the two organizations; maintaining a customer focus during the transition.
Objective	To gain a mandate to proceed, with targets for negotiation.	Board approval to consummate the deal.	Shape capital market reaction.	Resolve uncertainty; build support for the merger; motivate.
Special challenges	Balance analysis and advocacy: presenter needs approval and joint thinking on goals.	Can't say too much; limited bandwidth; risk of lawsuit for carelessness, disloyalty.	Can't say enough; risk of lawsuit for misrepresentation.	Greed and fear: dealing with threats and opportunities to employees posed by the merger. Rumors. Distraction caused by the deal, and resulting effect on productivity.
Tactics	Focus on the optionality in the concept development effort: explore uncertainty and its drivers, along with valuation.	Focus on the board's stakeholder perspectives, and their natural concern for risk exposure.	Speak to concerns of the lead steers, not just the average investor or other interested groups.	Build trust. Address concerns of employees through many channels; intervention by direct managers. Respond promptly to rumors. Be proactive in communicating facts.

CHAPTER 35—WORKBOOK QUESTIONS

Part I: What's Wrong with This Picture?

1. Consider the following:

   a. *At an industrial corporation, a senior associate in the strategic planning group is about to present to the CEO a proposal to acquire what he thinks is the "perfect target." He has worked hard all week to finally be ready with his presentation—a PowerPoint slide show containing 100 slides. In addition, a few days ago he submitted to the CEO a 387-page "pitch book" containing details about the target.*

   b. *At another company, a planner from the strategic business group has just started presenting his proposal to the CEO and other executive officers of the firm. He begins his presentation with a brief background about the potential target, followed by valuation, pricing, financial impact of the deal, and then its strategic rationale.*

Part II: Vignettes

1. You are the director of business development for Perra Delight, a consumer products company, and you have developed a merger idea. A month ago, the former CEO, Leroy Lazar, with whom you had worked for 10 years, retired and left the firm. The new CEO, Hillary Madison, whom you did not know prior to her arrival at the company, comes from a successful competitor firm. Madison has a good reputation and credibility in the industry, but she is younger than the prior CEO and thus perhaps a bit more ambitious—someone with her eye on becoming one of the "best CEOs."

   a. *What challenges might you face in presenting your merger idea to the new CEO?*

   b. *Could there be any greater opportunity for a successful deal presentation to Madison (versus one that would have been made to Lazar)? Why or why not?*

   c. *What could you do to increase the probability of a successful deal presentation to Madison?*

2. You are the director of business development for the Wermelt Wonders Corporation, which will be coming out with a press release announcing its merger with Daneker Diamonds. Right now, you are in a meeting with Wermelt's CEO, the CFO, director of investor relations, and the company's PR director. Collectively, you are deciding what to put in the press release, and specifically how much to include. The director of PR would like to limit the amount of information in the release. The CFO and the CEO are in disagreement on whether they should disclose certain financials; furthermore, the CEO believes the CFO's projections are overly conservative.

   What would you advise?

Part III: Cases

Hewlett-Packard and Compaq

On September 4, 2001, Compaq and Hewlett-Packard (HP) held their first joint investor presentation, in which they announced the merger between the two companies. The presentation—made in person and also available via conference call and webcast[1]—was delivered primarily for the investment community rather than for press reporters and the general public.

The intent of the investor presentation was to build on the press release from the previous day and to highlight what a few of the two companies' top executives (namely Carly Fiorina, HP chairman and CEO, and Compaq's chairman, Michael Cappellas) believed to be important aspects of the deal.

Read the following informal excerpts from the presentation (commentary from Carly Fiorina and Michael Cappellas) and then answer the questions that follow.

CARLY FIORINA: Michael and I first met at a public policy conference . . . and we figured out quickly that not only did we agree on public policy . . . but we also had a common vision of where the [technology] industry was going.

MICHAEL CAPPELLAS: Yes, I actually remember we were in such agreement. . . .

CARLY FIORINA: And we agreed on just about everything, I recall. . . .

MICHAEL CAPPELLAS: As [we] started to look at the vision of what we were doing, where we believe the Internet is going fundamentally, what the strategies were—it was clear that they overlapped. Then [we got] to the cultural issues—that the two companies believe in innovation, really painting the foundation, engineering excellence and a real drive. So in addition to the strategies, it was pretty clear that the culture was the same.

CARLY FIORINA: I think we realized very early on that we saw eye to eye, that we liked and respected each other, and I think it's going to be a terrific team. Not just at the top, but throughout the entire organization.

Michael mentioned culture. And, of course, culture is essential to a successful integration. There has been much written about the culture and the values of both of our companies. And, in fact, I think we've seen how closely those cultures and values are aligned just in how our teams worked together over the last several months.

I think as well I mentioned we share a commitment to innovation, to invention, to engineering excellence and prowess. We share a deep contribution to communities, and we share common values of how you ought to treat people: with respect, trust, and integrity.

We have a common strategy—this is not about a change in strategy. This is about a leapfrog move to accelerate our ability to continue on the strategy that we have been on, and the one Compaq has been on for the last two years as well.

If you go back and look at the presentations each company has made separately to the financial community over the last 18 months in particular, I think you will see a great deal of commonality. . . .

I want you to know that we take the integration challenge exceptionally seriously. This is a massive integration effort. One could argue it is the largest integration effort in the technology industry. And we are trying to integrate in a very difficult overall environment. . . .

We have a comprehensive integration plan in place. We've thought carefully about organizational rationalization. And we intend to be decisive. We intend to be disciplined and aggressive. And we intend to move with speed.

We have a set of early decisions already made, and we've identified the managers that we think are absolutely critical to this going forward. We already have retention plans in place. We will be appropriately leveraging outside expertise. . . . Each of us worked with McKinsey and Accenture to lay out what a mathematical model of the deal would look like. So we've done a lot of work and a lot of detailed planning before we ever said that this is a transaction that we were prepared to do.

We have chosen our executives very carefully.

We are helped by the fact that we have similar organizational models already in place: a go-to-market or front-end organization and a product development or back-end organization. And we are helped by the fact that our sales forces are structured around country management.

We have the same kind of structure around what we would call customer business managers, lead account reps to a customer, and then product specialization and technical consulting support underneath.

That helps with integration.

MICHAEL CAPPELLAS: And one of the interesting things as you think about the potential of this company, remember, both of us have not been sitting still for the last weeks and quarters. There is an awful lot of work being done, and what will now start to show up is the work we've accomplished. And I actually believe and think you'll start to see the things we've done as we've been bringing the companies together; you'll start to see not only the benefit of what we will do, but the benefit of what we have done. . . .

1. *Analyze the comments made by Fiorina and Cappellas. Based on the excerpts, what do you think they tried to convey to their shareholders, and how do you think they tried to "sell" the deal in the investor presentation?*

2. *The HP-Compaq merger was announced on September 4, 2001. Between the opening and closing of stock trading that day, HP's stock price fell from $20.40 to $18.33, a 10 percent drop in value. Does the drop in stock value convey a failure of HP-Compaq's deal presentation on September 4?*

Smucker

1. *Here is a press release from the J. M. Smucker Company[2] announcing its acquisition of the Jif and Crisco brands from the Procter & Gamble Company. As a shareholder, would you have thought this press release to be effective? Why? What does it do well or not do well? What themes and expectations are created in investors' minds as a result of these announcements?*

2. *The day the deal was announced, the chairman and president of Smucker also issued a memo to employees, informing them of the deal. The memo is reproduced here following the press release. What do you think of this move by the Smucker executives? What do you think of the memo?*

J.M. SMUCKER ANNOUNCES STOCK DEAL WITH P&G FOR JIF AND CRISCO[3]

—Smucker combines three #1 classic food brands—

ORRVILLE, Ohio and CINCINNATI, Ohio, October 10—The J.M. Smucker Company (NYSE: SJM) and The Procter & Gamble Company (NYSE: PG) today announced a definitive agreement to merge the JIF peanut butter and CRISCO cooking oils businesses into The J.M. Smucker Company in an all-stock transaction.

Prior to completion, the JIF and CRISCO brands and the associated assets will be spun off from the existing P&G Company and then immediately merged with The J.M. Smucker Company. Procter & Gamble shareholders will receive one share of new J.M. Smucker stock for every 50 shares they hold in Procter & Gamble in a tax-free transaction. Based on Smucker's closing stock price of $25.89 on October 9, 2001, this represents a pre-tax equivalent cash price of $1.0 billion or approximately 1.7 times net sales.

With successful closing of the transaction, Smucker expects its sales to approximately double, to $1.3 billion. For fiscal 2003, the first full year of integration, Smucker projects net earnings before one time costs associated with the transaction to be in the range of $95–105 million, almost three times current levels. This includes a provision for increased marketing support focused on the JIF and CRISCO brands.

Additionally, the Smucker Company said it expects the combined earnings power of the three brands to allow it both to continue its historic strong dividend practice, typically in the range of 40 to 50 percent of earnings, and to pursue new product development and acquisition opportunities while maintaining its investment grade rating profile.

For P&G, the transaction is expected to be slightly dilutive in fiscal 2002, but the company is comfortable with the current range of estimates. Dilution in fiscal 2003 is estimated at 6 cents per share. However, with the potential accretive impact of the pending Clairol transaction, P&G still expects to achieve its earnings goal of double-digit growth in 2003.

EXECUTIVE COMMENTS:

"The combination of these icon brands, SMUCKER'S, JIF and CRISCO—all with number one market positions—creates a new and exciting company with the strongest of positions in both the minds of consumers and in the center aisles of the nation's retail outlets," said Timothy Smucker, Smucker Chairman and Co-CEO.

"Not only is this transaction very accretive to earnings, it provides significant cash flows when coupled with our already strong balance sheet," said Richard Smucker, Smucker President and Co-CEO. "Just as important, it will strengthen our position to acquire other complementary leading food brands, providing opportunity for greater top- and bottom-line growth and clearly enhancing shareholder value."

"JIF and CRISCO are strong U.S. brands but they're no longer a strategic fit for P&G as we focus on building our big brands in core categories," said A.G. Lafley, President and CEO of Procter & Gamble. "At Smucker they will continue to enjoy a prominent position in another one of America's most admired companies, with an over 100-year proven track record of quality brand management."

According to Mr. Lafley, "This structure builds shareholder value very efficiently—a spin-off of JIF and CRISCO assets directly to our shareholders, and the opportunity for them to participate in the future growth of the new J.M. Smucker Company."

"Both these brands are an outstanding fit for Smucker," said Timothy Smucker. "CRISCO is very profitable and our singular focus on food will accrue to CRISCO'S benefit, and provide us an enabling platform leading to new categories and enhancing vertical integration."

"Combining JIF and SMUCKER'S," Richard Smucker explained, "brings number one brands together in the original, All-American comfort food—peanut butter and jelly. JIF also offers a broad and exciting menu of possibilities for product development and growth."

"In addition to the brands being market leaders, our companies possess similar management and employee cultures, common focus on customers, dedication to the highest standards of quality for consumers, and commitment to continually enhancing shareholder value. That is why both Richard and I, along with our entire board and management team, are so enthusiastic about this deal," Timothy Smucker concluded.

TRANSACTION DETAILS:

This spin-off and merger transaction (a "Revised Morris Trust" structure) effectively manages the tax implications to the parties. Procter & Gamble shareholders will own approximately 53 percent of the newly combined company, which will have approximately 49.3 million shares outstanding. The transaction is subject to regulatory and Smucker shareholder approvals, and the receipt of a ruling from the Internal Revenue Service that the transaction is tax-free to both companies and their shareholders. The transaction is expected to close during the second calendar quarter of 2002.

Following the completion of the transaction, the expanded company will include the JIF and CRISCO manufacturing plants in Lexington, Kentucky, and Cincinnati, Ohio, respectively, in addition to the existing Smucker facilities. Smucker will offer employment to all employees at these facilities 100% dedicated to these businesses.

TO: All Employees

FROM: Tim Smucker and Richard Smucker

DATE: October 10, 2001

AGREEMENT REACHED FOR JIF AND CRISCO BRANDS[4]

Today The J. M. Smucker Company reached a significant growth milestone in its more than 100-year history. We announced an all-stock transaction with Procter & Gamble for their JIF peanut butter and CRISCO cooking oil brands.

We are extremely excited about the combination of these three American icon brands (SMUCKER'S, JIF, and CRISCO), each with the number one market share position in their respective categories. It will create an even stronger company, doubling our sales to $1.3 billion and more than doubling our profits. Most importantly, this will provide us with a platform for even greater growth in the future.

The JIF and CRISCO brands are extremely compatible with our business. They have the same distribution channels and consumer appeal. All three brands are sold in the "center of the retail store" and complement our existing broker network giving us greater critical mass to serve our customers.

Included in this transaction are the CRISCO production facility located in Cincinnati, Ohio, and the JIF peanut butter plant located in Lexington, Kentucky. These facilities, along with support staff, will add about 450 new employees to the "family" of Smucker.

As we look to the future with this family of leading brands, we would expect our growth to continue to be generated from three major areas: (1) growing the core business and respective share of market of each of the brands, (2) the development of new products, and (3) the acquisition of additional brands. Since this is an all-stock transaction, we are not taking on any new debt, which positions us well for future acquisitions.

The closing of the transaction requires shareholder and regulatory approval, in addition to a private letter ruling from the IRS; therefore, we don't anticipate the transaction will close until our fiscal year's fourth quarter. As you would expect, this has and will require a great deal of effort by many people to complete. We would like to thank everyone involved for their efforts thus far and for the future efforts that will be required for a successful integration into our business.

As noted in our press release, there will be an investor relations conference call and Web cast later this morning. There will be many communication opportunities for our employees, and we would request that you not dial in to the call.

We are very excited to welcome JIF and CRISCO and the employees making these quality products into our family at Smucker.

TIM RICHARD

Raytheon

1. *Here is a press release issued by Raytheon Company, a large defense contractor, announcing a recent acquisition. How does it compare to the Smucker press release? Can you offer an explanation for the differences?*

RAYTHEON ACQUIRES HONEYWELL AEROSPACE AND DEFENCE SERVICES BUSINESS UNIT IN AUSTRALIA[5]

LEXINGTON, Mass., July 25/PRNewswire-FirstCall/—Raytheon Company (NYSE: RTN) announced today that it has acquired the Honeywell Aerospace and Defence Services (HADS) business unit of Honeywell (NYSE: HON) in Australia. With U.S. $20 million in revenue, HADS is a provider to the Australian Defence Forces of aviation life-cycle support operations in the form of avionics maintenance, logistics, and depot operations for fixed wing platforms.

"This acquisition establishes Raytheon as a principal provider of integrated aerospace support services to the Australian Defence Forces," said William H. Swanson, Raytheon chief executive officer and president. "It enhances our capabilities in two of our strategic business areas-Intelligence, Surveillance and Reconnaissance and Precision Engagement."

The terms of the transaction were not disclosed. HADS has become part of Raytheon Australia Pty Ltd, and is aligned with Raytheon Technical Services Company in Reston, Va.

Raytheon Company, with 2002 sales of $16.8 billion, is an industry leader in defense, government and commercial electronics, space, information technology, technical services, and business and special mission aircraft. With headquarters in Lexington, Mass., Raytheon employs more than 76,000 people worldwide.

NOTES

1. *References:* Link to full audiocast/webcast transcript: http://h18020.www1.hp.com/newsroom/presspaq/090401/transcript_investor.html; link to supporting PowerPoint presentation: http://h18020.www1.hp.com/newsroom/presspaq/090401/Investor_Doc.ppt.
2. A global manufacturer of food products. Its primary products are fruit spreads, dessert toppings, peanut butters, frozen peanut butter and jelly sandwiches, industrial fruit products, fruit and vegetable juices, beverages, syrups, condiments, and gift packages. (*Source:* Yahoo! Finance)
3. Press release as filed by Smucker with the SEC on October 10, 2003. Source: www.sec.gov/Archives/edgar/data/91419/000095015201504915/0000950152-01-504915.txt.
4. www.sec.gov/Archives/edgar/data/91419/000095015201504916/0000950152-01-504916.txt.
5. www.prnewswire.com/cgi-bin/micro_stories.pl?ACCT=149999&TICK=RTN&STORY=/www/story/07-25-2003/0001989212&EDATE=Jul+25,+2003.

36

Framework for Postmerger Integration

Postmerger integration is where expectations are fulfilled or broken. Failing to recognize integration issues at the bargaining table or in the analytic phase of the work can create enormous problems later on. More importantly, knowing what to do after the definitive agreement is signed is vital to the success of the deal.

- One must decide on an *integration strategy* early in the merger proceedings. Integration strategy must follow business strategy. The business strategy and merger rationale should be used as guides for designing integration strategy. Consider the strategic setting, turbulence, and motives for the deal. Integration strategy entails making a choice as to the level of autonomy, interdependence, and control of the target:
  - Autonomy is often reflected in the preservation of a culture, the continuation of a leadership team, and independence of decision making.
  - Interdependence is reflected in how closely the target meshes with the buyer's value chain and operations.
  - Control is reflected in the degree to which systems are imposed—financial control systems, quality control systems, governance mechanisms, and so on.

  Chapter 36 of the main text offers four integration strategies based on the choices made about autonomy, interdependence, and control. (See graphic on following page.)
- Integration planning is the first phase in integration implementation. Some factors to consider are:

Talent and intellectual capital	Who are the key employees? How do we retain them? What layoffs are necessary to achieve synergies and economies of scale from the combination? What strategic capabilities will be required by the firm for the future? How do we retain the knowledge base necessary for those capabilities? Should workforces be kept separate or be combined?
Production, logistics, and supply chain management	Where can we achieve cost reductions? How we can streamline operations to achieve those reductions? Should facilities be shut down? Should production processes be integrated or kept separate? Will suppliers be retained? What improvements can be made in the supply chain? Can customer service be integrated? How? What investments are necessary to achieve cost reductions?

(Continued)

Financial controls and management information systems	Are the reporting systems of the target congruent with ours? Do their reporting systems provide the information we need to advance our strategy? What must be done to align their systems with ours? What investments are necessary to achieve alignment? Which systems need to be phased out?
Compensation systems	Are our compensation systems aligned with those of the target? Do we want our compensation systems to be aligned with those of the target—might their culture be more responsive to a different compensation system than ours? How do we communicate any necessary adjustments in compensation?
Space	Should work spaces be integrated? What factors must we consider in work space design? What atmosphere do we want the work spaces to have?

- Execution is the second phase of integration implementation. Its success depends on:
  - Speed and decisiveness.
  - Communication.
- Seven deadly sins to avoid in postmerger integration, according to Michael Sweeney of UBS:[1]
  1. Poor due diligence (financial and human capital).
  2. Delay the start of integration and drag out the finish.
  3. Allow divergent initiatives.
  4. Take too long to answer "me" issues.

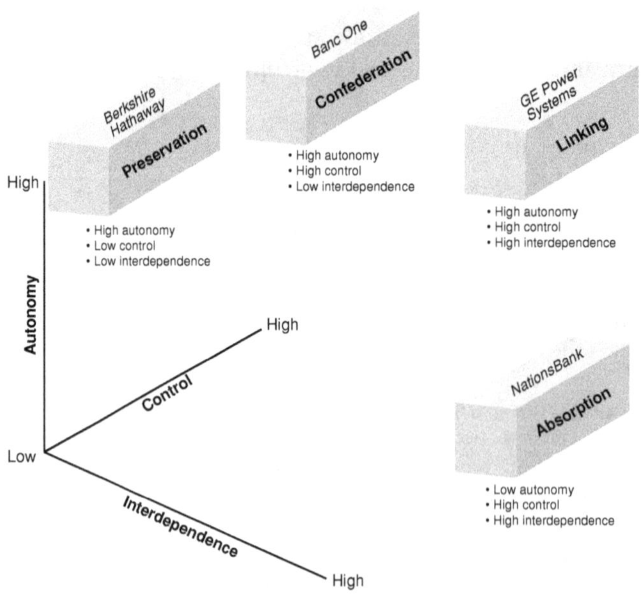

5. Undercommunicate.
6. Put no one in charge.
7. Ignore project management disciplines.

CHAPTER 36—WORKBOOK QUESTIONS

Part I: Integration Strategy

Chapter 36 of the main text discusses four integration strategies for postmerger integration: preservation, confederation, linking, absorption.

In each of the following cases, what would you recommend as the best integration strategy? What considerations about autonomy, interdependence, and control led to your recommendation?

1. In 1983, Brown-Forman Distillers, a U.S.-based manufacturer of top-selling whiskey brands, acquired in a hostile takeover Lenox China & Crystal, a maker of tabletop and other consumer products. Brown-Forman's strategy was to assemble a portfolio of businesses around the focus of high-quality consumer products with strong brands. John Chamberlin, chairman and CEO of Lenox, cited the acquisition as a poor fit, saying, "Lenox is a design company with 'aesthetics and mystique' that sells durables with a long purchase cycle and substantial department store distribution channels. . . . In contrast . . . Brown-Forman is a 'packaging and taste' company that makes consumable products with repeat-purchase cycles and liquor-store distribution channels."[2]

2. In September 2001, Hewlett-Packard Co. (HP) announced it would acquire Compaq Computer Corp. in a $25 billion stock swap transaction. The deal would bring together the world's second (Compaq) and third (HP) largest computer makers. Both companies were struggling to keep costs down and to stay competitive amidst a PC industry that had become commoditized. Cost savings were therefore a major rationale for the deal. The savings were to come from layoffs, office closures, shedding duplicate product lines, and consolidating supply chains. Some observers noted that it would be hard to create a unified culture within the merged entity. HP was known to have an entrepreneurial, "shoot-from-the-hip" culture, whereas Compaq had a reputation as a bureaucracy. During one HP reception an observer commented, "I could tell H-P folks from the Compaq folks right away. The former Compaq employees, in suits and ties, huddled on one side of the room. Polo-shirted H-P staffers stood on the other." The observer joked, "Those guys are going to kill each other."[3] However, Carly Fiorina, CEO of the combined company, asserted that melding the two cultures would "go smoothly, because there are many parallels between them."[4]

3. In May 1998, German firm Daimler-Benz AG and U.S.-based Chrysler Corp. announced a merger of equals that would create the fifth largest automotive company in the world by sales. A primary motive for the deal was the potential for cross-selling—the merger would enable Chrysler to sell more cars in Europe,

and Daimler to sell more Mercedes cars in the United States, where it had a less than 1 percent share.[5] The merger would create a global manufacturer with products ranging from economy cars to luxury sedans to sport utility vehicles to minivans—the merging companies had distinctly different product lines whose identities the CEOs would seek to maintain. Due to the different product lineups, assembly lines would be kept separate, no plants would be closed, and dealerships would not be combined. Dual headquarters would be maintained in Stuttgart, Germany, and Auburn Hills, Michigan. Cost reductions would be achieved by utilizing economies of scale in manufacturing, purchasing, new product development, and logistics. Jürgen Schrempp and Robert Eaton, chief executives of Daimler and Chrysler respectively, would be co-chairmen and chief executives of the merged company, with Eaton stepping down after three years. Many observers commented that melding the cultures would be difficult. Said one newspaper, "[Daimler] has been fed fat on success. . . . [Chrysler] still sees itself as scrappy following a brush with bankruptcy."[6] Other differences included corporate structures and the role of labor unions.

4. In July 1995, Walt Disney Co. announced it would acquire Capital Cities/ABC Inc., in what was then the second-largest merger in U.S. history. The motive for the deal was to integrate entertainment programming with distribution. Walt Disney would bring to the table its movies and television productions among others, while Capital Cities/ABC would bring its number one rated television network, which distributed programming to 225 affiliates reaching 99.9 percent of U.S. television households. Capital Cities/ABC also owned 80 percent of sports channel ESPN, which reached 67 million local households and 100 million households overseas.[7] An observer commented, "With one stroke of the pen, the ABC network is now assured [of] its supply of programming . . . and at the same time Disney has assured shelf spaces for its TV production."[8] Because the two companies' businesses were complementary, there were to be neither staff reductions nor shedding of assets. Michael Eisner, CEO of Disney, said, "None of the assets are duplicative; they all mesh together."[9]

5. In August 1995, Pharmacia AB (Stockholm, Sweden) and Upjohn Co. (Kalamazoo, Michigan) announced a merger of equals that would create the ninth largest pharmaceutical company in terms of worldwide drug sales. The firms had previously ranked 19th and 20th, respectively. Pharmacia was a niche drug manufacturer specializing in cancer and cardiovascular, infectious, and neurobiological diseases,[10] while Upjohn had several high-profile products including antibaldness treatment Rogaine, anti-anxiety drugs Xanax and Halcion, and pain reliever Motrin.

   Of late, Upjohn had been in a worrisome situation due to both a weak pipeline of drugs and patent expirations—four of its top drugs had lost U.S. patent protection in the prior three years.[11] In contrast, Pharmacia had a strong research pipeline, with a host of new products nearing the end of clinical trials and poised for launches. Marketwise, Upjohn had only a small presence in Europe, and Pharmacia had a relatively small presence in the United States. Jan Ekberg, chairman of Pharmacia, said, "Through the merger, Pharmacia gains access to Upjohn's strong U.S. sales, marketing, and distribution infrastructure to fully exploit the sale of Pharmacia products, while Upjohn gains additional sales and marketing support in Europe."[12] The merged company would be headquartered in London, although there would also be operational headquarters in Stockholm, Kalamazoo, and Milan. Only the chief executive and corporate officers would be based in London.[13]

Part II: Integration Implementation

1. *You are managing the postmerger integration for a company and notice that the progress in one division seems a bit behind schedule. The division manager pleads with you to understand—after all, the integration process just started one month ago; one must plan these things carefully and work out the details before moving. Do you agree with the manager? Why or why not? If you do not agree, what would you tell him?*

2. *You are part of a team of consultants hired to make sure integration is kept on target for a newly merged company. Several days into the job, you notice a palpable difference between two sales divisions. In division A, the atmosphere is optimistic and jovial, the team members are excited about the new direction of the company, and people from both the old target and buyer firms blend well. In division B, morale seems to be low, especially among employees of the target firm. They say they have no idea as to how the merger will impact their division. They also have neither seen nor been addressed by the new CEO. What might have gone wrong here?*

3. *Bank A (buyer) and Bank B (target) recently announced a merger. Each had been highly successful on its own, but trends in the banking industry led each to conclude that merging was the only way to survive. Most of the value would be created from cost synergies—financial and operating control procedures would be harmonized, and duplicate operations would be shed. Both banks had top-of-the-line information systems, but it was important to have only one unified system. The head of the postmerger integration team decided to test both systems for a few months to see which would work better. Do you agree with his strategy? Why or why not?*

NOTES

1. UBS AG internal document, Michael Sweeney, May 31, 2000.
2. "Lenox Rebuffs Brown-Forman Takeover Offer, Adopts Defense," *Dow Jones News Service*, June 15, 1983.
3. Pui-Wing Tam, "Merger by Numbers: An Elaborate Plan Forces H-P Union to Stay on Target," *Wall Street Journal*, April 28, 2003, p. A1.
4. Molly Williams, "H-P's Deal for Compaq Has Doubters As Value of Plan Falls to $20.52 Billion," *Wall Street Journal*, September 5, 2001, p. A3.
5. Brandon Mitchener and Steven Lipin, "Deal Sparks Enthusiasm for 'Global Reach'—Analysts See Team with Little Overlap and Synergies to Exploit," *Wall Street Journal Europe*, May 7, 1998, p. 6.

6. Ibid.
7. "Disney, Capital Cities/ABC Agree to Merge; $19 Billion Transaction Will Enhance Shareholder Value by Creating World's Leading Entertainment and Communications Company," *Business Wire*, July 31, 1995.
8. Laura Landro et al., "That's Show-Biz: Walt Disney's Merger with Cap Cities/ABC Stuns Global Industry," *Wall Street Journal Europe*, August 1, 1995, p. 1.
9. "News Roundup: Walt Disney–Cap Cities Merger Developments," *Dow Jones Newswires*, July 31, 1995.
10. "Pharmacia-Upjohn to Merge: Everybody Seems Happy," *Genesis Report-Rx*, vol. 4, no. 5, August 1, 1995.
11. Nigel Cope, "Pharmacia and Upjohn Merge," *Independent* (London), August 21, 1995, p. 15.
12. David Lawder, "Upjohn Co., Sweden's Pharmacia to Merge," *Reuters News*, August 20, 1995.
13. Eric Reguly, "Upjohn in $13Bn Swedish Merger—Pharmacia & Upjohn Inc.," *Times* (London), August 21, 1995.

37

Corporate Development as a Strategic Capability: The Approach of GE Power Systems

A significant development in the field of M&A is that active buyers are investing increasingly in business processes, human capital, and information technology to elevate the quality of their business development activities. The resulting infrastructure can contribute significantly to the successful execution of the corporate development strategy.

General Electric Power Systems illustrates how the business development function of a company can become a strategic capability.

- A *strategic capability* integrates a set of resources (such as human capital, financial capital, and physical property) in a special way to generate competitive advantages, yield high returns, and create organizational agility. Strategic capabilities are difficult to imitate.
- Chapter 37 of the main text presents a profile of General Electric's Power Systems (GEPS) division as an example of business development viewed as a strategic capability. The main strategy of GEPS was to survey the whole energy chain, focusing on oil and gas, power generation, and energy management technologies. From 1995 to 2000, GEPS was highly acquisitive. Key attributes of GEPS' business development contributed to both its overall excellence and to the high success rate of its mergers and acquisitions. Noteworthy examples include:
  - *Consistency of processes.* This included using common valuation models, presentation templates, and analytical frameworks that were applied to all business development projects. GEPS developed structured and standardized processes to provide a strong foundation and even playing field for comparative acquisition analysis and consistent, streamlined deal execution.
  - *Active knowledge management.* Strong electronic data systems allowed for an integrated M&A process, organized archiving of important materials, and strong communication between employees.
  - *Continuous improvement mind-set.* A strong dedication to process improvement, especially in deal origination, deal cycle time, due diligence, acquisition integration, and synergies, characterized GEPS. Five percent of the group's staff was focused solely on process improvement.

- *Top-down and bottom-up pipeline.* By taking this double-pronged approach, GEPS was able to develop rich business development ideas from various sources of the firm.
- *Senior management engagement.* Senior executives at GEPS personally reviewed the deals in progress and postacquisition integration activities on a weekly basis. The CEO of General Electric himself dedicated material time each month to review the business development process.
- *Careful and systematic acquisition screening* of potential targets, with a particular focus on:
  - *Strategic fit.* Acquisition to get better, not bigger.
  - *Technology.* Target should provide enhancing capabilities.
  - *Quality of human resources.* Significantly influenced the acquisition decision.
  - *Financial considerations.* Predetermined requirements (i.e., EBIT operating margins of 15 percent or more, accretive to GE earnings in the first year, double-digit revenue growth, etc.).
- *Integration of experts in a broad array of functional backgrounds.* Experts in areas such as intellectual property, environmental issues, human resources, finance, law, sales, technology, sourcing and manufacturing are immersed in GE's intense due diligence efforts.
- *Postmerger integration and audit.* GEPS was highly cognizant of the fact that a deal's success was contingent on the postmerger integration efforts.
  - Assigned integration team leaders.
  - Established Centers of Excellence (COEs) that focused on guiding integration in each function.

CHAPTER 37—WORKBOOK QUESTIONS

1. *What are the attributes that characterize business development at GEPS? Please identify and describe them.*

2. One of the hallmarks of GEPS' success in business development is its systematic processes. The division has built an M&A "factory" for business development that reduces variation.

   a. *Please describe GEPS' M&A factory. What components or features have contributed to the factory-like processes?*

   b. *Do you think there could be any drawbacks to GEPS' systematic process-focused approach? If yes, please explain.*

3. *Suppose you are the CEO of a company division similar to GEPS, and you have been mandated to hire three new employees: a black belt six sigma practitioner, a technology trainer, and a knowledge-management learning specialist. What are the important benefits that each professional would bring to your organizational division?*

4. *In GEPS' deal development process, a business development professional or operating unit CEO initiates contact with a top executive at a prospective target firm. If the response from the target firm is negative, would it make sense for GEPS to pursue further discussions, or would further solicitation be a waste of time? Explain.*

5. You are a management consultant who has just finished a six-week project on-site at GEPS. While you had been hired specifically to work on the integration of a recently acquired company, part of your project entailed learning more about GEPS' entire approach to making acquisitions.

   You have been asked by your manager, a senior consultant, to make a presentation about how a corporate business development process can become a strategic capability for a firm. Based on your close observance at GEPS, what would you highlight in your presentation?

CHAPTER 38

M&A "Best Practices": Some Lessons and Next Steps

Effective M&A practitioners take a proactive stance in understanding M&A and develop views about future cycles.

Learning about the different aspects of M&A is necessary but not sufficient for becoming a true deal leader. Deal leadership is achieved only when a business practitioner can synthesize the different parts of the M&A deal into a successful, integrated whole.

- Good M&A practices can be identified and adopted—and if employed well they can become part of a masterful repertoire of *best practices*. However, the field is too complicated and rapidly changing to offer a definitive expression of a single best practice approach. Rather, best practitioners commit to a process of ongoing study and learning in order to define for themselves the outlines of good practice.
- Some elements of best practice include:
  - Think like an investor.
  - Take a "whole deal" perspective.
  - Aim to create value rather than claim value.
  - Develop a view and play the game.
  - Find and use optionality.
  - Resist earnings management and momentum-acquiring.
  - Temper determinism with behaviorism.
  - Focus on process first, then outcome.
  - Master the tools and concepts, but also get help.
  - Practice with integrity.
- Our understanding of M&A remains imperfect. Chapter 38 of the main text outlines 10 areas for further research:
  1. The profitability of M&A.
  2. The relative merits of strategies of focus and diversification.
  3. Herd behavior of acquirers in producing cycles of M&A activity.
  4. The role of information asymmetries in M&A.
  5. The efficiency of trade-offs among terms in the design of deals.

6. The "management" of financial reports: why and how it happens.
7. The defining features of "good governance."
8. The costs and benefits of antitakeover defenses.
9. The costs and benefits of merger regulation.
10. The estimation of appropriate costs of capital for discounting in M&A.

- Many businesspeople will argue that *learning by doing* is the best process for ongoing professional development in M&A. But while the lessons obtained from learning by doing are usually highly instructive, they can also be costly. Chapter 38 of the main text emphasizes the benefits of professional development from other sources:
  - *Learning by watching.* Observing other M&A professionals at work conveys a great deal of tacit learning about the field.
  - *Learning by reading.* Chapter 38 offers a list of recommended books and articles. One could initiate a reading program, possibly in concert with others.
  - *Learning from current events.* Chapter 38 offers an approach to studying newly announced deals. This centers around valuing the target, interpreting stock price movements, and constructing a term sheet for the deal.

CHAPTER 38—WORKBOOK QUESTIONS

1. *The continuous increase in the automation of M&A analytical techniques allows for the deal designer to focus less on number crunching and more on the shaping of deals. What are the possible benefits and drawbacks of this? Please explain.*

2. *Victoria Nakagawa is the newly appointed managing director of a business development group at Best Ensemble Inc. Looking at its historical performance, she has concluded that the group has been slow to conclude deals and uneven in the quality of work completed on various deals, and has lost a number of acquisition opportunities to competitors. She has noticed that the professionals in the group define their contributions very narrowly: accounting, valuation, due diligence, law, and so on. Based on the reading in this and previous chapters, in what directions might she pursue the development of this group?*

3. *What can you learn from current events in M&A?*

PART

Two

Answers

1

Introduction and Executive Summary

1. Success in M&A is determined not only by structural factors, but also by conduct.
2. Organizational structure is just as important as managerial conduct and interpersonal skills. Organizational structure can have great impact on the ability of target and buyer to mesh, and as such affects postmerger success.
3. Managing legal exposure is important. But best practitioners also watch for opportunities to proactively *shape* laws and regulations in ways that benefit the public interest.
4. Success means more than avoiding criminal indictment: Best practitioners understand that it is important not only to do deals well, but also to do them *right*. For this to happen, best practitioners consciously promote the development of an ethical environment in their firms.
5. Success in M&A goes beyond being able to negotiate and consummate a deal. The ultimate measure of success in M&A is whether a deal is able to create value. Value creation entails being successful on many fronts—strategic planning, search, due diligence, deal design, negotiations, postmerger integration, communication, and process management.
6. Careful planning increases the likelihood of success in M&A. But human behavior and luck can also play a role.
7. Good due diligence goes beyond simply checking facts. An inquisitive mind-set that looks for patterns, synthesizes facts into valuable information, and answers "why" questions is important to the due diligence process.
8. Good process is crucial to developing good M&A practice because it lends discipline to thinking, provokes analysis, and invites reflection. Merely focusing on outcomes does not motivate the development of a mind-set that synthesizes, learns from past lessons, and continually builds on a body of knowledge.
9. It is unlikely that there is a single "best" design for each M&A deal. Instead, there may be several feasible designs because of the complex trade-offs among the many dimensions of a deal.
10. Market prices are useful data for valuation where markets are integrated and efficient. But where markets are inefficient and/or segmented, prices may be less helpful as indicators of intrinsic value.

CHAPTER 2
Ethics in M&A

1a. The following are hypothetical expressions consistent with the three perspectives:

- *David:* Disney should not have paid the greenmail to either Saul Steinberg or Irwin Jacobs. By paying greenmail, the company neglected its duty to maximize the wealth of its shareholders. Furthermore, if paying greenmail were actually ethical, it could be made into a universal rule. Such is not the case, however. If all corporations paid greenmail as a routine response to objections from shareholders about corporate policies, it would stifle debate and dissent, divert corporate resources away from the business mission of the firm, and create an environment of rule by intimidation. The investing public would lose confidence in companies neglecting their duty to maximize the wealth of shareholders.
- *Ulyssa:* David, I don't think greenmail can be deemed as a universal unethical act; whether it is good or bad depends on its consequences for those affected by the payment. Look at the positive outcome of paying greenmail in this particular case. I think the potential benefits here outweighed the drawbacks. Paying greenmail was the best action because Disney was preserved and left intact, which in the long run benefited the shareholders, the corporation, and employees. Now consider what could have happened if Disney had not paid greenmail: The company could have been handed over to a raider with less management experience and commitment to Disney's artistic and corporate visions. This in turn could have weakened the Disney brand and negatively altered company's operations, marketing, and corporate culture. This could have caused the stock to plummet, which would have destroyed value for shareholders.
- *Vera:* I think both of you are focusing on the wrong issues. You are not ethical simply because you follow your duties and evaluate the consequences of your actions. What we really need to consider is what paying greenmail portrays about Ron Miller and the Disney Company. Do you think that Miller could look at himself in a mirror or publicly address an audience of Disney's shareholders with pride, and feel confident that he did the right thing? I don't think he could. A person who pays greenmail disregards the fundamental virtues of fairness and equality. Greenmail is not what a person of character would do.

1b. This is not a math problem for which there is a strictly correct answer. A critical thinker would offer these observations:

- Did David weigh all of Ron Miller's duties? The duty to the welfare of shareholders is a legal obligation. But CEOs carry other duties as well, even though they may not have the blessing of law: These might include a duty to preserve and develop the artistic vision of Disney and a duty to promote the welfare of employees. Also, even if shareholder welfare is the highest responsibility, paying greenmail *might* best promote shareholder welfare, as Chapter 2 of the main text argued.
- Does Ulyssa really intend to suggest that an end justifies any means? A positive end might explain the means, but it neither justifies nor makes the means ethical. An additional flaw stems from the difficulty of assessing the probabilities of future results and consequences. The sequence of events requires making a decision with unpredictable outcomes before knowing the consequences in advance. Another time-based flaw concerns the trade-off between short-term and long-term consequences. A decision that considers "the greatest good for the greatest number" in the short term could be harmful to an even larger group of people in the long term. Consider an example that we see often in practice. A corporation may adopt certain operational or accounting policies to meet Wall Street analysts' earnings expectations and thus make its shareholders happy without careful consideration of the potential negative long-term consequences for the corporate entity, its shareholders, its employees, and other stakeholders.
- Vera's virtues-based approach urges one to think beyond duty, compliance, and results. She believes that ethics is about being a virtuous person. Vera's approach to making sound decisions emphasizes our ability to reason and judge based on our expectations of ourselves and of others. But whose virtues matter here? Is it sufficient to take a simply personal view, or are there overarching virtues that one should serve?

2. *Case #1: Power Electronics/SIC.* Settlement of escrow accounts is fertile ground for ethical issues. The postmerger audit may have exposed systematic "earnings management" by the target firm that the buyer justifiably wants to correct—and for which the buyer does not want to overpay. But the buyer could be playing an aggressive game of earnings management as well: essentially taking write-offs at the seller's expense that will make the buyer look good later on. The seller's abandonment of the arbitration process agreed upon in the contract is not consistent with the duty to fulfill contracts.

The *consequences* are pretty clear: One side's gain in this dispute is the other side's loss. The argument for *duties* seems to favor SIC: The contract specifies how disputes might be resolved through arbitration. Perhaps Power Electronics is trying to get SIC's attention with the lawsuit. The *virtues* consideration invites more information. What was the real situation at Power Electronics? Was SIC justified in withholding the payment from escrow or did Power Electronics really hide conditions at the firm?

(*Note:* This is based on an actual business case; names have been disguised.)

3. *Case #2: Hershey.* The controversy over the Hershey Trust's proposal to sell the company generated international attention. While the synopsis necessarily omits detailed information one might like to have, and though the ethical dilemmas in this case are not given to straightforward resolution, the perspectives raised in Chapter 2 of the main text suggest a number of ethical issues:

   - ***Duties.*** The directors of the Hershey Trust were obliged to preserve the financial standing of the trust and promote its mission—the proposed sale seems consistent with these duties. Even taking a stakeholder perspective, it is not clear that the sale of the company would impair the directors' obligation to other groups. A sale of the company could have been conditional upon guarantees of employment in the company's current locations. The loss of independence by senior management of Hershey Foods seems to be the most likely casualty—any formal or implied contract between the trust and management would need to be carefully weighed.
   - ***Consequences.*** The sale of Hershey Foods would probably generate a healthy premium for the trust's investment in the company and diversify its endowment base. The consequence for the company would be a loss of independence, which mattered particularly to management. The loss of independence triggered some fears that acquisition of Hershey Foods by another company might cause a shift of manufacturing to other locations, hurting the employees and community with a loss of jobs—there was no evidence to suggest that this was likely, but opponents of the sale made much of the speculation. On balance, it seems that the Hershey Trust (and other shareholders) would have gained from the sale, and management would have lost.
   - ***Virtues.*** The fight seems to have been toughest here. Promoting the survival and prosperity of a philanthropic organization seems virtuous. But opponents presented the proposal as an abandonment of a trust with the community. They argued that the Hershey Trust was unethical because it was acting out of self-interest and self-aggrandizement.

3

Does M&A Pay?

PART I: SHORT ANSWER

1. *Event studies.* These studies look at value creation for a firm and its shareholders surrounding the announcement of a merger transaction by examining its abnormal returns. The abnormal return of the merger is simply the raw return (the change in share price plus any dividend paid, divided by the closing share price of the previous day) less a benchmark of what investors required that day, such as the return on a large market index like the S&P 500.

   Advantages: These studies provide direct measures of value created for investors, and are forward looking.

   Drawbacks: This method assumes "capital market efficiency," which research finds is valid in developed financial markets on average and over time. But occasional anomalies can distort the returns. The analyst should seek to draw inferences from many studies with large samples on the assumption that many observations will overcome the effect of possible anomalies.

   Accounting Studies. These studies examine the reported financial results (i.e., quarterly or annual earnings reports) of acquirers before, during, and after acquisitions to see how financial performance changed. The focus of these studies could include: net income, return on equity, returns on assets, earnings per share (EPS), leverage, and liquidity of the firm. The best accounting studies compare acquiring firms with their nonacquirer peer firms.

   Advantages: These are based on financial statements that have been audited and certified. They are widely used by investors and considered a good indirect source of information regarding value creation. Also, they reflect the financial position of the company (leverage and liquidity, to name a couple of aspects).

   Drawbacks: Financial statements are backward looking in that they rely on historical data. Also, the data are based on accounting values, not market values. The reporting practices and structure of a company's financial statements can change over time, leading to noncomparable data for different reporting periods. Furthermore, companies and auditors have been known to "manage" financial reports (as discussed in the preceding chapter). In addition, the analysis of financial statements does not account for the value of intangible assets, and is sensitive to inflation and deflation because of the historic cost approach.

Surveys. These entail administering and analyzing the results of a standardized questionnaire, which asks a diverse pool of managers to answer whether particular acquisitions created value.

Advantages: As a form of primary research, these can offer more direct and insightful information relevant to specific deals.

Drawbacks: Surveys can be biased by managers' subjective views. Also, their recollections may not be entirely accurate. Furthermore, the worth and validity of surveys is often dependent on the level of response. M&A surveys typically yield a low rate of participation (2 to 10 percent).

Clinical studies. These are the most focused of all the research methods. Each clinical study examines in great depth either one deal exclusively or a small number of deals. These studies generally involve conversational, face-to-face primary research—field interviews with executives and knowledgeable observers.

Advantages: A clinical study can offer the most detailed and insightful information regarding specific deals. Given its inductive approach, much detail and factual background information can be gathered.

Drawbacks: Given the extremely focused nature of this approach, it is not well suited for hypothesis testing or other statistical analysis. The extreme specificity and potentially idiosyncratic results of these studies can make it difficult to draw insightful "big picture" conclusions.

2. The two approaches evaluate different metrics, and at different times. The accounting-based study looks at a company's financial reports, which reflect a company's operation results, highlight its financing and investing activities. The market return analysis, however, focuses more on a company's stock price (or market capitalization), a measure of what investors believe to be the present value of the firm's future cash flows. Market return analyses, therefore, are forward looking.

   As for differences in timing: Event studies look at market returns before, during, and after a deal *announcement*: This can be over any length of time, even measured in a short time frame of a few days. Accounting studies, however, compare reported data that are at least three months apart (quarterly reports).

PART II: QUESTIONS ON REAL BUSINESS SITUATIONS

1. Yes. The deal appears to have created new economic value for Smucker. This is evident in the sustained positive difference between Smucker's share price and the benchmark, the S&P 500 index. Smucker's positive returns could be due to several reasons:

   - *A focusing, not diversifying, investment for Smucker.* The buyer was familiar with consumer packaged foods. Jif and Crisco would complement the rest of the line.
   - *Synergies through economies of scale and purchasing.* For example, Smucker did not have a direct sales force and dealt solely with brokers. If Jif and Crisco already had a direct sales force, Smucker could leverage that new dis-

tribution channel and use it for a broader array of products. Even if Jif and Crisco did not have direct sales forces, the additional volume of these products would allow Smucker to spread its distribution costs, which should in turn still improve profit margins.

- *Increased market power for Newco owing to its greater size.* With larger size, Smucker might enjoy greater ability to position its products more favorably on retailers' shelves. Another concern about this deal is that it might have been executed to build market share. Research studies have shown that efforts to enhance market position through M&A yield flat to worse financial performance compared to predeal financial metrics. However, it is possible that M&A growth could actually enhance organic growth, and that the real warning from research is that M&A growth is *not a substitute* for organic growth.
- *Advantageous price.* Perhaps P&G simply sold cheap.
- *Issuance of shares by Smucker builds debt capacity for the firm.* There were a few aspects of this deal that could be seen as cautionary signs. One was the all-stock payment method. Studies referenced in Chapter 3 of the main text have shown that stock-based deals are associated with negative returns at deal announcements. In most cases, this is a logical result following theories that managers issue stock at the high point in the cycle of a company's market capitalization or in the overall stock market cycle. However, in the aftermath of September 11, Smucker's shares were trading at historically low points. As pointed out in the chapter, the announcement of an all-stock deal signals that management of the buying firm believe their shares are expensive and overvalued. In this particular case, however, it is questionable that Smucker's management or investors viewed the shares as overpriced.

2. In undiscounted terms, Quaker lost $1.4 billion on Snapple, while Triarc gained $700 million. Quaker's loss is notable especially in light of the expected synergies. Like Smucker's acquisition of Jif and Crisco, Quaker Oats was making a focused investment. In this instance, M&A did not pay off for Quaker.

   Quaker's effort to reposition Snapple in grocery stores and away from convenience stores was a flop. Resistance by independent bottlers and competitive responses by Coke and Pepsi turned a moneymaker into a money loser.

   Past success (such as Quaker's with Gatorade) is no indicator of future performance. M&A is not a profit machine that will automatically create value for the buyer. The buyer should enter each new deal with few preconceptions about success.

4
M&A Activity

1. The cycle of M&A activity and the cycle of the stock market are both driven by the same fundamental forces in the economy. When the stock market is buoyant, the economic activity in markets is probably good—at such times, companies may have more cash to spend on acquisitions, and CEOs may be more optimistic about the payoff from acquisitions. Also, companies might acquire with stock if they think their stock is overvalued. When stock prices rise, buyers can more easily offer stock as a form of payment over cash. Thus, a company's sheer ability to pay in stock rather than cash can stimulate and influence its decision to engage in M&A activity. Rapid development of a capital market in countries where it had been previously underdeveloped may spur M&A activity.

2. The entrepreneur is the key figure in keeping the capitalist engine in motion. He or she seeks to exploit profitable opportunities and thus becomes a steady agent of change. By exploiting an invention, new technology, or other type of innovation, entrepreneurs trigger new patterns of behavior in the business landscape. Changes spurred by the entrepreneur can relate to production, consumer behavior, distribution, and so on.

3. Innovations do arise because of consumers' needs or wants, although those needs or wants can be latent (not realized) or not yet developed in consumers. For example, the invention of the television was not a response to an existing demand from consumers, but rather a forward-looking anticipation of demand that could be created for the product. While producers may need to educate consumers on the attributes and benefits of new products and services, they do not force the products onto consumers. Because consumers often do resist change, producers have the burden of showing and convincing them of the worthiness of an innovation.

   Entrepreneurs, therefore, have the task of identifying and envisioning needs and wants that may not yet be met, realized, or developed. In addition, entrepreneurs can identify not only unmet demands, but also alternative methods for meeting existing demands. The railroad was not invented because consumers "took the initiative in displaying an effective demand for their service in preference to the services of the mail coaches." However, the railroad was an alternative method of meeting the demand for transportation, and the entrepreneur responsible for its invention envisioned a future demand for the railroad: a "want" and "need" for a faster transportation service that offered new advantages.

4a. The journalist's questions ask the CEO to respond to the view that M&A activity could be a product of self-serving managers who make deals happen if and when they are in their favor. Her questions convey skepticism about the reasons given by executives to explain M&A activity.

In contrast, the CEO's stance portrays the straight economic turbulence view: M&A activity is a product of market and industry conditions and turbulence, which all present attractive investment opportunities.

4b. While the journalist's questions raise some concerns about the motivations behind M&A activity, she has no more than anecdotal evidence to ground the argument that M&A activity is a product of self-serving managers. The deal process itself involves justification for the reasons of a merger. From extensive documentation, discussions, and due diligence, a company must convey the business reasons behind any merger.

The CEO's view that economic conditions and turbulence are the leading drivers of M&A is based on facts about macroeconomic conditions and turbulence in the communications industry. Much evidence supports the "turbulence view," which explains well the M&A activity across various industries and across time.

5. Potential sources of turbulence include:

   1. ***Overcapacity and collapsed demand for Internet services.*** Providers of Internet capacity seriously overinvested in plant and equipment. Falling demand bankrupted many companies whose businesses were predicated on rapid growth of the digital economy. Genuity's bankruptcy provided Level 3 with an opportunity to acquire capacity that would seem to fit well with Level 3's business strategy.
   2. ***Deregulation: the Telecommunications Act of 1996.*** The Act provided opportunities for "any entity to compete in the telecommunications market." This allowed companies like Level 3 Communications to enter, grow, and compete in a market that was previously much more regulated and restrictive. The Act was a source of turbulence in that it changed the landscape of the entire communications industry and provided growth and acquisition opportunities that were previously not possible.
   3. ***Globalization: international expansion.*** The globalization of communication services itself is a source of turbulence that likely motivated Level 3 to significantly expand in international markets through acquisitive growth. Before acquiring Genuity, the company had operational facilities in 27 U.S. markets and nine European markets. After the acquisition the company nearly doubled its number of markets: As of March 2003, it had 57 markets in the United States and 16 markets in Europe.
   4. ***Technological change: evolution and changing landscape of the Internet.*** Level 3 identified Genuity as a pioneer in the Internet, and realized that Genuity's assets and intellectual capital would complement its own, which were based more on later Internet developments (optical and IP-based services).

CHAPTER 5

Cross-Border M&A

1a. *Analysis:* A business manager must have a "view" about a country in which an investment is contemplated. To get a view on where the best place to invest is and how to invest, one needs to perform a strategic analysis of countries. The strategic analysis for a country should include macroeconomic conditions and trends, microeconomic strength, the health of institutions, and so on. The following commentary gives a strategic overview of Thailand and the Philippines. Its conclusions are that *Thailand is a better investment site for the business manager described in the case, and a joint venture is a practical and safer approach for entering the Thai market.*

Thailand

As reported in the World Bank write-up, Thailand began to implement deep reforms in the financial sector, corporate governance, and competition policy after the financial crisis in 1997. These reforms have helped the economy to hold up in spite of the global downturn. After the major crisis in 1998, Thailand's economy started the recovery process and grew at over 4 percent in 1999. The graph of real GDP growth shows that after the sudden slowdown in 2000 and the first half of 2001, which coincided with the global economic recession, economic growth showed a strong turnaround. Real GDP growth increased from lower than 2 percent in the third quarter of 2001 to almost 6 percent in fourth quarter 2002. A positive trade balance kept boosting foreign exchange reserves, which strengthen foreign investors' confidence and capital market stability. Although the fiscal budget turned to a slight deficit in 2002, in general the balance is healthy both in absolute terms and as a percentage of GDP. The Thai government implemented a slightly contractionary monetary policy to keep inflation at bay starting in mid-2001. But the overall inflation level over the past several years is definitely in control compared to the 1998 level. At the same time, the exchange rate between the Thai baht and the U.S. dollar has stabilized at around 40 to 45 due to the stability of inflation. Although foreign direct investment has not returned to the same level as before the crisis, domestic spending, consumer spending, and net exports have pushed overall GDP to grow at an accelerated level. Domestic industrial production growth also picked up its pace after 2002. Overall, economic recovery is under way and the government's fiscal and monetary policies continue to support growth and reduce external vulnerability.

As with most developing nations, Thailand seems to be undergoing a change from being an agricultural country to being a manufacturing country. After strong efforts by the government to help the poor and focus on education, Thailand's illiteracy rate dropped to 4 percent, which is among the lowest in this region. The high-savings habit of the Thais also helps to maintain a high level of investment that is essential to the country's long-term growth. After the 1998 crisis, the Thai government proactively kept foreign debt at a maintainable level. Besides financial industry reforms, structural reforms were also implemented in other areas as part of a broader strategy to improve the nation's competitiveness. The government strove to formulate a comprehensive strategy and to initiate new measures to promote productivity growth. Poverty reduction and balanced development are set forth as medium-term strategies in the government's Ninth Plan. Thailand's monarch has also attacked corruption and has advocated for the improved management of natural resources. In the telecom industry, Thailand seems to be lagging in terms of technological investment and wireless coverage, which offers a great opportunity for foreign investors to bring in much needed investment and technology, especially in the wireless sector. Although the government is devoted to battling poverty and corruption, the challenge remains for the government to convince the general public about governance and social stability. The move toward strengthening democratic institutions is, however, a step in the right direction.

The Thai government also advocated several industrial reforms to improve transparency in the banking industry (and although not mentioned in the information provided, to increase the speed of privatization and support several niche industries). The stock market has stagnated for several years, suggesting that this is a time of attractive valuations in terms of asset pricing compared to the mid-1990s' high-flying real estate prices.

Overall, Thailand is on the verge of economic recovery and has a stable government that has prioritized poverty reduction, which is essential for social stability and long-term domestic demand growth. GDP growth mainly relies on domestic demand and investment, which is the result of a high savings rate. A current account surplus boosts foreign exchange reserves and reduces total debt, which relieves the pressure on fiscal policy and capital investment by the private sector. A healthy macroeconomic environment, supportive microeconomic conditions, and efforts to improve corporate governance and government regulation all offer a great opportunity for foreign investors to enter the Thai market. The relatively well-integrated capital market, reasonable asset pricing levels, and growing industry demand make the timing favorable, too.

The Philippines

Similar to Thailand, the Philippines made much progress in reducing poverty during the early to mid-1990s. However, the Philippines went through a turbulent political period from 1999 to early 2001, leading to slowdowns in both economic growth and poverty reduction. However, public confidence was restored somewhat with the ascendance of a new administration in January 2001. This administration has attempted to pursue sound macroeconomic policies as well as governance and structural reforms.

Although several macroeconomic indicators show some bright spots, the overall economy in 2003 does not look very optimistic. Real GDP growth over the past three years has been around 3 to 5 percent, which indicates that the Philippines did not suffer as much as Thailand from the Asian crisis. Inflation was reduced from 12 percent in 1999 to less than 4 percent in 2002, because of an aggressive contractionary monetary policy. The Philippine government seems to have reversed this policy in the second quarter of 2002 to encourage private investment and consumer spending. Although the current account is in surplus, most of that is coming from positive net income received from abroad, whereas the other major component of the current account—the trade balance—is flat to negative. In addition, foreign direct investment has been erratic. As opposed to Thailand, the Philippines' GDP growth is mainly caused by consumer spending and government spending; the latter has resulted in a persistent budget deficit and increasing debt burden. The industrial production growth rate decreased to a negative level, which is not a promising sign.

The key challenge for the Philippines is to address its chronic fiscal deficit. But in order to do this while sustaining growth at the same time, private demand will have to take the lead. This will be possible if the government takes steps to create a favorable investment climate and to be persistent in its financial and corporate restructuring efforts. Although the Philippine government has done a great job managing inflation, the peso continues to weaken against major currencies, presenting another obstacle to foreign investors. Overall, the Philippines has shown modest growth in the past several years and did not experience a dramatic downturn, which may suggest it is a less integrated market.

The Philippines, like Thailand, undertook efforts to reduce poverty and to focus on education. The illiteracy rate is at 5 percent, which is low in this region. However, educational attainment is low, and the quality of education is poor. The Philippines also has a modest savings rate. Because of a long period of budget deficit, the country's debt-to-GDP ratio has increased to 74 percent, which imposes an annual interest burden amounting to 3.5 percent of GDP. To improve its fiscal position, the government is working on longer-term structural reforms, including finding ways to reverse the slide in revenues.

Nonperforming loans (NPLs) of the banking sector rose to 18 percent in June 2002 versus 17 percent in 2001. The Philippine government has been trying to improve the banking system, though efforts to deal with nonperforming loans have yet to bear fruit. The Philippine stock market has not done well, and volumes have been thin. Spreads on government bonds have risen. Although the low level of the stock market helps bring down overall asset pricing, the increasing credit spread indicates that there is a higher risk level associated with uncertainty in the future. In the telecommunications industry, the Philippines has adequate domestic service, which may mean stiffer competition for new entrants.

Overall, a moderate recovery is under way. However, the boost from the demand side has been from public spending, and income from abroad. Indications of increasing financial risk suggest that this may not be the right time to invest in the Philippines. Furthermore, political instability poses a challenge to foreign investors.

1b. ***Preliminary choice:*** Comparing the two countries, in mid-2003 one could conclude that Thailand is economically and politically more attractive as a country for investment than the Philippines. Economically, Thailand seems to have greater potential for sustainable economic growth supported by positive trends such as a higher savings rate, higher investment growth, net export growth, and so on. Nonetheless, Thailand still sustains some degree of political and economic risk; in addition, there is some uncertainty as to how government regulation will play out: Will reform efforts be successful? Because of these uncertainties, a joint venture investment may make more sense than a 100 percent acquisition. In fact, this is a very common method of investment for many cross-border deals in developing countries.

1c. The information obtained by your analyst has focused primarily on macroeconomic and institutional factors. While these areas lend important insights, the country analysis framework summarized in Exhibit 5.12 of the main text suggests research in two additional areas:

- *Microeconomy:* industry structure, the role of foreign direct investment, infrastructure, and factors suggested by Porter's "diamond" of country competitiveness.
- *Culture:* norms and practices in areas such as work ethic, risk bearing, leadership, and entrepreneurship.

Country analysis draws on the wide range of insights offered by macroeconomics, microeconomics, institutional analysis, and cultural analysis.

CHAPTER 6

Strategy and the Uses of M&A to Grow or Restructure the Firm

1. Strategy is a plan for fulfilling the mission and achieving the strategic objectives of a company. It is the road map that guides the day-to-day actions of a firm. To achieve a firm's objectives, then, strategy should be the engine driving M&A search, analysis, and implementation. M&A is a tactical instrument of strategy. Strategy should therefore influence decisions on issues like whether to grow organically or inorganically, how to grow, whether and how to restructure a company, and whether and how to exit a business.

2. Strategic analysis tools include:

    1. The Porter model is a useful guide and discipline for industry and competitor analysis. Based on your analysis of the five forces, you should be able to assess how fast a market will grow and how competitive the market will be.
    2. The strategic map and growth-share matrix are useful in this case, since they can help illustrate the relative positions of competitors. The map is helpful for identifying any areas that are unoccupied by competitors.
    3. The strategic canvas and the attractiveness-strength matrix can both be used in this case. The strategic canvas will allow you to compare the strategies of competitors on a number of dimensions in order for you to assess how well your business unit can compete. The attractiveness-strength matrix will allow you to evaluate the business unit relative to other units in your firm on the basis of industry attractiveness and the competitive strength of the unit within that industry.

3. Drivers of value include:

    - *High relatedness, in terms of industry of buyer and target.* Studies by Rumelt (1974, 1982) found that strategies motivated by "related" diversification purposes had higher returns on equity than strategies for unrelated diversification or for single-business focus. Perhaps a good example for this would be a company that strategically decides to acquire another company that is a supplier for the company. Acquiring a supplier could eliminate costs and improve operating efficiencies in the company's value chain, thus creating value and higher returns.
    - *Deregulation.* In industries experiencing deregulation, companies may seek to create value by merging with companies that they previously were not

able to—for example, the deregulation of the commercial banking industry allowed for convergence (mergers) between commercial banks and insurance companies.

- *Efficiency or inefficiency of internal capital markets.* Research studies have shown that some diversification mergers (of conglomerates) have realized greater efficiencies because their ability to allocate resources was better than that of the external capital market. Thus, a diversifying merger would be a more likely driver of value when the external capital markets are inefficient (i.e., where the more diversified company could create more efficiency and value internally than the capital markets would be able to do externally).
- *Special information-based assets.* There is evidence that when one or both firms in a diversifying merger have significant information-based assets, the diversified firm can transfer knowledge and intellectual capital more efficiently than the public markets could.

4. Organic growth is that which is "home grown" inside of a firm through internal investment. Inorganic growth, in contrast, is growth through investing or structuring an affiliation outside of the firm.

   Organic growth is particularly appropriate if a firm has a unique competitive advantage that will allow for superior returns on investment, such as patents/patent rights, proprietary technology, unique know-how, and core competencies (i.e., strategic capabilities that translate resources into special advantages for a firm). Organic growth is particularly appropriate if a firm has unique resources or capabilities, that are difficult to imitate and thus something the firm does not want to share or dilute by combining with another company.

   Inorganic growth is particularly appropriate for a company that does not currently have, but would like to acquire and benefit from, a unique competitive advantage of another firm. For example, a pharmaceutical company might want to buy another firm in the same industry that has a patent to develop/produce a new drug that the company believes will be very successful and profitable. Inorganic growth may be the best/only way a company can attain resources that are vital to its continued success. In fields such as biotechnology, computer software, defense electronics, and filmed entertainment, corporations may need to reach beyond their internal operations to acquire intellectual property, patents, creative talent, and managerial know-how. Also, inorganic growth is particularly appropriate if it gives a company significantly greater access to suppliers and buyers (which, not surprisingly, are two of Porter's five forces).

5. The conventional view that mergers for diversification destroy value has been challenged by critics who offer both theories and evidence to prove otherwise—that at least in some cases, diversification can and does create value.

   Salter and Weinhold (1979) argued that corporate diversification could do things that shareholder portfolio formation could not, such as: promote knowledge transfer across divisions, reduce costs, aggregate resources that can be shaped into core competencies that create competitive advantage, and exploit better transparency and monitoring through internal capital markets. The diversified firm "internalizes" the capital market by acting as an allocator of resources among its businesses.

Rumelt (1974) found that profitability varied by type of diversification strategy—that not all mergers driven by diversification motives have the same returns. Rumelt's findings reveal that a strategy of close relatedness in diversification yields the best returns. While his research was instrumental in demonstrating that strategic focus is important and creates value, it also shows that there is a wide range of returns that can result from diversification strategy, and that some types of diversification can create more value than others.

Four studies by Kruse (2002), Healey, Palepu, and Ruback (1992), Parrino and Harris (1999), and Cornett and Tehranian (1992) found improvements in operating performance following diversifying acquisitions.

Anslinger and Copeland (1996) performed research that found that some firms pursuing a conscious strategy of unrelated diversification have realized high abnormal returns for sustained periods.

6. Domestically, the main options for inorganic growth would include (1) a majority acquisition, (2) joint venture, or (3) minority investment. The majority acquisition, for instance, might entail buying out a different fast-food chain or some other business. Or, since location is important in this business, you may want to buy out those other restaurants or commercial establishments that are in prime spots in those locales where you don't have the best locations. Purchase of a direct competitor may encounter sharp antitrust restrictions. With joint venture or minority investments you could grow through partial engagement with other firms that would still carry influence for the protection of the brand and mitigation of risks.

   In developing countries the choices are broader where there is a strong local partner: franchising, strategic alliance, joint venture, and purchasing a minority stake. Among the four, franchising and joint venture agreements are the most attractive strategies. Depending on the particular conditions of a country, one can be more appropriate than the other. For instance, in a country where the political and economic risk is relatively high and consumer acceptance of foreign brands is high, franchising would be a better alternative because it would not require a large capital investment. It would also allow you to expand very fast, thereby capitalizing on the high customer acceptance of foreign brands. In contrast, in a country that is more economically and politically stable, but where people are not as open to foreign brands, a joint venture might be the better choice because it allows you more direct operational control necessary for promoting quality and brand image.

7. Restructuring the company in a way that creates more transparency about its business divisions may help reduce the diversification discount. Setting a division up as a separate entity from the holding company can help increase transparency. There are four ways of organizing a division as a separate entity: partial carve-out, partial spin-off, partial split-off, and tracking stock. The four differ from each other in terms of who ends up owning the shares in the new entity, and the degree of the control the parent retains. The specific choice will therefore depend on the strategy of the firm. For instance, if the firm wants to retain a high degree of control, issuing tracking stock may be the best option.

   Another way that restructuring can create value is by preventing the cross-subsidization of "loser" business units by successful units. This could be achieved by divesting the losers and by carve-out, spin-off, or split-off.

8. The framework for choosing an inorganic growth strategy would require the following steps:

    1. Identify the benefits from a relationship with the target business.
    2. Assess the need for ownership and control.
    3. Manage risk exposure.

    The thought process can be laid out in a decision tree format: The first question leads to an answer that sets up the second question, and the second to the third. By following the path of answers, one should be able to arrive at the inorganic growth strategy that best fits the company's needs. (Refer to Exhibit 6.20 in the main text.) In some cases, one may identify more than one attractive strategy. To decide which strategy is best, one can use these guidelines: retain a bias for simplicity, consider starting small, and remember value creation!

9. Input the data into the growth-share matrix in the Excel spreadsheet model "Growth Share.xls," which is found on the CD-ROM. You should come up with the following chart:

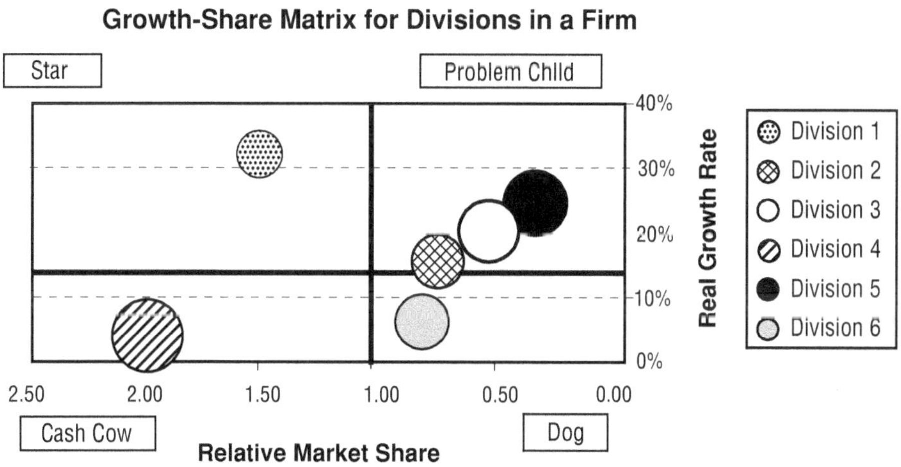

    [This spreadsheet can be found in the folder "Key Spreadsheets from the Workbook" located on the CD-ROM.]

    As can be seen from the graph, division 6 is a "dog" and would be the prime candidate for shedding. There may be hope for the "problem children" if the company can find a way to increase market shares of those divisions—they would then become stars. Division 4 is the cash cow, which can provide for the financial needs of your company.

10. Input the data into the spreadsheet model "Learning Curve.xls," found on the CD-ROM. The results should be:

		5% Cost Reduction	10% Cost Reduction	15% Cost Reduction
Slope		0.05	0.10	0.15
Base cost		$120.00	$120.00	$120.00
Time Period	Cumulative Production (000s)			
0	0	$120.00	$120.00	$120.00
1	5	$114.00	$108.00	$102.00
2	10	$108.30	$ 97.20	$ 86.70
3	20	$102.89	$ 87.48	$ 73.70
4	40	$ 97.74	$ 78.73	$ 62.64
5	80	$ 92.85	$ 70.86	$ 53.24
6	160	$ 88.21	$ 63.77	$ 45.26

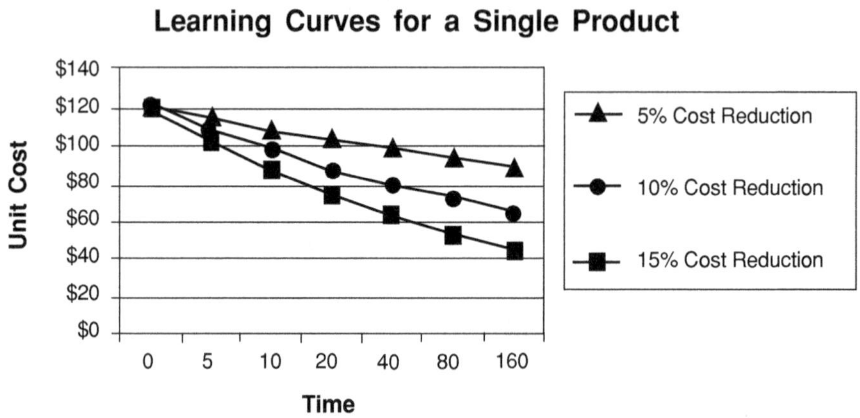

[This spreadsheet can be found in the folder "Key Spreadsheets from the Workbook" located on the CD-ROM.]

As the table shows, as the number of units produced doubles, the reduction in cost proceeds at a different rate under the different scenarios. For instance, for the 5 percent cost reduction scenario in time period 2, cumulative production doubles from 5,000 to 10,000, and the cost per thousand decreases from $114 to $108.30—a 5 percent reduction. In the 15 percent cost reduction scenario in time period 2, cumulative production doubles from 5,000 to 10,000, and the cost per thousand decreases from $102 to $86.70—a 15 percent reduction. Another important thing to note is the compounding effect of the learning curve. As time progresses and cumulative production increases, the difference in cost between different scenarios increases, too, due to the compounding effect. For instance, in time period 1, the difference in cost under the 5 percent and 10 percent reduction scenarios—$114 vs. $108—is 5 percent. By the time we get to time period 6, the difference in cost under these two scenarios is 28 percent ($88.21 vs. $63.77)!

11. The following are several alternatives for increasing Joy Company's self-sustainable growth rate, although there may be many more combinations of different strategies that will produce the targeted 16 percent rate of growth:

Change in Policy	New Policy Target	Existing Policy	Required Change
1. Increase debt/equity ratio. Finance the growth with debt.	D/E = 1.68	D/E = .30	Fivefold relevering
2. Sell equity.	DPO = –107% (i.e., sell about as much equity each year as you generate internally)	DPO = 40% (i.e., no equity sales)	Drop the dividend. Sell equity.
3. Improve internal profitability.	ROE = 26.77% ROTC = 21.44%	ROE = 15% ROTC = 12.46%	Margins almost double.
4. Improve internal profitability *and* increase debt/equity ratio.	ROTC = 17.33% D/E = .70	ROTC = 12.46% D/E = .30	Increase margins and leverage a lot.
5. Cut dividend payout ratio *and* improve internal profitability *and* increase debt/equity ratio.	DPO = 20% ROTC = 14.67% D/E = .50	DPO = 40% ROTC = 12.46% D/E = .30	Cut dividend in half. Increase leverage. Increase margins.

[This spreadsheet can be found in the folder "Key Spreadsheets from the Workbook" located on the CD-ROM.]

As can be seen in the table, the CEO can increase the sustainable growth rate to 16 percent by increasing leverage, selling equity or improving internal profitability. In addition, the CEO can combine these strategies to achieve the targeted growth rate. Comparing the different alternatives, some have advantages and some have disadvantages. For instance, increasing the debt ratio to 1.68 can achieve the goal, but is difficult to implement and also increases financial risks associated with huge increases in leverage. Or, although improving internal profitability can help achieve the target, it may be very difficult to implement. So among the five alternatives, the fifth choice may be the most reasonable because it balances the different approaches by reducing the dividend payout, modestly improving internal profitability, and increasing the debt equity ratio to a reasonable level.

12. The diversification discount can be calculated by comparing the company's total capital to the sum of the implied total capital of its divisions, which in turn can be estimated individually using the data on industry averages. The implied total capital of the divisions comes out to $133 million; therefore, there is a diversification discount of 9.86 percent:

	Implied Capital ($ MM)
Division 1	24.0
Division 2	56.3
Division 3	52.8
Total capital	133.1
Discount	9.86%

[This spreadsheet can be found in the folder "Key Spreadsheets from the Workbook" located on the CD-ROM.]

7

Acquisition Search and Deal Origination: Some Guiding Principles

PART I: TRUE OR FALSE

1. True.
2. True.
3. True.
4. True.
5. True.
6. False. If information about an acquisition opportunity is fully public, it will be difficult for the buyer to tailor the terms to greater advantage.
7. True.
8. True.
9. False. In some cases, an ideal target may become available unexpectedly. If there is a compelling argument for doing a deal, the unexpectedness of the target's appearance should not hinder a deal.
10. False. Deal-rich information is private.

PART II: SHORT ANSWER

1. The "Oracle of Bacon" game illustrates the "small world" concept. It is difficult to find actors/actresses separated by more than four links to Kevin Bacon. In fact, the average number of links is 2.94. The point is that people are more connected to each other than we may think. As an M&A practitioner, therefore, part of the game in acquisition search is to get good connections. Potential targets may very well come the M&A practitioner's way through such connections.
2. In studying how people find jobs, Granovetter discovered that personal connections were decisive. Granovetter found that three-quarters of successful connections to job offers were through "weak ties," people whom the job seeker saw occasionally or rarely. The point is that there is strength in weak ties, and that

the diversity and breadth of the network matter. The implication for an M&A practitioner is that it pays to build a network that extends beyond people in one's own circle. If an M&A practitioner limits his connections to people in the same circles, it may limit his chances of being in the "sweet spot"—finding a target that not many competitors know about.

3. The best navigators:
   - Have proprietary information, know-how, and connections.
   - Can innovate better than others.
   - Discover trends and sweet spots before others.
   - Enjoy a cost advantage over competitors.
   - Have positive reputations.

PART III: TARGET ASSESSMENT CASES

1. *Possible Answers:* Nine groups of students conducted this exercise in May 2003 and separately came up with the companies discussed here. Your results, of course, do not necessarily have to match what is in the list—in fact, they may not match at all. Go ahead and read about the suggested targets nonetheless. You may pick up some useful ideas regarding the acquisition search process/criteria/issues. You will also find for each suggested target how the buyer reacted to the proposal.

Campbell Soup Company

Profile

Campbell manufactures soups, juice beverages, sauces, crackers, and confectionery products. It operates under four business segments: North America Soup and Away from Home, North America Sauces and Beverages, Biscuits and Confectionery, and International Soup and Sauces. Popular brands are Campbell's and Swanson's for soups, Prego and Pace for sauces, Franco-American for pasta, V8 for vegetable juice, Pepperidge Farm for baked goods, and Godiva for premium chocolate.

2002 Revenues	$6.46 billion
2002 Operating margins	17.1%

Campbell's 2002 Revenue and Earnings Distribution

	Revenues	Earnings
North America Soup and Away from Home	41%	55%
North America Sauces and Beverages	19%	21%
Biscuits and Confectionery	25%	16%
International Soup and Sauces	15%	8%

Why Campbell's?

- Products fit the fast and portable meal kit concept (will fit the buyer's distribution system).
- Lines of "good for you" products: Campbell's Soup, Swanson, V8 vegetable juice.
- Growth opportunities in soup market: "ready to serve" market growth of 16 percent; Campbell's Soup's growth only 9 percent. Over 90 percent of consumers eat soup of some form.
- Dominance in North America.
- Strong presence in Europe.

Deal Rationale

- Synergies in the product line and distribution channels.
- Opportunities to grow Campbell's business internationally using the buyer's distribution capabilities.
- Expansion and diversification of the buyer's product line.
- Access to strong "ready to serve" and "good for you" brands.
- Opportunity to purchase undervalued company and change management to improve operations (Campbell's was undergoing some restructuring measures during this time).

Ownership Structure

Family trust and insiders	45.1%
Barclays Bank	2.7%
State Street Corp.	2.6%
Capital Guardian	2.3%
Mellon Bank	2.1%
Other institutions	23.0%
Free float	22.2%

Risks

- Ability to convince majority stock owners to sell.
- Regulatory approval. However, this risk was thought to be low because the product portfolios were complementary.
- Integration risk: Campbell's was founded in 1869, so there is a strong culture and sense of pride.

Buyer's Reaction

The buyer had already been monitoring this potential target and knew that the family was not interested in selling. However, the buyer said it would keep Campbell's on its watch list to be alert for possible interest in selling by the insiders.

Lifeway Foods

Profile

Lifeway Foods, Inc., manufactures probiotic, cultured, dairy, and nondairy health food products. The company's primary products are kefir, a dairy beverage similar to yogurt; a line of various drinkable yogurts under the name La Fruta and Tuscan, and a dairy-based immune-supporting dietary supplement beverage, Basics Plus. It also produces a soy-based alternative to dairy kefir. Finally, the company manufactures a line of various farmer cheeses sold under the name Lifeway Farmer Cheese.[1]

2002 Revenues	$12.2 million
2002 Operating margins	21.1%

Why Lifeway?

- Proprietary probiotic formula.
- The only product known in the kefir category.
- Growing brand names.
- Innovative product offerings.
- Consistent revenue and net income growth versus industry.
- High margins.
- High quality management.

Deal Rationale

- Enables the buyer to gain foothold in "good for you"/organics market, to participate in the trend toward health-consciousness.
- Provides opportunity for the buyer to enter high margin dairy and gut health sector.
- Provides stable of morning meal products and microsnacks.

Ownership Structure

Family	54.3%
Danone	20.4%
Institutional	1.3%
Other	24.0%

Risks

- Ability to convince major stockholders to sell.
- Cultural fit.
- Integration risk.
- Noncompetition agreement with Danone.

Buyer's Reaction

The buyer considered the target too small.

Hansen Natural Corporation

Profile

Hansen Natural Corporation is an alternative beverage company with products in several categories: natural sodas, fruit juices, soy smoothies, energy drinks, "functional drinks," sparkling lemonades and orangeades, noncarbonated ready-to-drink iced teas, children's multivitamin juice drinks, and noncarbonated lightly flavored energy waters.[2] It also sells nutrition bars and cereals under the Hansen's brand name.

2002 Revenues	$95.5 million
2002 Operating margins	5.8%

Why Hansen's?

- Seventy years in the natural beverage industry.
- Has 20 percent market share in energy drinks market.
- Five-year sales compound average growth rate of 16.5 percent.
- Was 2002 sales leader in new age carbonated beverages within California market.
- Leading brand in Southern California natural soda market for more than 25 years.
- Low-asset business—third-party suppliers.

Deal Rationale

- Allows buyer entry into fast-growing organic, soy, juice, and energy drinks markets:
    - Energy drinks are fastest-growing segment of beverage market.
    - Growth in sales of soy food in 2001 was 27 percent.
    - Organic beverage sales are expected to grow 24 percent annually until 2005.
    - Shelf-stable juices expected to grow 26 percent annually until 2005.
- Buyer has opportunity to grow the brand.

Ownership Structure

Insiders and 5%+ owners	42.0%
Institutional	14.0%
Other	44.0%

Risks

- Ability to convince majority stock owners to sell.
- Integration risk.

Buyer's Reaction

Hansen and its operating margins are too small.

Lance, Inc.

Profile

Lance manufactures, markets, and distributes a variety of snack-food products that include sandwich crackers, potato chips, nuts, popcorn, and other salty snacks, as well as cookies, cakes, and candy. Lance uses its own fleet of tractors and trailers to make weekly deliveries to sales territories. Lance also operates approximately 39,000 company-owned vending machines.

2002 Revenues	$538.4 million
2002 Operating margins	12.0%

Why Lance?

- Highly recognized brand name.
- Proven management team.

Deal Rationale

- Products complement the buyer's own snack foods lines.
- Feasible to push target's product lines through buyer's distribution channels.
- Buyer's product lines can be pushed through Lance's vending machines.

Ownership Structure

Top five shareholders:

Van Every Lance	5.4%
Philip Van Every	4.8%
Barclays Global	4.1%
PIMCO Equity	3.9%
American Century Investments	2.6%

Risks

- Ability to convince family members to sell stock.
- Regulatory approval.
- Cannibalization of buyer's own snack food brands.
- Potential perceived dilution of high-powered stable of buyer's brands.

Buyer's Reaction

Buyer felt that target's products too heavily overlapped with its own, and could not justify cannibalizing its own products, which were generating higher profit margins than those of the target.

Group Danone

Profile

Group Danone is a producer of fresh dairy products and packaged water, biscuits, and cereal products.[3]

2002 Revenues	$14 billion
2002 Operating margins	10.8%

Danone's Revenue Breakdown by Product	
Fresh dairy products	46%
Beverages	27%
Biscuits	24%
Other	3%

Danone's Revenue Breakdown by Geography	
France	23%
Rest of European Union	34%
Rest of world	43%

Why Group Danone?

- Global leader in cultured dairy products.
- Second largest producer of biscuits.
- Second largest bottled water producer.
- Strong international presence.
- Strong R&D.
- Little product overlap.

Deal Rationale

- Product line expansion.
- Fulfill buyer's objective of expanding into "good for you" products.
- Gain access to Danone's European and Asian distribution channels.
- Acquire expertise in chilled and refrigerated markets.

Ownership Structure

Danone has no large controlling shareholder; 40 percent of shares are held by shareholders outside of France.

Risks

- Willingness of foreign shareholders to sell to a U.S. company.
- Antitrust issues.
- Integration concerns—significant time might be required to realize gains due to size, with respect to both distribution channels and management structure.
- Supplier relationships for Danone products must be managed due to EU structure.

Buyer's Reaction

Interested. Margins are thinner than targeted, but would like to know more about possibilities to increase margins.

Lindt

Profile

Lindt is a company with more than 150 years of experience making premium Swiss chocolate.

2002 Revenues	$1.2 billion
2002 Operating margins	10.1%

Lindt's Revenue Breakdown by Geography

Europe	72%
United States	20%
North and South America (excluding U.S.)	4%
Rest of world	4%

Why Lindt?

- Strong brand awareness.
- Strong market share in Europe.
- Premium pricing.
- More than a 150 years of experience.
- Opportunity to improve market share in United States, where it has less than 1 percent of the market.

Deal Rationale

- Buyer would gain a new product line with captive premium markets.
- Buyer would gain exposure to European market.
- Lindt would provide a new platform for product innovation.
- Lindt's R&D capabilities could be used to develop buyer's line of snack-food products.
- Buyer could build Lindt into a strong brand, just like Campbell's has done with Godiva.

Ownership Structure

Fonds fur Pensionserganzungen der Chocoladefabriken Lindt & Sprugli AG owns 22.3 percent of shares. It is the only shareholder that owns more than 5 percent of the company.

Risks

- Willingness of foreign shareholders to sell to a U.S. company.
- Lindt operates in a mature, low-growth market.
- Chocolate would be a new market for the buyer, with new technologies and production processes.
- Failure of retail expansion of Lindt in the United States.

Buyer's Reaction

Margins are thinner than targeted, but strong brand may present opportunities for improvement in margins. Also, dedicated retail system may be too asset intensive for buyer's preferences. Still, buyer wanted to know more.

Tingyi (Cayman Islands) Holding Corp.

Profile

Tingyi is the best-known food and beverage company in China. It specializes in the production and distribution of instant noodles, beverages, and bakery products.

2002 Revenues	$1.2 billion
2002 Operating margins	12.6%

Revenue Breakdown by Product	
Instant noodles	54%
Beverages	38%
Bakery	7%
Other	1%

Why Tingyi?

- Strong brand:
  - Number one in instant noodles, with 35 percent market share.
  - Fifty-one percent market share in ready-to-drink tea market.
  - Number three player in fruit juice market, with 15 percent market share.
- Well-developed distribution network.
- Nationwide network of production.
- Instant noodles business is a cash cow.

Deal Rationale

- Acquisition will allow buyer to have a strong presence in China.
- Opportunity to push buyer's products through target's well-established distribution network.
- Expansion of buyer's product lines—major revenue enhancement.
- Little product overlap—new products can be source of growth.

Ownership Structure

Ting Hsin Holdings	33% (This parent company of Tingyi is a Taiwanese company.)
Sanyo Foods	33%
Public	34%

Risks

- Ability to convince major shareholders to sell.
- Lack of familiarity doing business in China.
- Oversupply of low-end products in China may lead to price wars.
- Stiff competition: There are many well-established local brands in China.
- Scalability of products in the Western world is questionable.
- Regulatory approval.
- Differences in management style and culture.
- Chinese consumers may not accept buyer's Western products.

Buyer's Reaction

Strong interest. Wants to know more about the "country bet" implicit in this acquisition.

Maruchan, Inc.

Profile

Maruchan, Inc., is a noodles manufacturer with $500 million in sales. It is a wholly owned subsidiary of Toyo Susian, a Japanese company.

2002 Revenues	$ 500 million
2002 Operating margins	9.4%

Why Maruchan?

- Strong brand—dominant market share in North America.
- Double-digit growth in North America.
- Leading low-cost capabilities.
- Has two manufacturing plants in the United States: one in Virginia and one in California.

Deal Rationale

- Instant noodles fit the buyer's desired product characteristics: convenient, ready to go, "good for you/better for you."
- Appeal to ethnic groups in the United States.
- Growth potential for instant noodle market in the United States (currently, Asia accounts for 88 percent of the market for instant noodles).
- About 42 percent of U.S. population is below 30 years old; thus, there is a large number of potential consumers of instant noodles.
- Revenue enhancement through extension of buyer's product line.

Risks

- Ability to convince Toyo Susian to sell.
- Instant noodles would be a new product/new market for the buyer.
- Instant noodle product line may not be compatible with buyer's products.
- Differences in management style and culture.

Buyer's Reaction

Low interest because of margins and strength of competition.

Yakult Honsha Co. Ltd.

Profile

Yakult Honsha makes the leading brand of probiotic drinks worldwide. It also manufactures other juices, sports drinks, teas, and coffees.

2001 Revenues	$1.9 billion
2001 Operating margins	9.9%

Revenue Breakdown by Product	
Food and beverages	85%
Cosmetics	6%
Pharmaceuticals and life sciences	9%

Why Yakult?

- Leading brand in probiotic drinks worldwide.
- Innovative technology.
- Product has proven medical benefits.

Deal Rationale

- Secure a strong international brand in a growing category (probiotics).
- Enhance good-for-you product portfolio.
- Growth potential through chilled distribution capabilities.
- Secure revenue streams from outside North America.
- Opportunity to build Yakult brand in the United States.

Ownership Structure

Top five shareholders:

Fedian PTE Ltd. (Danone)	19.3%
Fidelity Investments	7.5%
Matsusho Co.	6.5%
Chase Manhattan	5.5%
Capital Research Management	4.5%

It must be noted, however, that Yakult's ownership remains predominantly Japanese:

Japanese financial institutions	24%
Japanese individuals	21%
Other Japanese corporations	20%
Foreign institutions and others	35%

Risks

- Ability to convince Japanese shareholders to sell.
- Ability to manage cultural integration.
- Yakult may not "click" with American consumers—it has a very distinct taste.
- M&A rules in Japan may pose difficulties—for instance, share for share exchanges by non-Japanese firms are prohibited; thus, payment would need to be in cash.

Buyer's Reaction
Low interest because of low margins and likely demands of sellers.

NOTES

1. *Source:* Yahoo! Finance.
2. Ibid.
3. Ibid.

CHAPTER 8

Due Diligence

PART I: CONCEPT QUESTIONS

1. An investor mentality goes beyond mere data-fetching and list-checking. It seeks to gauge the risk exposure and investment attractiveness of the target. Thinking like an investor therefore expands due diligence toward a critical assessment of risk and returns.
2. A narrow due diligence review is brief, contained, and focused only on issues needed to get the deal done, such as legal and accounting issues. In a competitive setting, this may be the only feasible strategy. However, it does not serve the investor mentality very well; its main focus is simply deal consummation. In contrast, a broad review looks everywhere, takes the time it needs, and makes material demands on the target. A choice between narrow or broad due diligence often equates to a choice between "surprises now" and "surprises later." "Surprises now" entails higher expenditures for due diligence, but yields greater insight about the target.
3. The best due diligence efforts focus on acquiring knowledge rather than just amassing information or data. Knowledge is information that has been processed in order to be usable. Data are simply raw facts, and information consists of data that is concentrated and improved. Knowledge, in contrast, examines, ruminates on, and synthesizes data and information in order to extract patterns, trends, and insights. Knowledge presupposes *understanding*.

PART II: MINI-CASES

1. It seems reasonable to conclude that the due diligence process for this deal was wanting in no small measure. Given the size of the deal, it is surprising that the buyer was content to simply base due diligence on public information. Of course, no one can say for sure whether going beyond the public domain would have uncovered the fraud, even though the nature of the problems uncovered, the length of the time period during which fraud had been taking place, and the massiveness of the deception suggest that a discovery might have been possible with some digging. At the very least, it would have been known that CUC's accounting systems were outdated, and that might have raised some alarm bells.

2. Due diligence was probably one cause of the Quaker/Snapple merger failure, albeit not the only one. Hubris certainly seems to have been a factor in this case—it would explain why Quaker went forward with the deal in spite of clear indications that sales were much weaker than expected. But with respect to the distribution, excess inventory, and production problems, it appears that greater due diligence efforts might have prevented surprises. For instance, given the crucial role distribution would play in the success of the merger, could Quaker have consulted with Snapple's independent distributors to ensure their agreement with Quaker's distribution plan? Could interviews with Snapple's customers have helped uncover the slow turnaround time and the stuffing of the distribution pipeline with inventory? Could interviews with suppliers have revealed the contracts that required minimum quotas? Doing the legwork on these issues may have brought about more "surprises now" rather than "surprises later."

3. Although no definitive evidence can be given, it seems in this case that the acquirers failed to conduct enough due diligence on the infusion industry and on Critical Care's competitive position within it. The huge disparity between expectations of 30 percent earnings growth versus the actual results (flat earnings) suggests how little Medical Care's executives knew. It is difficult to understand how Medical Care could not have known about pricing pressures in the industry given how drastic they were. Careful industry study should have uncovered information such as this. Presumably, too, discussions with other players in the industry, such as competitors, insurers, and HMOs, might have led to the discovery that Critical Care was charging fees well above market and losing share because of it.

CHAPTER 9
Valuing Firms

1. The recommended action should be to buy shares of Sober Brews. At $32.8 apiece, Sober's market capitalization comes out to only $1,187.70, 25 percent lower than the estimated equity value of $1,586. This is a violation of value additivity (i.e., $V_{\text{Sum of parts}} > V_{\text{Market}}$). Securities analysts and corporate raiders are known to conduct this kind of analysis.

2. Corrected statements are:

   a. An opportunity to create value exists when price and intrinsic value differ.

   b. It is not necessary that *all* estimators be used. Indeed, it may be an inefficient use of your time. Only those that are applicable are relevant. One must not mechanically apply all estimators; rather, one should carefully select the most relevant estimators to use.

   c. Using point estimates ignores the fact that these values are estimated with uncertainty. It is better to pick a *range* of value within which the intrinsic value is believed to reside.

   d. Intrinsic value is unobservable; it can only be estimated.

3. Nothing will be left to the owner of Red Hill because the liquidation value of assets is less than debt outstanding. The resulting equity value is minus $394.1:

	Book Value ($000)	Percent Recoverable	Liquidation Value
Cash	$ 123.8	100	$ 123.8
Receivables	619.0	75	464.3
Inventory	309.5	55	170.2
PPE	879.0	60	527.4
Other assets	92.9	90	83.6
	$2,024.1		$1,369.2
Debt	1,763.3		1,763.3
Equity	$4,114.7		$ (394.1)

[This spreadsheet can be found in the folder "Key Spreadsheets from the Workbook" located on the CD-ROM.]

4a. The current enterprise market value of Pellagia is \$880.05 million:

Shares outstanding	135.00
Price per share	\$ 5.63
Equity market value	\$760.05
Debt market value	120.00
Enterprise market value	\$880.05

[This spreadsheet can be found in the folder "Key Spreadsheets from the Workbook" located on the CD-ROM.]

4b. Based on simple averages of the comparable firms' multiples (17.44 P/E and 1.09 P/S), the equity value using price-earnings is \$662.7 million, and the enterprise value using price-sales is \$690.4 million.

5a. The proper discount rate for free cash flows is the weighted average cost of capital (WACC), not the cost of equity.

5b. The proper discount rate for cash flows to equity holders is the cost of equity.

6. Calculating Tel-Talk's cost of equity:

$$\begin{aligned} K_e \text{ using CAPM} &= R_f + \text{Beta} \times \text{Market risk premium} \\ &= 5.63\% + 1.10 \times 5.9\% \\ &= 12.12\% \end{aligned}$$

$$\begin{aligned} K_e \text{ using the dividend growth model} &= \$2.31/\$46.25 + 6.2\% \\ &= 5.0\% + 6.2\% \\ &= 11.2\% \end{aligned}$$

The two methods yield estimated costs of equity that differ by 92 basis points. This is a common problem in valuation. If both estimators are credible, one should triangulate toward an estimate from them. To triangulate means to critically evaluate the assumptions behind each method, and to weigh each method according to its relevance to the company under consideration. For instance, the dividend growth model assumes a constant growth rate in dividends and ignores risk. One must ask whether such assumptions are reflective of the reality of the company being valued.

7. The bookseller's current beta reflects its current capital structure; therefore, beta has to be unlevered first:

$$\beta_u = \frac{\beta_L}{1 + \frac{(1-T)D}{E}}$$

$$= \frac{.98}{1 + \frac{(1-.35).095}{.905}}$$

$$= .92$$

Now the unlevered beta has to be relevered to reflect Trigeorgis' desired capital structure:

$$\beta_L = \beta_U\left[1+(1-t)\frac{D}{E}\right]$$

$$= .92\ [1 + (1 - 0.35) \times .30/.70]$$

$$= 1.18$$

In short, Trigeorgis' beta will rise from 0.98 to 1.18 if the firm increases its leverage as suggested.

8. Middlestates' free cash flows given in the problem need to be discounted at the cost of capital. In addition, terminal value has to be estimated.

 Terminal value comes out to $15,213, calculated as follows:

$$\text{Terminal value} = \frac{CF \times (1+g_\infty)}{K - g_\infty}$$

$$= \frac{924 \times (1+3.0\%)}{9.28\% - 3.0\%}$$

$$= 15{,}213$$

Where g is calculated using the Fisher formula:

$$g^{\infty}_{\text{Nominal}} = \left[(1+g^{\infty}_{\text{Units}})\times(1+g^{\infty}_{\text{Inflation}})\right]-1$$

$$= [(1 + 1.5\%) \times (1 + 1.5\%)] -1$$

$$= 3.0\%$$

The enterprise value, calculated by discounting the yearly free cash flows (given in the problem) and the terminal value ($15,213) at the cost of capital, comes out to $14,117. A valuable insight is that the terminal value makes up most of the enterprise value.

9.

	Year 1	Year 2	Year 3	Year 4	Year 5
EBIT	28.74	29.17	29.60	30.05	30.50
Taxes	9.77	9.92	10.07	10.22	10.37
NOPAT	18.97	19.25	19.54	19.83	20.13
Less: additions to net working capital	(5.75)	(5.83)	(5.92)	(6.01)	(6.10)
Less: capital expenditures	(28.74)	(29.17)	(80.30)	(62.20)	(30.50)
Plus: depreciation	52.68	53.47	54.27	55.09	55.91
Free cash flow	37.16	37.72	(12.41)	6.71	39.45
Terminal value					720.93
Total free cash flows	37.16	37.72	(12.41)	6.71	760.37
Discounted at WACC	34.38	32.28	(9.82)	4.91	514.91
Enterprise value	576.66				
Less debt	192.30				
Equity value	384.36				

(Continued)

	Year 1	Year 2	Year 3	Year 4	Year 5
Equity value per share	**7.46**				
Calculation of WACC:					
K_d	6.1%				
After-tax K_d	4.0%				
K_e	9.6%				
Market value of debt	192.30				
Market value of equity	540.75				
% debt	26.2%				
% equity	73.8%				
WACC	8.1%				

[This spreadsheet can be found in the folder "Key Spreadsheets from the Workbook" located on the CD-ROM.]

The equity value per share, according to this valuation, is $7.46.

10. The equity value of the bookseller is $1.865 billion or $24.88 per share.

Step 1: Unlever the beta:

.98(1+((1-.35) × (.095))/.905 = 0.92

Note: This step has already been performed in the answer to Problem 7.

Step 2: Compute the CAPM for unlevered K_e 10.50%

Step 3: Discount free cash flows at the unlevered cost of equity.

	1	2	3	4	5
EBIT	171.4	191.9	210.3	235.9	238.0
Plus: depreciation and amortization	83.5	95.3	96.2	103.0	112.0
Less: additions to net working capital	(32.7)	(37.3)	(17.7)	(41.6)	(39.7)
Less: capital expenditures	(159.2)	(141.2)	(90.7)	(100.0)	(120.0)
Subtotal	63.0	108.7	198.1	197.3	190.3
Terminal value					2,612.2
Free cash flows	62.99	108.73	198.11	197.35	2,802.49
Discounted at unlevered ke	57.00	89.04	146.82	132.35	1,700.77
Enterprise value, unlevered	$2,126.0				

Step 4: Evaluate financing effects.

Total debt:	400.0
Interest rate:	6.0%
Annual interest expense	$ 24.0
Tax shield	$8.4
PV of perpetual debt tax shields	$ 140.0

Total enterprise value = Value of enterprise (unlevered) + Value of debt tax shields
= $2,126.0 + $140 = $2,265.98

Less debt	400.00
Equity value	$1,865.98
Equity value per share	**$ 24.88**

[This spreadsheet can be found in the folder "Key Spreadsheets from the Workbook" located on the CD-ROM.]

10
Valuing Options

1a. To calculate the payoff, one needs to translate Mr. Jones' requirement into numerical cash flows. The minimum return of 30 percent means that he wants a payoff of at least \$104 [\$80 × (1 + 30%)]. Because he is willing to give up the excess returns over 50 percent, the maximum payoff for Mr. Jones will be \$120 [\$80 × (1 + 50%)]. Therefore, if the stock trades at between \$104 and \$120 at the end of two years, he will get an amount equivalent to whatever the stock price is.

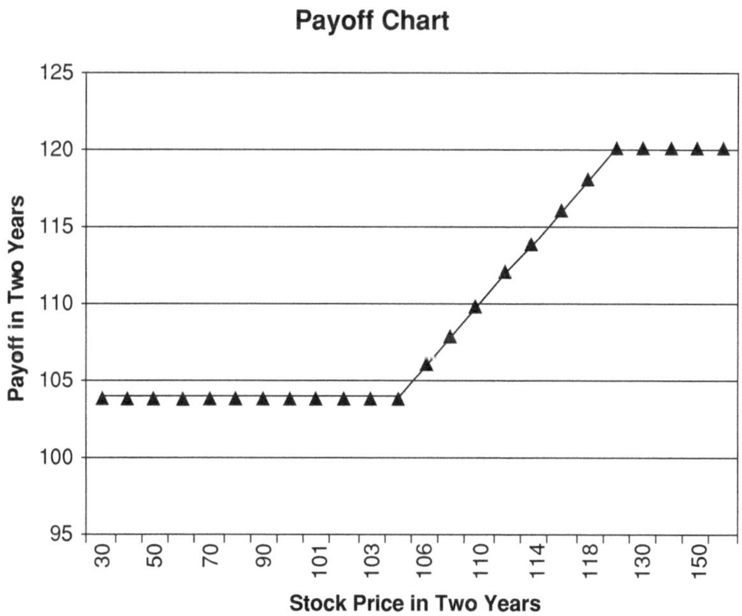

[This spreadsheet can be found in the folder "Key Spreadsheets from the Workbook" located on the CD-ROM.]

1b. From the payoff chart, one can recognize a "bull spread" as discussed in Chapter 10 of the main text. To hedge his position, Mr. Jones has to buy a put option to protect himself from downside risk if the stock trades below \$104. At the same time, he can sell a call option with a strike price of \$120, giving up some upside but also reducing the cost he incurs to protect himself from the downside risk (i.e., the cost of his put option). This payoff can therefore be decomposed into a combination of a short call option with an exercise price of $120 and a long put option with an exercise price of $104.

2. Black-Scholes is a common approach to valuing European options when the distribution of the value of the underlying asset is lognormal, in which case the binomial method is not appropriate. Here, the uncertainty of the value of the underlying asset—the total sales from the well—follows a normal distribution. Therefore, the Black-Scholes model is a useful approach in this example.

Step 1	Insert parameters into the model
Stock price	$10,000,000
* The expected value of the well.	
Exercise price	$8,000,000
* The cost to exercise the option.	
Risk-free rate	7%
Volatility	40%
Time (years)	5
Step 2	Calculate the option value using template.
Call value	$5,365,623

Black-Scholes ***European: No Dividend***	
Call value	$5,365,623
Call delta (hedge ratio)	0.862
Call elasticity	1.606
Using put-call parity	
Put value	$1,003,127
Delta	–0.138
Elasticity	–1.379
S underlying asset price	$10,000,000
X exercise price	$8,000,000
rf risk-free rate	7%
sd volatility	40%
t years to expiration	5
Cumulative Standard Normal Function	
d1 from Black-Scholes	1.088
N(d1)	0.862
d2 from Black-Scholes	0.194
N(d2)	0.577

[This spreadsheet can be found in the folder "Key Spreadsheets from the Workbook" located on the CD-ROM.]

The right to drill is a call option that has an expected value of $10 million (the underlying asset price). The value of the option is $5,365,623.

3a. Draw the tree and calculate the payoff of options at the expiration.

	Time: Now		Time: One Year Later	Probability	Call Option Payoff Ex. Price: $100	Put Option Payoff Ex. Price: $100
		Up 20%	$120.00	50%	$20.00	$–
Stock price	$100.00					
		Down 15%	$85.00	50%	$–	$15.00

3b. Then, use the Goal Seek feature in Excel to find the appropriate risk-free rate that makes C – P – [S – Ex × exp(–rt)] equal to zero. In this case, the implied risk-free rate is 2.47 percent.

Expected call option payoff at expiration	\$ 10.00
Expected put option value at expiration	\$ 7.50
Stock price	\$100.00
Exercise price	\$100.00
Call value	\$ 9.76
Put value	\$ 7.32
$C - P$	\$ 2.44
$S - \text{Ex} \times \exp(-rt)$	\$ 2.44
$C - P - [S - \text{Ex} \times \exp(-rt)]$	\$ (0.00)
Risk-free rate	2.47%

[This spreadsheet can be found in the folder "Key Spreadsheets from the Workbook" located on the CD-ROM.]

4. The way to find an arbitrage opportunity is to identify a violation of put-call parity. The simple way to do this is to estimate the value of the put option using the three other components of put-call parity. If the estimated price is the same as the quoted price, then there is no arbitrage opportunity.

   Using put-call parity, the value of the put option in this case can be calculated as:

$$\text{P} = \text{C} + \text{Ex} \times \exp(-\text{r} \times \text{t}) \times \text{S}$$
$$? = 0.50 + \$55 \times \exp(\ \times 8\% \text{ x } 1/12) \times \$50$$
$$? = \$5.13$$

This indicates that the put option (quoted at \$6.00) is overvalued. By selling one put option and shorting one stock, you can get \$56.00 cash. Use this money to buy one call option (\$0.50) and put the rest (\$55.50) in Treasury bills to earn the risk-free rate of return, and you will lock in a return of \$0.87 in one month without any cost and risk.

Payoff Diagram

Decomposed position
One short put option
One short stock
One long call option
One long Treasury bill

Stock Price in One Month	Payoff of Short Put	Payoff of Short Stock	Payoff of Long Call	Payoff of T-bills	Net Payoff
\$35.00	\$(20.00)	\$(35.00)	\$ —	55.87124	\$0.87
\$40.00	\$(15.00)	\$(40.00)	\$ —	55.87124	\$0.87
\$45.00	\$(10.00)	\$(45.00)	\$ —	55.87124	\$0.87
\$50.00	\$ (5.00)	\$(50.00)	\$ —	55.87124	\$0.87
\$55.00	\$ —	\$(55.00)	\$ —	55.87124	\$0.87
\$60.00	\$ —	\$(60.00)	\$ 5.00	55.87124	\$0.87
\$65.00	\$ —	\$(65.00)	\$10.00	55.87124	\$0.87
\$70.00	\$ —	\$(70.00)	\$15.00	55.87124	\$0.87
\$75.00	\$ —	\$(75.00)	\$20.00	55.87124	\$0.87
\$80.00	\$ —	\$(80.00)	\$25.00	55.87124	\$0.87
\$85.00	\$ —	\$(85.00)	\$30.00	55.87124	\$0.87

[This spreadsheet can be found in the folder "Key Spreadsheets from the Workbook" located on the CD-ROM.]

Under parity, you should get the same payoff no matter whether the price of the underlying asset rises or falls. You can demonstrate this with a table of payoff results as shown.

5a. When a call option is deep in the money, with little chance of the stock moving back below the strike price before expiration, the option might be exercised early. This generally occurs where the dividend the investor would receive on the underlying stock, if he were to exercise the option, is greater than the interest expense incurred in buying the shares ahead of the expiration date. Generally this exercising of the call option occurs only in the period right before the ex-dividend date.

5b. Let's take a non-dividend-paying stock as an example. In this case, call option values for both American and European options will be the same because it would never be optimal to exercise the American option early. But in the case of put options, an American put option might be exercised early if it is deep in the money because of a put option's insurance purpose. Therefore, an American put option has greater value than a European put option with the same terms. Putting these two values in the put-call parity equation, one will find that one side of the equation changes in value while the other side doesn't. Therefore, put-call parity will not hold.

6. Drivers of option values:

Decrease In	Call Option Value Will	Put Option Value Will
Underlying asset price	Decrease	Increase
Exercise price	Increase	Decrease
Time to expiration	Decrease	Decrease
Risk (volatility)	Decrease	Decrease
Dividend yield	Increase	Decrease
Risk-free rate	Decrease	Increase

7. The beta of an option can be calculated by using the same regression method used for stocks. As with stocks, the beta of an option is a measure of movement relative to the market—but it is not the same as volatility (which is the standard deviation of returns). Generally speaking, the beta of an option is much greater than that of the corresponding underlying stock because the option offers a much greater return for the same market movement—this is a more levered return, is riskier, and will have a higher beta than the underlying stock.

8. The option values can be calculated using the Black-Scholes equation. The example illustrates the calculation for the call option in problem 8a using "Option Valuation.xls."

Step 1	Insert parameters into the model
Stock price	$80.00
Exercise price	$90.00
Risk-free rate	9%
Volatility	25%
Time (years)	1
Call value	$6.99

Black-Scholes European: No Dividend	
Call value	$6.99
Call delta (hedge ratio)	0.506
Call elasticity	5.783
Using put-call parity	
Put value	$9.25
Delta	–0.494
Elasticity	–4.278
S underlying asset price	$80.00
X exercise price	$90.00
rf risk-free rate	9%
sd volatility	25%
t years to expiration	1
Cumulative Standard Normal Function	
d1 from Black-Scholes	0.014
N(d1)	0.506
d2 from Black-Scholes	–0.236
N(d2)	0.407

[This spreadsheet can be found in the folder "Key Spreadsheets from the Workbook" located on the CD-ROM.]

a. $6.99.

b. $3.02.

c. $16.20, which is made up of the call option value of $11.54 and the put option value of $4.66. This kind of portfolio can be used to capture the returns from an increase in volatility of the stock. If the stock swings more than $16.20 (the likely price of the position) in either direction in the next year, the holder of this portfolio will earn a profit.

d. $5.59 for call, $3.76 for put, $15.26 total.

9. First, calculate the payoff from senior and junior debt for a range of different asset market values. Then, graph the payoffs:

Book value of assets	$10,000,000.00	New Debt	$5,000,000.00
Market value of equity	$30,000,000.00		
Book value of debt	$10,000,000.00		
Market value of asset	$40,000,000.00		

Asset Value (in Millions)	Senior Debt Payoff	Junior Debt Payoff
$ —	$ —	$ —
$ 2.50	$ 2.50	$ —
$ 5.00	$ 5.00	$ —
$ 7.50	$ 7.50	$ —

(Continued)

Asset Value (in Millions)	Senior Debt Payoff	Junior Debt Payoff
$10.00	$10.00	$ —
$12.50	$10.00	$2.50
$15.00	$10.00	$5.00
$17.50	$10.00	$5.00
$20.00	$10.00	$5.00
$22.50	$10.00	$5.00
$25.00	$10.00	$5.00
$27.50	$10.00	$5.00
$30.00	$10.00	$5.00
$32.50	$10.00	$5.00
$35.00	$10.00	$5.00
$37.50	$10.00	$5.00
$40.00	$10.00	$5.00

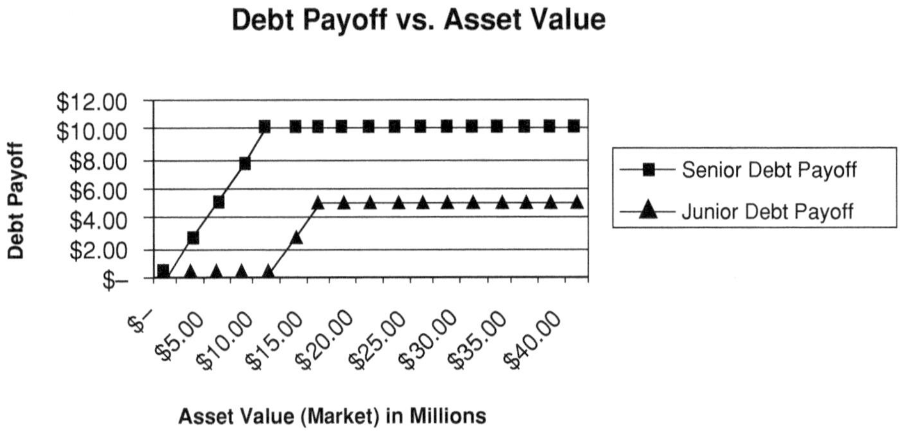

[These spreadsheets can be found in the folder "Key Spreadsheets from the Workbook" located on the CD-ROM.]

From the graph, it is clear that a positive payoff on junior debt begins when the asset value exceeds the obligation to senior creditors, and that the junior debt payoff behaves like a bond when asset value exceeds the combined obligations to senior and subordinated creditors. Note that the sloping portions of the senior and junior debt functions in the graph suggest that, over some range, the creditors will feel like equity holders. When the asset value drops below $15 million, junior debt creditors will have a payoff similar to a short put option—

this short put estimates the default risk discount for the debt. Therefore, when Mr. Brian is considering this loan, he needs to price this option into the terms of the loan. One way to do so is to find the quoted price for a put option with an exercise price for total assets at $15 million and add that into the yield. In addition, Mr. Brian's risk level will affect his decision. Even if this loan offers a higher return because of the extra discount caused by the embedded put option, it also brings higher risk.

CHAPTER 11

Valuing Synergies

1. Preferred discount rates:
   a. Cost-saving synergies are typically considered to be fairly predictable, with a level of risk about as variable as EBIT; therefore, K_d could be used as the discount rate.
   b. The revenue synergies are speculative. Other mergers of content providers and channels of distribution (such as AOL/Time-Warner and Sony/Columbia) that were premised on revenue synergies failed to deliver them. Even K_e may not be high enough to capture the risk. A venture capitalist's required rate of return may be appropriate.
   c. Again, cost synergies are considered to be fairly predictable and might be discounted at K_d; revenue synergies are less certain, so a higher discount rate such as the cost of equity may be more appropriate.

2.	Year 0	Year 1	Year 2	Year 3	Year 4	Year 5
Revenues		297.0	308.9	321.2	334.1	347.4
Cost savings		5.9	6.2	6.4	6.7	6.9
Cost savings after tax		3.9	4.0	4.2	4.3	4.5
Initial investment	(50.0)					
Terminal value						187.9
Free cash flows	(50.0)	3.9	4.0	4.2	4.3	192.4
Net present value	**$98.1**					

3. The present value of after-tax synergies is $8.2 billion:[1]

	1999F	2000F	2001F	2002F	2003F
Revenue enhancements	3,489.6	3,749.9	4,014.8	4,278.5	4,559.8
Operating income from revenue enhancements	425.8	457.5	489.8	522.0	556.3
Cost savings	400.0	412.0	424.4	437.1	450.2
Total incremental operating income	825.8	869.5	914.2	959.1	1,006.5
Taxes	289.0	304.3	320.0	335.7	352.3
After-tax incremental income	536.7	565.2	594.2	623.4	654.3
Terminal cash flow					9,626.8
Total incremental income	536.75	565.19	594.23	623.42	10,281.09
Present value	$8,211.06				

4. The entire gain is predicated upon a reduction in cost of capital that stems from lower-than-anticipated covariance in returns between the two firms. Specific questions to ask are:

   - Why is this covariance *unanticipated* by investors? The merging companies are both public and have a sizable analyst following. What makes you suppose that the analysts are not already aware of this?
   - Is there some *information asymmetry* between insiders and the public? Is there something you would like to tell me that I don't already know?
   - What is the basis for your estimated covariance reduction? Why is it likely to be –0.15, and not –0.20 or –0.10? Is there some rigor behind this estimate, or is it just a guess?
   - What prevents public shareholders from creating this value on their own by combining the two firms in a securities portfolio?
   - If public shareholders can create this value on their own, why should my firm pay your shareholders for the right to create this value?

5. By trial and error or the Excel "solver" function, back-solve to find that annual revenue enhancements should be at least \$2.7 billion:

Year		0	1	2	3	4	5
Revenue enhancements, constant dollars			\$2,702	\$2,702	\$2,702	\$2,702	\$2,702
Expected inflation rate			2%	2%	2%	2%	2%
Growth rate of FCF (nominal), in perpetuity	3%						
Discount rate	10%						
Ongoing investment revenue (year 1)	2%						
Operating cost revenue	90%						
Revenue enhancements, current dollars			\$2,756	\$2,812	\$2,868	\$2,925	\$2,984
Operating costs to support revenue enhancements			(2,481)	(2,530)	(2,581)	(2,633)	(2,685)
Tax expense (@ .38)			(105)	(107)	(109)	(111)	(113)
After-tax cost savings			171	174	178	181	185
Less: investment necessary to realize the added revenue		\$ (400)	(55)	(56)	(57)	(59)	(60)
Subtotal		(400)	116	118	120	123	125
Terminal value							1,844
Free cash flow		\$ (400)	\$ 116	\$ 118	\$ 120	\$ 123	\$1,969
Net present value of cost savings		\$1,200					

6. The present value of savings is $2.6 billion. See the following chart:

Year		0	1	2	3	4	5
Pretax cost savings, constant dollars			$ 63	$118	$183	$183	$ 183
Expected inflation rate	2.5%						
Discount rate	6.0%						
Tax rate	35.0%						
Pretax cost savings, current dollars			$ 63	$118	$183	$188	$ 192
Gain on sale of assets			$ 63	$ 48			
			$126	$166	$183	$188	$ 192
Tax expense			(44)	(58)	(64)	(66)	(67)
After-tax cost savings			19	60	119	122	125
Less: investment necessary to realize the savings		$ (480)					
Subtotal		(480)	19	60	119	122	125
Terminal value							3,660
Free cash flow		$ (480)	$ 19	$ 60	$119	$122	$3,785
Net present value of cost savings		**$2,616**					

7. An investment in Leonid could be regarded as an option on uncertain product development activities. This investment could be valued as a European option. Inserting the following inputs into the Black-Scholes option pricing model yields a value of $167.3 million.

Underlying asset value	$388
Strike price	$272
Term	.667 years
Volatility	90%
Risk-free rate	4.5%

8. No, Leonid is not worth $270 million to Sirius. The expected value of cash flows from existing operations is $88.9 million. Adding to that the value of the contingent synergies, $167.3 million, totals only $256.2 million, less than the asking price.

	Year 1	Year 2	Year 3	Year 4	Year 5
Operating income	$ 6.38	$ 7.54	$ 8.14	$ 6.97	$ 7.32
Cost savings	8.00	8.41	9.05	9.99	11.30
	$ 14.38	$15.95	$17.19	$16.96	$ 18.62
Taxes	5.03	5.58	6.02	5.94	6.52
	$ 9.35	$10.36	$11.18	$11.02	$ 12.10
Capex	—	—	(20.00)	—	—
Depreciation	1.74	2.26	2.71	2.99	3.14

	Year 1	Year 2	Year 3	Year 4	Year 5
Change in net working capital	(2.32)	(3.02)	(3.62)	(3.98)	(4.18)
	$ 8.77	$ 9.61	$ (9.73)	$10.03	$ 11.06
Terminal value					119.30
	$ 8.77	$ 9.61	$(9.73)	$10.03	$130.36
Present value of cash flows	88.91				
Add value of contingent synergies	167.30				
Value of Leonid to Pritzker	$256.21				

NOTE

1. On announcement day, shares of both Citicorp and Travelers soared, adding roughly $30 billion to the combined market value of the two companies.

CHAPTER 12

Valuing the Firm across Borders

1. The problem here is a mismatch between the growth rate of cash flows (stated to be in real terms) and the discount rate (nominal). The rates and cash flows should be expressed in consistent terms, either real/real or nominal/nominal. In ideal settings the two approaches should yield the same NPV. But where depreciation expense is based on historical asset values, the two approaches will differ. Chapter 12 in the main text argues that the nominal/nominal approach gives a correct estimate of NPV where depreciation expense is based on historical book values.

   To complete the valuation, the cash flow forecast must be expressed in nominal terms to be consistent with the cost of capital. The sales growth rate must therefore be adjusted to reflect a nominal rate. Using the Fisher equation, the rate would be $[(1.05 \times 1.03) - 1] = 8.15$ percent, and the NPV would be 89,338.

		Year 1	Year 2	Year 3	Year 4	Year 5
Sales		68,776	74,381	80,443	86,999	94,090
Cost of goods sold		45,048	48,720	52,690	56,985	61,629
Gross profit		23,728	25,662	27,753	30,015	32,461
Operating expenses		16,850	18,223	19,709	21,315	23,052
EBIT		6,878	7,438	8,044	8,700	9,409
Taxes		2,201	2,380	2,574	2,784	3,011
After-tax EBIT		4,677	5,058	5,470	5,916	6,398
Change in net working capital		(344)	(372)	(402)	(435)	(470)
Subtotal		4,333	4,686	5,068	5,481	5,928
Perpetual growth rate	8.15%					
Terminal value						132,181
Free cash flows		4,333	4,686	5,068	5,481	138,108
Discount rate	13.0%					
Discounted cash flows		3,834	3,670	3,512	3,362	74,960
NPV	89,338					

[This spreadsheet can be found in the folder "Key Spreadsheets from the Workbook" located on the CD-ROM.]

2a. The one-year forward rate would be US\$1:PhP33.1. The solution is obtained from the no-arbitrage condition:

$$\$1 \times (1 + R_{\text{Dollar}}) = \$1 \times SPOT_{\frac{\text{Peso}}{\text{Dollar}}} \times (1 + R_{\text{Peso}}) \times \frac{1}{FWD_{\frac{\text{Peso}}{\text{Dollar}}}}$$

$$\text{One-year rate: } (1 + .0552) = \text{PhP}30.4 \times (1 + .15) \times 1/FWD_{\text{1-yr}}$$

$$FWD_{\text{1-yr}} = \text{PhP}33.1$$

(The actual rate one year later was US\$1:PhP43.56—a 32 percent difference from the rate projected. In fact, the Asian crisis broke out in September 1997 and set off rounds of devaluations across Southeast Asia.)

2b. One-year forward rate:

$$\begin{aligned} FWD_{\frac{\text{Peso}}{\text{Dollar}}} &= SPOT_{\frac{\text{Peso}}{\text{Dollar}}} \left[\frac{(1 + Inf_{\text{Peso}})^n}{(1 + Inf_{\text{Dollar}})^n} \right] \\ &= \text{PhP}30.4 \times (1.08/1.025) \\ &= \text{PhP}32.0 \text{ one year from now} \end{aligned}$$

2c. The modest difference between the two estimates of forward exchange rates is due to the large difference in the implied real rates of return in the two countries. The equation implicitly assumes that the two rates are equal. However, the real rates of return implied when one works backward using the Fisher equation are 2.9 percent for the United States and 6.5 percent for the Philippines; hence the nonequivalency of results. It is not unusual for developing countries to offer higher real rates of return than developed countries—it is by this means that capital is attracted from developed to developing countries.

3. This is an illustration of the equivalence of the nominal/nominal and real/real approaches:

	Year 1	Year 2	Year 3	Year 4	Year 5
a. Without inflation, at nominal rate					
Depreciation	50	50	50	50	50
Depreciation tax shield	20	20	20	20	20
NPV of depreciation tax shields	\$79.85				
b. With inflation, at nominal rate					
Depreciation	51.5	53.0	54.6	56.3	58.0
Depreciation tax shield	20.6	21.2	21.9	22.5	23.2
NPV of depreciation tax shields	\$86.94				
c. Without inflation, at real estate					
Depreciation	50	50	50	50	50
Depreciation tax shield	20	20	20	20	20
NPV of depreciation tax shields	\$86.94				

[This spreadsheet can be found in the folder "Key Spreadsheets from the Workbook" located on the CD-ROM.]

Note: The nominal discount rates in both (a) and (b) were calculated using the Fisher equation: $(1.03 \times 1.0485) - 1 = 8.0$ percent.

Notice that the answers to (b) and (c) are the same. In effect, when one discounts depreciation tax shields at the real rate, it is as if the historical cost basis of depreciation was actually allowed to inflate. This is why we say that the real/real approach of discounting cash flows ignores the distortion of using historical cost assets as the basis of depreciation.

4.

(U.S.$, in Millions)		2003	2004	2005	2006	2007	2008
Exchange rate (reals per dollar)	R$3.54	3.75	3.97	4.20	4.45	4.71	4.98
Free cash flows		$402	$502	$637	$709	$803	$1,650
Terminal value						$21,940	
Cash flows including terminal value		$402	$502	$637	$709	$22,743	
Present value in U.S. dollars	$17,677						

[This spreadsheet can be found in the folder "Key Spreadsheets from the Workbook" located on the CD-ROM.]

First, forecast forward exchange rates using the given inflation rates. Then, use the forecasted forward rates to convert the Brazilian cash flows into U.S. dollar cash flows. To come up with the same values between the approaches, the dollar flows must be discounted at the nominal discount rate in U.S. dollars, which is equal to 7.52 percent, calculated as $[(1 + 5\%) \times (1 + 2.4\%) - 1]$. The key underlying assumptions are that inflation is the only differing variable between the U.S. and Brazilian nominal discount rates, and that the real discount rate in Brazilian reals is the same as that in U.S. dollars. Inflation is already reflected in the exchange rate and in the U.S. dollar cash flows; therefore it is necessary only to discount the U.S. dollar cash flows using the real rate of return. These assumptions are consistent with interest rate parity.

5. Based on the data provided, one could use the adjusted CAPM to estimate K_e:

$$k_e = R_f^{US} + \pi + (\beta_i^{Foreign} \cdot \beta_{Foreign}^{US}) \cdot (R_m^{US} - R_f^{US})$$

$[R_f(\text{US})$ + Country credit spread$] = R_f$(foreign country)	7.25%
Beta of target versus foreign country stock index	0.97
Beta of foreign country stock index versus U.S. index	1.28
Market risk premium, U.S.	6.00%
$\mathbf{k_e}$	**14.7%**

[This spreadsheet can be found in the folder "Key Spreadsheets from the Workbook" located on the CD-ROM.]

6a. The cost of equity of Singapore Airlines is estimated to be 10.4 percent, based on the following calculations:

Singapore Airlines	
R_f	4.5%
$R_m - R_f$	5.8%
Beta	1.02
K_e	10.4%

6b. The costs of equity of Southwest Airlines and American Airlines are estimated to be 9.8 percent and 13.7 percent respectively based on the following calculations:

Southwest Airlines	
R_f	3.8%
$R_m - R_f$	5.6%
Beta	1.07
K_e	9.8%
American Airlines	
R_f	3.8%
$R_m - R_f$	5.6%
Beta	1.77
K_e	13.7%

[These spreadsheets can be found in the folder "Key Spreadsheets from the Workbook" located on the CD-ROM.]

6c. In general, the costs of equity between Singapore Airlines and the two U.S. airlines are not comparable because the numbers are denominated in different currencies, and their betas are against different indexes. Also, the equity market risk premiums are slightly different. In short, this is an apples-versus-oranges comparison.

7. Calculating U.S. dollar cost of equity:

   a. The globally diversified nature of the investment firm's holdings would argue for the use of the international CAPM (ICAPM), where the beta of the firm is measured against a global index, and the risk premium used is a world risk premium as opposed to a country risk premium:

$$k_e = R_f + \beta_i^w \times (R_m^w - R_f)$$

   b. Using a CAPM estimate based on a country equity market risk premium might be reasonable if the country is a major component of the global equity market portfolio (as is the United States) and one believes that the global and country equity market risk premiums are similar (as is the case between the United States and Canada). A U.S.-based CAPM could be used if there are comparable U.S. companies that are actively traded on which to base an estimate of beta. Otherwise, given the integration of the United States and Canada, one could estimate a cost of equity from CAPM using Canadian data, or the ICAPM, with betas of comparable companies (making adjustments, where necessary for differences in inflation).

8a. 7.18 percent.

8b. 9.84 percent.

8c. Comparing the results between (a) and (b), the K_e using the adjusted CAPM method is higher because of the country credit spread and also because Telekom Malaysia has a much higher beta against its home market than against the world market, which itself is probably due to a low correlation between equity returns in Malaysia and the global market.

13

Valuing the Highly Levered Firm, Assessing the Highly Levered Transaction

1. To calculate Deep-Sea Tuna's terminal value, you first need to calculate the residual cash flows. Assume that no more debt is repaid. The terminal value for 1992 is derived from the residual cash flow in 1993, capitalized at $K_e - g$. Assume the residual cash flow in 1993 is equal to the net income in 1992 multiplied by $(1 + g)$ (or \$12.2mm × 1.025). Other assumptions are $g = 2.5\%$; $K_e = 13.93\%$.

Solution 1: DCF Analysis Using Circularity Method

	1985	1986	1987	1988	1989	1990	1991	1992
Risk-free rate	12.00%	12.00%	12.00%	12.00%	12.00%	12.00%	12.00%	12.00%
Market premium (equity)	6.00%	6.00%	6.00%	6.00%	6.00%	6.00%	6.00%	6.00%
Book value of the debt ($ MM)	$59.0	$55.4	$49.8	$42.2	$34.7	$29.4	$18.9	$7.0
DCF value of equity ($ MM)	$32.7	$38.6	$45.3	$52.9	$61.6	$71.6	$82.9	$95.8
D/E (market)	180.30%	143.57%	109.91%	79.72%	56.29%	41.06%	22.81%	7.33%
Unlevered beta	0.57	0.57	0.57	0.57	0.57	0.57	0.57	0.57
Levered beta	1.10	1.00	0.90	0.81	0.74	0.69	0.64	0.59
Cost of equity	18.63%	17.97%	17.37%	16.84%	16.42%	16.15%	15.83%	15.55%
Cumulative cost of equity								**16.84%**
Discount factor	84.30%	71.46%	60.88%	52.10%	44.76%	38.53%	33.27%	28.79%
Residual cash flows	$ —	$ —	$ —	$ —	$ —	$ —	$ —	$ —
Terminal value							Note 1	$95.8
Net present value ($ MM)	**$27.6**					Perpetual growth =		2.50%

Note 1: Assumes no more debt is repaid. The terminal value for 1992 was calculated as the residual cash flow in 1993, capitalized at $K_e - g$. The residual cash flow in 1993 was assumed equal to the net income in 1989 times $(1 + g)$ (or 12.2 × 1.025).
Other assumptions: $g = 2.5\%$; $K_e = 13.93\%$.

Using the circularity method illustrated in Exhibit 13.4 of the main text, you can start with an (approximate) fixed equity value (this can be hard-coded in the cell) and then derive the debt-to-equity ratio.

With the unlevered beta of 0.57 (given), you can determine the levered beta (B_L) for the equity as well as the cost of equity.

$$B_L = B_U \times [1 + (1 - t) \times (\text{Debt}_{\text{Book}}/\text{Equity}_{\text{Market}})]$$

The resulting estimated levered beta varies from 1.10 in 1985 to 0.59 in 1992—this is due entirely to the changing mix of debt and equity over time. With estimates of the levered beta, it is now possible to estimate the cost of equity using the CAPM model.

The terminal value can be estimated using the cost of equity in the final year[1] (15.55 percent), the residual cash flow, and the perpetual growth rate (2.50 percent), based on the following equation:

$$\text{Terminal value} = \text{Equity cash flow}_{1992} \times (1 + g)/(k_e - g)$$

From this end point, you can iterate back to the present with circularity calculations to determine the various years' discount rates and annual equity values. Finally, you arrive at the net present value of the equity valuation equal to $27.59 million.

2. To determine what the deal is worth to a senior mezzanine investor, lay out the expected cash flows of the equity, principal, and interest for each year from 1985 to 2000 (as in the Solution 2 chart) and then determine the internal rate of return (IRR) from the total cash flows, which equals 26.67 percent.

Solution 2: Valuing the Senior Mezzanine Participation

Year	Equity	Principal	Interest	Total Cash Flow
1985	$ (1.00)	$ (7.00)		$(8.00)
1986	$ —	$ —	$1.12	$ 1.12
1987	$ —	$ —	$1.12	$ 1.12
1988	$ —	$ —	$1.12	$ 1.12
1989	$ —	$ —	$1.12	$ 1.12
1990	$ —	$ —	$1.12	$ 1.12
1991	$ —	$ —	$1.12	$ 1.12
1992	$19.16	$ —	$1.12	$20.28
1993	$ —	$ —	$1.12	$ 1.12
1994	$ —	$ —	$1.12	$ 1.12
1995	$ —	$ —	$1.12	$ 1.12
1996	$ —	$ 1.40	$1.12	$ 2.52
1997	$ —	$ 1.40	$0.90	$ 2.30
1998	$ —	$ 1.40	$0.67	$ 2.07
1999	$ —	$ 1.40	$0.45	$ 1.85
2000	$ —	$ 1.40	$0.22	$ 1.62
NPV of 20% equity:				**$ 4.52**
IRR				**26.67%**
Benchmark for evaluating IRR			Weight	
K_e		16.84%	12.50%	
i		16.00%	87.50%	
Weighted average			**16.11%**	

Then determine a hurdle rate against which to compare this IRR by taking a weighted average of the geometric mean cost of equity, 16.84 percent (estimated across time from the equity costs found in the first part of the analysis) and the required return on the notes (assume this is 16 percent, for the purpose of this example), weighted according to their proportion in the strip (i.e., 1/8 for equity and 7/8 for notes. The hurdle rate is 16.11 percent. In comparison, the IRR on the strip is larger by about 10 percent.

3.

Solution 3: Valuing the Bank Participation

Year	Equity	Principal	Interest	Total Cash Flow
1985	$ (2.00)	$(37.00)		$(39.00)
1986		$ 0.57	$5.92	$ 6.49
1987		$ 3.62	$5.83	$ 9.45
1988		$ 5.10	$5.25	$ 10.35
1989		$ 5.01	$4.43	$ 9.44
1990		$ 0.30	$3.63	$ 3.94
1991		$ 10.47	$3.58	$ 14.06
1992	$38.33	$ 11.90	$1.91	$ 52.13
NPV of 40% equity:				$ 9.03
IRR				**22.93%**
Benchmark for evaluating IRR			Weight	
K_e		16.84%	5.13%	
i		16.00%	94.87%	
Weighted average			**16.04%**	

You can take the same approach as the one used in answer 2. The difference between hurdle rate of 16.04 percent and the IRR on the strip (22.93%) is about 7 percent.

4. The following chart summarizes both the investment and expected returns of each of the parties involved in this case:

Party	Investment ($ MM)		Return of Equity ($ MM)	IRR	Required Rate of Return
Management	Equity	$ 0.30	$38.30	12,675.0%	16.8%
Senior	Equity	$ 1.00	$19.16	1,816.0%	16.8%
subordinated	Debt	$ 7.00		16.0%	16.0%
notes investors	Total	$ 8.00		26.7%	16.1%
Bank	Equity	$ 2.00	$38.30	1,816.0%	16.8%
	Debt	$37.00		16.0%	16.0%
	Total	$39.00		22.9%	16.0%

Under the assumptions they set forth, the management team of Felicity will earn the highest rate of return on the buyout of Deep-Sea Tuna, which is consistent with the fact that they also bear the highest risk in this investment. The

IRR on the investment is astonishingly high. As argued in Chapter 13 of the main text, there is no straightforward quantitative benchmark against which to assess the adequacy of this IRR—the geometric mean of 16.8 percent is imperfect because the levered beta model assumes no default risk. However, on the basis of sheer size one might conclude that the management team is capturing most of the profit in this investment.

The investors in the senior subordinated (mezzanine) notes take on more risk than the bank does because their debt is junior to that of the bank: They have secondary claims on the repayment of debt. In order to compensate for this additional risk, these investors would receive an opportunity to purchase 20 percent of the equity in Deep-Sea Tuna. So the overall returns on their investment are higher than those for the bank's investment.

From the perspective of the bank, having a mezzanine investor creates a buffer of sorts; to these senior lenders, the mezzanine layers look like equity.

Overall, this case illustrates the different grades of investment based on risk levels; the higher the risks, the higher the returns. The senior subordinated note seems to be the "plug" security in the transaction, designed to supply the financing and meet investors' required returns without overburdening the firm financially.

[The spreadsheets in this chapter can be found in the folder "Key Spreadsheets from the Workbook" located on the CD-ROM.]

NOTE

1. By implication, using the final year's cost of equity to estimate the terminal value suggests no further changes in the mix of debt and equity for the firm. The analyst should test this assumption for reasonableness. But in general, it is not an unreasonable assumption: The firm is unlikely to reduce its debt to zero.

14

Real Options and Their Impact on M&A

1. Real options may appear in the field of M&A in strategic planning, deal design, and postmerger integration:
   - In strategy, real options appear in decisions about flexibility versus irreversibility of actions; insurance; learning and competencies; and corporate strategic planning. Possible applications of real options in strategy might be buying a minority interest before completing the acquisition; buying a built-up company versus building up the same assets yourself; choosing to be a second mover; acquiring the rights to exploit an uncertain resource; and searching for acquisition targets.
   - Real options often appear in deal design through the exchange offer, breakup terms, liquidity and control features, contingent payment schemes, transaction risk management, and takeover tactics.
   - In postmerger integration, real options may appear in the organizational design and operational architecture of the firm, the structuring of contracts for human resources, and selection among competing capabilities.
2. There are four possible approaches for valuing options:
   1. Value the real option in the framework of an existing equation.
   2. Value the option using the framework of a binomial lattice.
   3. Value the option in a decision tree framework.
   4. Value the option using simulation analysis.

   The Black-Scholes option pricing model is the simplest to use. It can be helpful when the parameters are easy to define and the assumptions for underlying asset returns are met. The binomial lattice is more flexible than the Black-Scholes equation; therefore it can be best used for simplified staging problems. But it is tedious to use it to model many periods, and use of the binomial distribution may result in oversimplification. The decision tree method is the most commonly used model for real option valuation because of its flexibility and transparency. Its drawbacks are that it is difficult to use for more complex problems, and it entails estimating probabilities accurately. Finally, Monte Carlo simulation is the most advanced and comprehensive method. It not only values options, but it also provides a complete risk profile. Similar to the decision tree and binomial methods, the difficulty of assessing the appropriate distribution function to use makes it a subjective method, too.

3. Among the four choices, the court upgrade and flexible lighting and sound system give you options. They have extra value compared to the seating upgrade and the multimedia center because they give you the *flexibility* to change the use of the stadium. The luxury rooms and the multimedia center projects do not provide the same flexibility.

4.

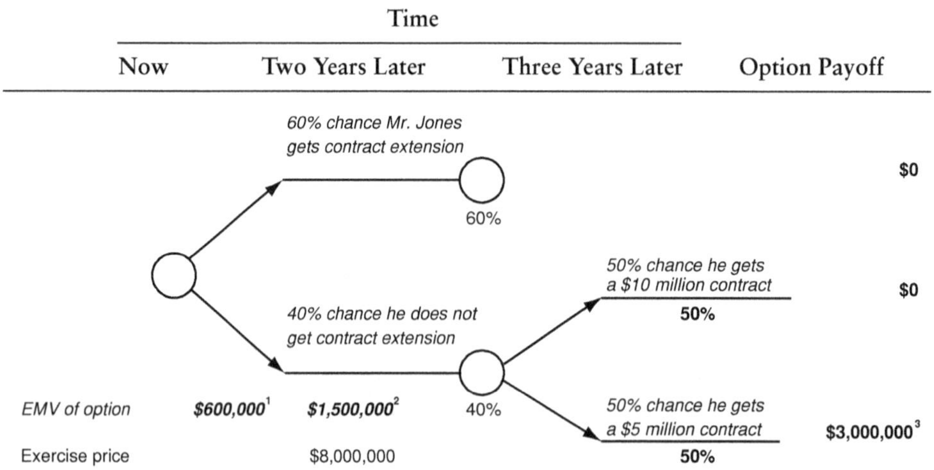

1. $600,000 = 60% × $0 + 40% × $1,500,000.
2. $1,500,000 = 50% × $0 + 50% × $3,000,000. $1.5 million is the expected monetary value of this option after two years.
3. $3,000,000 = $8,000,000 – $5,000,000. If Mr. Jones manages to get only the $5 million contract, he would want to exercise his extension option with the current team to earn a salary of $8 million. Therefore, the payoff of the option is the difference between the $5 million contract he could get and the $8 million guaranteed extension contract.

Folding back the tree to the present, we come up with a value of $600,000 for the extension option.

5.

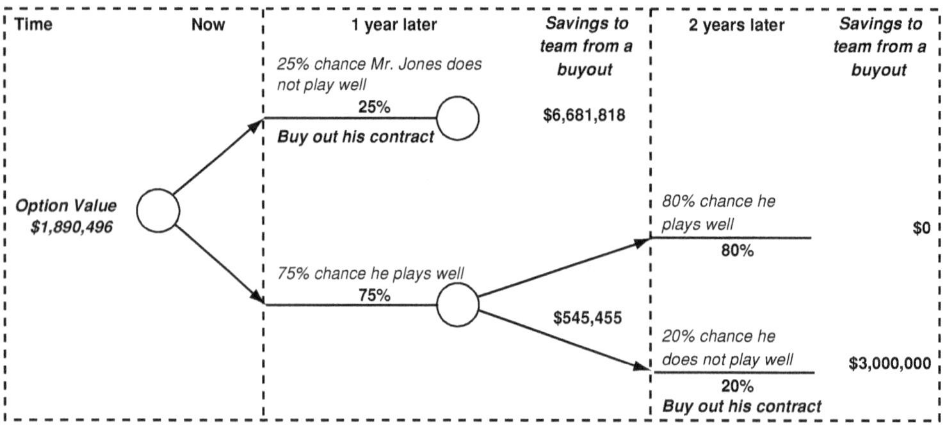

(Continued)

The payoff of \$3,000,000 at the end of two years is calculated based on the fact that the team will buy his contract out at \$6 million instead of paying him \$9 million. The savings of \$6,681,818 after the first year is calculated by following the same logic and accounting for the time value of money.

\$6,681,818 = \$9,000,000/(1 + 10%) + \$8,500,000 – \$10,000,000
\$545,455 = (80% × \$0 + 20% × \$3,000,000)/(1 + 10%)
\$1,890,496 = (25% × \$6,681,818 + 75% × \$545,455)/(1 + 10%)

Payment schedule: Discount rate 10%

Year	Salary		
1	\$7,500,000	Exercise price in year 1	\$10,000,000
2	\$8,500,000	Exercise price in year 2	\$ 6,000,000
3	\$9,000,000		

Based on the preceding calculation, the total present value of the buyout option = \$1,890,496.

6.

Step 1 ***Insert parameters***

Underlying asset value (The current value of the patent)	**\$8,000,000**
Exercise price (The purchase price for the patent after three years.)	**\$10,000,000**
Risk-free rate	**7.5%**
Volatility	**25.0%**
Time (years)	**3**
Resulting call value	**\$1,377,415**

Black-Scholes
European: No Dividend

Call value	**\$ 1,377,415**
Call delta (hedge ratio)	0.587373404
Call elasticity	3.411454722
Using put-call parity	
Put value	\$ 1,362,577
Delta	–0.412626596
Elasticity	–2.422625293
S underlying asset price	\$ 8,000,000
X exercise price	\$10,000,000
rf risk-free rate	7.5%
sd volatility	25.0%
t years to expiration	3
Cumulative Standard Normal Function	
d1 from Black-Scholes	0.220793636
N(d1)	0.587373404
d2 from Black-Scholes	–0.212219066
N(d2)	0.415968097

7.

Step 1 ***Grow the tree***

Parameters needed:

Volatility (annualized)	20%
Length of period (year)	1
Up percentage (u)	1.221402758
Down percentage (d)	0.818730753

Now	Year 1	Year 2	Year 3	Year 4	Year 5
					$ 54,365,637
				$44,510,819	
			$ 36,442,376		**$ 36,442,376**
		$ 29,836,494		$29,836,494	
	$24,428,055		**$ 24,428,055**		**$ 24,428,055**
$ 20,000,000		$ 20,000,000		$20,000,000	
	$16,374,615		$16,374,615		$16,374,615
		$ 13,406,401		$13,406,401	
			$10,976,233		$10,976,233
				$ 8,986,579	
					$7,357,589

A: $24,428,055 = $20,000,000 × U (1.221)
The binomial approach assumes that each year, the value of the firm will move up by *u* (*u*= e^(1 × 20%) = 1.221) or down by *d* (*d* = e^(−1 × 20%) = 1/*u* = 0.818). This means that at the end of the first year, the value of the joint venture will be either $24,428,055 (*u* × $20,000,000) or $16,374,615 (*d* × $20,000,000)

Step 2 ***Assess the probabilities of an up or down movement***

— These will be used in step 5 to fold back the tree.
Pu = [(1 + Rf)−d)]/(u−d) 0.574336542— 57.43% chance of moving up
Pd = [u−(1 + Rf)]/(u−d) 0.425663458— 42.57% chance of moving down
Rf = 5%

Step 3 ***Assess the states in which the options will be exercised***

In the table above, the shaded numbers indicate when the option will be exercised. In these cases, the value of the joint venture is greater than the exercise price — $20,000,000 for 100% ownership or $5,000,000 for 25% of the joint venture.

Step 4 ***Estimate the payoffs associated with these end-states.***

Exercise price $20,000,000 for 100% 25% 25%

Now	Year 1	Year 2	Year 3	Year 4	**Year 5**
					$8,591,409
				—	
			$4,110,594		**$4,110,594**
		—		—	
	—		**$1,107,014**		**$1,107,014**
—		—		—	
	—		—		—
		—		—	
			—		—
				—	
			—		—

Step 5 ***Calculate the present expected value of future payoffs.***

Now	**Year 1**	**Year 2**	**Year 3**	**Year 4**	**Year 5**
			B		**$8,591,409**
				$6,365,800	
			$8,686,041		**$4,110,594**
		$5,897,539		**$2,697,219**	
	$3,907,369		**$2,827,833**		**$1,107,014**
$2,539,822		**$1,681,060**		**$605,522**	
	$992,963		**$331,213**		—
		$181,169		—	
			—		—
				—	
					—

$8,686,041 = ($6,365,800 × Pu + $2,697,219 × Pd)/(1 + rf) + $4,110,594
(B): Taking the example of $8,686,041, one would take the expected value of the *Pu* × *$6,365,800* + *Pd* × *$2,697,219*, or (.5743 × $6,365,800) + (0.4257 × $2,697,219) to yield $4,804,219—discounting this by one year at the risk-free rate, 0.05 yields $3,814,374, then add $4,110,594 from Step 4 for a total option payoff in year 3 of $8,686,041. This process is repeated for each cell to arrive at a value of $2,539,822 for the option portfolio.

8.

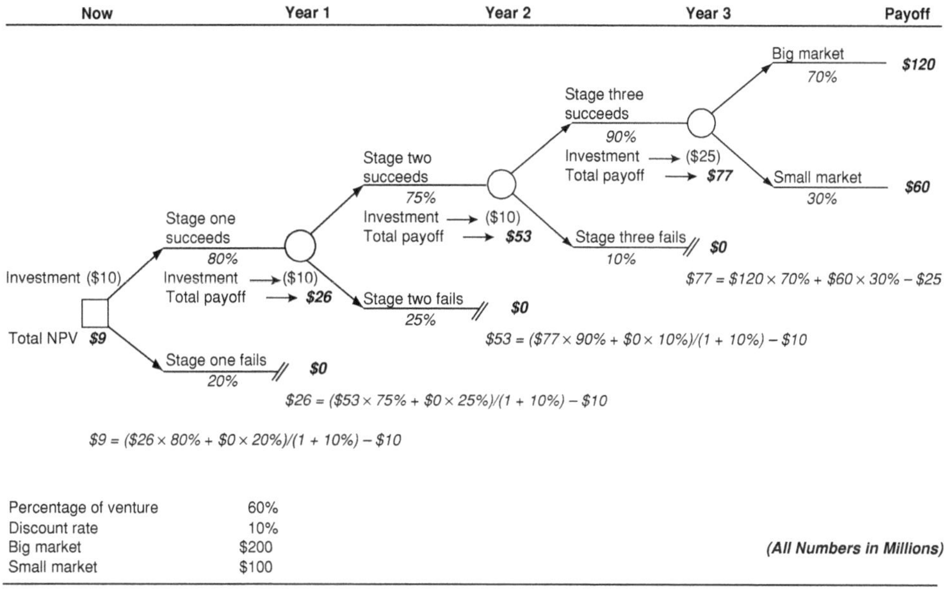

In the decision tree, the terminal payoffs are calculated by multiplying 60 percent by the forecasted profits because ABC is purchasing 60 percent of XYZ. Then, the payoffs are discounted according to the corresponding time period to obtain the expected monetary value (EMV). The investment for each period is deducted from EMV to obtain the net present value for each period.

9a. To arrive at the conclusion about whether to invest in this project, one needs to calculate the net present value. First, the cash flow model is built as shown. Then, the uncertainty distribution about the revenues is specified: a normal distribution with a mean of $50 million and a standard deviation of $25 million. (Revenues have a minimum value of zero as sales cannot be negative.) NPV is calculated by discounting all cash flows by 25 percent, and the probability distribution of NPV is simulated by running the model 5,000 times. The results reveal a mean NPV of $10.58 million for company ABC.

			Now	Year 1	Year 2	Year 3
Capital expenditure	10 in millions					
Period	3 years	Capex	−10.0			
Mean of year 1 revenue	50 in millions	Revenues		39.5	41.4	43.5
Standard deviation of revenue	25 in millions	Profit		7.9	8.3	8.7
Revenue growth for years 2 and 3	5%	Total cash flows	−10.0	7.9	8.3	8.7
Profit margin	20%	NPV of project		6.1		
Discount rate	25%					

Statistics	Value
Trials	5,000
Mean	$10.58
Median	$10.21
Mode	—
Standard deviation	$ 9.63
Variance	$92.67
Skewness	0.25
Kurtosis	2.74
Coefficient of variability	0.91
Range minimum	($9.98)
Range maximum	$44.70
Range width	$54.68
Mean standard error	$ 0.14

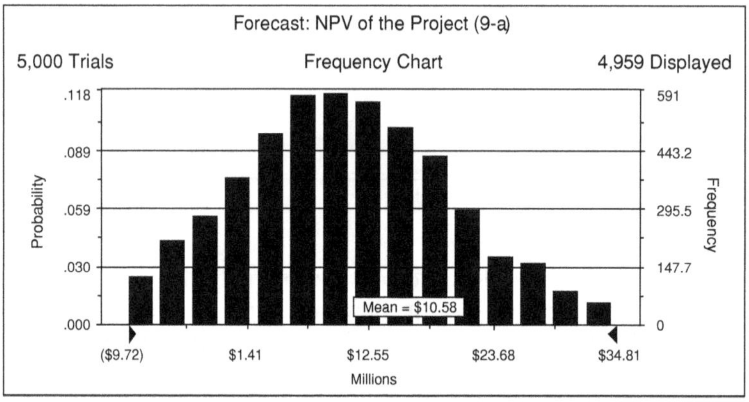

9b. Similar to (a), a cash flow model is built. Then, the uncertainty distribution about the revenues in year 1 is specified: a normal distribution with a mean of $50 million and a standard deviation of $25 million. (Revenues have a minimum value of zero as sales cannot be negative.) Finally, the expansion option is modeled by assuming that if revenues exceed $50 million, the cash flows for years 2 and 3 are calculated by using a new revenue growth rate (20 percent on top of 5 percent) for the excess over $50 million, and a new profit margin (21 perent). NPV is calculated by discounting all cash flows by 25 percent. Running the model 5,000 times, the simulation generates a mean NPV of $11.18 million for company ABC. Compared to the result in (a), it indicates a $0.50 million increase in the project NPV, the value of this expansion option.

			Now	Year 1	Year 2	Year 3
Capital expenditure	10 in millions					
Extra capital expenditure for expansion	1.5 in millions	Capex	–10.0	0.0		
Period	3 years	Revenues		26.9	28.3	29.7
Mean of year 1 revenue	50 in millions	Profit		5.4	5.7	5.9

			Now	Year 1	Year 2	Year 3
Standard deviation of revenue	25 in millions	Total cash flow	–10.0	5.4	5.7	5.9
Revenue growth for years 2 and 3	5%	NPV of project		1.0		
Extra revenue growth from expansion for years 2 and 3	20%					
Profit margin (without expansion)	20%					
Profit margin (with expansion)	21%					
Discount rate	25%					

Statistics	Value
Trials	5,000
Mean	\$ 11.18
Median	\$ 10.17
Mode	—
Standard deviation	\$ 10.11
Variance	\$102.16
Skewness	0.37
Kurtosis	2.90
Coefficient of variability	0.90
Range minimum	(\$ 9.99)
Range maximum	\$ 49.11
Range width	\$ 59.11
Mean standard error	\$ 0.14

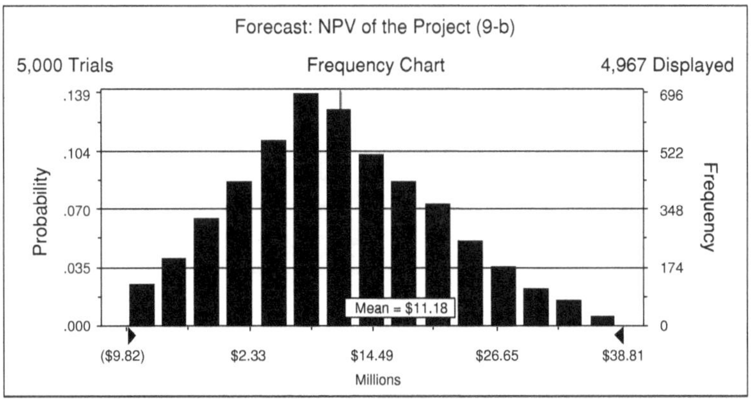

[All spreadsheets in this chapter can be found in the folder "Key Spreadsheets from the Workbook" located on the CD-ROM.]

CHAPTER 15

Valuing Liquidity and Control

1. Liquidity and control are rights, and as option theory shows, rights are valuable. You paid a premium or discount because of the presence or absence of these rights.

2. The following table gives the calculations based on the binomial option-pricing model. The inability to exit is like forgoing the value of a put option for the next three years. The calculation estimates the value of this put option to be \$5.85 million, or 11.7 percent of the value of the company.

Step 1 Grow the tree

Parameters needed:

Volatility (annualized)	22%
Length of period (year)	1
Up percentage (u)	1.2460767
Down percentage (d)	0.8025188

Now	Year 1	Year 2	Year 3
	(A)		\$96.74
		\$77.64	
	\$62.30		\$62.30
\$50.00		\$50.00	
	\$40.13		**\$40.13**
		\$32.20	
			\$25.84

(A) – \$62.30 = \$50 × U = \$50 × 1.246

The binomial approach assumes that each year, the value of the firm will move up by *u* (*u* = e^(1 × 22%) = 1.246) or down by *d* (*d* = e^(−1 × 22%) = 1/*u* = 0.803). This means that at the end of the first year, the firm's value will be worth either \$62.30 million (*u* × \$50 milllion) or \$40.13 (*d* × \$50 million)

Step 2 Assess the probabilities of an up or down movement. (These probabilities will be used in step 5 to fold back the tree.)

Pu = [(1 + Rf) – d)]/(u – d)	51.29%	= chance of the firm value moving up
Pd = [u – (1 + Rf)]/(u – d)	48.71%	= chance of the firm value moving down

(Rf = 3%)

Step 3 Assess the states in which the options will be exercised

In the above table, the shaded numbers indicate when the put option will be exercised. In these cases, the payoff is less than the exercise price of \$50,000,000.

Step 4 Estimate the payoffs associated with these end-states.

Now	Year 1	Year 2	Year 3	
			—	
		—		
	—		—	
—		—		
	—		**\$9.87**	(\$50 – \$40.13)
		—		
			\$24.16	(\$50 – \$25.84)

Step 5 Calculate the present value of expected future payoffs.

Now	Year 1	Year 2	Year 3
			—
		—	
			—
	\$2.21		
\$5.85		**\$4.67**	
	\$10.05		**\$9.87**
		\$16.34	
	(B)		**\$24.16**

(B) — \$10.05 = (\$4.67 × Pu + \$16.34 × Pd)/(1 + Rf)

For instance, to arrive at (B), \$10.05 million, one would take the expected value of (*Pu × \$4.67 + Pd × \$16.34)*, or (.513 × \$4.67) + (0.487 × \$16.34) to yield \$10.35. Discounting this by one year at the risk-free rate, 3%, yields \$10.05. This process is repeated for the other cells. Folding the expected values back to the present, we arrive at a value of \$5.85 million for this put option.

Step 6 Calculate the liquidity discount.

Net value of the firm (Value of the firm – Put option value)	\$44.15
Liquidity discount	11.7%

3. The solution is similar to problem 2, except that the binomial tree is grown out to five years instead of three years. Now the put option is worth \$6.39 million or 12.8 percent of the base value of the firm. See the chart:

Step 1 Grow the tree

		Now	Year 1	Year 2	Year 3	Year 4
						\$120.54
Parameters needed:		(A)			\$96.74	
				\$77.64		\$77.64
Volatility (annualized)	22%		\$62.30		\$62.30	
Length of period (year)	1	\$50.00		\$50.00		\$50.00
			\$40.13		\$40.13	
Up percentage (u)	1.2460767			\$32.20		\$32.20
Down percentage (d)	0.8025188				\$25.84	
(A) — \$62.30 = \$50 × U = \$50 × 1.246						\$20.74

The binomial approach assumes that each year, the value of the firm will move up by *u* (*u* = e^(1 × 22%) = (1.246)or down by *d* (*d* = e^ (–1 × 22%) = 1/*u*= 0.803). This means that at the end of the first year, the firm's value will be worth either \$62.30 million (*u* × \$50 milllion) \$40.13 (*d* × \$50 million)

Step 2 Assess the probabilities of an up or down movement. (These probabilities will be used in step 5 to fold back the tree.)

Pu = [(1+Rf)-d)]/(u–d)	51.29% =	chance of the firm value moving up
Pd = [u–(1+Rf)]/(u–d)	48.71% =	chance of the firm value moving down
Rf = 3%		

Step 3 Assess the states in which the options will be exercised

In the above table, the shaded numbers indicate when the put option will be exercised. In these cases, the payoff is less than the exercise price of \$50,000,000.

Step 4 Estimate the payoffs associated with these end-states.

Exercise price \$50

Now	Year 1	Year 2	Year 3	Year 4	Year 5	
					—	
				—		
			—		—	
		—		—		
	—		—		—	
—		—		—		
	—		—		**\$9.87**	(\$50 – \$40.13)
		—		—		
			—		**\$24.16**	(\$50 – \$25.84)
				—		
					\$33.36	(\$50 – \$16.64)

Step 5 Calculate the present value of expected future payoffs.

	Now	Year 1	Year 2	Year 3	Year 4	Year 5
						—
					—	
				—		—
			\$1.04		—	
		\$3.29		***\$2.21***		—
	\$6.39		**\$5.85**		***\$4.67***	
		\$10.04		***\$10.05***		**\$9.87**
			\$15.07		***\$16.34***	
				\$21.29		**\$24.16**
(B) — \$10.04 = (\$5.87 × Pu + \$15.07 × Pd)/(1 + Rf)		*(B)*			***\$27.80***	
						\$33.36

For instance, to arrive at (B), \$10.04 million, one would take the expected value of (*Pu* × *\$5.85* + *Pd* × *\$15.07)*, or (.513 × \$5.85) + (0.487 × \$15.07) to yield \$10.35. Discounting this by one year at the risk-free rate, 3%, yields \$10.04. This process is repeated for the other cells. Folding the expected values back to the present, we arrive at a value of \$6.39 million for this put option.

Step 6 Calculate the liquidity discount.

Net value of the firm (Value of the firm – Put option value)	\$43.61
Liquidity discount	12.8%

Extending the term of illiquidity will result in a higher liquidity discount. The liquidity option becomes more valuable because of the longer term. However, although you will pay less now, the risk is also greater due to more uncertainty for a longer term.

4. The implied volatility can be found using Excel's Goal Seek function, but to do so, one must first know the value of the option:

Step 1 Determine the implied option values for both buyer and seller.

			Implied option value for each party:
DCF valution:	$10,000,000		
Buyer's bid price:	$8,500,000	***Buyer***	***$1,500,000***
Seller's ask price:	$9,000,000	***Seller***	***$1,000,000***

Step 2 Insert the parameters into the model and then use Goal Seek to calculate implied volatility.
(The illustration below calculates the implied volatility from the point of view of the seller. To calculate the implied volatility from the buyer's viewpoint, simply replace the put value of the seller with that of the buyer.)

Stock price	$10,000,000
* DCF value of the company.	
Exercise price	$10,000,000
* The cost to exercise the option.	
Risk-free rate	7%
Put value	$1,000,000
Time (years)	1
Implied volatilities:	
Buyer's view:	47.6%
Seller's view:	34.2%

Black-Scholes European: No Dividend	
Call value	$1,676,062
Call delta (hedge ratio)	0.646431209
Call elasticity	3.856845901
Using put-call parity	
Put value	$1,000,000
Delta	–0.353568791
Elasticity	–3.535687914
S underlying asset price	$10,000,000
X exercise price	$10,000,000
rf risk-free rate	7%
sd volatility	34.2%
t years to expiration	1
Cumulative Standard Normal Function	
d1 from Black-Scholes	0.375703313
N(d1)	0.646431209
d2 from Black-Scholes	0.033955554
N(d2)	0.51354376

The implied volatility from the buyer's valuation is greater than that for seller. As the results show, the volatility implied by the buyer's view is 47.6 percent and by the seller's view is 34.2 percent. Therefore, the buyer's assessment of the risk level of the company is higher than that of the seller. Thus, the value of the put option is greater to the buyer than to the seller.

[The spreadsheets for questions 1 to 4 can be found in the folder "Key Spreadsheets from the Workbook" located on the CD-ROM.]

5. Your options position can be decomposed into two options: a long call option expiring in five years and a short put option expiring in two years. Therefore, the value of your options is the difference between the call and put option values.

Valuation of Call		
Assumptions:		
Stock price	$	40
Exercise price	$	40
Risk-free rate		8%
Volatility		20%
Time (years)		5
Call value	**$**	**14.15**

(Continued)

Valuation of Put		
Assumptions:		
Stock price	$	40
Exercise price	$	40
Risk-free rate		6%
Volatility		20%
Time (years)		2
Put value	$	2.36
Long call	$	14.15
Short put	$	2.36
Net value of one share	$	11.79
Total value of options	$1,179,000.00	

[This spreadsheet can be found in the folder "Key Spreadsheets from the Workbook" located on the CD-ROM.]

6a. The Shapley Values for the oceanic shareholders are given in the following table—this table assumes that the oceanic shareholders own 50 percent of the votes.

A	% Voting control shareholder 1								
% Voting Control Shareholder 2	5	10	15	20	25	30	35	40	45
45	0.18	0.20	0.22	0.24	0.28	0.32	0.38	0.44	0.50
40		0.32	0.35	0.38	0.41	0.44	0.48	0.50	0.44
35			0.42	0.44	0.47	0.49	0.50	0.48	0.38
30				0.48	0.49	0.50	0.49	0.44	0.32
25					0.50	0.49	0.47	0.41	0.28
20						0.48	0.44	0.38	0.24
15							0.42	0.35	0.22
10								0.32	0.20
5									0.18

Notice that the power index for oceanic shareholders is highest when the balance of shares is divided equally between the major shareholders; for example, each has 25 percent. Notice also that the increase or loss in power is not linear. Going from a 25–25 split between shareholders 1 and 2 to a 20–30 split results in a .02 decrease in power for the oceanic shareholders. However, going from a 20–30 split between shareholders 1 and 2, to a 15–35 split results in a greater decrease in power—.06—for the oceanic shareholders. In general, the more lopsided the balance between shareholders 1 and 2 becomes, the higher the rate at which the oceanic shareholders lose power.

6b. The following table assumes that the oceanic shareholders own only 10 percent of the votes.

B	% Voting control shareholder 1								
% Voting Control Shareholder 2	41	42	43	44	45	46	47	48	49
49	0.18	0.20	0.22	0.24	0.28	0.32	0.38	0.44	0.50
48		0.32	0.35	0.38	0.41	0.44	0.48	0.50	0.44
47			0.42	0.44	0.47	0.49	0.50	0.48	0.38
46				0.48	0.49	0.50	0.49	0.44	0.32
45					0.50	0.49	0.47	0.41	0.28
44						0.48	0.44	0.38	0.24
43							0.42	0.35	0.22
42								0.32	0.20
41									0.18

Notice that the power indexes for the oceanic shareholders in this scenario follow the same pattern as in problem 6a. This illustrates that voting power derives from *relative* distribution of votes rather than the absolute percentage held.

7.

			Percentage Return				Total Capital			
			Now	Year 1	Year 2	Year 3	Now	Year 1	Year 2	Year 3
Step 1	Grow the tree									
	Parameters needed:		(A)			**24.60%**				$174.37
					20.14%				$139.95	
	Volatility (annualized)	20%		**16.49%**		**16.49%**		$116.49		$146.83
	Length of period (year)	1	13.50%		13.50%		$100.00		$126.05	
				11.05%		11.05%		$111.05		$139.98
	Up percentage (u)	1.221403			9.05%				$121.10	
	Down percentage (d)	0.818731				7.41%				$130.07

(A) – 16.49% = 13.5% × u = 13.5% × 1.221

The binomial approach assumes that each year, the index return will move up by *u*(*u* = e^(1 × 20%) = 1.221) or down by *d* (*d* = e^(–1 × 20%) = 1/*u* = 0.818). This means that at the end of the first year, the S&P 500's return will be either 16.49% (*u* × 13.5%) or 11.05% (*d* × 13.5%)

Step 2 Assess the probabilities of an up or down movement. (These probabilities will be used in step 5 to fold back the tree.)

Pu = [(1 + Rf) – d)]/(u – d) 62.40% = chance of index return moving up
Pd = [u – (1 + Rf)]/(u – d) 37.60% = chance of index return moving down
Rf = 7%

Step 3 Assess the states in which the options will be exercised

In the above table, the shaded numbers indicate when the incremental benefit will be obtained. In these cases, the return on the S&P 500 index is greater than the "exercise percentage" of 15%.

Step 4 Estimate the percentage and monetary payoffs associated with these states.

Trigger percentage 15%

Percentage payoff				*Monetary payoff*			
Now	**Year 1**	**Year 2**	**Year 3**	**Now**	**Year 1**	**Year 2**	**Year 3**
			9.60%				**$13.43**
		5.14%				**$5.99**	
	1.49%		**1.49%**		**$1.49**		**$1.88**
—		—		—		—	
	—		—		—		—
		—				—	
			—				—

The percentage return is calculated by deducting the trigger return — 15% — from the return on the S&P 500. The monetary pay off is calculated by multiplying the percentage payoff with the corresponding year's beginning total capital.

Step 5 Calculate the present value of expected future payoffs.

Now	**Year 1**	**Year 2**	**Year 3**
		(B)	
			$13.43
		$14.48	
	$10.32		**$1.88**
$6.24		**$1.09**	
	$0.64		—
		—	
			—

(B) — $14.48 = ($13.43 × Pu + $1.88 × Pd)/(1 + Rf) + $5.99

For instance, to arrive at (B), $14.48 million, one would take the expected value of (*Pu* × *$13.43* + *Pd* × *$1.88)*, or (.6240 × $13.43) + (0.3760 × $1.88) to yield $9.09. Discounting this by one year at the risk-free rate, 7%, yields $8.49, to which we add $5.99 to arrive at the value of $14.48 million for year 2. This process is repeated for the other cells. Folding the expected values back to the present, we arrive at a value of $6.24 million for control. This is the present value of the incremental benefits from the aggressive trading strategy.

8.

Step 1 Build an Excel spreadsheet model. A finished model, "SP 500 CHPT15.xls," can be found on the CD-ROM.

S&P 500 Return	
Mean	13.50%
Volatility	20%

Starting capital	$100.00
Risk-free rate	7%
Trigger return	15%

Time	Now	Year 1	Year 2	Year 3
SP 500 return	13.50%	15.27%	11.82%	10.48%
Standard deviation	2.700%	3.053%	2.364%	2.095%
Total capital	$100.00	$115.27	$128.89	$142.39
Incremental profit		$0.27	$ —	$ —
Present value of incremental profit				$0.25

Step 2 Go to cells with uncertain distributions and specify the distribution. In this problem, this has been done for you: The distribution is normal with a mean of 13.5% and a standard deviation of 2.7%.

Step 3 Run Crystal Ball 5,000 times (or any number of times you want), and you will get a result like the following:
Forecast: PV of incremental profit

Summary:

Display range is from $0.00 to $16.95 million.
Entire range is from $0.00 to $43.97 million.
After 5,000 trials, the Standard error of the mean is $0.07.

Statistics	Value
Trials	5,000
Mean	$2.84
Median	$0.00
Mode	$0.00
Standard deviation	$5.20
Variance	$27.07
Skewness	2.60
Kurtosis	10.85
Coefficient of variability	1.83
Range minimum	$0.00
Range maximum	$43.97
Range width	$43.97
Mean standard error	$0.07

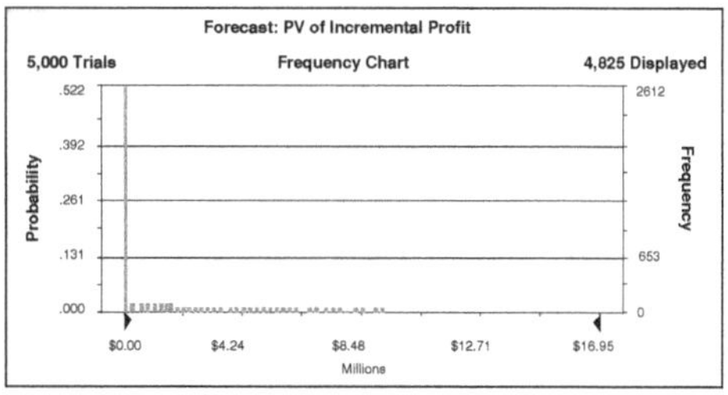

In this particular run, the value of control is calculated at $2.84 million with a standard deviation of $5.20 million. This mean is much lower than the result calculated using the binomial model because of the smoothing effect of a normal distribution. In addition, we obtain a risk profile by using Monte Carlo simulation as opposed to the binomial model. Our simulation tells us that the payoff has a very high standard deviation, indicating that the value of the control right will be very uncertain.

Note that simulation results will not always return the exact numbers. However, in general, the results should be pretty consistent.

9.

Step 1	Insert parameters into the model
Stock price	$20
Exercise price	$25
Risk-free rate	8%
Volatility	25%
Time (years)	2
Call value	*$2.22*

Control gives the owner the right to take on this co-branding project. The total value of the control right is $2.22 million. Therefore, the buyer can pay $2.22 million for this "control" premium.

Black-Scholes European: No Dividend	
Call value	$2.22
Call delta (hedge ratio)	0.487992
Call elasticity	4.405481
Using put-call parity	
Put value	$3.73
Delta	–0.512008
Elasticity	–2.743084
S underlying asset price	$20
X exercise price	$25
rf risk-free rate	8%
sd volatility	25%
t years to expiration	2
Cumulative Standard Normal Function	
d1 from Black-Scholes	–0.030105
N(d1)	0.487992
d2 from Black-Scholes	–0.383658
N(d2)	0.350616

10.

Base case value of the equity[1] (in millions)	$100.00
Adjustment for illiquidity[2]	–25%
Value of equity adjusted for possible illiquidity[3] (in millions)	$ 75.00
% premium for control	20%
Size of controlling block[4]	51%
Value of controlling block[5] (in millions)	$ 45.90
Value of minority block[6] (in millions)	$ 29.10
Value of equity adjusted for control asymmetry and illiquidity[7] (in millions)	$ 75.00
Total share outstanding in millions	50
Controlling block price per share[8]	$ 1.80
Minority block price per share[9]	$ 1.19

1. The base value of the company is the value of the firm with marketable shares but without any control blocks. This is in effect the value of the firm calculated from the DCF model.
2. When you take the firm private, the shares are going to be illiquid, hence a discount—in this case, 25%. Illiquidity is assumed to affect all shares equally.
3. Base value × (1 – % discount for illiquidity).
4. Percentage ownership of the major shareholder.
5. Value of equity adjusted for possible illiquidity × (1 + Control premium) × Size of controlling block.
6. The difference between the value of equity adjusted for possible illiquidity and the value of the control block.
7. The law of conservation of value requires that the value of minority and control blocks sum up to the value of equity adjusted for possible illiquidity.
8. Value of the controlling block divided by the number of shares for the controlling block.
9. Value of the minority block divided by the number of shares for the minority block.

The price per share for the controlling block is $1.80, and the price per share for the minority block is $1.19.

[The spreadsheets for questions 6 to 10 can be found in the folder "Key Spreadsheets from the Workbook" located on the CD-ROM.]

CHAPTER 16

Financial Accounting for Mergers and Acquisitions

1. Consolidated statements for 100 percent stock transaction:

Consolidated Balance Sheet (FY 2001)	BB&B	Entries	Consolidated
Assets			
Current assets:			
Cash and equivalents	239.3	46.8	286.2
Merchandise inventories	606.7	310.7	917.4
Other current assets	39.7	119.5	159.2
Total current assets	885.7	477.1	1,362.8
Investment securities	—	—	—
Property and equipment, net	302.7	212.1	514.7
Identifiable intangible assets		500.0	500.0
Goodwill		1,020.6	1,020.6
Other assets	7.4	46.6	53.9
Total assets	1,195.7	2,256.4	3,452.1
Liabilities and Shareholders' Equity			
Current liabilites:			
Accounts payable, accrued expenses and other current liabilities	321.2	144.1	465.3
Current portion of long-term debt		—	—
Income taxes payable	32.0	—	32.0
Total current liabilities	353.2	144.1	497.3
Long-term debt		25.0	25.0
Deferred rent and other liabilities	25.5	34.7	60.2
Total liabilities	378.7	203.8	582.5
Shareholders' equity:			
Common stock	183.9	2,052.5	2,236.4
Retained earnings	633.2	—	633.2
Cumulative other comprehensive income			
Treasury stock			
Total shareholders' equity	817.0	2,052.5	2,869.5
Total liabilities and shareholders' equity	1,195.7	2,256.4	3,452.1

All accounts on the balance sheet simply add the preexisting balances for BB&B and Pier 1, except for "Identifiable intangible assets," "Goodwill," and "Common Stock."

Identifiable intangible assets: ← Given in the problem

Goodwill: ← Goodwill is calculated as follows:

Implied market value of firm (bid price + Pier 1's liabilities)	2,256.35
Book value of Pier 1 assets	735.71
Identifiable intangible assets	500.00
Goodwill	1,020.64

Common stock: ← Pier 1's equity accounts do not appear in the consolidated statement. Additional common stock is recorded based on the value of the new shares issued by BB&B for the acquisition.

Consolidated Income Statement (FY 2002) ($ Millions)	BB&B	Entries	Consolidated
Net sales	2,928.0	1,548.6	4,476.5
Cost of sales	1,720.4	898.8	2,619.2
Gross profit	1,207.6	649.8	1,857.3
SG&A (incl. depreciation & amortization)	861.5	490.9	1,352.4
Extra depreciation & amortization		25.0	25.0
Operating profit	346.1	133.8	479.9
Interest income (expense)	11.0	0.2	11.2
Earnings before taxes	357.1	134.0	491.1
Provision for taxes	137.5		186.6
Net income	219.6		304.5
EPS	0.76		0.87
Shares outstanding	289.7	60.5	350.2

All accounts on the income statement are simply added together, except for the line that shows amortization expense for "Identifiable intangible assets."

Provision for taxes: ← Taxes are based on the 38% tax rate applied to earnings before taxes.

[These spreadsheets can be found in the folder "Key Spreadsheets from the Workbook" located on the CD-ROM.]

2. See answer 4.

3. Consolidated statements for 60 percent stock, 40 percent cash transaction:

Consolidated Balance Sheet (FY 2001)	BB&B	Entries	Consolidated
Assets			
Current assets:			
Cash and equivalents	239.3	46.8	286.2
Merchandise inventories	606.7	310.7	917.4
Other current assets	39.7	119.5	159.2
Total current assets	885.7	477.1	1,362.8
Investment securities	—	—	—
Property and equipment, net	302.7	212.1	514.7
Identifiable intangible assets		500.0	500.0
Goodwill		1,020.6	1,020.6
Other assets	7.4	46.6	53.9
Total assets	1,195.7	2,256.4	3,452.1
Liabilities and Shareholders' Equity			
Current liabilites:			
Accounts payable, accrued expenses and other current liabilities	321.2	144.1	465.3
Current portion of long-term debt		—	—
Income taxes payable	32.0	—	32.0
Total current liabilities	353.2	144.1	497.3
Long-term debt (Pier 1 existing debt)		25.0	25.0
Long-term debt (for acquisition payment)		821.0	821.0
Deferred rent and other liabilities	25.5	34.7	60.2
Total liabilities	378.7	1,024.8	1,403.5
Shareholders' equity:			
Common stock	183.9	1,231.5	1,415.4
Retained earnings	633.2	—	633.2
Cumulative other comprehensive income			
Treasury stock			
Total shareholders' equity	817.0	1,231.5	2,048.5
Total liabilities and shareholders' equity	1,195.7	2,256.4	3,452.1

In coming up with the balance sheet, all procedures are the same as with the 100% stock transaction, except for the addition of debt used to fund the acquisition.

Debt assumed is 40% of the total purchase price.

Pier 1's equity accounts do not appear in the consolidated statement. Additional common stock is recorded based on 60% of the total purchase price.

Consolidated Income Statement (FY 2002) ($ Millions)	BB&B	Entries	Consolidated
Net sales	2,928.0	1,548.6	4,476.5
Cost of sales	1,720.4	898.8	2,619.2
Gross profit	1,207.6	649.8	1,857.3
SG&A (incl. depreciation & amortization)	861.5	490.9	1,352.4
Extra depreciation & amortization		25.0	25.0
Operating profit	346.1	133.8	479.9
Interest income (expense)	11.0	(57.3)	(46.3)
Earnings before taxes	357.1	76.5	433.6
Provision for taxes	137.5		164.8
Net income	219.6		268.8
EPS	0.76		0.82
Shares outstanding	289.7	36.3	326.0

For the income statement, all procedures are the same as with the 100% stock transaction, except for the interest expense on the debt used to fund the acquisition.

4. Answers to problems 2 and 4:

Ratios for Bed Bath & Beyond	Without Merger	With Merger: 100% Stock	With Merger: 60% Stock, 40% Cash
Gross margin	41.2%	41.5%	41.5%
Operating margin	11.8%	10.7%	10.7%
Net margin	7.5%	6.8%	6.0%
EPS	0.76	0.87	0.82
% Dilution/(accretion)	—	14.7%	8.8%

- Gross margins increase slightly, but operating margins decrease due to the amortization of intangible assets. Remember, however, that we have not factored in any synergies. Synergy can trump dilution!
- Net margin declines much more significantly in the part-stock, part-cash transaction owing to the interest expense associated with the debt raised for the acquisition.

5. Financial statements for 40 percent stake:

Bed Bath & Beyond Balance Sheet		**2001**	
Assets			
Current assets:			
Cash and equivalents	429.5		429.5
Merchandise inventories	754.0		754.0
Other current assets	43.2		43.2
Total current assets	1,226.7		1,226.7
Investment securities	51.9		51.9
Investment in Pier 1	—	821.0	821.0
Property and equipment, net	361.7		361.7
Other assets	7.2		7.2
Total assets	1,647.5		2,468.5
Liabilities and Shareholders' Equity			
Current liabilites:			
Accounts payable	270.9		270.9
Accrued expenses and other current liabilities	190.9		190.9
Income taxes payable	49.4		49.4
Total current liabilities	511.3		511.3
Deferred rent and other liabilities	41.9		41.9
Total liabilities	553.2		553.2
Shareholders' equity:			
Common stock	241.6	821.0	1,062.6
Retained earnings	852.8		852.8
Total shareholders' equity	1,094.4		1,915.4
Total liabilities and shareholders' equity	1,647.5		2,468.5

Under the equity method, the buyer's investment in the target is reflected on the balance sheet at the buyer's acquisition cost. This investment is captured in an "Investment" account on the asset side.

The common stock account is increased by the value of shares issued to acquire 40% of the target.

Bed Bath & Beyond Income Statement ($ Millions)	BB&B	2002 Entries	New Balance
Net sales	2,928.0		2,928.0
Cost of sales	1,720.4		1,720.4
Gross profit	1,207.6		1,207.6
SG&A	861.5		861.5
Operating profit	346.1		346.1
Interest income/(expense)	11.0		11.0
Earnings before taxes	357.1		397.2
Provision for taxes	137.5		137.5
Income from equity investment		40.1	40.1
Net earnings	219.6		259.7
EPS	0.76		0.83
Shares outstanding	289.7	24.2	313.9

Under the equity method, the buyer's share in the target's earnings is simply reflected in one line, "Income from equity investment."

This is calculated by multiplying the target's *net* income by the buyer's proportionate share.

[These spreadsheets can be found in the folder "Key Spreadsheets from the Workbook" located on the CD-ROM.]

17

Momentum Acquisition Strategies: An Illustration of Why Value Creation Is the Best Financial Criterion

1. Tyco probably stopped acquiring because it "hit the wall," having realized that the pace of growth by acquisition was unsustainable. Tyco had experienced tremendous growth since the 1980s through aggressive acquisitions. The firm's stock price fell sharply when investors realized that the firm's growth momentum was ending.

   The alleged fraud at the company offers a related explanation. Like unrealistic earnings momentum, tax and accounting fraud are eventually discovered. The restructuring may have been an attempt to cover the accounting trail. Both motives (momentum or fraud) spring from the exploitation of illusion and should be condemned by best practitioners.

2. Corporate managers and directors sometimes argue that investors want earnings momentum, and that all they are doing is giving investors what they want. But what investors want is the creation of value, not momentum. Research finds that momentum produces no supernormal returns for investors. Momentum is unsustainable indefinitely; it invites a focus on accounting cosmetics rather than on economic reality. And finally, momentum distracts management from focusing on value creation.

3. In simple terms, dilution occurs when shares outstanding increase faster than earnings in an acquisition; also, dilution occurs if the P/E ratio paid for the target exceeds the P/E ratio of the buyer. Accretion, on the other hand, occurs where the offered P/E ratio is smaller. Large size amplifies the dilution/accretion effect; small size dampens it. The factors that drive EPS dilution are the growth rate of the buyer's shares relative to the target's percentage addition to the buyer's earnings, the P/E ratio embedded in the bid relative to the P/E ratio of the buyer, and the size of the target relative to the size of the bidder.

4.

Financial Data on Merging Firms		Before Merger Buyer	Before Merger Target	After Merger Newco	After Merger % Change	Cash Deal Newco
1 Purchase-related charges (in thousands)	0.5%			$ (120)		$(120)
2 Net income (in thousands)		$3,000	$1,000	$3,880	29%	$2,710.00
3 Number of shares (in thousands)		1,500	1,000	1,980	32%	1,500
4 Earnings per share (EPS)		$2.00	$1.00	$ 1.96	–2%	$1.81
5 Current stock price		$50.00	$20.00			$43.36
6 Price/earnings ratio		25.00	20.00			24.00
7 Ratio of earnings of target to buyer			0.33			
Terms of share-for-share offer						**In Cash**
8 Dollar value of bid				$24.00		$24.00
9 Premium over target's prebid price				20%		20%
10 Ratio of P/E paid to P/E of buyer				0.96		0.96
Dilution to the buyer resulting from the deal						
11 Dollar accretion (dilution) in buyer EPS				$(0.04)		$(0.19)
12 Percentage accretion (dilution)				–2.0%		–9.7%
					Interest rate	5%
					Tax rate	35%

a. As seen in the table, the earnings per share for Newco after the merger is $1.96 (line 4). This implies dilution of 2.0 percent from the buyer's EPS before the merger.

b. Note that the EPS for Newco is estimated to be $1.81, which indicates a 9.7 percent dilution.

c. As seen in the following table, an increase in the target's earnings will reduce dilution and enhance accretion when premiums are low. As premiums grow larger, deals become *more* dilutive as target earnings increase—this reflects the "double whammy" of a bigger target and higher premium, both of which require more shares to be issued.

Dilution/Accretion for the Buyer in a Share-for-Share Deal

		Premium over Target's Prebid Price (%)						
		0%	5%	15%	20%	25%	35%	45%
Earnings of the target (in thousands)	$ 500	1.5%	0.8%	–0.5%	–1.1%	–1.8%	–3.0%	–4.3%
	$1,000	2.6%	1.4%	–0.9%	–2.0%	–3.1%	–5.3%	–7.3%
	$1,500	3.6%	1.9%	–1.2%	–2.7%	–4.2%	–7.0%	–9.7%
	$2,000	4.3%	2.4%	–1.4%	–3.3%	–5.0%	–8.3%	–11.5%
	$2,500	5.0%	2.7%	–1.7%	–3.7%	–5.7%	–9.4%	–12.9%
	$3,000	5.6%	3.0%	–1.8%	–4.1%	–6.3%	–10.3%	–14.1%
	$3,500	6.0%	3.2%	–2.0%	–4.4%	–6.7%	–11.1%	–15.1%

5. From the tables and chart following, it can be seen that a deal with Company A is immediately dilutive (–23.7 percent) and a deal with Company B is immediately accretive (16.3 percent). But the deal with Company A offers faster growth in earnings after the merger. In roughly six years, it will yield the higher EPS. Valuation analysis should determine which target creates more value for shareholders. It may be that Company A creates more value even though it would dilute earnings.

	Buyer Before	Target A Before	Buyer after Acquiring Target A	Target B Before	Buyer after Acquiring Target B
Financial Data on Merging Firms					
Number of shares	5,000	2,000	9,571	2,000	6,286
Net income	$6,500	$3,000	$9,500	$3,000	$9,500
Earnings per share	$ 1.30	$ 1.50	$ 0.99	$ 1.50	$ 1.51
Current stock price	$28.00	$40.00	$64.00	$15.00	$18.00
Price/earnings ratio	21.54	26.67	64.48	10.00	11.91
Ratio of earnings of target to buyer		0.462		0.462	
Earnings growth rate	10%	25%		5%	
Terms of share-to-share offer					
Dollar value of bid			$64.00		$18.00
Premium over target's prebid price			60%		20%
Ratio of P/E paid to P/E of buyer			1.98		0.56
Resulting accretion (dilution)					
Dollar accretion (dilution) in buyer EPS			($ 0.31)		$ 0.21
Percentage accretion (dilution)			–23.7%		16.3%

Earnings forecasts

	Now	Year 1	Year 2	Year 3	Year 4	Year 5	Year 6	Year 7	Year 8	Year 9	Year 10
Income for buyer before	$6,500	$7,150	$7,865	$8,652	$9,517	$10,468	$11,515	$12,667	$13,933	$15,327	$16,859
EPS for buyer alone	$1.30	$1.43	$1.57	$1.73	$1.90	$2.09	$2.30	$2.53	$2.79	$3.07	$3.37
Target A before	$3,000	$3,750	$4,688	$5,859	$7,324	$9,155	$11,444	$14,305	$17,881	$22,352	$27,940
Income for buyer after acquiring target A	$9,500	$10,900	$12,553	$14,511	$16,841	$19,624	$22,959	$26,972	$31,815	$37,678	$44,799
EPS after merger	$0.99	$1.14	$1.31	$1.52	$1.76	$2.05	$2.40	$2.82	$3.32	$3.94	$4.68
Growth rate for Newco		14.74%	15.16%	15.60%	16.06%	16.52%	17.00%	17.48%	17.96%	18.43%	18.90%
Target B before	$3,000	$3,150	$3,308	$3,473	$3,647	$3,829	$4,020	$4,221	$4,432	$4,654	$4,887
Income for buyer after acquiring target B	$9,500	$10,300	$11,173	$12,124	$13,163	$14,297	$15,535	$16,888	$18,366	$19,981	$21,746
EPS after merger	$1.51	$1.64	$1.78	$1.93	$2.09	$2.27	$2.47	$2.69	$2.92	$3.18	$3.46
Growth rate for Newco		8.42%	8.47%	8.52%	8.57%	8.61%	8.66%	8.71%	8.75%	8.79%	8.84%

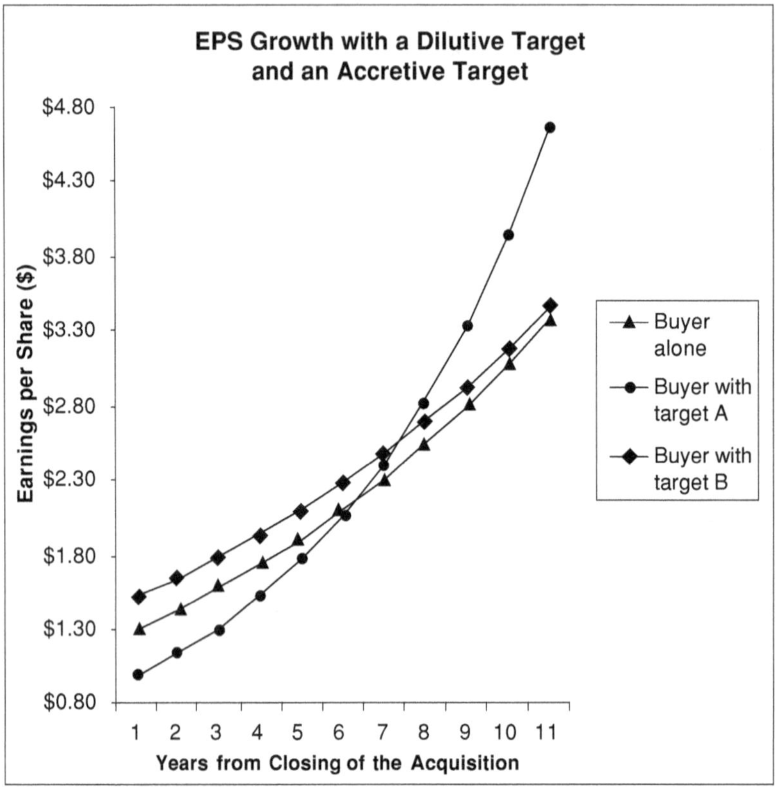

[All spreadsheets in this chapter can be found in the folder "Key Spreadsheets from the Workbook" located on the CD-ROM.]

CHAPTER 18

An Introduction to Deal Design in M&A

PART I: MINI-PROBLEMS

1a. Both sides have strong motivations for doing a deal: R_x wants the co-marketing rights to the new drugs for strategic reasons. Genesis needs funding. But the uncertainty surrounding approval of the drugs puts an equity investment at risk. The CEO of Genesis is optimistic, but approval and success of the drug are not certain. The design problem is one of how to deal with different assessments of risk. There are at least two design solutions:

1. Genesis could issue a convertible bond to R_x rather than shares of equity. The proceeds of a convertible bond issue could provide Genesis the funding it needs, while granting some downside protection to R_x in the event that the drugs do not receive approval. Later, if the drugs succeed, R_x could convert the debt to equity. The option embedded in the convertible bond helps to bridge the differing views of risk.
2. R_x could purchase Genesis equity in stages, after Genesis passes the various milestones of regulatory approval. Staged investing commits R_x to providing additional funds as uncertainty about the new drugs is resolved. This scheme amounts to creating a stream of options—these help to bridge the differing views of risk.

1b. The parties could bridge the gap through the use of an earnout, an arrangement where a portion of the purchase price would be paid by R_x only if Genesis attains agreed-upon performance goals within some time frame.

2a. If maintaining its credit rating is valuable to Company A, then A could extend a choice to the shareholders of B: accept a fully valued offer, paid in stock, or a less than fully valued offer in cash—the discount would be equivalent to the loss in value sustained by A arising from any damage to its credit rating.

2b. Company B can insist on a floor. If Company A's stock price falls below a certain level, the exchange ratio ought to be adjusted upward, or Company B must be remunerated in some other form. Company A in turn can insist on a cap. If its stock rises beyond a certain level, it can ask for a downward readjustment of the exchange ratio. The resulting structure—one with both a cap and a floor—is called a collar.

2c. Company A can use a variety of methods to keep Company B in the deal. One solution is to impose a walk-away or termination fee if Company B withdraws from the agreement. Another solution might be to agree on a "lock-up" option, where Company A gains the right to buy a block of shares in Company B should the latter enter into a merger agreement with another party. (Usually, both parties are subject to these terms—in this case, Company A would most likely be subject to the walk-away fee or lock-up option too if it withdraws from the deal agreement.)

2d. Company A could negotiate private agreements with Company B's managers. These agreements might entail commitments about titles, perquisites, and side payments (in the form of options, bonuses, employment contracts, consulting contracts, golden parachutes, etc.).

PART II: MINI-CASE

1. The control structure was highly advantageous to NCNB. Despite being a minority shareholder and putting up only 20 percent of equity, NCNB obtained control as the only shareholder to hold voting shares. One can guess that the FDIC accepted this structure because its main interest lay in saving First Republic from failing rather than in actively running the bank.
2. NCNB not only had a staggered purchase option, it also had exclusive rights to acquire more equity in Newco within the next five years. The staggered purchase terms effectively gave NCNB a number of long call options on Newco. NCNB had the right, but not the obligation to buy more stock. Having the staggered purchase option allowed NCNB to have more *time* to gain more *information* on Newco. The advantage of time was offset somewhat by the ratcheting price, which served as an incentive for NCNB to complete its acquisition of Newco earlier rather than later. The exclusivity clause bought NCNB time to bring Newco back to health without threat of a competitor or some other outside party benefiting from ownership of Newco.
3. NCNB was allowed to transfer bad loans originated under old management to the Special Asset Division, and was reimbursed by the FDIC for these loan losses. In addition, the FDIC paid NCNB the costs of administering the division. NCNB did not share in any losses suffered by the Special Asset Division, but did share in any gains made by the division. For NCNB, the agreements with respect to the Special Asset Division virtually eliminated any exposure to bad loans originated under previous management.
4. It was an attractive deal from NCNB's viewpoint. NCNB obtained title to the largest bank in Texas, with plenty of protection from the FDIC. NCNB virtually had no exposure to First Republic's bad loans. The control structure allowed NCNB 100 percent control over Newco, yet NCNB was never required to commit to buying the whole company. The staggered payment option gave NCNB the chance to opt out of the deal if its attempt to restructure First Republic did not work out. The deal design insulated NCNB from many risks.

CHAPTER 19

Choosing the Form of Acquisitive Reorganization

1. Sam should take party B's offer. The all-cash deal is not tax-efficient since it would require Sam and his shareholders to pay taxes immediately on the gain from the sale of shares. In contrast, the all-stock deal can be organized to be tax-free under any of the following structures:

   Statutory merger ("A" reorganization).
   Forward triangular merger ("A" reorganization).
   Reverse triangular merger ("A" reorganization).
   Voting stock-for-stock ("B" reorganization).
   Voting stock for assets ("C" reorganization).

2. No. Mr. Welch used the book value of the assets as the basis for his tax calculation. He should have used market value (as long as he can justify to the IRS that the economic value of the assets is $511,000). The correct answers are:

Market value	$511,000
Useful life	8
Depreciation expense	$ 63,875
Tax savings	**$ 21,718**
Discount rate	10%
Present value of savings	**$115,861**

3. The possible forms of reorganization are those in which the target (or the Newco into which the target merges) becomes a subsidiary of Escape. Since the deal will definitely involve some exchange of stock, the possible forms of reorganization are:

   Forward triangular merger ("A" type reorganization).
   Reverse triangular merger ("A" type reorganization).
   Voting stock-for-stock acquisition ("B" type reorganization).
   Voting stock-for-assets acquisition ("C" type reorganization).

4.

Type of Reorganization	Requirements for Tax-Free Qualification
Forward triangular merger ("A" type reorganization)	• Escape must acquire at least 70 percent of the fair market value of Grupo Viva's gross assets, and 90 percent of the FMV of net assets. • Payment must consist of at least 50 percent of Escape's parent corporation stock.
Reverse triangular merger ("A" type reorganization)	• At least 80 percent of the consideration must be paid in Escape's parent corporation voting stock. • As in the forward triangular merger, Escape must control "substantially all" of the Grupo Viva's assets.
Voting stock-for-stock acquisition ("B" type reorganization)	• Escape must pay only in voting stock, and afterward control at least 80 percent of the votes.
Voting stock-for-assets acquisition ("C" type reorganization)	• Escape must pay at least 80 percent of the consideration in voting stock. • Escape must not have had an ownership interest in Grupo Viva prior to the transaction. • At least 70 percent of the fair market value of the gross assets and 90 percent of the FMV of net assets of Grupo Viva must be transferred to Escape.

All of these forms of reorganization are tax-free to the seller. The two "A" type reorganizations dominate the others by permitting freeze-outs.

5. Under the forward triangular merger ("A" type reorganization), Escape cannot pay more than 50 percent of the consideration in cash. Under the reverse triangular merger ("A" type reorganization) Escape cannot pay more than 20 percent of the consideration in cash. Thus the forward triangular merger appears to offer the greatest design flexibility.

6. The possible forms of reorganization are:

   Statutory merger ("A" type reorganization).
   Voting stock-for-assets acquisition ("C" type reorganization).

7. Yes. The voting stock-for-assets acquisition does not allow tax-free status if the buyer had an ownership interest in the target prior to the transaction. Therefore, the only remaining option is a statutory merger (the "A" type reorganization).

8. To force Leonardo Fox out, Decadence should acquire Bright Ice for cash, thus leaving no shares in Fox's ownership. This entails a two-step transaction, an acquisition of a voting majority of Bright Ice shares for cash, followed by a "minority freeze-out" merger of Bright Ice with a subsidiary of Decadence, also for cash. Thus, the transaction should be structured using cash as the form of payment and entailing a merger with a subsidiary of Decadence. A triangular cash merger, either reverse or forward, would achieve Decadence's goal. As long as the buyer can attract a voting majority of the target's shares, the merger can be effected and the dissenting shareholders can be forced to exit.

9. A minority freeze-out seeks to eliminate direct interests in the target firm held by minority shareholders following the completion of the deal. This is ordinarily accomplished by merging the target into the buyer or a subsidiary of the buyer.

CHAPTER 20

Choosing the Form of Payment and Financing

PART I: TRUE OR FALSE

1. True.
2. False. Payment in stock is associated with higher returns to targets.
3. True.
4. False. Taxable deals are for cash, and "tax-deferred" deals are for stock.
5. False. In cash deals, target shareholders must pay taxes immediately on their capital gains, whereas in stock deals, taxes can be deferred until shares are sold.
6. True. This is called expropriating creditor wealth. A bidder can bid aggressively if part of the cost of possible overpayment is borne by the creditors of the firm.
7. True.
8. True.
9. False. The acquirer will prefer to offer stock (due to its contingent-pricing characteristics) if it thinks the target knows more than it does.
10. True.
11. False. Because the discipline imposed by creditors presumably results in better performance, bidders' announcement returns have been found to be positively related to the fraction of acquisition value funded by bank debt.

PART II: QUESTIONS

1. Factors that favor either a cash or a stock payment are present. On one hand, one could argue for a cash payment on the grounds of the CEO's optimism about the value of synergies, available debt capacity, and favorable interest rate environment. On the other hand, one could say a stock payment is better given the uncertainty about the target's stand-alone value.

2. Given the CEO's view that current market valuations may not last, this seems to be an opportune time to use stock as a medium of currency. However, an issuance of stock may signal a belief that the stock is overvalued, and may produce a negative reaction from the market.

3. If Company A issues shares to pay for the acquisition, Smith would still be the largest shareholder by far, though Pierce would also hold a sizable stake. Smith would own a percentage stake slightly more than twice as large as Pierce's; on the grounds of Smith's requirement that his stake be *at least* twice that of Pierce, the stock payment would be acceptable to Smith.

	% Ownership in Newco
Smith	38.5%
Pierce	18.5%
Other major stockholder of Company A	15.4%
Oceanic shareholders	27.7%

4. Offer to pay as high a premium for the target as consistent with the buyer's analysis of the target's intrinsic value, offer to pay in cash, and use internal sources of funds (such as cash on hand or unused debt capacity). These will increase Company A's chance of success in its hostile bid.

5. Issuing new debt of higher seniority than current creditors enjoy can allow buyers to bid more than their assessment of the intrinsic value of the target. This imposes part of the cost of possible overpayment on the creditors of the firm; it represents an expropriation of creditor wealth.

6. The period 1998–2000 was a period of economic strength and a buoyant stock market, whereas 1990–1992 represented a period of economic weakness. As discussed in the chapter, stock payments tend to be used with greater frequency during economic booms.

7a.

		With Merger	
Ratios	Without Merger	100% Stock	100% Cash
Gross margin	41.2%	41.5%	41.5%
Operating margin	11.8%	10.7%	10.7%
Net margin	7.5%	6.8%	4.8%
EPS	$0.76	$0.87	$0.66
% Accretion/(dilution)		14.7%	–12.8%
Debt-equity ratio	—	0.9%	251.2%
Interest cover (EBIT/Interest expense)	Net interest income	Net interest income	3.6×

- Gross and operating margins are the same regardless of the form of payment chosen.
- Net margins are much lower under the 100 percent cash transaction due to interest expense on the debt used for funding the acquisition.
- EPS is accretive under the 100 percent stock transaction, suggesting that the incremental income from the merger is more than enough to offset the impact of new share issuance. However, EPS is dilutive under the 100 percent cash payment scenario, suggesting that the additional income from the synergies of the deal is not high enough to offset interest expense on the acquisition debt.
- Obviously, under the all-cash transaction, Bed Bath & Beyond's debt-equity ratio shoots up, and it moves to a net interest expense rather than net interest income situation. (Interest coverage of 3.6×, however, is still respectable.)

7b.

100% Cash

Purchase Premium	EPS ($)	% Dilution
20%	0.675	–11.0%
25%	0.661	–12.8%
30%	0.647	–14.7%
35%	0.633	–16.5%
40%	0.620	–18.3%

100% Stock

Purchase Premium	EPS ($)	% Accretion
20%	0.875	15.5%
25%	0.869	14.7%
30%	0.863	13.9%
35%	0.858	13.1%
40%	0.852	12.3%

In general, the higher the purchase premium, the lower the accretion (in the all-stock transaction) and the greater the dilution (in the all-cash transaction). In addition, EPS is more sensitive to changes in the purchase premiums under the 100 perent cash transaction.

7c.

100% Stock

Purchase Premium	Exchange Ratio	New Shares Issued	% Ownership by BB&B Shareholders	% Ownership by Pier 1 Shareholders
20%	0.60	58.12	83.3%	16.7%
25%	0.63	60.55	82.7%	17.3%
30%	0.65	62.97	82.1%	17.9%
35%	0.68	65.39	81.6%	18.4%
40%	0.70	67.81	81.0%	19.0%

The higher the purchase premium, the higher the exchange ratio required, and thus the greater the number of shares that need to be issued. Accordingly, a higher purchase premium means Bed Bath & Beyond will need to give up more control.

[All spreadsheets for problem 7 can be found in the folder "Key Spreadsheets from the Workbook" located on the CD-ROM.]

CHAPTER 21

Framework for Structuring the Terms of Exchange: Finding the "Win-Win" Deal

1. The task here is to find the crossover point for the deal boundaries because that is the minimum point of the win-win region. By preparing a graph or table of the deal boundaries, one can identify the crossover point. In this case, Newco must trade at around 21 times or higher in order for there to exist the possibility of a deal acceptable to both parties.

	P/E Model Assumptions	
Buyer's share price	P1	$ 25.96
Target's share price	P2	$ 38.31
Buyer's net income	E1	$ 9,600
Target's net income	E2	$15,400
Net income from synergies	Es	$ 1,250
Buyer's shares outstanding	S1	10,700
Target's shares outstanding	S2	6,680

Results Based on P/E of Newco	Maximum Acceptable ER1	Minimum Acceptable ER2
16	0.82	2.50
17	0.97	2.15
18	1.12	1.89
19	1.27	1.69
20	1.43	1.52
21	1.58	1.39
22	1.73	1.27
23	1.88	1.18
24	2.03	1.10
25	2.18	1.02

2. As can be seen from the following hypothetical numbers, right now Microsoft is willing to pay a maximum exchange ratio of 1.12, but the minimum ExxonMobil will accept is 1.27. To make the deal work, Microsoft must be convinced to increase the exchange ratio to 1.27—which means ExxonMobil must convince Microsoft that Newco will trade at a minimum of 19 times.

MSFT

	P/E Model Assumptions	
Buyer's share price	P1	$ 25.96
Target's share price	P2	$ 38.31
Buyer's net income	E1	$ 9,600
Target's net income	E2	$15,400
Net income from synergies	Es	$ 1,250
Buyer's shares outstanding	S1	10,700
Target's shares outstanding	S2	6,680
Expected P/E ratio of Newco	PE12	18.00

Results Based on P/E of Newco		
	Maximum Acceptable **ER1**	
	1.12	

← The maximum that Microsoft is willing to pay given its view that Newco will trade at a P/E of 18x

XOM

	P/E Model Assumptions	
Buyer's share price	P1	$ 25.96
Target's share price	P2	$ 38.31
Buyer's net income	E1	$ 9,600
Target's net income	E2	$15,400
Net income from synergies	Es	$ 1,250
Buyer's shares outstanding	S1	10,700
Target's shares outstanding	S2	6,680
Expected P/E ratio of Newco	PE12	22.00

Results Based on P/E of Newco		
		Minimum Acceptable **ER2**
		1.27

← The minimum that Exxon is willing to accept given its view that Newco will trade 22x

Feasible Deal for Microsoft

	P/E Model Assumptions	
Buyer's share price	P1	$ 25.96
Target's share price	P2	$ 38.31
Buyer's net income	E1	$ 9,600
Target's net income	E2	$15,400
Net income from synergies	Es	$ 1,250
Buyer's shares outstanding	S1	10,700
Target's shares outstanding	S2	6,680
Expected P/E ratio of Newco	PE12	19.00

← Microsoft must believe that Newco will trade at 19x before it will be willing to pay Exxon's asking price. This P/E ratio can be found by using Goal Seek to solve for the P/E ratio that will give a maximum acceptable exchange ratio of 1.27.

Results Based on P/E of Newco		
	Maximum Acceptable **ER1**	
	1.27	

3. As can be seen from the following hypothetical numbers, Microsoft is willing to pay a maximum exchange ratio of 1.57, but the minimum ExxonMobil will accept is 1.68. To make the deal work, Microsoft must convince ExxonMobil to lower its minimum to 1.57. This means Microsoft must convince ExxonMobil that Newco will have a DCF value of at least $517 billion.

MSFT

DCF Model Assumptions	
P1	$ 25.96
P2	$ 38.31
S1	10,700
S2	6,680
DCF12	$550,000

Maximum Acceptable ER1
1.57

← Microsoft is willing to pay at most an exchange ratio of 1.57 given its view that Newco will have a DCF value of $550 billion . . .

XOM

DCF Model Assumptions	
P1	$ 25.96
P2	$ 38.31
S1	10,700
S2	6,680
DCF12	$500,000

Minimum Acceptable ER2
1.68

← . . . but Exxon thinks Newco will have a DCF value of only $500 billion. As a result, its minimum acceptable payment is above what Microsoft is willing to pay.

XOM

DCF Model Assumptions	
P1	$ 25.96
P2	$ 38.31
S1	10,700
S2	6,680
DCF12	$516,997

Minimum Acceptable ER2
1.57

← Microsoft must convince Exxon that Newco will have a DCF value of $517 billion in order for Exxon to accept Microsoft's maximum offer. This DCF value is found by using Goal Seek to find the DCF value that will result in a minimum acceptable ratio of 1.57.

4. This is still the same deal; only the currency used for the acquisition has changed. Newco must still trade at around 21 times or higher in order for a deal to be attractive. (See problem 1.)

	P/E Model Assumptions	
Buyer's share price	P1	$ 25.96
Target's share price	P2	$ 38.31
Buyer's net income	E1	$ 9,600
Target's net income	E2	$15,400
Net income from synergies	Es	$ 1,250
Buyer's shares outstanding	S1	10,700
Target's shares outstanding	S2	6,680

Results Based on P/E of Newco

PE12	Maximum Acceptable ER1	Minimum Acceptable ER2
19	33.08	38.31
20	37.01	38.31
21	40.94	38.31
22	44.87	38.31
23	48.80	38.31
24	52.73	38.31
25	56.66	38.31

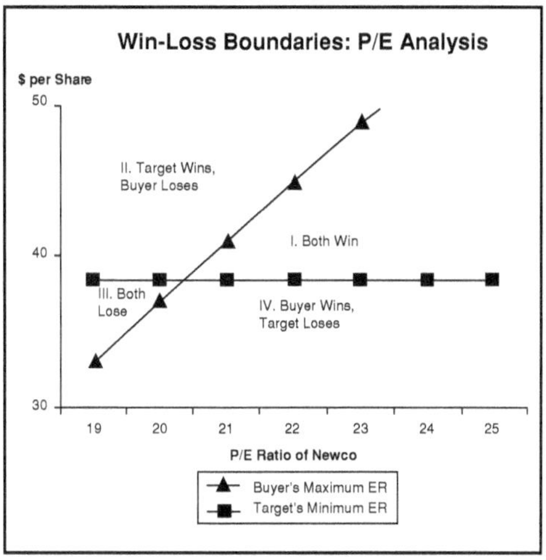

5. The crossover point can be found by preparing a data table of the deal boundaries. In this case, the data table reveals that the deal becomes feasible at a DCF value of between $500 and $550 billion. The exact number is $537 billion.

DCF Model Assumptions	
P1	$ 25.96
P2	$ 38.31
S1	10,700
S2	6,680
DCF12	$550,000

DCF	Maximum Acceptable ER1	Minimum Acceptable ER2
$400,000	$18.30	$38.31
$450,000	$25.78	$38.31
$500,000	$33.27	$38.31
$550,000	$40.75	$38.31
$600,000	$48.24	$38.31
$650,000	$55.72	$38.31
$700,000	$63.21	$38.31
$750,000	$70.69	$38.31
$800,000	$78.18	$38.31

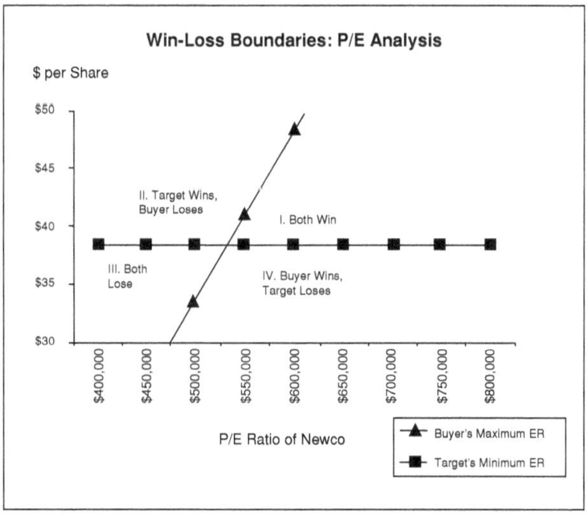

6. In a cash-for-stock transaction, the minimum price paid is the target's market price.

7. A win-win deal is not feasible at an expected P/E ratio of 11 times.

		P/E Model Assumptions
Buyer's share price	P1	$35.00
Target's share price	P2	$20.00
Buyer's net income	E1	$ 200
Target's net income	E2	$ 150
Net income from synergies	Es	$ 10
Buyer's shares outstanding	S1	80
Target's shares outstanding	S2	80
Expected P/E ratio of Newco	PE12	11

Results Based on the P/E of Newco

PE12	Maximum Acceptable ER1	Minimum Acceptable ER2
11	0.41	0.68
12	0.54	0.59
13	0.67	0.52
14	0.80	0.47
15	0.93	0.42
16	1.06	0.38
17	1.19	0.35

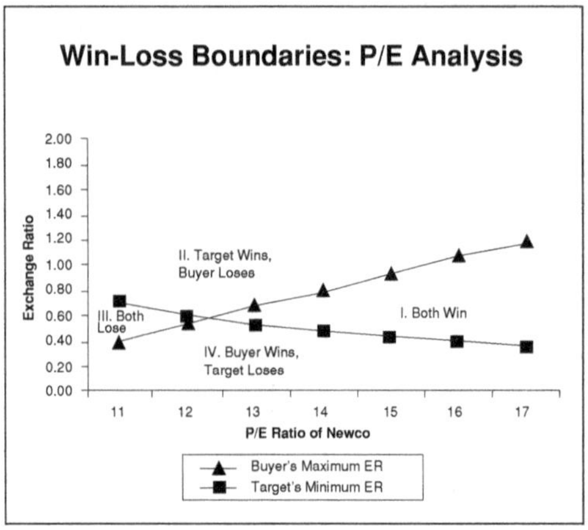

8. They must achieve $50 million in synergies in order to make this a win-win deal at a P/E ratio for Newco of 11 times. The impact of synergies can be seen in the graph: with only $10 million in synergies, there is no zone of potential agreement at a P/E ratio of 11 times; the seller's maximum is below the target's minimum. The deal will become feasible only if the P/E is at around 13 times or higher. With the increase in synergy value, a deal becomes possible at a P/E of 11 times.

		P/E Model Assumptions
Buyer's share price	P1	$35.00
Target's share price	P2	$20.00
Buyer's net income	E1	$ 200
Target's net income	E2	$ 150
Net income from synergies	Es	$ 50
Buyer's shares outstanding	S1	80
Target's shares outstanding	S2	80
Expected P/E ratio of Newco	PE12	11

← Use Goal Seek to find the value of synergies that will make the deal work if Newco trades at 11x.

Results Based on the P/E of Newco

PE12	Maximum Acceptable ER1	Minimum Acceptable ER2
9	0.29	0.80
10	0.43	0.67
11	0.57	0.57
12	0.71	0.50
13	0.86	0.44
14	1.00	0.40
15	1.14	0.36

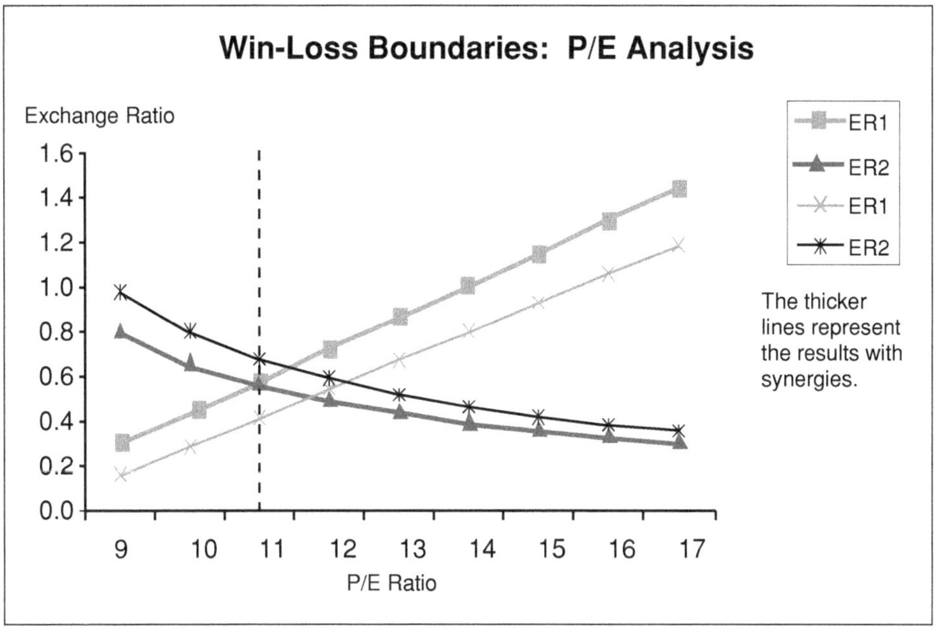

[The spreadsheets for problem 1 to 8 can be found in the folder "Key Spreadsheets from the Workbook" located on the CD-ROM.]

9. A deal is feasible if DCF value is projected at $5 billion.

DCF Model Assumptions	
P1	$35.00
P2	$20.00
S1	80
S2	80

DCF12	Maximum Acceptable ER1	Minimum Acceptable ER2
$3,000	0.0714	1.1429
$3,500	0.2500	0.8421
$4,000	0.4286	0.6667
$4,500	0.6071	0.5517
$5,000	0.7857	0.4706
$5,500	0.9643	0.4103
$6,000	1.1429	0.3636
$6,500	1.3214	0.3265
$7,000	1.5000	0.2963

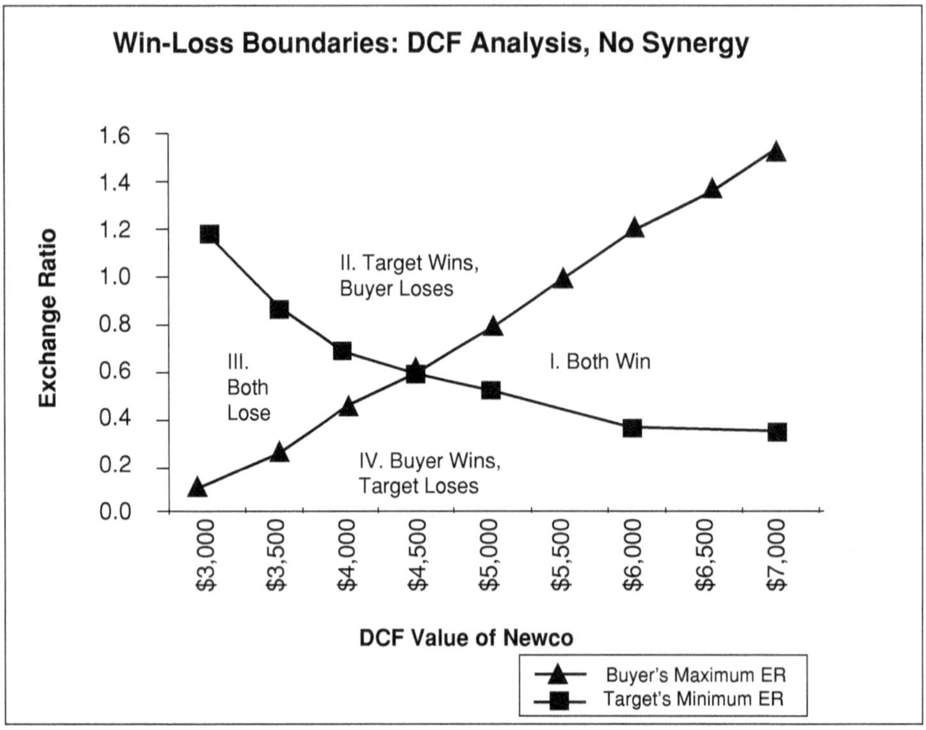

10. The graph in problem 9 does not change. Only the positions of the parties change: Looking at the x-axis, the parties are now at a DCF value for Newco of $6 billion due to the addition of the $1 billion in synergies. As can be seen from the graph, the zone of potential agreement widens as the DCF value of Newco increases.

11. The proportion of Oracle's net income in Newco is 92.4 percent. This contribution ratio for Oracle would imply an exchange ratio of 1.36 Newco shares for each PeopleSoft share. This number can be calculated using the following formula:

$$ER = \frac{\frac{N_{\text{Buyer}}}{C_{\text{Buyer}}} - N_{\text{Buyer}}}{N_{\text{Target}}}$$

However, based on Oracle's bid price and its current market price, the implied exchange ratio is 1.2. The difference is due to the fact that the exchange ratio of 1.36 is based on accounting values, whereas the exchange ratio of 1.2 is based on market prices. These two differing perspectives may suggest why PeopleSoft chose not to accept this offer: It underestimates the contribution of PeopleSoft to Newco's earnings.

12. At this new bid price, the implied exchange ratio is 1.46—higher than what is implied by the contribution analysis. Therefore, this bid is more attractive from PeopleSoft's point of view—but there remain the knotty *social* issues created by Oracle's hostile bid.

22

Structuring and Valuing Contingent Payments in M&A

1. An earnout can provide a number of benefits to both parties if it is properly structured. For the seller, an earnout can provide additional payments if the acquired business does as well as expected. In addition, an earnout will benefit the buyer by making additional payments necessary only if the business does significantly better than expected. Although earnouts are quite useful in bridging the valuation gap and retaining and motivating shareholders or managers, they also pose challenges in postacquisition integration and in the definitions of the earnout formulas and performance goals.

2.

		Now	Year 1	Year 2	Year 3	Year 4	Year 5
Step 1 Grow the tree							
							$57.55
						$40.55	
Parameters needed:		(A)			$28.58		$28.58
				$20.14		$20.14	
Volatility (annualized)	35%		$14.19		$14.19		$14.19
Length of period (year)	1	$10.00		$10.00		$10.00	
			$7.05		$7.05		$7.05
Up percentage (u)	1.419068			$4.97		$4.97	
Down percentage (d)	0.704688				$3.50		$3.50
(A) -- $14.19 = $10 × U = $10 × 1.419						$2.47	
							$1.74

The binomial approach assumes that each year, the value of the firm will move up by *u* (*u* = e^(1 × 35%) = 1.419) or down by *d* (*d* = e^(−1 × 35%) = 1/*u* = 0.705). This means that at the end of the first year, firm value will be worth either $14.19 million (*u* × $10 milllion) or $7.05 (*d* × $10 million).

	Now	Year 1	Year 2	Year 3	Year 4	Year 5
Profit margin	10%	10%	10%	10%	10%	10%
						$5.75
					$4.06	
				$2.86		**$2.86**
			$2.01		$2.01	
		$1.42		$1.42		$1.42
	$1.00		$1.00		$1.00	
		$0.70		$0.70		$0.70
			$0.50		$0.50	
				$0.35		$0.35
					$0.25	
						$0.17

Step 2 Assess the probabilities of an up or down movement. (These probabilities will be used in step 5 to fold back the tree.)

Pu = [(1 + Rf) − d)]/(u − d)	49.74%	= chance of the firm value moving up
Pd = [u − (1 + Rf)]/(u − d)	50.26%	= chance of the firm value moving down
Rf = 6%		

(Continued)

Step 3 Assess the states in which the options will be exercised.

In the table, the shaded numbers indicate when the earnout will be awarded.
In these cases, the profit is more than the exercise price of $1,500,000.

Step 4 Estimate the payoffs associated with these end-states.

Exercise price $1.50

Now	Year 1	Year 2	Year 3	Year 4	Year 5	
					$4.25	(= $5.75 – $1.50)
				—		
			—		$1.36	(= $ 2.86 – $1.50)
		—		—		
	—		—		—	
—		—		—		
	—		—		—	
		—		—		
			—		—	
				—		
					—	

Step 5 Calculate the present value of expected future payoffs.

Now	Year 1	Year 2	Year 3	Year 4	Year 5
				(B)	
					$4.25
				$2.64	
			$1.54		$1.36
		$0.86		$0.64	
	$0.47		$0.30		—
$0.25		$0.14		—	
	$0.07		—		—
		—		—	
			—		—
				—	
					—

(B) — $2.64 = ($4.25 × Pu + $1.36 × Pd)/(1 + Rf)

For instance, to arrive at (B), $2.64 million, one would take the expected value of (*Pu × $4.25 + Pd × $1.36*), or (.4974 × $4.25) + (0.5026 × $1.36) to yield $2.80. Discounting this by one year at the risk-free rate, 6%, yields $2.64. This process is repeated for the other cells. Folding the expected values back to the present, we arrive at a value of $0.25 million for this earnout plan. Although in this case, the total value of the earnout plan is just about 5% of the value of the total deal, it is a good illustration of how to value the earnout plan by the binomial approach. In reality, the earnout plan will generally be a much greater percentage of the value of the deal.

[This spreadsheet can be found in the folder "Key Spreadsheets from the Workbook" located on the CD-ROM.]

3. As with problem 2, build a binomial lattice laying out the outcomes. Then calculate the payoffs for each outcome. Fold back the expected value of the payoffs to arrive at the value of the option. The answers are:

Profit	Volatility of Revenue Growth				
Margin	25%	30%	35%	40%	45%
8%	$0.082	$0.124	$0.161	$0.194	$0.225
9%	$0.130	$0.171	$0.207	$0.240	$0.272
10%	$0.178	$0.217	$0.253	$0.287	$0.333
11%	$0.225	$0.263	$0.313	$0.364	$0.413
12%	$0.283	$0.338	$0.392	$0.443	$0.493

From the table, it is clear that the value of the earnout increases directly with volatility and profit margins.

4. The solution is the same as in problem 2, except that the binomial tree goes only as far as three rather than five periods.

			Now	Year 1	Year 2	Year 3
Step 1	Grow the tree					
	Parameters needed:		(A)			**$28.58**
					$20.14	
	Volatility (annualized)	35%		$14.19		$14.19
	Length of period (year)	1	$10.00		$10.00	
				$7.05		$7.05
	Up percentage (u)	1.419068			$4.97	
	Down percentage (d)	0.704688				$3.50

(A) – $14.19 = $10 × U = $10 × 1.419

The binomial approach assumes that each year, the value of the firm will move up by u ($u = e$^(1 × 35%) = 1.419) or down by d ($d = e$^(–1 × 35%) = 1/u = 0.705). This means that at the end of the first year, firm value will be worth either $14.19 million ($u$ × $10 milllion) or $7.05 ($d$ × $10 million).

	Now	Year 1	Year 2	Year 3
Profit margin	**10%**	**10%**	**10%**	**10%**
				$2.86
			$2.01	
		$1.42		$1.42
	$1.00		$1.00	
		$0.70		$0.70
			$0.50	
				$0.35

Step 2 Assess the probabilities of an up or down movement. (These probabilities will be used in step 5 to fold back the tree.)

Pu = [(1 + Rf) – d)]/(u – d) 49.74% = chance of the firm value moving up
Pd = [u – (1 + Rf)]/(u – d) 50.26% = chance of the firm value moving down
Rf = 6%

Step 3 Assess the states in which the options will be exercised.

In the above table, the shaded numbers indicate when the earnout will be awarded. In these cases, the profit is more than the exercise price of $1,500,000.

Step 4 Estimate the payoffs associated with these end-states.

Now	Year 1	Year 2	Year 3
			$1.36 (= $2.86 – $1.50)
		—	
	—		—
—		—	
	—		—
			—

Step 5 Calculate the present value of expected future payoffs.

Now	Year 1	Year 2	Year 3
		(B)	
			$1.36
		$0.64	
	$0.30		—
$0.14		—	
	—		—
		—	
			—

(B) — $0.64 = ($1.36 × Pu + 0 × Pd)/(1 + Rf)

For instance, to arrive at (B), $0.64 million, one would take the expected value of (*Pu × $1.36 + Pd × $0)*, or (.4974 × $1.36) + (0.5026 × $0) to yield $0.675. Discounting this by one year at the risk-free rate, 6%, yields $0.64. This process is repeated for the other cells. Folding the expected values back to the present, we arrive at a value of $0.14 million for this earnout plan.

[This spreadsheet can be found in the folder "Key Spreadsheets from the Workbook" located on the CD-ROM.]

5. The results are:

Profit Margin	Volatility of Revenue Growth 25%	30%	35%	40%	45%
8%	$0.028	$0.057	$0.081	$0.104	$0.124
9%	$0.059	$0.086	$0.111	$0.133	$0.155
10%	$0.089	$0.116	$0.140	$0.163	$0.185
11%	$0.120	$0.146	$0.170	$0.193	$0.215
12%	$0.151	$0.175	$0.199	$0.223	$0.246

From this table, it is clear that the value of the earnout increases with increases in volatility and profit margins. At the same time, as compared to problem 3, notice that the value of the earnout plan decreases with the shortening of the earnout period.

6. Build the five-year forecast as shown, and model the uncertainties about revenue growth and profit margins as normal distributions. Running Crystal Ball 5,000 times, the result is shown. From the buyer's point of view, the value of the proposed deal has an expected value of $4.56 million ($2 million cash and $2.56 million expected value of the earnout); this is lower than the buyer's estimation of the value of the firm. Therefore, it is an attractive deal to the buyer.

Buyer Valuation

				Year 1	Year 2	Year 3	Year 4	Year 5
Base Year Sales			$12,000					
Earnout Period, in Years			5					
Sales				$13,849	$15,429	$17,092	$18,021	$19,547
	Growth Rate	Mean	12%					
		Standard deviation	3%	15%	11%	11%	5%	8%
Profit				$1,510	$1,885	$1,917	$2,091	$2,790
	Profit Margin	Mean	12%	11%	12%	11%	12%	14%
		Standard deviation	2%					
Earnout Target for Profits				$500	$1,000	$1,500	$2,000	$2,500
Annual Earnout Value				$1,010	$885	$417	$91	$290
	Present Value of Earnout, Discounted at 7%			**$2,333**				
	Dollars at Closing			$2,000				
	Enterprise Valuation of Proposed Earnout			**$4,333**				

[This spreadsheet can be found in the folder "Key Spreadsheets from the Workbook" located on the CD-ROM.]

Note that this result is a deterministic estimate of value, which differs from the probabilistic estimate given in the next table. Because the probabilistic estimate accounts for the entire range of outcomes, it is superior to the deterministic estimate.

Summary:
Display range is from \$2,995 to \$6,129 thousands
Entire range is from \$2,605 to \$7,063 thousands
After 5,000 trials, the standard error of the mean is \$9

Statistics	Value
Trials	5,000
Mean	\$ 4,557
Median	\$ 4,519
Mode	—
Standard deviation	\$ 609
Variance	\$371,107
Skewness	0.29
Kurtosis	3.01
Coefficient of variability	0.13
Range minimum	\$ 2,605
Range maximum	\$ 7,063
Range width	\$ 4,458
Mean standard error	\$ 8.62

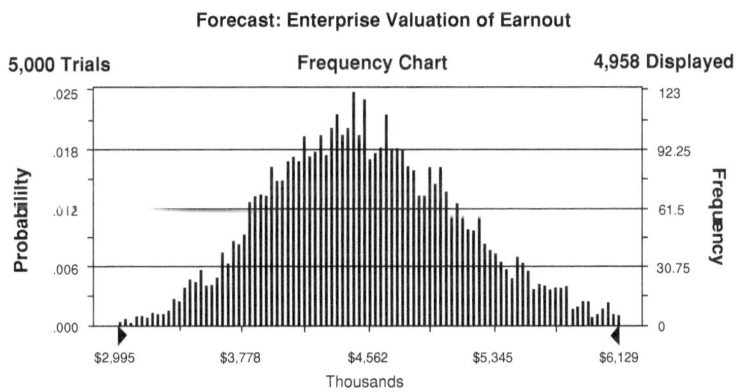

In conclusion, the deterministic approach yields an estimated value of \$4,333, while the probabilistic approach gives a mean estimate of \$4,557.

7. Build the five-year forecast as shown, and model the uncertainties about revenue growth and profit margins as normal distributions. Running Crystal Ball 5,000 times, the result is shown. From the seller's point of view, the valuation of the proposed earnout has a mean of \$8.14 million, which is higher than the seller's estimation of the value of the firm. Therefore, it is an attractive deal to the seller.

Seller Valuation				Year 1	Year 2	Year 3	Year 4	Year 5
Base Year Sales			$12,000					
Earnout Period, in Years			5					
Sales				$13,364	$15,506	$18,606	$21,854	$26,126
	Growth Rate	Mean	20%					
		Standard deviation	5%	11%	16%	20%	17%	20%
Profit				$2,027	$2,210	$2,376	$3,790	$3,920
	Profit Margin	Mean	14%	15%	14%	13%	17%	15%
		Standard deviation	3%					
Earnout Target for Profits				$500	$1,000	$1,500	$2,000	$2,500
Annual Earnout Value				$1,527	$1,210	$876	$1,790	$1,420
	Present Value of the Earnout, Discounted at 7%			**$5,576**				
	Dollars at Closing			$2,000				
	Enterprise Valuation of Proposed Earnout			**$7,576**				

[This spreadsheet can be found in the folder "Key Spreadsheets from the Workbook" located on the CD-ROM.]

Note that this result is a deterministic estimate of value, which differs from the probabilistic estimate given in the next table. Because the probabilistic estimate accounts for the entire range of outcomes, it is superior to the deterministic estimate.

Summary:
Display range is from $4,440 to $11,951 thousands
Entire range is from $3,538 to $14,334 thousands
After 5,000 trials, the standard error of the mean is $20

Statistics	Value
Trials	5,000
Mean	$ 8,137
Median	$ 8,079
Mode	—
Standard deviation	$ 1,406
Variance	$1,977,696
Skewness	0.26
Kurtosis	3.15
Coefficient of variability	0.17
Range minimum	$ 3,538
Range maximum	$ 14,334
Range width	$ 10,796
Mean standard error	$ 19.89

(Continued)

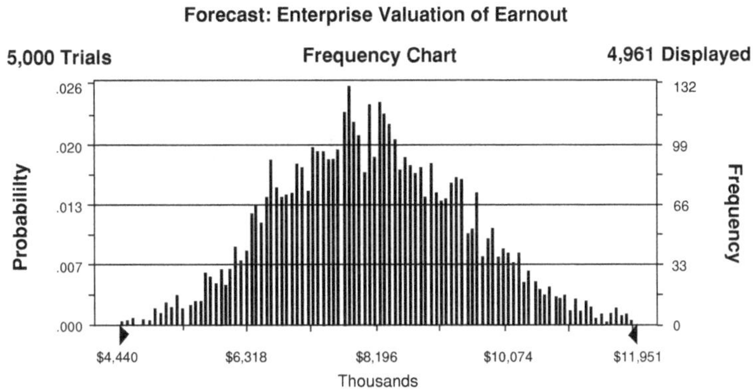

8. Use the model you built in problem 6, using the Decision Table tool in Crystal Ball to estimate the value of the earnout plan under different revenue growth rates and profit margins. The results will be similar to those shown in the following table:

Mean Profit Margin	Mean Revenue Growth				
	10%	11%	12%	13%	14%
10%	$3,376	$3,462	$3,552	$3,675	$3,779
11%	$3,771	$3,875	$4,023	$4,172	$4,340
12%	$4,229	$4,393	$4,579	$4,756	$4,953
13%	$4,753	$4,965	**$5,185**	**$5,405**	**$5,629**
14%	**$5,345**	**$5,560**	**$5,800**	**$6,090**	**$6,344**

Shaded portions are where the buyer will not take the deal.

9. Use the model you built in problem 7, using the Decision Table tool in Crystal Ball to estimate the value of the earnout plan under different revenue growth rates and profit margins. The results will be similar to those shown in the following table:

Mean Profit Margin	Mean Revenue Growth				
	16%	18%	20%	22%	24%
12%	**$5,503**	**$5,760**	**$5,989**	**$6,248**	**$6,515**
13%	**$6,231**	**$6,496**	**$6,751**	$7,054	$7,283
14%	**$6,919**	$7,210	$7,546	$7,849	$8,158
15%	$7,697	$8,012	$8,301	$8,672	$9,001
16%	$8,454	$8,766	$9,096	$9,485	$9,827

Shaded portions are where the seller will not take the deal.

[These spreadsheets from problems 8 and 9 can be found in the folder "Key Spreadsheets from the Workbook" located on the CD-ROM.]

CHAPTER 23

Risk Management in M&A

1. There are many kinds of transaction risks in M&A:
   - Decline in the buyer's share price or financial performance.
   - Preemption by a competing bidder.
   - Disappointed sellers.
   - Appearance of formerly hidden product liabilities.
   - Loss of key customers by the target.
   - Problems in the target's accounting statements.
   - Regulatory intervention.
   - Litigation by competitors.
   - Disagreements over social issues.
   - Failure to get shareholder approvals.
   - Controversy or lack of credibility.
2. The lockup option gives the buyer the right to buy the Baltimore factory if another bidder acquires Fine-Machinery. Therefore, it is a call option with a payoff of \$5 million (value of \$20 million, less the exercise price of \$15 million) if there is a competing successful bid, and zero if there is no competing successful bid. The decision tree is drawn as follows, and the value of this call option is calculated at \$1,250,000.

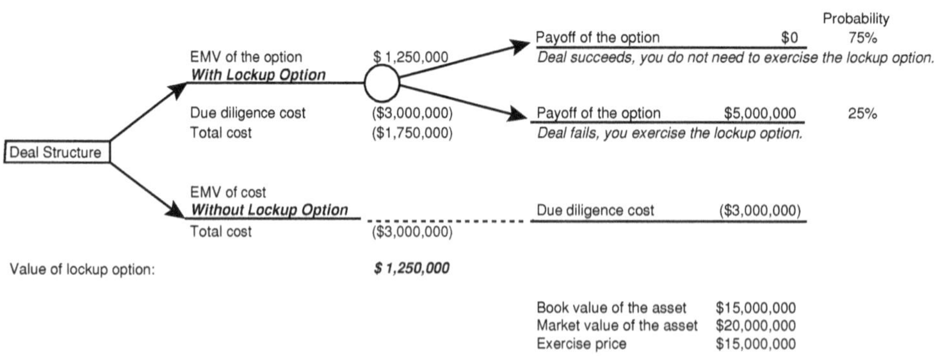

3. An exit clause is a very common risk management tool to reduce the buyer's risk. In this problem, the exit clause gives the buyer the right, not the obligation, to abandon the purchase if the deal becomes unattractive. The value of the exit clause is $1 million, computed as the difference between the expected monetary value (EMV) of the deal with, and without, the exit clause.

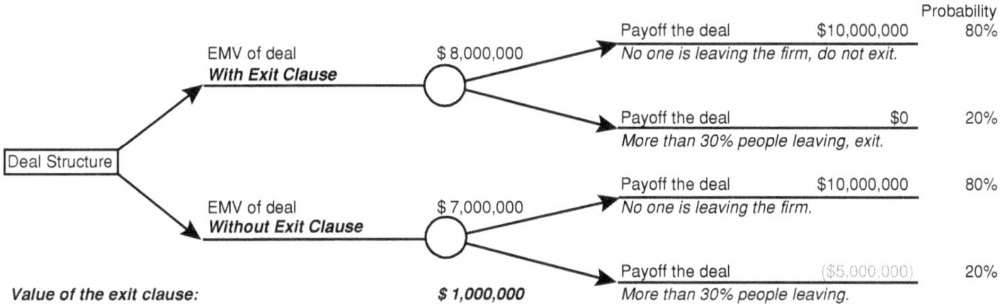

4. As noted in Chapter 8 of the main text, due diligence is a risk management device. In combination with the exit clause, investing in due diligence acquires a *put option* in this case; the audit provides more accurate information about the accounting of the target, which gives the buyer the right to withdraw from an economically unattractive deal. By drawing the decision tree, one can compute the value of this option at $1.5 million. After deducting the cost of option from the value of the option, the net value of the option is estimated to be $1 million.

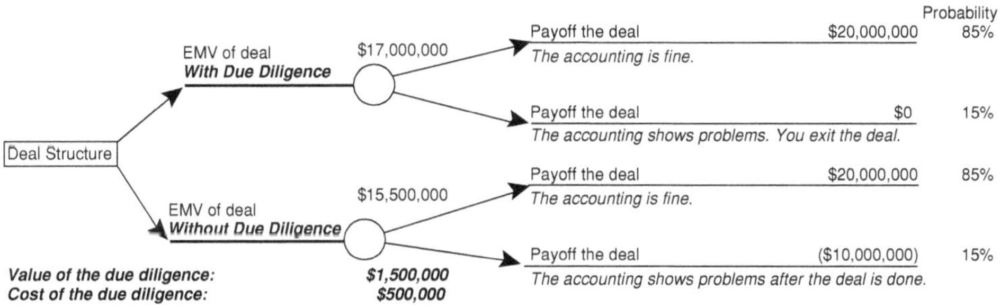

5. Insert the parameters into the model. You should obtain the following results:

		Buyer's Stock Price	Value of Bid with Collar	Number of Buyer Shares Issued per Target Share with Stock Collar
Fixed exchange ratio	1.40	$ 0.01	$28.00	2,800.00
Collar upper strike	$40.00	$ 5.00	$28.00	5.60
		$10.00	$28.00	2.80
Exchange ratio above upper strike	Upper strike/buyer's stock price	$15.00	$28.00	1.87

(Continued)

		Buyer's Stock Price	Value of Bid with Collar	Number of Buyer Shares Issued per Target Share with Stock Collar
Collar lower strike	$20.00	$20.00	$28.00	1.40
		$25.00	$35.00	1.40
Exchange ratio below lower strike	Lower strike/buyer's stock price	$30.00	$42.00	1.40
		$35.00	$49.00	1.40
		$40.00	$56.00	1.40
		$45.00	$56.00	1.24
		$50.00	$56.00	1.12

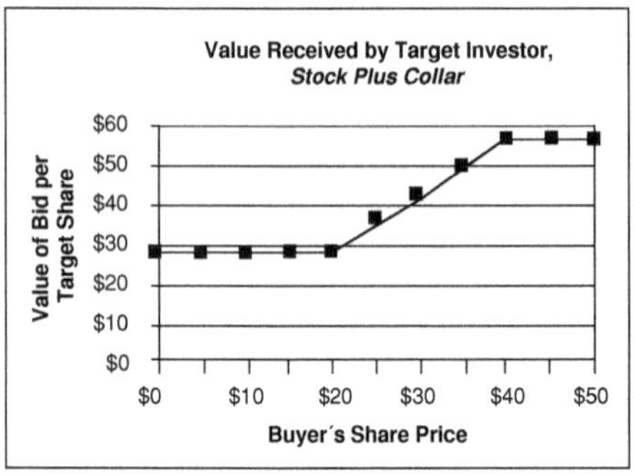

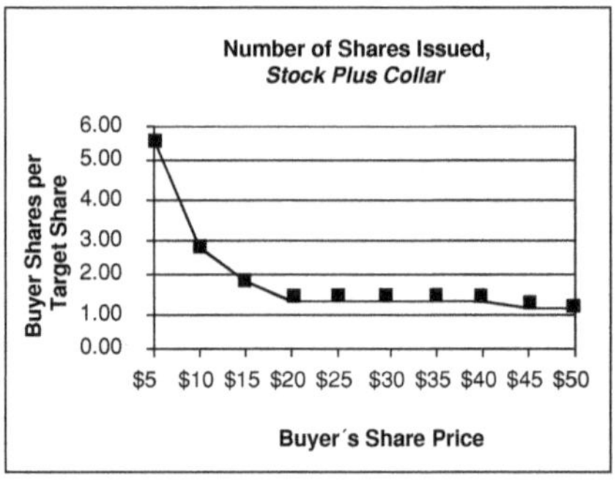

From the standpoint of the target investor, the collar for this fixed exchange ratio deal essentially consists of a long put option (with a strike price of $20) and a short call option (with a strike price of $40). When the collar is combined with the stock position, the graph of payoffs presented to the target shareholders corresponds to the floating collar.

6. Insert the parameters into the model. You should obtain the following results:

		Buyer's Stock Price	Value of Bid with Collar	Number of Buyer Shares Issued per Target Share with Stock Collar
Fixed value per target share	$40.00	$ 0.01	$ 0.02	2.00
Collar upper strike	$60.00	$10.00	$20.00	2.00
Exchange ratio above upper strike	0.667	$20.00	$40.00	2.00
Collar lower strike	$20.00	$30.00	$40.00	1.33
Exchange ratio below lower strike	2.00	$40.00	$40.00	1.00
		$50.00	$40.00	0.80
		$60.00	$40.00	0.67
		$70.00	$46.67	0.67

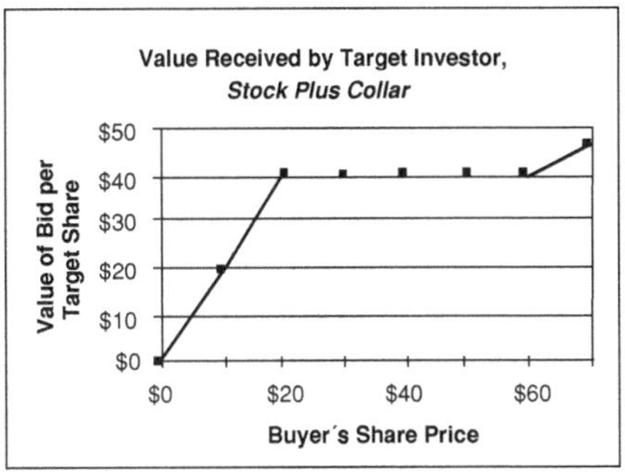

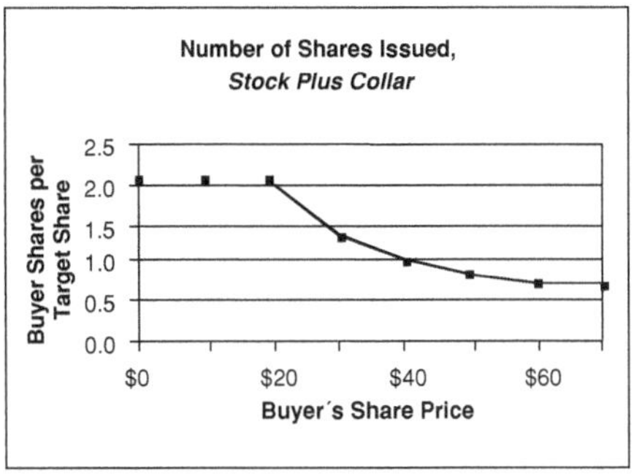

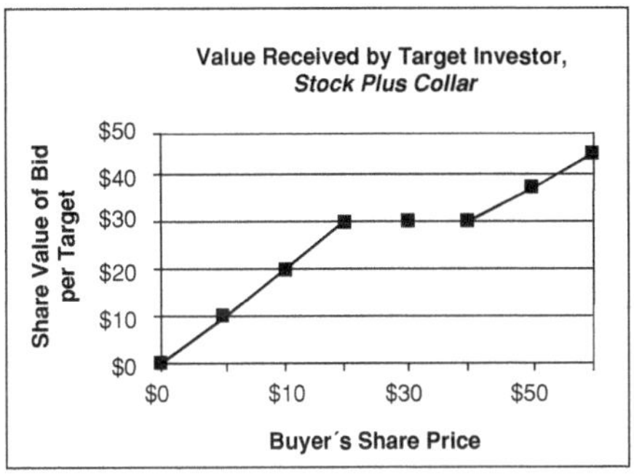

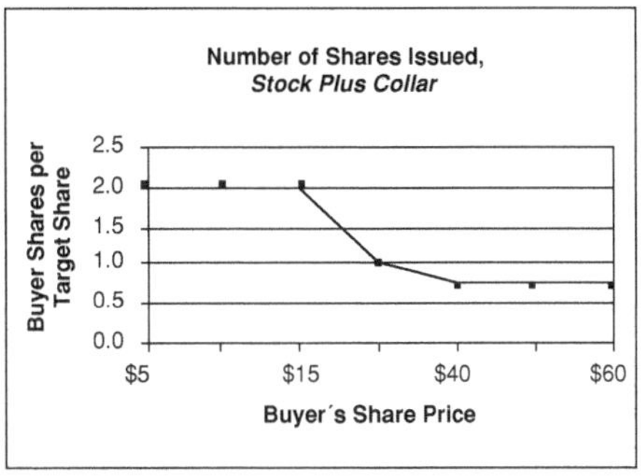

The diagrams of the combined position given in the preceding charts correspond to the fixed collar.

7. This problem is a simple illustration of how the Monte Carlo simulation can be used to calculate the value of a staged investment. The distribution of the value of the potential drug follows a normal distribution as shown:

	Time		
	Now	**After More Information**	**Total**
Payment	$15	$5	$20
Uncertainty		61.55518	
Trigger price		$50	

Running Crystal Ball 5,000 times, a $19 million mean total payment is obtained. It indicates that the buyer can save an expected value of $1 million by structuring the acquisition as a staged payment plan.

Statistics	Value
Trials	5,000
Mean	$ 19
Median	$ 20
Mode	$ 20
Standard deviation	$ 2
Variance	$ 5
Skewness	–1.20
Kurtosis	2.43
Coefficient of variability	0.11
Range minimum	$ 15
Range maximum	$ 20
Range width	$ 5
Mean standard error	$0.03

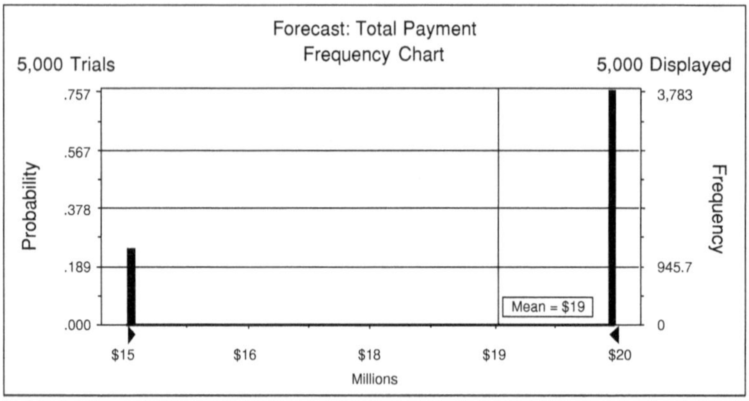

Source: Output as produced from Crystal Ball software simulation.

8a. To arrive at the true value of the deal, one needs to calculate the value of the contingent value right—the CVR is essentially a collar that lives beyond the closing of the acquisition. This collar consists of a long put with the strike price at $42 and a short put with the strike price at $32, which allows a maximum cash payment of $10 ($42 – $32). By using "Collars Analysis.xls" in the CD-ROM, one can arrive at the option value of the individual put options. The net value of one collar comes out to $7.88. Since each target share will be exchanged for two shares of your firm's stock, the offer in terms of one target's share is worth $55.89, which is equal to $45.00 + $10.89 (cash plus the value of the collar times 1.4).

Life of collar:	365
Structure of collar:	
If one component is a long call:	
Strike price:	$—
Payoff formula (text):	Maximum of (stock price minus strike price) or zero
Payoff calculated:	0
If one component is a short call:	
Strike price:	$—
Payoff formula (text):	Zero minus the maximum of (stock price minus strike price) or zero
Payoff calculated:	$—
If one component is a long put:	
Strike price:	$42.00
Payoff formula (text):	Maximum of (strike price minus stock price) or zero
Payoff calculated:	$ 7.89
If one component is a short put:	
Strike price:	$32.00
Payoff formula (text):	Zero minus the maximum of (strike price minus stock price) or zero
Payoff calculated:	$—
Buyer's share price today	$30.00
Annualized volatility of buyer's share price	15.0%
Forecast of return of buyer's share price at closing of deal	12.84%
Forecast of buyer's share price at closing of deal	$34.11
Risk-free rate of return today	4.8%
Annualized volatility of risk-free rate of return	16%
Standard deviation of annualized risk-free rate of return	0.8%
Forecast of risk-free rate of return	7%
Calculated value of the collar (sum of four payoffs)	$7.39

Note: The calculated value in this table reflects just one draw from the various distributions. Please refer to the next table for an estimate of the mean of the entire distribution.

Forecast: Value of Collar

Statistics	Value
Trials	5,000
Mean	$7.88
Median	$9.46
Mode	$0.00
Standard deviation	$2.61
Variance	$6.81
Skewness	–1.60
Kurtosis	4.56
Coefficient of variability	0.33
Range minimum	$0.00
Range maximum	$9.80
Range width	$9.80
Mean standard error	$0.04

(Continued)

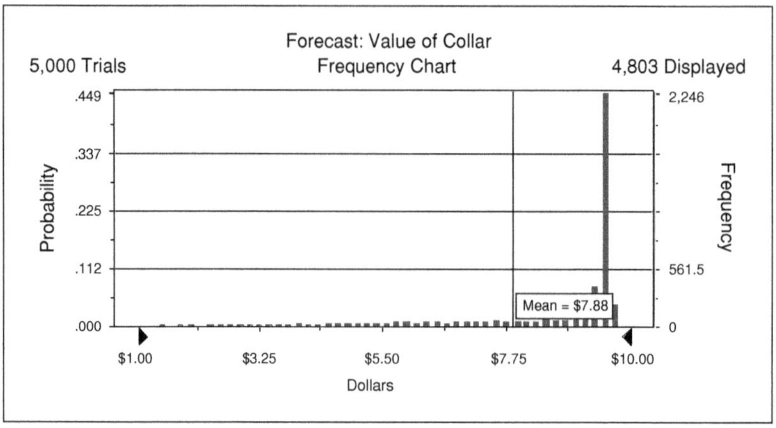

8b.

Life of the collar:	
Best guess days	730
Maximum days	1,095
Minimum days	365
Forecast of life of collar:	628.1783
Structure of the collar:	
If one component is a long call:	
Strike price:	$ —
Payoff formula (text):	Maximum of (stock price minus strike price) or zero
Payoff calculated:	0
If one component is a short call:	
Strike price:	$ —
Payoff formula (text):	Zero minus the maximum of (stock price minus strike price) or zero
Payoff calculated:	$ —
If one component is a long put:	
Strike price:	$50.00
Payoff formula (text):	Maximum of (strike price minus stock price) or zero
Payoff calculated:	$15.89
If one component is a short put:	
Strike price:	$35.00
Payoff formula (text):	Zero minus the maximum of (strike price minus stock price) or zero
Payoff calculated:	(0.89)
Buyer's share price today	$40.00
Annualized volatility of buyer's share price	18.0%
Forecast of return of buyer's share price at closing of deal	7.50%
Forecast of buyer's share price at closing of deal	$43.12
Risk-free rate of return today	6%
Annualized volatility of risk-free rate of return	20%
Standard deviation of annualized risk-free rate of return	1.2%
Forecast of risk-free rate of return	6%
Calculated value of the collar (sum of four payoffs)	$13.63

Note: The calculated value in this table reflects just one draw from the various distributions. Please refer to the next table for an estimate of the mean of the entire distribution.

Forecast: Value of Collar

Statistics	Value
Trials	5,000
Mean	$12.65
Median	$13.22
Mode	$ 0.00
Standard deviation	$ 1.79
Variance	$ 3.22
Skewness	–2.93
Kurtosis	13.45
Coefficient of variability	0.14
Range minimum	$ 0.00
Range maximum	$14.55
Range width	$14.55
Mean standard error	$ 0.03

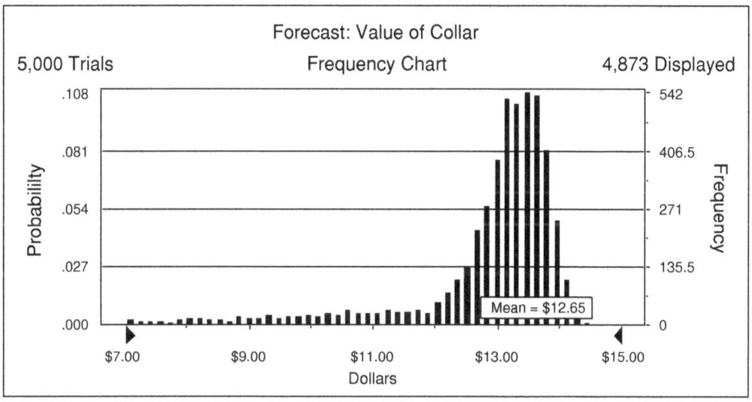

By using a triangular distribution for the time period of the option, the value of the collar can be calculated. A trial run of 5,000 times results in a mean value of the collar of $12.65 per buyer's share. Therefore, the total payment for one share of the target's stock is $62.71 ($45 + 1.4 × $12.65).

9.

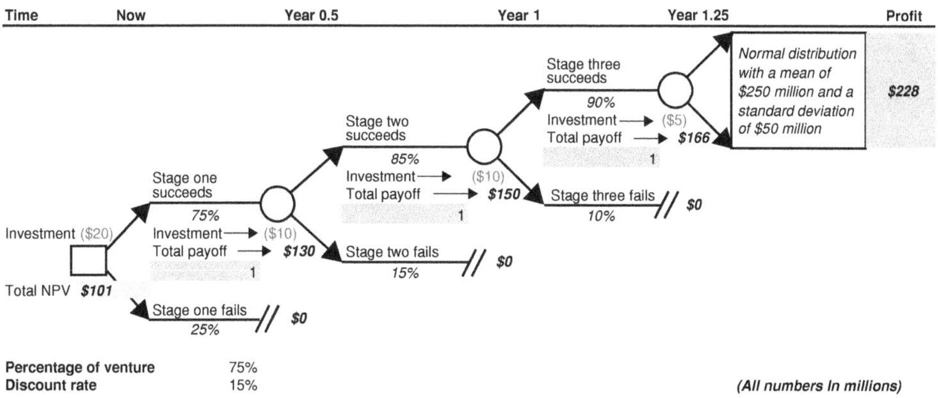

In the tree, the terminal payoffs are calculated by multiplying 75 percent by the forecasted profits, which follows a normal distribution with a mean of $250 million and a standard deviation of $50 million because Macrosofft is purchasing 75 percent of Red Dragon. Then, the payoffs are discounted according to the corresponding time period to obtain the expected monetary value (EMV). The investment for each period is deducted from EMV to obtain the net present value for each period. Given that the profit at the end of year 1.25 ($228 million) is uncertain, it should be simulated to generate a distribution and an expected value. The following table completes this analysis, and finds the expected NPV today is $57 million.

Statistics	Value
Trials	5,000
Mean	$ 57
Median	$ 82
Mode	($ 20)
Standard deviation	$ 73
Variance	$5,402
Skewness	–0.05
Kurtosis	1.38
Coefficient of variability	1.28
Range minimum	($ 38)
Range maximum	$ 223
Range width	$ 261
Mean standard error	$ 1.04

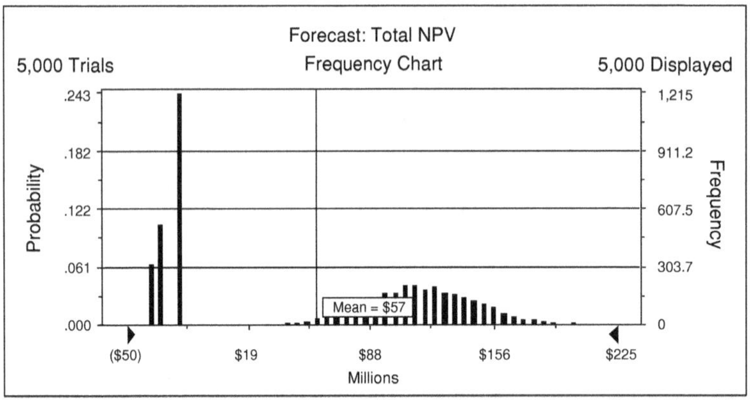

24

Social Issues

1a. There were several key social issues included in the DaimlerChrysler merger agreement:

- *Joint name:* DaimlerChrysler.
- *Country of incorporation:* Germany.
- *Operational Headquarters:* in Germany and the United States.
- *Common language:* English.
- *CEO:* A structure of two co-CEOs.
- *Board seats:* Chrysler and Daimler would each hold half of the board seats of the Newco board of directors.
- *Executive compensation:* The compensation for German executives was significantly lower than that for their American counterparts. It was known that the CEO of Daimler made the equivalent of $2.5 million a year, while Chrysler's CEO made $16 million in 1997. However, Daimler disclosed pay only on an aggregate basis.

1b. By and large, these terms reflect a merger of equals. Two headquarters, two co-CEOs, and a board of directors for Newco with equal representation from both Daimler and Chrysler are strong indications of this.

1c. The issue of the new company name was a point of contention that became resolved only in the final merger discussions. CEO Jürgen Schrempp really wanted the Newco name to be Daimler-Benz; Robert Eaton, the CEO of Chrysler, insisted on having his company name included. The issue of the new company name appeared to be one that would make or break the deal.

The choice of English as the common language was controversial among German DaimlerChrysler employees. But English was widely used in business across Europe and DaimlerChrysler wanted to be a truly global firm.

1d. There is always a risk that any social issue can create problems after a merger deal closes. In this case, an issue that could become problematic is the discrepancies between German and U.S. executive compensation structures. The differences could make German employees feel they are not being treated fairly. Furthermore, the structure of co-CEOs could become problematic as each CEO may be accustomed to taking the lead, rather than conceding and negotiating decisions with a partner on equal footing.

2. Social issues can create value. Spending on social issues may be positively correlated with incentive effects: The more a company spends on social issues, the better the returns from improved employee motivation.

   Social issues can also destroy value: Because negotiations on social issues may give a prospective buyer favorable consideration by a target firm, other potential bidders may be discouraged from making a higher competing bid. A target firm may end up settling on an acquisition price with the favored buyer that is lower than what target shareholders might have received from another bidder. The difference in value represents an opportunity cost to the target shareholders.

3. Best Homes, Inc., may have a golden parachute program in place that would give Roberta a sizable sum of money if there were a change in corporate control (i.e., if Urban Living acquired the company). Even if Best Homes did not have golden parachute provisions, its severance package could be significant for Roberta, and something that she believes is worth receiving if her job is indeed terminated. The formula for severance packages at Best Homes is a month's salary for every year worked at the firm; this means that Roberta would receive a severance payment worth 75 percent of her current annual salary. Given that Roberta is very marketable and skilled, she could stay until she receives a severance payment and then easily get a comparable job if and when she leaves Best Homes.

4. The merger bears many of the characteristics of a merger of equals:
   - Each firm was to have equal representation on the board of the new company.
   - The former CEOs would occupy the top two executive positions.
   - Each firm was bound to a $250 million breakup fee.
   - Each firm would give the other an option to acquire 19.9 percent of its currently outstanding shares if a higher bidder came along.
   - The proposed new blended name, Morgan Stanley Dean Witter Discover, conveyed an appearance of equality.
   - The two firms would retain their respective headquarters locations.
   - The deal was structured as a merger with an exchange of shares.
   - The acquisition premium was low.

25

How a Negotiated Deal Takes Shape

1. The CEO of Family Mart may be exposing his company to risk by showing the buyer the books before signing a confidentiality agreement. If the parties do not intend to sign a confidentiality agreement, it may be advisable for the CEO of Family Mart to release private information in stages.
2. The CEO of Family Mart is making a promise before even discussing the transaction with his directors. Such a commitment may expose the CEO to legal liability. The advisable procedure is to gain approval of the board first.
3. It is not uncommon for CEOs to engage in preliminary discussions prior to informing a larger group. However, Olsen is taking an unnecessary risk by going far along the process without informing his directors. No matter how attractive the deal seems to him, the board may not grant its approval, and Olsen may end up wasting precious time and resources.

   This happened in merger discussions between Coca-Cola and Quaker. Coca-Cola had begun negotiations with Quaker without informing its board. Coca-Cola delivered a written proposal to Quaker discussing the terms of its offer, and the two parties signed a confidentiality agreement, conducted due diligence reviews, and even got an auditing firm's opinion that the merger could be accounted for under the pooling method. When Coca-Cola brought the matter up for approval in a board meeting, the directors unanimously rejected the combination.
4. Olsen could resort to either a bear hug or a hostile tender offer. In a bear hug, Olsen would send a merger proposal directly to Little Pete's board of directors, bypassing the CEO. In a hostile tender offer Olsen would send the proposal directly to Little Pete's shareholders.
5. If the acquisition is material and probable, Little Pete's has an obligation to disclose.
6. A standstill agreement protects the target against the buyer gaining control or accumulating voting power in the target in the open market while negotiations are proceeding.
7. A letter of intent would probably trigger the need to make a public announcement (because the deal is certainly material and highly probable). Given the concern that outside parties may derail the deal, the two parties might simply proceed to negotiate the definitive agreement, gain support of the two firms' boards of directors, and simultaneously issue a merger proxy statement, submit the antitrust filings with the government, and make a public announcement. This approach leaves as little time as possible for potentially hostile parties to react.

CHAPTER 26

Governance in M&A: The Board of Directors and Shareholder Voting

1. The laws of the state of incorporation govern when challenging directors' decision to sell a firm.

2. Under straight voting, the shareholder wields votes equal to the number of shares held. Under cumulative voting, a shareholder is granted votes equal to the number of shares held times the number of directors to be elected.

3a. Echo has no chance under straight voting. The Addams family can outvote Echo 700,000 to 100,000 for each director.

3b. Assuming that the public does not vote straight for Addams' Apple directors, Echo has a chance under cumulative voting. The Addams family has a total of 5.6 million votes, which when divided by eight comes out to 700,000 votes per director. Echo can vote his nominee in if he votes all of his 800,000 shares for his nominee.

4. The duty of care is violated. See Smith vs. Van Gorkom.pdf on the CD-ROM for description of an instance similar to this.

5. The directors have a clear conflict of interest in this situation and would arguably violate the duty of loyalty in approving the proposal.

6. Tom Kane has an obligation to do more under the duty of care. Financial statements are detailed presentations requiring careful and thorough attention. Tom should not slacken in his oversight of Walking Shoes' financial systems.

7. The Revlon duties are probably triggered in this case. Directors must commence an auction unless strong strategic reasons exist (as in *Time Warner v. Paramount*) as to why the directors should "just say no" to a superior bid.

8. Under the business judgment rule, courts are unlikely to intervene if directors and officers have fulfilled their duties in good faith, are not conflicted, are informed, and act in rational belief, all of which seem to be true in this case.

27

Rules of the Road: Securities Law, Issuance Process, Disclosure, and Insider Trading

1. Joe is not right. The aim of securities laws is to inform investors, prevent manipulation, produce more efficient markets, and achieve a level playing field.
2. Pearl has already violated the Williams Amendment. Although she personally did not cross the 5 percent threshold, the investor group of which she is a part owns 24.95 percent. The Williams Amendment states that upon crossing the 5 perent threshold, the buyer (the pool) has to file notice with the SEC within 10 days. She will also violate the Williams Amendment by discriminating among the shareholders, and by keeping her offer open for less than 20 business days.
3. This does not violate the Williams Amendment since both back-end and front-end offers have equal economic value. A court challenge may succeed if a plaintiff can argue that Ronaldman's shares are worth less than $10 each.
4. Fitness Buff should have disclosed the merger negotiations or responded, "We do not comment on rumors in the market." By denying the rumor, Fitness Buff went against the SEC pronouncement that "If the issuer is aware of nonpublic information concerning acquisition discussions . . . at the time the statement is made, the issuer has an obligation to disclose sufficient information concerning the discussions to prevent the statements made from being materially misleading."
5. Denver has clearly violated the laws of insider trading by misappropriating the information provided by Siegel. Siegel, although he may not have been intending to, may have also violated regulations for disclosure of information by providing confidential information to one outsider and not the public.
6. Yes. Myer-Goodwill-Milo is engaging in a public offering of unregistered stock, in violation of the 1933 Act. Myer-Goodwill-Milo has jumped the gun by making an offering before the registration of securities is effective.
7. No, not if the issuance qualifies as a private placement. To qualify as a private placement, there must be a small circle of offerees (which there is in this case), and 18th Century's five owners would need to qualify as "accredited investors" for which status as high-net-worth individuals is a key criterion.

CHAPTER 28

Rules of the Road: Antitrust Law

1. If the price of X increases, demand for Y will decrease. Some examples of products that might exhibit negative cross elasticities are:

   - *DVD player prices and DVDs.* If the prices of DVD players fall, demand for DVDs increases.
   - *Gasoline prices and cars.* If gasoline prices rise, demand for cars may fall.
   - *Mobile phone usage rates and handsets.* If charges for mobile phone usage increase, demand for mobile phone handsets may fall.

   Goods that exhibit negative cross elasticities tend to be complementary; that is, they tend to be used together.

2.

% Change in demand for lamb chops(*a*)	0.0025
% Change in price of beefsteaks (*b*)	0.01
Cross elasticity of demand (*a*/*b*)	**0.25**

   The positive cross elasticity suggests that lamb chops and beefsteaks are substitutes rather than complements. But demand for lamb chops is not very sensitive to changes in the price of beef.

3. The calculation of pre- and post-transaction HHI indexes is:

Summary	
Market HHI before the deal	3,108.8
Market HHI after the deal	3,196.4
Change in market HHI	87.6

HHI Indexes before the Contemplated Transaction

	Based on Revenues		
Market Players	FY 2000 Revenue ($ MM)	% Market Share	(Market Share)^2
Best Buy Co. Inc.	12,494.0	40.7	1,656.4
Circuit City Stores Inc.	10,599.4	34.5	1,192.1
RadioShack Corporation	4,794.7	15.6	243.9

(Continued)

Market Players	FY 2000 Revenue ($MM)	% Market Share	(Market Share)^2
	Based on Revenues		
The Good Guys Inc.	860.5	2.8	7.9
Intertan Inc.	484.2	1.6	2.5
Rex Stores Corp.	464.3	1.5	2.3
Tweeter Home Entertainment	404.7	1.3	1.7
Ultimate Electronics Inc.	385.0	1.3	1.6
Sound Advice Inc.	177.3	0.6	0.3
Harvey Electronics Inc.	34.4	0.1	0.0
Total	30,698.5	100.0	3,108.8 HHI

HHI Indexes after the Contemplated Transaction

Market Players	Revenues	% Market Share	(Market Share)^2
	Based on Revenues		
Best Buy Co. Inc.	12,494.0	40.7	1,656.4
Circuit City Stores Inc.	10,599.4	34.5	1,192.1
Intertan Inc.	484.2	1.6	2.5
Rex Stores Corp.	464.3	1.5	2.3
Tweeter Home Entertainment	404.7	1.3	1.7
Ultimate Electronics Inc.	385.0	1.3	1.6
Sound Advice Inc.	177.3	0.6	0.3
Harvey Electronics Inc.	34.4	0.1	0.0
RadioShack & Good Guys	5,655.2	18.4	339.4
Total	30,698.5	100.0	3,196.4 HHI

Note: "(Market Share)^2" indicates the resulting value when "% market share" has been raised to the second power.

The merger certainly increases the already high concentration among the sample of firms selected. But it might be argued that RadioShack and The Good Guys operate in different market segments. One specializes in the do-it-yourself private-label market, while the other specializes in brand-name systems. The problem here illustrates that market definition is at least as important as the calculation of HHIs.

4.

Market HHI before the deal	7,204
Market HHI after the deal	7,675
Change in market HHI	471

These results show the sports-drink market as being highly concentrated. The HHI is well above the 1,800 threshold, and the change in market HHI is also well above the 50-point mark. The FTC commissioners were actually split on this issue. Two of the commissioners voted to investigate further the proposed merger between PepsiCo and Quaker Oats, while two others voted against taking any further action.

5. Yes, Firm A is required to file a report. The Hart-Scott-Rodino Act requires a filing if a buyer has assets over $100 million and a target has assets over $10 million.

6. Yes. The post-transaction concentration may be very high, but because Eagle is a failing firm, the FTC might approve the deal. Specifically, if the effect of the deal on competition (if the two companies merge) is less deleterious than the effect of letting Eagle go bankrupt, the FTC may approve the deal. This is the "failing company defense" to possible antitrust objections.

7. Yes, Satellite and Alpha can consummate the deal. No response from the FTC or the DOJ within 30 days of filing gives clearance for firms to complete mergers and acquisitions.

29

Documenting the M&A Deal

1. Sally can ask Harry to sign a standstill agreement, which seeks a commitment on Harry's part not to purchase more target shares without the approval of Close Call's board. By limiting the Motley Players' shares, the standstill agreement prevents Motley Players from accumulating voting power. A standstill agreement helps Close Call prevent loss of control during negotiations.
2. The financial adviser may have been thinking that in exchange for signing a confidentiality agreement, Harry could ask Sally to sign an exclusivity agreement to prevent competitors from entering the picture. The financial adviser could also be thinking of having Sally sign a termination agreement in which Close Call would pay a fee or reimburse Motley's expenses if it terminated negotiations. This would increase the chances of a successful negotiation.
3. Predator's insistence on a "tail provision" is common practice, though the four-year time frame that Predator requests seems rather long.
4. The engagement letter has not included a provision that specifies the scope of the engagement. The services sought by the client can cover a potentially wide range, from providing a fairness opinion to advising on deal structure and even performing other services up to and including closing. The scope of the adviser's services should be clearly laid out in the engagement letter.
5. The complexity of the target in terms of scope of operations would dictate a longer due diligence period than two weeks. Harry's request is more reasonable.
6. No, Harry has no obligation to comply with the terms set out in the earlier documents. The term sheet and the letter of intent are nonbinding.
7. The parties to the deal are PayPal, Inc. (the target), eBay Inc. (the buyer), and Vaquita Acquisition Corp. (a wholly owned subsidiary of eBay).
8.

Purchase Price	
Implied price per share	No share price given for eBay
Resulting PayPal ownership of eBay	7.6% (students will need to calculate)
Transaction fees	Not given
Exchange ratio	0.39
Cap	None

(Continued)

Form of Payment	
Consideration	100% stock
Number of shares to be issued	26.14 million shares (you will need to calculate)
Form of Transaction and Tax Considerations	Section 368(a) Reverse Triangular Merger. Tax-deferred to the sellers.
Transaction Process Requirements	
Termination penalties	PayPal pays eBay $5 million if the agreement is terminated by eBay. PayPal pays eBay $45 million pursuant to conditions set out in Section 8.5(c).
Shareholder vote	PayPal shareholders must approve the deal. Shareholder approval is not required for eBay.
Closing date	No specific date given. "Occurs after all the conditions in the merger agreement have been fulfilled."
Social Issues	
Organization structure	PayPal becomes a stand-alone subsidiary of eBay.
Executives	The officers of the company at the effective time shall, from and after the effective time, be the officers of the surviving corporation until their successors have been duly elected or appointed and qualified.
Board seats	The directors of merger subsidiary at the effective time shall, from and after the effective time, be the directors of the surviving corporation until their successors have been duly elected or appointed and qualified.
Headquarters	Not mentioned.
Name	Subsidiary will remain PayPal Inc.
Workforce	eBay and PayPal shall work together to retain selected key employees of PayPal, including new employment terms as appropriate.

9. The merger agreement was dated July 7, 2002. The closing date occurs after all the conditions in the merger agreement have been fulfilled. The effective date is when a certificate of merger has been filed with and accepted by the secretary of state of Delaware (the state in which both buyer and target are incorporated).

   The merger is a reverse triangular merger. PayPal will merge into the eBay subsidiary Vaquita, and will emerge as the surviving entity.

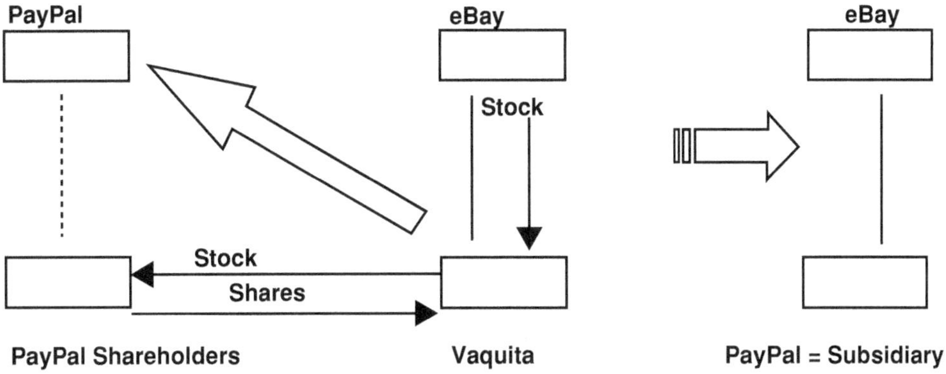

10. The "Recitals" section tells us that the boards of both target and acquirer have already approved the deal, and that they deem the deal to be in the best interest of shareholders. The "Recitals" section also suggests that certain conditions—such as stockholders' agreements and employment agreements—have been put in place. These agreements make it more difficult for each party to back out of the deal.
11. PayPal's bylaws will apply.
12. The directors will be those of Vaquita Acquisition Corp., and the officers will be those of PayPal. As a result, eBay retains control of the board and keeps PayPal management in place.
13. The deal is a share-for-share exchange. Each PayPal share will be exchanged for 0.39 shares of eBay.
14. The chief representations and warranties issues include:
    - Proper incorporation and valid existence of the company, and warranty of good standing. (This prevents fraud.)
    - Class and number of shares outstanding, including any options outstanding. (This fixes the number of shares to be included in the exchange, preventing unexpected dilution.)
    - No violations of governmental filings. (This prevents surprise over violations of rules and laws.)
    - Integrity of financial statements. (This prevents surprise due to accounting fraud or error.)
    - Existing and expected litigation and liabilities. (This prevents surprise over unexpected lawsuits and legal obligations.)
    - Employee benefit plans and labor matters. (This prevents surprise over labor matters.)
    - Compliance with company bylaws and any contracts entered into. (This prevents unexpected lawsuits due to noncompliance.)

- Potential environmental litigation. (This limits exposure arising from unexpected environmental liabilities.)
- Sufficiency of corporate authority for merger approval. (This prevents corporate authorities from obstructing the deal.)

15. Examples of covenants are:
    - The agreement to conduct business as usual until the effective date protects both buyer and target from material adverse effects arising from business disruption.
    - Agreements prohibiting the target from doling out additional awards under employee benefit plans, from selling any capital stock and/or paying extraordinary dividends, and from commencing litigation all protect the buyer from potential additional liabilities.
    - The agreement by the target not to solicit any other merger offers protects the buyer from competing bids.
    - Prohibitions against making misleading statements and omitting material facts protect both the target and buyer from potential liabilities arising from fraud or from consummating a bad deal.
    - Agreements to convene shareholder meetings, to file registration/proxy statements promptly, and to take any actions needed to consummate the merger protect both parties from any foot-dragging.
    - Agreements to provide target employees with benefits no less favorable than those previously provided and to retain key employees protect the target's employees and ensure smoother consummation of the deal.

16. Some of the conditions include:
    - Obtaining the necessary stockholder approval.
    - Expiration of the waiting period under the Hart-Scott-Rodino Act.
    - No governmental litigation prohibiting the consummation of the merger.
    - S-4 registration statements (these register with the SEC new shares to be issued) should have become effective.
    - Blue-sky approvals should have been obtained.

    The preceding conditions give the buyer and/or target an exit in the event that some outside party (e.g., shareholders, government) fail to complete important prerequisites.

    - Reps and warranties made by buyer and target should be true as of agreement and closing dates.
    - Both buyer and target should have performed all obligations agreed upon in the merger agreement.
    - Submission of "comfort letters" from accountants.

    The preceding conditions manage risk by preventing fraud and by allowing either party to exit in the event that the other party fails to complete an important condition for the merger.

- No material changes in financial condition, business, or results of operations of both buyer and target.
- Submission of tax opinions stating that the merger will be treated for federal income tax purposes as desired by the parties.

The preceding conditions manage risk by allowing the target or buyer to exit if outside conditions render the merger unable to bring about the expected financial benefits.

17. Termination is possible when:
    - There is mutual written consent by the respective boards of eBay and PayPal.
    - The merger is not consummated by December 31, 2002, or, if an extension is needed, by March 31, 2002, at the latest.
    - There has been a breach of any representation, warranty, covenant, or other term of agreement by either party.
18. The buyer, SPX Corporation, is filing the proxy statement.
19. SPX wants Echlin's shareholders to call for a special shareholders' meeting. SPX needs at least 35 percent of the votes for a special meeting to be called.
20. Common stock.
21. According to the Business Combination Statutes,

    a. a corporation may not engage in any business combination with an "Interested Shareholder" (defined as the beneficial owner of 10% or more of the voting power of a company) for five years following the date on which the Interested Shareholder became such unless the acquisition which resulted in the Interested Shareholder becoming such or the business combination is approved by the board of directors and by a majority of the non-employee directors, of which there shall be at least two, before the date of the 10% acquisition.

    b. any business combination with an Interested Shareholder that was not approved by the board of directors prior to the 10% Acquisition must be approved by the board of directors, 80% of the voting power and two-thirds of the voting power not controlled by the Interested Shareholder or meet certain conditions regarding minimum price and type of consideration.

    These conditions limit the ability of SPX to accumulate shares if board approval is not obtained. If SPX accumulates 10 percent *before* board approval is obtained, SPX will need to gain approval from an even wider constituency.
22. Echlin has a "Rights Agreement" that allows each right holder (in Echlin's case, all common stockholders except the potential buyer) to buy Echlin shares at a predetermined exercise price once a potential buyer obtains 20 percent or more of Echlin's shares. Once a potential buyer has accumulated 20 percent of shares, the rights may be redeemed only if there are "Continuing Directors" in office and a majority of such "Continuing Directors" concurs in

authorizing redemption of the rights. If a potential buyer commences a tender offer, Echlin's board of directors will no longer be able to amend the Rights Agreement after the 10-business-day period after commencement of the tender offer, unless the board of directors takes action to extend such period.

The Rights Agreement hinders SPX's attempt to acquire Echlin by severely diluting SPX's equity stake and voting power. The provision that only continuing directors can redeem the rights makes it virtually impossible for SPX to revoke the Rights Agreement unless it can get its own nominees on the board before it accumulates 20 percent of Echlin's shares, or before it commences a tender offer.

23. Probably Connecticut is not friendly to hostile takeovers. According to the proxy statement, the Connecticut House of Representatives recently introduced a bill that would (1) restrict the ability of shareholders of a public company to remove directors, (2) require the approval of a majority of "continuing directors," rather than the approval of the board of directors, and (3) provide that approval of a majority of "continuing directors," rather than the board of directors, would be required.

24. SPX is proposing a reverse triangular merger in which a subsidiary of SPX would be merged into Echlin. However, SPX reserves the right to amend the terms of the exchange, including the surviving entity in the merger.

25. SPX is proposing a part-stock, part-cash deal where Echlin shareholders would receive for each Echlin share $12.00 in cash and 0.4796 share of SPX common stock. The transaction will be taxable to exchanging shareholders. The offer represents around a 32 percent premium to Echlin's share price. SPX has filed a registration statement with the SEC, but the registration is not yet effective.

26. Echlin shareholders will own 70 percent of SPX if the deal is consummated. The deal is a reverse takeover, in effect.

27. SPX's conditions:

- *Minimum condition.* The number of shares tendered must represent at least $66^2/_3$ percent of the shares outstanding on a fully diluted basis.
- *Rights condition.* The Rights Agreement must have been suspended or otherwise be inapplicable to the exchange offer. The rights condition is to prevent triggering the poison pill, which would allow Echlin shareholders to acquire shares cheaply, thereby diluting SPX's equity stake.
- *Business Combination Statutes condition.* SPX must be satisfied that the restrictions contained in the Business Combination Statutes (see problem 21) will not apply to the proposed business combination. This is to relieve SPX of having to overcome inordinate obstacles (e.g., approval of directors/continuing directors, 80 percent vote, etc.).
- *Financing condition.* SPX must have obtained sufficient financing to enable the exchange offer and the merger to be consummated. This is to avoid the risk that the merger cannot be consummated due to lack of funding.
- *SPX stockholder approval condition.* Since SPX needs to issue more than 20 percent of its outstanding common stock to consummate the exchange offer,

it needs the approval of its stockholders. This is in compliance with New York Stock Exchange rules.

28. SPX estimates it will need $2.4 billion in funding and has received a "highly confident" letter from CIBC Oppenheimer that the necessary financing will be raised.

29. This is an escape clause that would allow SPX to start negotiating again if the opportunity arises. In effect, this clause prevents SPX from being compelled to go through with its offer if it changes its mind.

30. SPX is proposing:

    - *Repeal of bylaws adopted subsequent to April 3, 1997.* SPX wants to repeal Echlin's bylaws to prevent its directors from taking action permitted by its bylaws to block SPX's acquisition of Echlin.
    - *Removal of directors of the company and replacement with SPX nominees.* SPX wants to remove all of Echlin's current directors from the board and replace them with its own nominees. SPX needs to remove Echlin's directors because they have shown no interest in pursuing a merger with SPX and are likely to prevent SPX from consummating its offer. SPX has put up five nominees for election to the board.
    - *Amendment of the bylaws of the company.* SPX wants to amend Echlin's bylaws to reduce the number of directors from nine at present to five.

31. There must be a quorum at the special meeting, and the number of votes cast in favor of removal of a director must exceed the number of votes cast against removal.

CHAPTER 30

Negotiating the Deal

1. Nova was trying to "anchor" at a price that was clearly too low and probably insulting to the CEO of Seattle Springs. Anchoring works as long as the quoted price is credible.
2. Maybe not. Opening at one's reservation price commits one to a "take it or leave it" strategy—you retain no flexibility for further bargaining. Furthermore, such a strategy ignores the fact that bargaining is a process of *discovery* of prices and other terms. Nova might have anchored at a lower price. By opening right at the high end of its estimate of the target's value, Nova may be setting itself up for overpayment.
3. The CEO of Nova Water should get a grip on reality. The CEO's reason for continuing to bid is "sunk cost" logic—economics teaches that this is a bad basis for making financial decisions. If, as assumed in problem 1, Nova's reservation price was $330 million, how does the entry of Rings of Saturn into the bidding change that? Without further sound justification, the CEO of Nova should be counseled to drop out of the bidding.
4. Sprouse is ignoring cultural influences on bargaining outcomes. Given what he has been advised, to leave the CEO of the Taiwanese concern negotiating with anyone less than the CEO of Sea Horse may be considered disrespectful.
5. The CEO is using single-issue serial bargaining rather than multi-issue parallel bargaining. In general, single-issue serial bargaining is associated with greater likelihood of deadlocks. Multi-issue parallel bargaining allows the parties greater room for finding mutually agreeable trade-offs.
6. The soft drink company may have ignored its BATNA. The $2 billion acquisition of the target was clearly more expensive in present value terms than building its own noncarbonated beverages business.
7. Settles is not paying attention to the fact that he is a repeated buyer in a small market and that he depends on positive rapport with sellers. His reputation may cost him deals in the future.
8. Bailey did not manage the approval process on his side effectively. He could have called the CEO to report that the other side insisted on locating headquarters in Toledo. He could have insisted on going over a list of points with the CEO prior to the negotiations. He could have avoided shaking hands on the agreement until he got the approval of his CEO.

31
Auctions in M&A

1. The English auction method is most advisable if bidders are affiliated. Although it may be vulnerable to collusion, it is less vulnerable than other methods and is the most transparent method.
2. The asset is unique/scarce; hence, an auction is preferred over other methods. If the bidders know each other, an English auction would be most advisable.
3. An auction is *not* recommended. There are only two potential bidders—if one decides not to bid, Selectiv will suffer loss of reputation by trying to hold a competitive auction and failing. Also, the goal of the founders is clearly not just revenue maximization, but also fit, stability, and ability to help the company grow. A private negotiated sale seems more appropriate.
4. A Dutch auction does not "leave money on the table," as opposed to an English auction. Because prices start from the top in a Dutch auction, the seller can fetch the highest price that any of the bidders is willing to pay. In an English auction, the winning bid is not necessarily the maximum price that the winner is willing to pay.
5. Because a second-price sealed-bid auction lets the winning bidder pay the second highest bid instead of the winning bid, it gives bidders an incentive to raise their bids. Thinking that they will never have to pay what they bid, bidders may be willing to bid their maximum or even beyond. In a first-price sealed-bid auction, bidders are unlikely to go beyond their maximum, or even to bid at maximum, for fear of the "winner's curse." Thus, a second-price sealed bid auction may have greater potential to fetch higher prices.
6. Two effects seem to have a role in this outcome. First, Virginia, Inc., may have been victimized by the "winner's curse." Winning an auction reveals that everyone else estimated the value of the asset to be less than the winner estimated—thus, the implication is that the buyer may have overpaid. Second, the fact that Virginia, Inc., bid higher than its reservation price suggests that it succumbed to bidding frenzy.
7. In theory, Virginia, Inc., has the power to abandon the negotiation at this point, though to do so might damage Virginia's reputation. Abandonment is threatening to the target, as it may signal new negative information about the target that may turn other interested parties away. Culpeper, Inc., though, has the advantage of still having other interested parties (bidders), the monopoly on the assets being sold, and inside information about the target.

8. A target's strategy would be to maximize revenues and the number of bidders. To do so the target must build credibility about the auction; that is, the target must disclose all rules clearly, and stick to them at all costs.

   The strategy of a bidder upon learning of an auction would be to pressure the target board to negotiate directly with it. This may be done through a host of tactics such as "bear hugs," "Saturday night specials," and others. The bidder will aim to drag the target away from an auction, or if that is not possible, to break down the rules of the auction.

32

Hostile Takeovers: Preparing a Bid in Light of Competition and Arbitrage

1. Yes, under Rule 14d-7(a)(1) target shareholders may withdraw their tenders for any reason in the first 15 days of a tender offer.
2. Not necessarily. If the highest offer is associated with a longer expected time to consummation, the arbitrageur may achieve higher *annualized returns* by taking a lower offer and a shorter holding period.
3. A two-tiered offer is one in which the terms of the offer are different for shareholders who tender earlier than for those who tender later. The difference might be in the actual value of the offer or in the form of payment (e.g., cash versus stock). The first tier often receives more value than the second tier as an incentive to compel shareholders to tender, such as when there are competing bids or time is of the essence, or if it is necessary to gain majority control quickly.
4.

	Two-Tiered Offer	Prisoner's Dilemma
The Incentive	The first tier in a two-tier offer is usually more attractive than the second tier (e.g., cash in first tier and stock in second tier). This creates an incentive for shareholders to tender as soon as they can.	The prisoner (let's call him Prisoner A) who confesses gets a shorter time in jail.
The Dilemma	If shareholders hold out, they may get a better deal through a competing offer. But at the same time, if they hold out, they may end up having no choice but to accept the less attractive part of the deal (the second tier) if other shareholders completely take up the first tier. As a result, the shareholders may choose to tender in order to receive the more attractive part of the deal. As with a prisoner's dilemma, a two-tiered offer exploits the shareholders' (prisoners') inability to work in concert with each other and to communicate.	If Prisoner A confesses he will get a shorter sentence *as long as* Prisoner B does not implicate him. However, Prisoner A cannot tell what Prisoner B will do. If Prisoner A does not confess (shareholders hold out) and Prisoner B squeals on him (other shareholders tender), he will get a longer sentence than Prisoner B (shareholders that held out will get the less attractive part of the deal).

5. Shareholders should communicate and collaborate, such as by forming ad hoc committees of target shareholder groups, and by taking action together to achieve a maximum bid. Shareholders could also try to buy more time. This will allow the target to search for a white knight, develop a recapitalization plan, or mount other defenses.

6. Blended value per share = (.30 × \$58.00) + (.70 × \$52.00) = \$53.80

Times number of shares	× 10,000
	\$538,000

   [This spreadsheet can be found in the folder "Key Spreadsheets from the Workbook" located on the CD-ROM.]

7. A leveraged recapitalization entails borrowing substantially and paying a large one-time dividend to shareholders and/or executing a large one-time share repurchase. The result is a highly levered acquisition target that is probably less attractive to a hostile bidder.

8a. Based on the last closing, the effective purchase price for Compaq would be \$14.69, representing a 19 percent premium to its market price. The premium seems modest and consistent with the merger-of-equals tone of the transaction.

8b. According to the following calculations, Siegel's holding period return and annualized return were 105 percent and 160 percent respectively.

Days in Holding Period		240
Assumptions		
Position and Payoff in Target Shares		
Buy target shares at		\$ 12.35
Payoff on target shares at end (exchange ratio × price of buyer's shares)		\$ 11.48
Gross spread per share on target shares		\$ (0.87)
Total value of gross spread on target shares (times # shares =	125,000	\$(108,925.00)
Position and Payoff in Buyer Shares		
Short buyer shares at		\$ 23.32
Payoff on buyer shares at end		\$ 18.22
Gross spread per share on buyer shares		\$ 5.10
Total value of gross spread on buyer shares	32,000	\$ 637,500.00
Total Assets of the Arbitrage Position		\$1,543,750.00
Short position in buyer shares		\$ 746,240.00
Borrowed shares of buyer		\$(746,240.00)
Debt @ % assets	70%	\$1,080,625.00
Capital employed		\$ 463,125.00
Total Liabilities and Capital of the Arbitrage Position		\$1,543,750.00
Net Spread Calculation		
Gross spread		\$ 528,575.00
– Interest @	6%	\$ (42,632.88)
– Short dividends forgone		\$ —

(Continued)

+ Long dividends received	$ —
Net spread	$ 485,942.12
Days in holding period	240
Results	
Return on capital for holding period only	105%
Return on capital annualized	160%

[This spreadsheet can be found in the folder "Key Spreadsheets from the Workbook" located on the CD-ROM.]

9. To decide on its bid price, CleanPack should consider things from the investor's point of view. The investor has to decide whether to tender to CleanPack. If the investor decides not to tender to CleanPack, she is faced with three scenarios, as illustrated in the following investor's decision diagram:

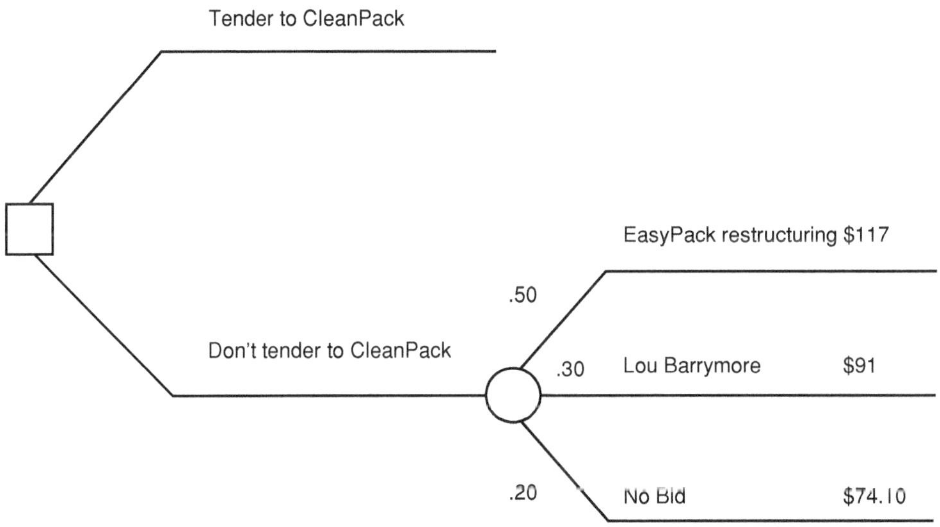

The expected value of not tendering (EVNT) = (.50 × $117) + (.30 × 91) + (.20 × 74.10) = $100.62.

Therefore, CleanPack must bid a price above $100.62 to attract shares into its tender offer.

CHAPTER 33

Takeover Attack and Defense

1. "Good" firms are those with not only strong financial performance, but also strong corporate governance and company management teams. Takeover defenses can leverage the bargaining power of good firms' managing executives for extracting high prices from bidders. However, takeover defenses more deeply entrench managers of "bad" firms—those whose managers are inept or pursuing private benefits; shareholders will react negatively when these firms announce antitakeover defenses. The primary implication is ironic: The firms that are most vulnerable to takeover (poorly managed and poorly performing firms) are those in which shareholders may be most hurt by defenses instituted, whereas the strong firms become even better guarded when takeover defenses are adopted.

2. There are four main types of charter amendments:

    1. *Classified board.* A classified board is a "staggered" one, in which board members are not elected all at once annually, but instead only a few each year. In general, the announcement of a classified board has little impact on shareholder wealth or firm performance, as investors react neutrally.
    2. *Supermajority provision.* This amendment specifies that mergers must be approved by an extra-large majority of votes (e.g., 75 to 85 percent of the votes, versus a 51 percent majority). The intended purpose of this amendment is to give a minority of shareholders a stronger voice to veto a merger, as well as delay a merger from being consummated. Scholars (Johnson and Rao 1999; Ambrose and Megginson 1992) have found that putting a supermajority provision in place has little effect on firms and shareholder value.
    3. *Fair price provision.* This provision requires that all selling shareholders receive the same price from the buyer. This prevents discriminatory practices like greenmail, where a bidder may seek to buy a majority of shares by offering a more attractive purchase price. Many states in the United States now require a takeover bid to carry a "fair price" for all shareholders. Some early research suggested that adopting a fair price amendment has a neutral to slightly negative effect on stock price. Ambrose and Megginson (1992) found that firms with fair price amendments are not much more likely to attract takeover bids.
    4. *Dual-class recapitalization.* This amendment creates two classes of stock with different voting rights (weightings): Class A stockholders may have five votes per share, whereas Class B stockholders may have one vote per share.

Some research on dual-class recapitalization shows a statistically negative impact on shareholder wealth, due to the loss of voting rights. However, Shum, Davidson, and Glascock (1995) found neutral to positive market reaction due to the loss of voting rights, provided that the shareholders received some form of compensation (e.g., increased dividends). Ambrose and Megginson (1992) found that dual-class recapitalization does not decrease the likelihood of a takeover bid.

3. You can use the following equation to test the profitability to the buyer of a takeover attack.

$$[\pi \text{ (Intrinsic value} - \text{Price} - \text{Transaction costs)} + (1 - \pi)\text{Transaction costs}] > 0$$

Probability of successful takeover	60%
Target intrinsic value (in $ millions)	$460.00
Investment banking adviser fee	2%
Legal fee	$ 10.00
Total transaction cost	$ 19.00
Buyer's planned bid price (in $ millions)	$450.00
Test	$ (1.40)

From the calculation the test gives a negative value, which indicates that the takeover attack would not create value for the buyer.

4.

Estimate of Dilution Imposed on the Bidder from a Poison Pill

Assumptions		
Stock price of target before pill is triggered	$30.00	
Number of shares outstanding before attempted raid:	1,500,000	
Discount at which nonraider shareholders have the right to purchase shares:	80%	
Purchase shares worth	$200	
By paying	$40	
Poison pill "trigger":	12%	
Assumption about whether pill exercise proceeds will be dividended to shareholders	No Dividend	Dividend
Market value of equity before trigger	$ 45,000,000	$ 45,000,000
Cash received upon exercise of poison pill rights	$ 52,800,000	$ 52,800,000
Dividend paid	$ —	$(52,800,000)
Market value of equity after trigger	$ 97,800,000	$ 45,000,000
Number of shares held by the raider when the pill is triggered	180,000	180,000
Number of shares held by investors other than the raider after the pill is triggered	10,120,000	10,120,000
Total number of shares outstanding after the pill is triggered	10,300,000	10,300,000
Price per share after trigger	$ 9.50	$ 4.37
Dilution in price per share	68%	85%

(Continued)

Estimate of Dilution Imposed on the Bidder from a Poison Pill *(Continued)*

Analysis of voting dilution imposed on raider			
Raider voting interest just before pill is triggered		12%	
Raider voting interest after pill is triggered		2%	
Economic dilution imposed on raider if pill is triggered and bid fails			
Change in raider's value of shares after pill is triggered		$ (3,690,874)	$ (4,613,592)
Raider's share of dividend from pill exercise proceeds		$ —	$ 922,718
Raider's total economic dilution after pill is triggered		$ (3,690,874)	$ (3,690,874)
Raider's total economic dilution as a percent of outlay		–68%	–68%
Economic dilution imposed on raider if pill is triggered and bid succeeds			
Value of nonraider shares before pill is triggered	$39,600,000		
Value of nonraider shares after pill is triggered	$96,090,874		
Change in raider's cost to acquire rest of shares		$(56,490,874)	$ (4,613,592)
Raider's share of dividend from pill exercise proceeds			$ 922,718
Raider applies cash from rights toward purchase price		$ 52,800,000	$ —
Raider's total economic dilution after pill is triggered		$ (3,690,874)	$ (3,690,874)
Raider's total economic dilution as a percent of outlay pretrigger		–68%	–68%
Change in cost to acquire remaining 88%		8%	8%

[This spreadsheet can be found in the folder "Key Spreadsheets from the Workbook" located on the CD-ROM.]

Using the model "Poison Pill Dilution.xls," you will need to input the assumptions at the top of the spreadsheet, namely the stock price before the pill is triggered, the number of shares outstanding before the attempted raid, the trigger percentage, the discount at which the nonraider shareholders have the right to purchase shares, and the total dollar worth of possible shares, that each share is eligible to buy.

As a result of triggering the poison pill, the raider's wealth in the target is diluted 68 percent. The raider's voting interest drops from 12 percent to 2 percent. And the raider will need to pay 8 percent more to acquire the remaining shares of the target.

34

The Leveraged Restructuring as a Takeover Defense: The Case of American Standard

1. American Standard (AS) decided to restructure when its prearranged takeover defenses were breached by court intervention. Originally, the company contemplated a leveraged recapitalization. But as the raider's bid price rose, AS signed a merger agreement with Kelso & Company, a white knight. The deal was effectively an LBO with an ESOP investment made with excess pension assets. It was only after American Standard had undergone this drastic restructuring that Black & Decker (B&D) retreated.

2. A leveraged recapitalization could be considered a synthetic MBO because it yields similar benefits to shareholders as those provided by an MBO, but without taking a firm private. Both MBOs and leveraged recaps provide preexisting shareholders with a large one-time cash payout, which is financed by a dramatic releveraging of the company. In addition, both restructurings also involve a significant change in operations and management incentive compensation.

3. Announcements of a company's shark repellent defenses are sometimes followed by declines in stock price because investors may suspect that incumbent management is adopting such provisions to protect their own interests over those of shareholders. Announcements of leveraged recaps and MBOs, however, are followed by substantial rises in share prices. Both involve a dramatic increase in corporate leverage, which can add value to a company in various ways: the value of debt tax shields, greater alignment of managers with shareholder interests, and improved operational efficiency. Furthermore, shareholders receive direct cash payouts from recaps and MBOs, which provide them with a quantitative, tangible method to value the company.

4. Being proactive is generally better than being reactive. But making a precautionary commitment to a full line of defense can have several disadvantages. First, it can lull management and the board into a false sense of security. As Chapter 32 of the main text noted, well over half of all targets of takeover attempts lose their independence. Second, defenses can entrench poor management to the disadvantage of shareholders: Takeover defenses may not al-

ways be in the interests of shareholders. And third, as the American Standard case suggests, success depends in large part on defensive reaction while the takeover contest is in progress. What matters most is *how you play the game.*

5a. You can set up a spreadsheet model like the following one, as outlined in Chapter 13 of the main text. In this base-case assumption, the value per American Standard share (line 24) rises from $50 to $68 (see line 24).

	Before Recapitalization	Changes	After Recapitalization
Book Value Balance Sheet			
1 Net working capital	$ 450,164		$ 450,164
2 Fixed assets & goodwill	$ 968,472		$ 968,472
3 Other	$ 81,812		$ 81,812
4 Total assets	$1,500,448		$1,500,448
5 Long-term debt	$ 279,506	$ 1,486,201	$1,765,707
6 Deferred tax, etc.	$ 370,316		$ 370,316
7 Preferred stock	$ 1,046		$ 1,046
8 Common equity	$ 837,722	$(1,486,201)	$ (648,479)
9 Other	$ 11,858		$ 11,858
10 Total capital	$1,500,448		$1,500,448
Market Value Balance Sheet			
11 Net working capital	$ 450,164		$ 450,164
12 Fixed assets & goodwill	$1,574,061		$1,574,061
13 Other	$ 81,812		$ 81,812
14 Tax shield	$ 104,815		$ 662,140
15 Total assets	$2,210,852		$2,768,177
16 Long-term debt	$ 279,506	$ 1,486,201	$1,765,707
17 Deferred tax, etc.	$ 370,316		$ 370,316
18 Preferred stock	$ 1,046		$ 1,046
19 Common equity	$1,548,126		$ 619,250
20 Other	$ 11,858		$ 11,858
21 Total capital	$2,210,852		$2,768,177
22 Cash	$ —		$ 48.00
23 Value of the share	$ 50.00		$ 20.00
24 Total per share	$ 50.00		$ 68.00

[This spreadsheet can be found in the folder "Key Spreadsheets from the Workbook" located on the CD-ROM.]

5b. By using the Goal Seek feature of Excel, you can back-solve for the new debt required to offer a restructuring value equal to Black & Decker's successively higher bids. The resulting findings show that beyond $68 per share, American Standard exceeds its maximum amount of external new borrowings.

	B&D's Bid	AS New Borrowing Required to Produce Total Value Equal to B&D's Bid	Value per Stub Share	Ratio of Long-Term Debt to Market Value of Common Equity
Prebid	$50.00	N/A	N/A	0.18
B&D's Bid	$65.00	$1,238,501	$25.00	1.96
	$68.00	$1,486,201	$20.00	2.85
	$73.00	$1,899,034	$11.67	6.03
	$77.00	$2,229,301	$ 5.00	16.21

[This spreadsheet can be found in the folder "Key Spreadsheets from the Workbook" located on the CD-ROM.]

These results are roughly consistent with the facts of the case: AS was able to boost its recapitalization plan to a total value of $74 to $75, but when Black & Decker raised its bid to $73, AS moved to formulate a leveraged buyout proposal that would pay AS shareholders $78. Operating as a public company, AS had less debt capacity than as a private firm.

5c. Unused debt capacity is an instrument of takeover defense used in the context of a restructuring or leveraged buyout proposal. But large unused debt capacity may be an inducement for the raider to attack in the expectation of a profit whether the target restructures or sells to the raider. Thus, unused debt capacity is a two-edged sword.

35

Communicating the Deal: Gaining Mandates, Approval, and Support

PART I: WHAT'S WRONG WITH THIS PICTURE?

1a. Keep the presentation simple. Too much material can obscure one's message. Most CEOs will probably not have the time (or the patience) to sit through a 100-slide presentation, much less read a nearly 400-page pitch book. The message has to be presented in a convincing but *concise* form.

1b. A deal presentation should emphasize its strategic rationale before getting into financial details. It would be difficult for a CEO (or anyone else for that matter) to absorb financial details without first understanding why and how a deal might fit with the company's overall business strategy.

PART II: VIGNETTES

1a. You have the challenge of communicating an idea to someone you do not know well and have not worked with in the past. Without a strong frame of reference (e.g., having already made other merger pitches to her) you probably do not have a sense of what aspects of a merger deal could be important to her and what kinds of ideas would be unattractive. Furthermore, even though you have a long tenure at the firm, you do not necessarily have buy-in or credibility with the new CEO. Perhaps you have done a good job at establishing yourself at the firm, but you have not yet personally proven yourself to Madison.

If you had a good relationship and working history with former CEO Lazar, it would probably be less difficult to present a merger deal to him, if only because you and he would have already had extensive conversations and communication on other matters. You probably would already know some of Lazar's ideas and viewpoints on different business matters (and what his important issues were) even before you pitched your specific merger idea to him.

1b. Yes, the circumstances could actually yield a better opportunity for deal approval. Consider this: The absence of a preexisting relationship with the new CEO may motivate or require you to take more formal preparation time to develop your merger idea and to sharpen your presentation skills. The extra time and effort could pay off if they result in a better overall presentation, which

would in turn increase your chances of successfully getting the merger idea approved by Madison.

There could be another reason for an increased probability for making a successful deal presentation, one in which your idea is approved. If Madison were very eager to make her mark at the new company and biased toward doing a merger even before seeing the specifics of a deal, you may have a greater opportunity for success. (This would be a clear example of managerial hubris at play in the merger decision-making process.)

1c. To improve your chances for making a successful deal presentation to the new CEO, you could do research on Madison and read about her background. If Madison does indeed have a good reputation and credibility in the industry, you would probably be able to find some good sources of information about her. In addition, you could just spend some time getting to know the new CEO before making a merger deal pitch to her. If you were to talk with Madison informally and develop a relationship with her, you would have a better sense of how to present your merger idea(s) in a way that would be successful.

2. Public disclosures of mergers should be prepared with legal counsel. It is important to disclose pertinent terms of the deal (such as the deal size, payment form, expected financial implications and synergies, etc.). While there may be an argument that "less is more" with respect to an initial press release about a merger for liability reasons as well as others, investors also have a right to learn the important facts about the deal up front. If shareholders are the ones whose votes you need to win, they will not likely support the deal if they do not have enough information, or if they learn about the deal in a piecemeal fashion well after the initial press release. The firms involved should use the press release as an opportunity to see how investors react up front, so they can gauge what they are up against as they prepare a formal deal presentation to shareholders.

   At the same time, the company must at all times be conscious of managing legal exposure and minimizing risk. Given the inherent risk of changing deal conditions, it would be wise to *not* include more information than necessary, and to *not* say anything that might be misleading or even construed/claimed to be misleading.

PART III: CASES

Hewlett-Packard and Company

1. The excerpts have two strong themes that Fiorina and Cappellas both convey repeatedly to market the deal as an attractive one.

   First and foremost, they both speak of the two companies as having a great deal "in common," including cultures, organizational models, sales force design, structures of customer support and account management, strategies, visions, and values. The two CEOs also speak of sharing a similar commitment to innovation, invention, and engineering excellence, as well as a deep contribution to communities. The two executives delineate the firms as two parts of an (already) integrated whole, and with all the descriptions of what the two companies have in common, the impression one gets is that they are in many ways the same company.

Second, both Fiorina and Cappellas speak about their comprehensive integration plan. What is particularly noteworthy in their commentaries is not the discussion of what they intend to do, but rather their testimonies about the great deal *that they have already done.*

Fiorina stated, "We have a set of early decisions already made. . . . We've done a lot of work and a lot of detailed planning before we ever said that this is a transaction that we were prepared to do."

Along the same lines, Cappellas noted, "I actually believe and think you'll start to see the things we've done as we've been bringing the companies together; you'll start to see not only the benefit of what we will do, but the benefit of what we have done. . . ."

What is particularly effective about these commentaries is that they make a strong impression and reinforce that a great deal of work has already been done, and that therefore the deal is far along and very much under way. This could have a strong influence on how shareholders decide to vote (i.e., for versus against the merger). It would be easier to vote for a merger that had already made a great deal of progress versus one that seemed to be in its infancy. Likewise, it would be much harder (presumably) to vote against a merger that is further developed than against one in which the wheels have barely been put into motion.

2. The drop in HP's stock value does not necessarily convey a failure on the part of HP and Compaq in communicating and presenting the deal to the investing community. An investor's decisions to buy or sell HP may be completely independent of the HP-Compaq press release and deal presentation. Some of those shareholders may have decided to sell even without spending (much) time reading the release or attending/listening to the investor presentation by the two companies. Regarding the investors who decided to sell HP after having taken a more active role in evaluating the deal—reading the news, listening to the investor presentation, and paying attention to Wall Street analysts' views—they did not necessarily sell because HP-Compaq management did a poor job of presenting the deal. The actual quality of the deal presentation will not always dictate the shareholders' reactions or receptivity to the deal, even though it seeks to influence them in a positive way. The quality of the presentation should enhance the probability and level of investors' receptivity to the deal, but even a good presentation will not suffice when a deal is perceived to destroy value.

Smucker

1. The Smucker press release on the Jif/Crisco acquisition is short and clear, provides enough detail, and has an upbeat tone. It has all the elements of a good press release.

- *Provides the strategic rationale for the deal:*

    SMUCKER

    "Combining JIF and SMUCKER'S," Richard Smucker explained, "brings number one brands together in the original, All-American

comfort food—peanut butter and jelly. JIF also offers a broad and exciting menu of possibilities for product development and growth."

"Just as important, it will strengthen our position to acquire other complementary leading food brands, providing opportunity for greater top- and bottom-line growth. . . ."

"Both these brands are an outstanding fit for Smucker."

P&G

"JIF and CRISCO are strong U.S. brands but they're no longer a strategic fit for P&G as we focus on building our big brands in core categories."

- *Gives details on price, form of payment, reorganization plan, and the resulting shareholder structure:*

Prior to completion, the JIF and CRISCO brands and the associated assets will be spun off from the existing P&G Company and then immediately merged with The J.M. Smucker Company. Procter & Gamble shareholders will receive one share of new J.M. Smucker stock for every 50 shares they hold in Procter & Gamble in a tax-free transaction. Based on Smucker's closing stock price of $25.89 on October 9, 2001, this represents a pre-tax equivalent cash price of $1.0 billion or approximately 1.7 times net sales.

This spin-off and merger transaction (a "Revised Morris Trust" structure) effectively manages the tax implications to the parties. Procter & Gamble shareholders will own approximately 53 percent of the newly combined company, which will have approximately 49.3 million shares outstanding.

- *Describes the financial impact of the transaction and the EPS impact for both Smucker and P&G shareholders:*

With successful closing of the transaction, Smucker expects its sales to approximately double, to $1.3 billion. For fiscal 2003, the first full year of integration, Smucker projects net earnings before one time costs associated with the transaction to be in the range of $95–105 million, almost three times current levels. . . .

Additionally, the Smucker Company said it expects the combined earnings power of the three brands to allow it both to continue its historic strong dividend practice, typically in the range of 40 to 50 percent of earnings. . . .

"Not only is this transaction very accretive to earnings, it provides significant cash flows when coupled with our already strong balance sheet," said Richard Smucker.

For P&G, the transaction is expected to be slightly dilutive in fiscal 2002, but the company is comfortable with the current range of estimates. Dilution in fiscal 2003 is estimated at 6 cents per share.

However, with the potential accretive impact of the pending Clairol transaction, P&G still expects to achieve its earnings goal of double-digit growth in 2003.

- *Discusses the expected timing of deal consummation, and the approvals required:*

  The transaction is subject to regulatory and Smucker shareholder approvals, and the receipt of a ruling from the Internal Revenue Service that the transaction is tax-free to both companies and their shareholders. The transaction is expected to close during the second calendar quarter of 2002.

- *Conveys a focus on creating shareholder value:*

  Smucker

  "Just as important, it [the transaction] will strengthen our position to acquire other complementary leading food brands, providing opportunity for greater top- and bottom-line growth and clearly enhancing shareholder value."

  P&G

  "This structure builds shareholder value very efficiently—a spin-off of JIF and CRISCO assets directly to our shareholders, and the opportunity for them to participate in the future growth of the new J.M. Smucker Company."

  Both

  "In addition to the brands being market leaders, our companies possess . . . commitment to continually enhancing shareholder value."

- *Addresses social issues:*

  "In addition to the brands being market leaders, our companies possess similar management and employee cultures, common focus on customers, dedication to the highest standards of quality for consumers, and commitment to continually enhancing shareholder value."

  Smucker will offer employment to all employees at these facilities 100% dedicated to these businesses.

- *Conveys enthusiasm:*

  ". . . both Richard and I, along with our entire board and management team, are so enthusiastic about this deal," Timothy Smucker concluded.

2. Issuing a memo to employees to inform them of a transaction may help to improve the chances of getting their buy-in. The Smucker memo conveys enthusiasm and starts out with a strong message: that the deal is beneficial for the company and therefore for its employees.

   It will create an even stronger company, doubling our sales to $1.3 billion and more than doubling our profits. Most importantly, this will provide us with a platform for even greater growth in the future.

The memo also briefly discusses the strategic rationale for the deal. In addition, the memo emphasizes that the employees are key to the success of this transaction; it recognizes and thanks the employees for their past and future efforts:

> *As you would expect, this has and will require a great deal of effort by many people to complete. We would like to thank everyone involved for their efforts thus far and for the future efforts that will be required for a successful integration into our business.*

Finally, there is a tacit message to Smucker employees to welcome their new colleagues into the "family":

> *Included in this transaction are the CRISCO production facility located in Cincinnati, Ohio, and the JIF peanut butter plant located in Lexington, Kentucky. These facilities, along with support staff, will add about 450 new employees to the "family" of Smucker.*

Raytheon

1. In contrast to the Smucker press release, the Raytheon release is very short and does not provide much detail. However, this is understandable since the target is small: $20 million in revenue. This makes up only 0.1 percent of Raytheon's $16.8 billion in revenue. The key point is that the quality and degree of disclosure need not be belabored if a transaction is relatively immaterial.

CHAPTER 36

Framework for Postmerger Integration

PART I: INTEGRATION STRATEGY

1. Preservation would seem to be an appropriate integration strategy in this case:
   - *Low interdependence.* The two companies have such different businesses that there would be scant opportunity for meshing the target's and the buyer's operations.
   - *Low control.* Likewise, the unrelated nature of the two businesses' operations would warrant separate financial, quality, and other operational control systems.
   - *High autonomy.* Given Brown-Forman's lack of experience in Lenox's business area, it would be advisable to keep Lenox's leadership team intact and allow them relatively wide discretion/independence in decision making.
2. Absorption into a new culture would be the best integration strategy in this case:
   - *Low autonomy.* Given that a key rationale for the deal is to achieve cost savings by integrating duplicate businesses, a unified culture is probably necessary. As Chapter 36 in the main text states, some researchers have concluded that in scale-driven deals (typically focused intently on improving efficiency), the successful acquirers tended to impose their culture on the target company.
   - *High control.* Because integration is key to the success of this deal, there needs to be a unified system of controls. Also, because the businesses of the two companies are similar, it is possible to operate under a unified system of controls.
   - *High interdependence.* Again, because the two companies operate in similar business areas, there are many opportunities for integrating operations.
3. The need for economies of scale would argue for an integration strategy of absorption. Yet the CEOs seek to maintain lines of differentiated products, which would suggest the need for some autonomy in product design and development. Linking might be an appropriate integration strategy:

- *High autonomy.* The wide divergence between Daimler's and Chrysler's product lines, the vast cultural gap, and the existence of dual headquarters and dual CEOs all call for each party to have a high degree of autonomy.
- *High control.* Being both automobile manufacturers, quality control systems, purchase control systems, asset allocation processes, and other logistical control systems could be unified.
- *High interdependence.* Coordinated business processes, especially in purchasing and manufacturing is necessary to achieve synergies contemplated in the deal.

4. This is a vertical merger with Disney the supplier and Cap Cities/ABC the distribution channel. Linking is a classic strategy for integrating firms in a value chain: high control, high interdependence, and high autonomy. The high control and interdependence are warranted where high coordination within the value chain is necessary to achieve economies of scale and high quality. But also, high autonomy may be justified where the businesses are different enough to warrant separate managerial oversight.

5. An integration strategy of confederation seems to be consistent with the business strategy and rationale for this deal:

   - *High autonomy.* The areas of specialty of the two drug firms seem to have little in common; in addition, the two companies are based in countries with significantly different cultural heritages. These would warrant a high degree of autonomy for both companies.
   - *High control.* Being both drug manufacturers, it seems plausible that control systems such as accounting and financial controls, quality controls, laboratory and resource allocation procedures would easily render themselves to unified systems.
   - *Low interdependence.* Although cross-selling using each other's sales and marketing forces was one of the main merger arguments, in terms of manufacturing operations little interdependence can be achieved, at least initially, due to the divergence in product specializations and the geographic distance.

PART II: INTEGRATION IMPLEMENTATION

1. Speed is crucial to the success of postmerger integration. This is not to say that integration should not be planned carefully—rather, the planning should be completed before the deal is consummated. Once integration is begun, it needs to be implemented quickly. Delay breeds uncertainty, and uncertainty paralyzes the course of business. It also often drains morale. Some consultants have argued that a merger is won or lost within the first 90 days after the merger announcement.

2. The difference in morale between the two divisions could be due to many things (differences in layoffs and other "me issues" are prime candidates). But confusion about the strategic direction of division B also suggests a

communication problem. Has the rationale for the merger been explained there? Have the new organization and strategy been communicated? Above all, is management *listening* to the employees?

3. The manager's approach ignores the need for speed and determination in completing postmerger integration. Not only will the duplicate systems hamper the unification of the two banks in various operational ways, but the strategy also signals to the organization the acceptability of redundancy and delay.

CHAPTER 37

Corporate Development as a Strategic Capability: The Approach of GE Power Systems

1. Business development at GEPS is characterized by:

- *Consistency of processes.* GEPS streamlined its approach to deals by using common valuation models, presentation templates, and common decision frameworks.
- *Active knowledge management.* GEPS was committed to sharing knowledge across staff and across time. Data retrieval system and Web-based tools helped to manage business planning, the deal process, and work coordination.
- *Continuous improvement mind-set.* GEPS (and GE at large) was committed to Total Quality Management and made use of the six sigma approach to map processes and to encourage ongoing process improvement.
- *Top-down and bottom-up deal pipeline.* GEPS took these two different approaches to generate deals: The bottom-up approach started with ideas from sales and marketing, and worked its way up to senior management, and the top-down approach began with ideas from senior management and moved down the hierarchical chain.
- *Senior management engagement.* GEPS senior leadership actively participated in weekly meetings, and the CEO of GE reviewed GEPS' business development activities monthly.

2a. The GEPS M&A "factory" is a metaphorical description of its streamlined and standardized business development processes. The "factory" eliminated variation and used the same methods across different deals.

The electronic digitization of information was a key contribution to the factory-like processes. These included:

- An e-deal room, which was a Web-based system that tracked deal progress and allowed for chat room conversations among professionals.
- A company tracker system of "wish list" target companies and their competitors.
- An equity tracker system that allowed executives to follow GEPS' equity investments and to see board meeting and deal progress notes.

- Due diligence tools, such as a question bank to promote an effective and thorough due diligence process.

2b. While GEPS' systematic processes have proved to be highly effective, there is perhaps an inherent risk that the factory-like approach could limit or discourage independent thinking that could be beneficial. When processes become so systematic, people may be prone to think uniformly, rather than creatively and "out of the box." Active, independent thinking may be highly important for working through the intricacies and nuances that are specific to different deals. Just because a standardized system can help streamline the processes for various deals does not mean that all of the deals should always be handled in exactly the same way.

3. A black belt six sigma practitioner is a full-time team leader who is responsible for measuring, analyzing, improving, and controlling key processes that contribute to Total Quality Management. A black belt would help create an environment and mind-set for continuous process improvement and operational efficiency.

   A technology trainer and knowledge-management learning specialist would add value to your division by training employees on how to use and master technological tools. A trainer and learning specialist would increase the value of your human capital by improving employees' skill sets and know-how.

4. It depends on the particular target company and the circumstances, and also on the judgment of the GEPS' business development team. It is logical to assume that if a cold call—an initial conversation with a potential target—is negative, it would be better to move on to other cold calls that might lead to better prospects.

   However, sometimes circumstances change such that an unlikely prospect becomes a strong candidate for a deal. For example, the mini-case describing GEPS' acquisition of Alpha Company (in Chapter 37 of the main text) depicts a situation where a follow-up call was worth making. The first call received a negative response from an elderly owner who was the original inventor of Alpha's proprietary technology. Three years after an initial cold call, GEPS contacted Alpha Company again and spoke to a different executive at the firm: a co-owner who was interested in possibly selling the company. The new circumstances ultimately allowed GEPS to make a successful acquisition.

5. You could describe the key attributes of GEPS' business development process, which, when executed well and taken collectively, translate to a strategic capability. These include:

   - *Strategic mind-set.* Effective, value-creating business development begins with a strategic view that guides the entire process. At GEPS, the business development efforts were highly focused and strategic in nature, as manifested in their matrix grid for deal sourcing.
   - *Integrated teams.* As depicted by GEPS, a "best practice" business development approach is integrating the work of individuals through team formation and integrating the efforts across teams.

37

- *Strong commitment.* A key component of good business development is commitment-building and commitment-giving. Notable at GEPS is the commitment and involvement of the CEO of GE.
- *Good information technology (IT) infrastructure.* GEPS shows the advantage of having good IT systems and know-how.
- *Knowledge management.* Often used in conjunction with IT systems, knowledge management allows for learning and information sharing across business units and across different deals. This was instrumental for GEPS business development processes.
- *A disciplined process focus.* Systematic process focus leads to great operating efficiency and total quality management. According to Dave Tucker at GEPS, a process discipline did not lead to a rigid and robotic mind-set; it actually allowed for great flexibility in creating deal design.
- *Early integration planning.* GEPS shows the effectiveness of early integration planning—which can help to make smoother transitions and to realize synergies.

CHAPTER 38

M&A "Best Practices": Some Lessons and Next Steps

1. Possible benefit(s) of automation include allowing the deal designer to spend more time on the creative aspects of the deal, and producing multiple and more varied quantitative analyses (i.e., employing different valuation techniques for comparison) in a short period of time.

   A possible drawback could be an overreliance on "opaque box" tools to do quantitative analyses—M&A practitioners should all have a strong conceptual understanding of the analytics and tools and should be able to question quantitative data and even perform some basic modeling and number crunching to test results and findings from more complex systems.

2. The group lacks process leaders—professionals who are in charge of pursuing a deal from beginning to end—and a "whole deal" perspective. She might begin with mapping the deal development processes and engaging professional counsel in improving the process at Best Ensemble. Also, hiring some process managers to carry the deals along and complement the work of the specialists might generate some improvement in performance.

3. Current events in M&A can be instructive in certain areas:

   - *Turbulence and activity:* As discussed in Chapters 3, 4, 5, and 6, the M&A practitioner will benefit greatly from "listening" not only to individual firms but also to different markets: the capital markets, industry markets, and the macro economy at large. Listening to both firms and markets is important in the process for identifying the drivers of economic turbulence and, in turn, good opportunities for mergers and acquisitions.

     The relationship between listening to firms and listening to markets is straightforward: The events and conditions of individual firms may reflect or have an impact on their industries and the capital markets, while the events and conditions of a particular industry (deregulation, consolidation) or the economy at large (interest rates, stock market) will have an impact on individual firms.

   - *Valuation analysis and deal design.* These two activities are highly interrelated. The target valuation will directly affect certain aspects of the deal design—the price, payment, and financing method. At the same time, certain aspects of the deal design such as social issues—side payments, golden parachutes, a "merger of equals" deal structure—will often dictate adjustments to initial valuation analysis.

A deal leader could enhance the transaction development process by assigning cross-functional roles to employees or by creating small deal teams comprised of members working on the different discrete parts of the deal. These small teams could share information and connect the different discrete transaction activities and results. In order to promote fluidity and dynamic interaction, a deal leader should try to break down barriers that divide different functional groups without disturbing the efficient processes in place within the various functional areas.